Malaysia

Land of Eternal Summer

Text and Photographs
by
Debbie and David Cook

WP
WILMETTE PUBLICATIONS

Malaysia, Land of Eternal Summer
First published 1995

Edited by Debbie Cook
Cartography by Debbie and David Cook

Published by Wilmette Publications Sdn. Bhd.,
Unit 19.03, 19th Floor,
Menara Promet,
Jalan Sultan Ismail,
50250 Kuala Lumpur.

Printed by Consolidated Press Sdn. Bhd.,
Lot 22 & 24, Jalan Segambut Atas,
Resource Industrial Park, Segambut,
51200 Kuala Lumpur.

ISBN 983-99908-1-0 (hardback)

Cover: *A yacht sailing through the waters of the idyllic Langkawi archipelago off Peninsular Malaysia's west coast. (Photograph by S.K. Chong)*
Overleaf: *A group of women from Sarawak dressed in their traditional costumes. The women are from the state's main indigenous groups (left to right): Bidayuh, Orang Ulu, Iban, Malay. (Photograph taken at the Sarawak Cultural Village)*
Page 6: *Malaysia is located at the crossroads of South East Asia, perhaps the world if this signpost on Pulau Sibu in the South China Sea is anything to go by.*

PRIME MINISTER
MALAYSIA

PREFACE

In the last decade Malaysia has become a popular destination for visitors from all over the world. They are drawn in ever increasing numbers by the country's many and varied attractions, whether historic sites like Melaka, tropical islands such as Pulau Langkawi, or the virgin rain forests of Taman Negara and Sarawak.

At the same time Malaysia has caught the world's attention because of the country's economic success. Malaysians are justifiably proud of their achievements and feel confident that the goal of Vision 2020, developed status for Malaysia within thirty years, will be realised.

This publication depicts the rich heritage of the Malaysian people and their land, highlighting their past, their various cultures and religions, and their myths and legends, while directing visitors to what they can see and do throughout the country. There has been a need for such a publication for some time. Not only is it an invaluable guide for visitors to our shores, it is also to be recommended for all Malaysians who want to know more about their country. I would like to congratulate Wilmette Publications and Debbie and David Cook for producing a book of this importance and quality.

DR. MAHATHIR BIN MOHAMAD
Kuala Lumpur
3rd January 1995

FORWARD

In the 19th century the renowned naturalist, Charles Darwin, referred to the tropics as a 'topsy turvy world'. He certainly had a point with regard to Malaysia. Here is a land where it can rain an inch in an hour, but be completely dry an hour or so later. Water is called *air.* There are plants which can eat rats, fish that walk, leaves which can jump about, and flowers which are bigger than a football, indeed a lot bigger, that is if you can find them. This is also a land where rivers are roads, there are houses with horns, buildings with brains and pocket-sized deer.

These conundrums are answered in the course of this book, which we hope both informs and interests Malaysia's many visitors and general readers alike. For two years we travelled back and forth across Peninsular and East Malaysia, researching and photographing the material for the book, exploring towns, *kampungs,* forests, islands and historic sites, talking to the local people, checking details and, not least, trying out the many foods and drinks on offer in Malaysia. The results of those thousands of miles in aeroplanes, trains, cars, not forgetting quite a few on foot, are contained within these pages.

This is a tourist guidebook in the conventional sense of the word with a great deal on what to see and do in the various states of Malaysia, while at the end of the book there is a travel information section. At the same time this book is more than just a guidebook. It aims to portray and bring to life the diversity of Malaysia, with its pot-pourri of peoples, through their cultures, religions and history. In this way the book sets out to capture the essential character of the country. This has not always proved a straightforward task. For instance, the country's history has not been easy to unravel. It is liberally sprinkled with legends and folklore, in themselves a vital aspect of the country's many cultures, as well as being rather shadowy in some areas. Nevertheless, we have tried to present the important events of Malaysian history in as informative and lively a fashion as possible, while relating them to what can be seen around the country today.

Special attention has been given to several figures from the past, who contributed more than most to the shaping of Malaysian culture and history. These men are mostly heroes, but there are one or two villains. Malaysian history also has its famous women, none more so than Cik Siti Wan Kembang and her adopted daughter Puteri Saadong. One of the most obscure historical characters is Ferdinand Magellan's Malay servant and friend, Enrique of Melaka, possibly the first man to circumnavigate the globe. There are also a few Chinese millionaires, men like Yap Ah Loy who effectively founded Kuala Lumpur. Finally, there are the colonial figures, from Alfonso d'Albuquerque to Frank Swettenham, men who opened up the country in the pursuit of wealth and exploitation.

The basic approach of the book is to examine the Malaysian states in turn and bring out their individual characteristics, while developing the many features of Malaysia that are common to all of them. The accompanying maps identify the principal sites of interest in all the states and the leading towns. A glossary giving the Malay words used in the text is located at the back of the book. All that remains is for us to say ***Selamat Datang ke Malaysia,*** or 'Welcome to Malaysia'.

Debbie and David Cook.

SOUTH
NORWAY 10105 KM.
SWEDEN 9692 KM.
SINGAPORE 135 KM.
DENMARK 10013 KM.
AUSTRALIA
U.KINGDOM 10695 KM.
SWITZERLAND 10422 KM.
CZECHOSLOVAKIA 9891 KM.
GERMANY 10406 KM.
KUALA LUMPUR 353 KM.
ITALY 10055 KM.
BELGIUM 10597 KM.
LUXEMBOURG 10486 KM.
AUSTRIA 9748 KM.
HOLLAND 10537 KM.
FRANCE 10772 KM.
SPAIN 11419 KM.
POLAND 9446 KM.
SIBU CABANAS

CONTENTS

MA
(NC
PERLIS
PULAU
LANGKAWI
KANGAR
ALOR SETAR
KEDAH
KOTA
BHARU
GEORGETOWN
PENANG
KELANTAN
KUALA
TERENGGANU
PERAK
TERENGGANU
IPOH
PAHANG
KUANTAN
SELANGOR
SOUTH
KUALA
LUMPUR
SHAH ALAM
STRAITS OF MALACCA
SEREMBAN
NEGERI
SEMBILAN
PULAU
TIOMAN
MELAKA
MELAKA
JOHOR
JOHOR
BAHRU
SINGAPORE
SUMATRA
(INDONESIA)
KUC

LAYSIA
RAWN TO SCALE)
NA SEA
SULU SEA
KOTA KINABALU
LABUAN
BRUNEI
SABAH
SARAWAK
CELEBES SEA
KALIMANTAN (INDONESIA)

INTRODUCTION

Land of Eternal Summer

'Imagine yourself transported to a land of eternal summer, to that Golden Peninsula, 'twixt Hindustan and Far Cathay, from where the early navigators brought back such wondrous stories of adventure. A land where nature is at her best and richest: where plants and animals, beasts and forests, birds of the air, and every living thing, seem yet inspired to a feverish desire for growth and reproduction, as though they were still in the dawn of creation.'

Frank Swettenham, 1895.

Malaysia is situated just north of the equator in the heart of South East Asia and covers an area of over 330,000 sq km. The country is divided by the South China Sea into Peninsular or West Malaysia, which forms the south-eastern extremity of the Asian land mass, and the northern part of the island of Borneo. Peninsular Malaysia contains eleven states. On the west coast are Melaka, Kedah, Perlis, Penang, Johor, Perak, Selangor and Negeri Sembilan, in addition to the Federal Capital Territory of Kuala Lumpur, known affectionately as 'K.L'. Along the east coast are Kelantan, Terengganu and Pahang. The Borneo lands of East Malaysia are composed of Sarawak, Sabah and the Federal Territory of Labuan.

Malaysia is truly a *Bumi Abadi Musim Panas,* or 'Land of Eternal Summer'. The tropical **climate** is uniformly hot and sunny, with temperatures ranging from 22°C to 32°C, except in the mountains and hill resorts where the weather is cooler. Due to the country's proximity to the equator, the sun rises and sets at roughly the same time throughout the year. The passing of the seasons is not characterised by any variations in temperature, but by changes in the level of rainfall, related to the cycle of monsoons. The annual rainfall is very high, ranging from 2,000 mm to 3,000 mm. No part of Malaysia has a really dry season, but most regions do have a time of the year when the level of rainfall rises considerably. For the west coast of the Malay Peninsula the wet season is from September to November, with another period of high rainfall in the months of April and May. The mornings tend to be fine, but convectional storms occur in the late afternoon. There is nothing in the temperate parts of the world to compare with a tropical storm. The heavens open and the rain pours down in torrents, often accompanied by thunder and lightning, and then, as quickly as the storm came, it has gone and the sun has reappeared. The rain is more persistent during the wet season on the east coast and in East Malaysia, which lasts from November to February. The level of humidity tends to hover at around 80% throughout the year in all parts of the country.

The **topography** of both Peninsular and East Malaysia is remarkably similar.

National flag**: The fourteen stripes signify the equal status in the Federation of the thirteen states and the Federal Government. The blue represents the unity of the people, yellow is the royal colour, while the star and crescent are the traditional symbols of Islam, the country's official religion. The star has fourteen points, representing the unity of the Federation.* ***Opposite: *These three schoolgirls reflect Malaysia's racial diversity, a factor which has led to the country being dubbed a 'mini Asia'.*

Coastal plains give way to a rugged mountainous interior. The spine of the peninsula is formed by the granite Main Range, or Banjaran Titiwangsa, which runs from the border with Thailand south for over 450 km to Negeri Sembilan. A considerable part of the interior of Pahang, Terengganu and Kelantan is also mountainous, much of this area forming Taman Negara, Malaysia's largest national park. One of the principal highlights of Taman Negara is Gunung Tahan (2,187 metres), the highest peak in the Malay Peninsula. A striking feature of the peninsular landscape is the dramatic limestone hills to be found near Kuala Lumpur, and at many places in the north and north-west of the country. These hills, rising abruptly from the surrounding countryside, are honeycombed with caves, some of which were home to ancient man. East Malaysia is dominated by vast and remote areas of jungle-clad mountains, through which runs the border with Kalimantan, the name for Indonesian Borneo. The most dramatic of all Malaysian peaks is Mount Kinabalu in Sabah, its rocky pinnacles rising to a height of 4,101 metres, making it the highest mountain in South East Asia.

As a result of the country's heavy rainfall, the mountainous interiors of both Peninsular and East Malaysia form the headwaters for numerous rivers. Until the 20th century the rivers in the peninsula were the principal arteries for travel and trade. This is perhaps best illustrated by the fact that nearly all the peninsular states take their names from the major river. The longest of these is the Pahang River (475 km). In East Malaysia the rivers remain to this day the principal means of moving around the country. The greatest and the busiest of these is the mighty Rejang (563 km) in Sarawak.

The typical soil of the country, a bright red, yellow or brown clay, is generally not very fertile, but the high temperatures and abundant rainfall provide ideal conditions for the growth of tropical rain forests. In spite of extensive logging operations and the opening up of the country for agricultural and urban development, over

half of Malaysia is still covered with forest, a great deal being so inaccessible that it will probably remain uncleared.

The Malaysian rain forests date back 130 million years, making them among the oldest in the world and far older than the jungles of the Amazon Basin or Equatorial Africa. While these and other rain forests were subjected to the ravages of the climatic changes brought about by the Ice Ages, the Malaysian forests were left untouched, producing the remarkably complex and diverse ecosystem of today. Nature is indeed at her 'best and richest' in these forests where the almost constant climate over millions of years has allowed the evolution of literally thousands of species of trees, plants and flowers. As many as two hundred different types of tree can be found in a single hectare of the rain forest. Animals and birds also thrive in what is an ideal habitat for them.

Sheltered parts of the coast in Borneo and the western side of the peninsula have another form of vegetation, mangrove swamps, though many of these have been cleared in the interests of tourism and development. Where the coast is more exposed to the open sea, notably along the east coast of the peninsula, long sandy beaches have been formed, with casuarina trees and coconut palms completing the image of a tropical paradise. Malaysia is also famed for its idyllic offshore islands. Along the west coast of the peninsula are the popular holiday destinations of Penang, the Langkawi archipelago and Pulau Pangkor, while off the east coast and Sabah lie a host of beautiful coral-fringed islands. These include Pulau Tioman, the setting for the Hollywood musical *South Pacific*, and Pulau Sipadan, with its spectacular coral cliffs.

Malaysia is a relatively young country, if a land with a long history. The eleven states of Peninsular Malaysia gained their independence from British

colonial rule in August 1957, with the creation of the Federation of Malaya. A strong central government was established in Kuala Lumpur, while certain powers were retained by the individual states. Six years later, the expanded **Federation of Malaysia** was formed, when the peninsular states were joined by Sarawak, Sabah and the island of Singapore. The name *Malaysia* was adopted to reflect the diverse ethnic make-up of the new country's population. Singapore left the Federation in 1965, becoming an independent nation, though both countries have since worked closely together in ASEAN (Association of South East Asian Nations). ASEAN has six member nations, the others being

Opposite: *Malaysia is renowned for its beautiful beaches. This is Pantai Cenang on Pulau Langkawi.* ***Above:*** *A changeable lizard demonstrating its acrobatic skills. Commonly found in the north of the Malay Peninsula, the lizard is so-named because the male changes colour during the breeding season.*

Indonesia, Thailand, the Philippines and Brunei, and was formed to promote greater economic, social and cultural cooperation in the region. Malaysia is a constitutional monarchy, and is the only country in the world to have a rotating system of kingship. There are hereditary rulers, called sultans, in nine of the peninsular states, who elect one of their number to be king, or Yang di-Pertuan Agong, for a period of five years. This way they all have a chance of being king during their lifetimes.

In little more than a decade Malaysia has been transformed from a provider of raw materials and cheap labour into one of the fastest growing economies in the world. A key factor in this economic miracle has been the political leadership of the fourth Prime Minister, Dato' Seri Dr Mahathir Mohamad, who has been in power since 1981. He is the inspiration behind **Vision 2020**, the plan to make Malaysia a fully developed nation within thirty years. This has presented Malaysians with an immense challenge, in simple terms an annual growth rate of at least 7% until 2020. Dr Mahathir is confident that the country can meet this target and has sealed a message to his people in a time capsule, buried at the head office of Public Bank in Kuala Lumpur, which will be opened in 2020.

The initial signs are very encouraging, and any visitor to Malaysia will be immediately confronted by signs of the country's rapid economic growth, whether in the constantly changing skyline of the capital, Kuala Lumpur, or in the many housing and light industrial developments to be found in Selangor and the other west coast states. All of this is a far cry from the early 1980s when the Malaysian economy was undermined by the collapse in commodity prices. These included tin and rubber, the latter of course being almost synonymous with the country since the heyday of the British Empire at the end of the 19th century. The lesson was learned and Dr Mahathir directed the country's efforts into expanding light industry and manufacturing, particularly in the field of electronics and electrical goods. During the

last decade the share of manufacturing in Malaysia's gross domestic product has increased from 19% to 30%, while agriculture has fallen from 23% to 16%. In the wake of this economic revolution has come a rise in incomes, virtually full employment and, perhaps most important of all, a new self-confidence amongst the people.

In a blaze of publicity Dr Mahathir launched the latest model of the Proton, Malaysia's national motor car, in 1993. More than any other product, the Proton range of cars has symbolised the manufacturing success of the Malaysian economy in the last decade. When Dr Mahathir first announced the project in 1982, many commentators poured scorn on it and predicted financial disaster. Today every other car on Malaysian roads is a Proton, models are exported abroad to twelve countries, and production at the factory in Shah Alam, the state capital of Selangor, continues to rise every year.

Malaysia has a diverse ethnic, religious and cultural make-up, and as a result has been dubbed a 'mini Asia'. The country has a **population** of 18.6 million people, of whom 62% are known as *bumiputeras,* or 'sons of the soil'. These include the Malays who number over 9 million, making them the largest group in the country, and the *orang asli,* or the original people of Peninsular Malaysia. The indigenous peoples of East Malaysia, the largest groups being the Ibans and Kadazans, also belong to the *bumiputera* class. The 5.4 million Chinese are Malaysia's largest non-indigenous group, followed by the Indians who total 1.5 million. Both China and India have had trading links with the Malay Peninsula since ancient times, but large scale migration only came during the second half of the 19th century, when the British required

Opposite: *Work on the production line at the Proton factory in Shah Alam.*
Above: *The Prime Minister of Malaysia, Dato' Seri Dr Mahathir Mohamad, and his wife, Datin Seri Dr Siti Hasmah, greeting guests at their 'open house' during Hari Raya Puasa.*

cheap labour to work the tin mines and rubber estates. Most of the Chinese in Malaysia originated from southern China and belong to the Hakka and Hokkien dialect groups, while the Indians are predominantly Tamils from southern India. Other minority groups in Malaysia include Eurasians, Europeans and Sinhalese.

The official **language** is Bahasa Malaysia, a standardised form of Malay. English is a compulsory subject in Malaysian schools and is therefore widely spoken throughout the country. Radio and television programmes are presented in Malay, English, Chinese (Mandarin) and Tamil, reflecting the ethnic diversity of the country.

In the wake of the various migrations to the Malay Peninsula have come all the world's major **religions**. Islam, the faith of the Malays, is the country's official religion, but freedom of worship is allowed for the many Buddhists, Hindus and Christians. One popular result of this tolerance is the frequency of religious festivals, several of which are public holidays. The Malaysian

Government has never espoused a fundamentalist form of Islam. An effective balance has been established between the moral code of Islam and the requirements of a modern, developing nation. Many Islamic values, such as peace, democracy, justice and non-discrimination, play an obvious role in shaping any modern country, but economic development at the end of the 20th century requires the active involvement of non-Islamic influences and institutions. Some compromises have had to be made. For instance, Islam preaches against usury, the cornerstone of the international banking and financial world. Prohibiting usury would clearly deal a very serious blow to any modern economy, though Muslim financial experts are already developing the concept of interest-free banking and examining acceptable ways of replacing the lost income.

Islam is an integral part of the Malay identity, shaping their whole way of life. It is still far from clear when the first Muslims came to the Malay Peninsula. The earliest evidence for the presence of Islam is the Terengganu Stone, which is inscribed with a series of Muslim laws and dates from the beginning of the 14th century. In the course of the following century Islam became established in Melaka. Like Buddhism and Hinduism in earlier times, and Christianity later in the 16th century, Islam was carried to the Malay Peninsula by merchants and seafarers. They flocked to Melaka where the trading facilities were so good, particularly after the sultan and his people had themselves become Muslims.

Ancient mariners once knew the Malay Peninsula as 'the land where the winds meet', the place where the monsoons that sweep across the Indian Ocean and the South China Sea at different times of the year converge. During the centuries when sailing ships ruled the waves, the monsoons determined the time and direction of sea travel, in the process turning the

peninsula into the crossroads of the East and the natural meeting point of two different civilisations, 'Hindustan and Far Cathay'. To the west across the Bay of Bengal lies India, while away to the east is China. The south-west monsoon affects the peninsula between May and September, while the north-east monsoon blows across the South China Sea from November to February. In the days of sail, vessels from India came to the peninsula on the south-west monsoon, stayed there in the intervening months and then returned home on the north-east monsoon. For the Chinese junks it was vice versa. During the period the ships were in the Malay Peninsula, they required docking facilities, a place to store or sell their cargoes, and supplies and amenities for their crews, leading to the growth of the Malay *entrepôts*, the greatest being Melaka.

Malaysian **history** can be conveniently divided into four distinct phases. The dark ages before the 15th century were a time of small city-states. These were mostly to be found in the north of the country, being located either by the side of the major rivers or along the coastal plains. Their prosperity was dependent on trade. The status and boundaries of these city-states were constantly fluctuating, and for long periods ultimate authority was imposed from outside, principally by Srivijaya in Sumatra.

The southern part of the peninsula was mostly a wilderness of swamp and jungle. The first important settlement was Melaka, founded by Parameswara at the beginning of the 15th century. The next hundred years proved to be the greatest period in Malay history. The Melaka Sultanate came to dominate trade and politics in South East Asia, wielding a power and authority as great as the earlier Srivijayan empire.

Opposite: *The domed minarets and graceful arches of the Kuala Lumpur Railway Station make it one of the great sights in the city.* ***Above:*** *The stunning golden domed Masjid Ubudiah in the royal town of Kuala Kangsar in Perak.*

The colonial phase of Malaysian history began abruptly in 1511 with the fall of Melaka to Alfonso d'Albuquerque and the Portuguese. They were followed by the Dutch, and finally the British, who left the most lasting impression on the country. This is still visible today in the style of architecture to be found in several of the leading towns, the *padangs,* the use of the English language, Malaysian law and administration, and the fact that Malaysians drive on the left-hand side of the road. British rule came to an end in 1957, ushering in the period of independence.

The Malay Peninsula was known to Ptolemy and the other early geographers as the 'Golden Khersonese', a name later used by the 17th-century poet John Milton in his epic work *Paradise Lost.* From the beginning the Golden Khersonese was one of those names which excited the minds of adventurers and romantics, a name around which legends and dreams mixed freely with reality. Tales told of a land of abundant gold, tales which persisted well into the 19th century. Unfortunately for most prospectors, the finds were disappointing. Yet in many other ways this is indeed a 'Golden Peninsula', for Malaysia is a land with endless sunshine, long golden beaches, ripened gold coloured *padi* fields, golden domed mosques and gold threaded *songket* cloth.

Many of the old beliefs and legends persist to this day in the *kampungs,* or villages, of rural Malaysia. In spite of the spread of Islam and the other established religions, the *bomoh,* or medicine man, many of whose practices are based on animistic beliefs, remains a central figure in *kampung* life. For instance, prior to important events such as weddings, the spiritual powers of the *bomoh* are called upon by the villagers to keep away the rain. On more than one occasion, so they tell, rain clouds have built up ominously in the sky, but, thanks to the *bomoh,* not a drop has fallen until the event in question has reached its conclusion.

The *kampung* is a world away from the city. There is no rushing about, no traffic jams, no exhaust fumes and no crowds. Life carries on much as it has always done, from the call to prayer before dawn, through the hours of daylight and toil, to sunset and evening prayer. As the sun slips peacefully beneath the horizon towards Mecca, the chant *'Allahu Akbar',* or 'God is Great', rings out from the mosque. Another day is over, as sunset, rather than midnight, is traditionally regarded as the end of the day in the rural areas of the country.

Eating is something of a national pastime in Malaysia and visitors will quickly realise that they are never far from some tasty dish or refreshing drink. Malaysia benefits from having the best in Malay, Chinese and Indian **cuisine**. The basis of most Malaysian meals is *nasi,* or rice, sometimes enriched with coconut milk, while *mee,* or noodles, provide a tasty

alternative. There are no hard and fast rules about eating certain dishes at specific times of the day. Rice and noodles are just as much a breakfast staple as they are for lunch and dinner.

Many Malaysians eat out at hawker stalls or restaurants during the weekdays, only cooking at home at the weekend. The hawker stalls occupy virtually every available public space in the towns and offer possibly the best fast food on earth. Steaming stoves, sizzling woks and smoking barbecues are surrounded by tables and chairs, where everybody tucks in heartily. Many of the stalls are housed in the various hawker centres, which are now a feature of several of the shopping complexes and office blocks in Kuala Lumpur. They also sell delicious fruit juices, essential thirst quenchers in the hot and humid climate. Virtually any fruit is obtainable in Malaysia and most can be turned into a refreshing drink with the addition of water, sugar and ice. The 'king' of all the country's fruits is the durian, a greenish spiky object resembling a medieval mace, for which Malaysians have an undying appetite, being prepared to part with large sums of money for the very best. Experts on the subject of durians are to be found in every town and *kampung*. They treat prized varieties, such as the D2, the D96 or, the very best, the D24, with the reverence which wine connoisseurs reserve for Chateau Lafite or Latour. The wide range of food and drinks available in Malaysia has given the country a deserved reputation as a paradise for gourmets and gluttons. Bon appétit!

Opposite: *The replica of a 16th-century Portuguese galleon on display in the historic town of Melaka.* ***Above:*** *Malaysia is not only a land of eternal summer, it is also a land of stunning sunsets.* ***Overleaf:*** *A 17th-century French map of the Malay Peninsula, Borneo, Java and Sumatra. The Malay Peninsula is simply called Malacca (the English spelling of Melaka), signifying the town's great historical importance. Several of the other Malay states are also referred to by name.*

LES ISLES
DE LA SONDE.
entre lesquelles sont
SVMATRA, IAVA,
BORNEO, &c.
Par le Sr. Sanson d'Abbeville
Geographe du Roy.
Avec privilege pour 20 ans
1651.
Mille Pas Geometriqu
Lieues commu. de Fran
Lieues grandes de Fran
Lieues comm. d'Alemag
Degrés de Longit. et Lati
135
140
145
Oc
MER
l'Equateur ou
Occident
Ligor
P. Cara
Coete in ficos
Tyamaiasi
P. Cosyn
Pulo
Siano
Nicubar
P. Sambilaon
P. Ponde
P. Butun
Gomes Pole
Achem
Daya
Laria
Pulo Sambilaon
P. Capas
Malacca
Pahang
Cocos I.
Verkens I.
P. Gaina
Baras
Bancalis
Terra d'Aru
Camper
P. Boren
P. Nays
Calappes I.
P. Mintaon
Goede Fortuyn I.
Saledoe
I. Nassau
Batacapas
Palangay
Palimbam
Tamby
I. d'Engano
d'Estroit de Iao
I. du Prince
Selam
Bintam
Pedra
Bruca
P. Timaon
P. Tingo
Laor

EAN
INDIENNE.
BORNEO
Equinoctiale
Borneo
Cimbabon
I. de S. Maria
Calamianes ou Paragoya
Palon
I. S. Miguel
Pracel
I. de S.a Maria
Zolo
P. Tigaon
P. Tiga
M. de S. Pedro
Canceirao Canciaro
Marudo
Monpracem
Baquaia Bacasa
Tanjong baran
Malano
Domilhano
Puchavaraon
Tamenacerin
Sambas
Tamanatos
Soucelouban
Monpaon
Adamantes
I. de S. Ioan
Boquenano
Temahe
Crimata
Sourenton
Dondongan
Succadano
Tanjong Sanbaur
Lave
Cotaring
Sampit
R. Succadano
Bendarmassin
Puerto Aror
Caburo
Celebes
Orient
Sabacuan
Mamoy
Quiqui
Mandor
Supa
Mintam
Maliquie
Tello
Macassar
CELEBES
Lambu
Plateo
Calandua
Tamaru
P. Lant
Sapy
a. Graciosa
Luboc
Corimaniao
Cariman Iava
Hitiam
Mulusiira
Tuban
Brandan
Aresbay
De Valgront
Madura
Panaru
Pater Noster
Bali
I. Gevapy
Flores
Bomnu
Arom
Biena
Pecato
Cunbava
Gevapy
Sufu
Estr. de Bali
Lambuan
Balamboam
IAVA
Materan
Batavia
Peyrounin sculp.
Midy
60 120 180 240 300
25 50 75 100 125
20 40 60 80 100
15 30 45 60 75
1 2 3 4 5
150
155
160

MELAKA

The Legendary Malay Kingdom

The town of Melaka, which has given its name to the state, was once the greatest emporium in the East and centre of the valuable spice trade. Famed for its opulence and exotic grandeur, Melaka became known as the 'Babylon of the Orient', a kingdom much coveted, and eventually conquered by ambitious colonial powers. In later years this once great trading centre gained the rather unflattering reputation of being a 'sleepy hollow'. 'The noise of the modern world reaches it only in the faintest echoes', commented one 19th-century traveller, in describing Melaka as 'a land where it is always afternoon - hot, still, dreamy'. Today Melaka has awoken from its slumber, and the noise of our modern world is all around. The roads are packed with cars, taxis seem to be constantly cruising past, ever on the look out for custom, while motor cycles dodge in and out of the lines of traffic. Yet the charm of the old town has been preserved. Melaka conjures up the past more than any other place in Malaysia, and rightly so, for Melaka is for most people the cradle of Malay history and culture.

Melaka was the leading port in South East Asia during the 15th century, the meeting place for merchants and seafarers from as far away as India, China and the Middle East. As many as eighty-four languages were said to be spoken in the market, while hundreds of ocean-going vessels were reputed to drop anchor in the harbour each year. Melaka prospered and grew, while life at the royal court in the town became ever more lavish and splendid, providing the ideal setting for some of the great characters of Malay folklore. If Melaka was the Malayan Camelot, then Hang Tuah was a warrior firmly in the mould of the knights of the Round Table, and Tun Perak a statesman as clever and wily as Merlin.

It was only fitting that five hundred years later Tunku Abdul Rahman should choose the ***Padang***, or sports field, at Melaka to proclaim the independence of Malaysia. Cries of '*Merdeka*', or independence, greeted his proclamation, where once the inhabitants of Melaka had cheered the feats of Hang Tuah and Tun Perak. Overlooking the *Padang*, the **Independence Memorial Building**, in British times a club for planters and officials, contains an exhibition depicting the struggle for nationhood. The *Padang* is also the venue for the nightly 'Sound and Light Show', an entertaining history 'lesson' on Melaka, which uses a dramatic soundtrack and synchronized spotlights to bring to life the various sites around **St Paul's Hill**.

The life of Hang Tuah can only be described as the stuff of which legends are made. He was born at **Kampung Duyong**, just outside Melaka. Here there is a well which Hang Tuah is said to have dug

State crest: *The star and crescent represent Islam and form part of a number of the state crests of Malaysia. The kris symbolise the 'Five Companions' from the great days of the Melaka Sultanate. The tree is a melaka tree from which the state derives its name, while the mousedeer represent the incident that prompted Parameswara to found his kingdom there. The state motto is 'unity in strength'.*
Opposite: *The statue of the Virgin Mary being borne aloft during the Good Friday celebrations at St Peter's Church in Melaka.*

himself. It is still used by the locals, who would have you believe that it contains a white crocodile, the *keramat,* or spirit, of Hang Tuah. If a person is spiritually pure, he or she should be able to see the *keramat.* As a boy Hang Tuah dreamed of performing great feats in the service of the sultan of Melaka and, together with four of his friends, he set about mastering the Malay art of *silat,* or self defence. They were exceptional students. At the age of sixteen, the 'Five Companions', as they became known, clashed with a band of pirates in the Straits of Malacca, emerging triumphant. Further training followed from the famed 'Guru of the Mountain', Adi Petra, who lived on Gunung Ledang, and taught them 'a quick wrist, a keen eye, and the marrow that makes a man'.

The 'Five Companions' showed all of these skills and more when they saved Tun Perak, the *bendahara* or chief minister, from four men who had run amok in the streets. An extremely grateful Tun Perak immediately arranged for them to enter the royal bodyguard, where Hang Tuah soon became a favourite of Sultan Mansur (1459-1477). His fame quickly spread. If one account is to be believed, 'wherever he went he caused a sensation, so struck were the people by his bearing,...married women tore themselves from the embraces of their husbands, so they could go and see him!' It seemed that the whole world lay at his feet, but Hang Tuah himself sounded a note of caution, asking one of his friends, Hang Lekir, 'what ocean is waveless? What person is blameless?' He continued, 'there is a saying, Lekir, 'When the lower coconut fronds fall, the upper fronds should not laugh'. You never know when it will be our turn!' His words proved only too prophetic.

Hang Tuah had made many enemies at court. They plotted against him and informed Sultan Mansur that he was consorting with one of the queen's ladies-in-waiting. The Sultan was outraged at such a public insult to the crown and ordered Tun Perak to have Hang Tuah put to death for treason. Tun Perak suspected a plot, but knew better than to try to dissuade the Sultan when his temper was aroused. Instead he hid Hang Tuah in a prison. For a month Hang Tuah was incarcerated in a small dark cell, living on meagre rations of rice and water. All thought him dead, particularly as Tun Perak had given Hang Tuah's *kris,* called *Tameng Sari,* to Sultan Mansur. A *kris* is the traditional Malay weapon, closely resembling a dagger, but usually with a wavy blade. Famed throughout Melaka, *Tameng Sari* was reputed to possess magical powers.

The Sultan gave *Tameng Sari* to another of the 'Five Companions', Hang Jebat, and appointed him chief of the royal bodyguard in succession to Hang Tuah. An alarming change immediately came over Hang Jebat. Angered at Hang Tuah's wrongful execution, he set out to avenge his friend's death, behaving in a manner calculated to insult Sultan Mansur. His voice and looks had always attracted women in droves, but now his ardour was almost uncontrollable, while his arrogance seemed limitless. The Sultan's patience had more than run out when Hang Jebat was discovered in the palace with one of his wives. The problem was that no one could match the fighting skills of Hang Jebat, not least because he was armed with *Tameng Sari.*

That is until Tun Perak produced Hang Tuah. Sultan Mansur was overjoyed and promptly pardoned him. Hearing of Hang Jebat's treacherous behaviour, Hang

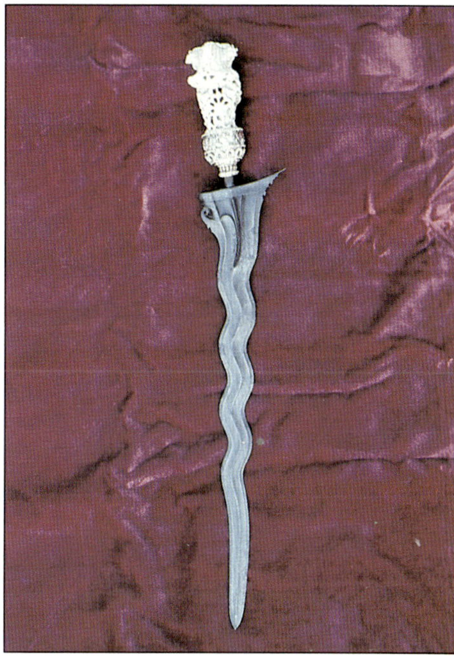

COURTESY OF THE MALAYSIA TOURISM PROMOTION BOARD

Left:** A bullock cart on the Padang in Melaka. Visitors can take a ride on this traditional Malay form of transport, which was first introduced into the state during the great days of the Melaka Sultanate.* ***Above: *A kris.*

Tuah knew what he had to do. The effects of a month's imprisonment could not easily be shaken off, but, after only two day's recuperation, Hang Tuah went to confront his former friend. He was armed with a *kris* given to him by the Sultan.

The duel between Hang Tuah and Hang Jebat is one of the epic events in Malay history. It was more than just a clash of personalities, it was also one of opposing principles. Hang Tuah would never compromise his loyalty to the Sultan, whereas Hang Jebat put greater faith in his sense of justice and friendship. Twice they fought each other to a standstill and had to take a rest, before Hang Tuah was able to wrench *Tameng Sari* from his opponent. Always a man of honour, he offered the Sultan's *kris* to Jebat, who gratefully accepted it. Hang Tuah now fought like a man reborn. The furious exchanges continued until Jebat lunged at Hang Tuah, missed, and buried his *kris* deep into a wooden door post. Hang Tuah seized his chance and mortally wounded Jebat in the stomach. The honour of Sultan Mansur had been avenged.

In gratitude Sultan Mansur appointed Hang Tuah his *laksamana,* or admiral of the fleet. Hang Jebat's body was said to have been thrown into the sea, though two fine graves, one in Jalan Kampung Kuli in Melaka town, and the other at Terendak Camp, an army base in the north-west of the state, have been associated with him. Hang Tuah's own grave is believed to be at **Tanjung Kling**, some 15 km to the west of Melaka. For centuries the tomb was known simply as an ancient grave, probably in the first instance to hide its identity from the Portuguese, who conquered Melaka in 1511.

Hang Tuah's career did not end with his defeat of Hang Jebat. Further glorious triumphs still lay ahead. He secured peace with the Siamese by worsting their champion, first cutting off his ear, then the tip of his nose, and finally his head. In this and many other ways Hang Tuah loyally served Sultan Mansur, undoubtedly the greatest of the Melaka rulers in the 15th century. The success of

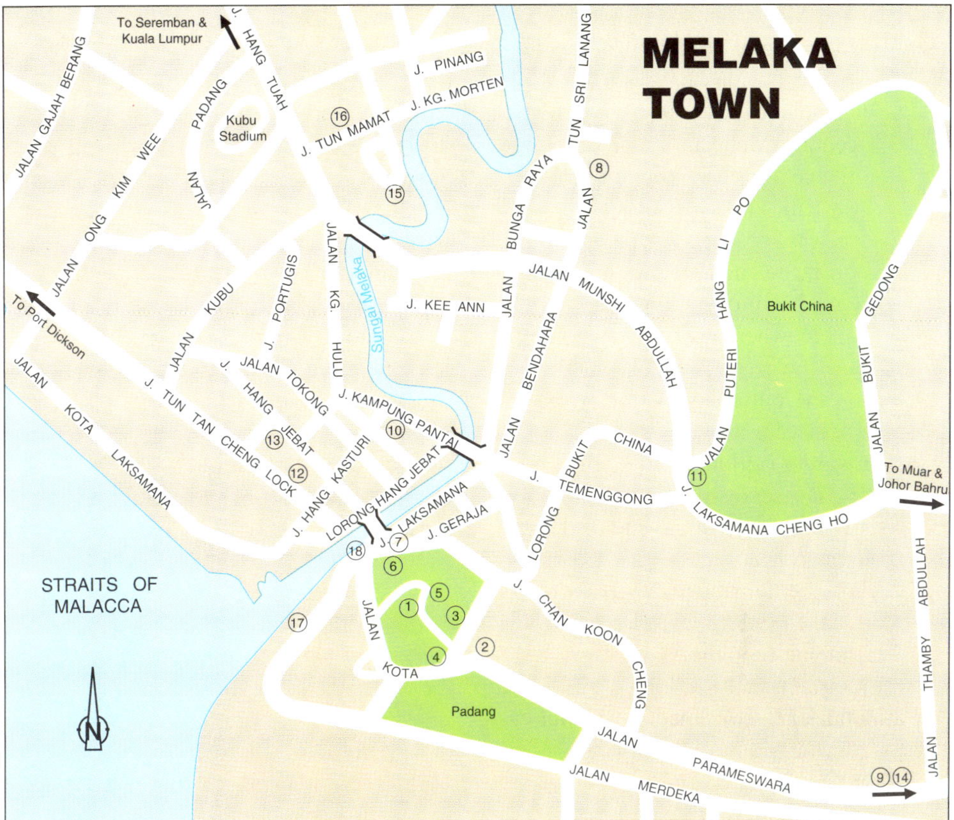

KEY

1. ST PAUL'S HILL
2. INDEPENDENCE MEMORIAL BUILDING
3. SULTANATE PALACE (MELAKA CULTURAL MUSEUM)
4. PORTA DE SANTIAGO
5. ST PAUL'S CHURCH
6. STADTHUYS (MELAKA HISTORY MUSEUM)
7. CHRIST CHURCH
8. ST PETER'S CHURCH
9. ST JOHN'S FORT
10. MAKAM HANG JEBAT
11. SAM POH'S WELL
12. BABA NYONYA HERITAGE MUSEUM
13. ANTIQUE SHOPS
14. PORTUGUESE SQUARE
15. EXPRESS BUS STAND
16. LOCAL BUS STATION
17. PORTUGUESE GALLEON
18. TOURIST INFORMATION CENTRE

the reign was symbolised by the magnificent palace Mansur had built for himself and his family. It was the marvel of the age. Today visitors to Melaka can see a replica of the **Sultanate Palace**, constructed in 1985 and located at the bottom of St Paul's Hill. It houses the Melaka Cultural Museum and includes displays depicting life in the 'real' palace during the 15th century.

Mansur built the palace when Melaka was the greatest *entrepôt* in the region and at the height of its power. The principal import from India was textiles, which were then traded in Melaka for eastern goods, such as spices from the Moluccas, silk and porcelain from China, gold and pepper from Sumatra, camphor from Borneo, sandalwood from Timor and tin from Perak. The authority of Melaka ran far and wide, over Pahang, Johor, the Riau and Lingga archipelagos, parts of Sumatra and the west

Opposite: *The Melaka Cultural Museum, built in the style of Sultan Mansur's palace.*

coast of the Malay Peninsula. At the heart of this commercial empire was the town itself. No illustrations have survived, but the written sources leave us a vivid picture of 15th-century Melaka. The river flowed through the centre of the town, overlooked by Melaka Hill, later St Paul's Hill, where the palace was located. At the foot of the hill was a large mosque, with the royal mausoleum behind. A wooden bridge, probably somewhere near the existing one, connected the royal buildings with the market on the other side of the river. The town stretched for a further 5 km along the coast towards Tanjung Kling, in a maze of narrow, crowded streets. All this was a far cry from the town at the end of the 14th century, when Melaka comprised no more than a poor settlement of 20 to 30 fishermen. How then did Melaka rise to its position of dominance in the Malay world?

The traditional version of the founding of Melaka is contained in the *Sejarah Melayu,* or the Malay Annals, probably the greatest surviving example of classical Malay literature. After tracing the descent of all Malay kings from Alexander the Great, the author recounts the well-known story of Parameswara. A prince from Palembang in Sumatra, Parameswara and his followers were driven out of Singapore, fleeing first to Muar, and then up the coast to the mouth of a river called Bertam. Here Parameswara relaxed with a spot of hunting. While standing beneath a *melaka* tree, he witnessed a curious scene. A startled mousedeer turned and kicked one of his hunting dogs, driving the animal into the water. Parameswara promptly decided to settle at the place, telling his followers, 'this is a fortunate land, where even the mousedeer are full of fight!' For good measure he named the land Melaka after the tree he was standing under.

It is a wonderful story, but there are more practical reasons for the rise of Melaka under the Malay sultans. The men at the top, the rulers and their ministers, were extremely able and quite ruthless in their pursuit of power and wealth. The site of the town also had several advantages. Situated on the maritime route between India and China, Melaka was ideally placed where the north-east and south-west monsoon winds meet. The harbour provided a sheltered anchorage, while the prominent hill overlooking the river had obvious defensive qualities. Such potential was turned into prosperous fruition by the trade links with China and India, which Parameswara and his successors strenuously fostered.

One of the many fascinations of modern day Melaka is to witness the enduring legacies of these ancient links. To the east of the river, there lie some 12,500 Chinese graves on **Bukit China**, in reality a series of low hills rather than one. From the highest point there are spectacular views of St Paul's Hill, and beyond over the red roofs of the town to the Straits of Malacca. Far away to the east Gunung Ledang is often visible.

The Chinese emperor began trading directly with Melaka early in the 15th century. The ties grew and reached a peak in the reign of Sultan Mansur, with his marriage to the emperor's daughter, Hang Li Poh. The *Sejarah Melayu* contain an unusual explanation for the emperor agreeing to such an alliance with a far less prestigious ruler. He despatched a large ship, laden with gold needles, as a gift to Sultan Mansur. An accompanying message revealed all: 'we hear that the Sultan of Melaka is a great ruler....(but) there are no rulers in this world greater than ourselves, and there is no one who knows the number of our subjects. We have asked for one needle from every household in our

Opposite: *Fishing boats moored on the Melaka River, once the site of bloody battles.*

realm!' Mansur could be just as clever, though sacks of sago would have to do in place of gold needles. The ship was filled with the sacks and sent back to the emperor. The Melakan explanation was as follows: 'our ruler ordered that each of his subjects should roll out a grain of sago until there were enough to fill a ship. That will indicate how many are the subjects of Melaka, no man knows their number!' Suitably impressed, the emperor allowed the marriage to go ahead.

When Hang Li Poh arrived in Melaka, she astonished Sultan Mansur with her beauty, while presenting Tun Perak with the thorny problem of where to accommodate her five hundred ladies-in-waiting. As always Tun Perak found a solution. Pointing to the low hill to the east of the town, he announced, 'houses will be built for the princess on that hill. We are going to call it Bukit China'. The site today covers over 106 acres. At the foot of the hill is the oldest known well in Melaka. Among the local Chinese it is called **Sam Poh's Well** after the famed Chinese envoy Admiral Cheng Ho. He visited Melaka several times in the early 15th century and, according to legend, took a drink from the well. From then on the water became renowned for its great purity. Those who drank from the well, so locals believed, would return to Melaka at least once during their lifetime. Today the purity of the water is questionable and visitors instead toss in a coin or two in the hope of returning to Melaka. The stout walls around the well reflect its strategic importance when it was a vital source of drinking water.

In its long history Bukit China has not only been associated with the Buddhist religion. There are as many as sixty Muslim graves to be found there. The most northerly of the hills has two imposing Muslim graves on its summit overlooking the new and striking **Masjid Al Azim**, the state mosque. Cheng Ho himself was a Muslim. Islam performed a vital role in the success of the Melaka Sultanate. The *Sejarah Melayu* correctly saw the acceptance of Islam in the early 15th century as

a watershed in the history of Melaka, an event which confirmed the kingdom's superior status. Muslim beliefs in self-reliance, the brotherhood of man, and involvement in the outside world and trade found an instant response in Melaka. The faith also strengthened the institution of kingship, for a Muslim ruler was 'the Shadow of God upon the Earth' and head of a religious hierarchy that stretched down to village level. The material benefits were not lost on the Malays, for Islam was also the religion of numerous foreign merchants, who now came to trade in Melaka and even to settle there.

Islam rapidly became the state religion and, as Melaka expanded territorially, so its new subjects followed suit. This process was not carried out by violence, but through alliances, trade and preaching. The commercial success of Melaka did as much as anything to further the cause of Islam in the area. The new religion became so closely identified with Malay society in Melaka, that to turn Muslim was to *masuk Melayu,* or 'enter the culture of the Malay'.

The gravestone of Sultan Mansur is on display in the Melaka History Museum and contains the following inscription: 'The world is but transitory; the world has no permanence; the world is like a house made by a spider'. Empires have always risen and fallen and Melaka was to be no different. By the reign of Sultan Mahmud (1488-1528), the royal court had declined dramatically from the great days of Sultan Mansur. Profligacy, corruption and even treason now held sway. The *bendahara,* Tun Mutahir, was typical of the times. There is no doubting his ability, whether as an administrator or a military leader, but he was intensely arrogant and never missed an opportunity to line his own pocket. Reputed to change his clothes as often as seven times a day, that is when he was not admiring himself in a full length mirror, he became extremely wealthy. Needless to say, he fell out with Sultan Mahmud, who later had him and his family murdered.

COURTESY OF MUZIUM NEGARA

Far beyond Melaka the world was also changing. In Europe this period is known as the 'Age of Discovery', that time in history when intrepid seafarers, like Christopher Columbus, Vasco da Gama and Ferdinand Magellan set out across the oceans in search of new lands and wealth. The Portuguese were the first Europeans to arrive in Melaka. A small fleet of ships, commanded by Diego Lopez de Segueira, sailed into the harbour in 1509. The local people were friendly, if rather curious of the new arrivals, one account describing how 'all the Malays crowded round in wonder at the appearance of the

Opposite: *The replica of the sultan of Melaka holding court in the Audience Hall, which is on display in the Melaka Cultural Museum.* ***Above:*** *Alfonso d'Albuquerque, the Portuguese commander who took Melaka in 1511.*

Portuguese', calling them 'white Bengalis'. Curiosity soon turned to animosity. When a Portuguese emissary called to pay his respects to Sultan Mahmud, he showed a marked lack of protocol. Some of the courtiers wanted to kill him and were only restrained with difficulty. Violence though had been postponed rather than prevented.

The Malays planned to capture Segueira and his men during a banquet on the beach, but they reckoned without the power of love. A Javanese girl swam out to the Portuguese ships, moored in the harbour, and warned her lover of the danger. The alarm was raised and the Portuguese at the banquet fled, making a frantic rush for their boats. In the chaos that ensued, twenty sailors were taken prisoner, before the remaining Portuguese were able to reach the ships, weigh anchor and take to the high seas. They would not return for two years.

Unfortunately for the Malays, Melaka weakened rapidly during those two years. After ordering the death of Tun Mutahir, Sultan Mahmud was overcome with remorse and became a virtual recluse. Effective power now lay with his son Ahmad. The Portuguese returned in 1511 led by Alfonso d'Albuquerque, an outstanding commander whose exploits established the basis of Portuguese power in the region. He began by demanding the release of the prisoners and a site on which to build a trading post, but the Malay leaders were in no mood to make any concessions. Albuquerque would have to take Melaka by force.

The Malay defenders could muster thousands of men, but the vast majority were poorly trained and inadequately equipped, in stark contrast to Albuquerque's 800 Portuguese veterans and 600 Indian auxiliaries. He could also call upon the cannons of his eighteen men-of-war, anchored in the harbour. His plan was to capture the bridge between the royal town and the merchant quarter, thus dividing Malay resistance. The initial attack came at dawn on 25th July, but it was a disaster. The Malays resisted ferociously, raining down showers of spears,

arrows and poisoned darts on the Portuguese. Ahmad set a stirring example to his men, charging into the attack on the back of an elephant. Some of the Portuguese wanted to give up after this first failure, but Albuquerque persuaded them to try again, promising great honour and untold wealth if they could take Melaka.

Following a heavy bombardment from the guns on the ships, the Portuguese launched their second major assault on 10th August. Albuquerque had decided to attack the bridge from the river, using a junk in which he placed four of his largest cannons. The junk initially became stuck on a sand bar, but sailed off at high tide and proceeded up the river to the bridge, where the Portuguese guns wrought havoc among the Malay defenders. The bridge was soon covered in bodies and, by nightfall, it was in Portuguese hands, sealing the fate of Melaka. Within a matter of days, all further resistance had collapsed.

The Portuguese were destined to hold the town until January 1641 when the Dutch captured it. They were in control for a slightly longer period, just over 150 years, before the British arrived in 1795. Many of the historical sites in Melaka relate to the colonial period, and yet the town will always, first and foremost, be associated with the story of the Malay Sultanate. In the Independence Memorial Building a poem, entitled *Our Fight for Freedom* by Syed Zulfida Shahabaddin, contains the following lines:

'From the ashes of Melaka's fall
Arose the phoenix of patriotism,
Strong and tall.'

Many made the ultimate sacrifice in the defence of the Malay Sultanate. Others, like Sultan Mahmud, would continue the struggle, for the Malay cause was undying, and perhaps the greatest monument to its strength are the remnants of the mighty colonial fortifications at Melaka. Only by

Opposite: *Large granite gravestones line the walls of St Paul's Church.* ***Below:*** *A mousedeer, the smallest hoofed animal in the world.*

walling themselves in did the Portuguese and Dutch survive for so long.

Albuquerque had a stone fortress, A Famosa, constructed within weeks. Walls and bastions were later added, encircling the hill overlooking the river, and by the end of the century Melaka was the strongest fortified town in South East Asia. On the summit of the hill, where the royal palace had proudly stood, a Portuguese nobleman, Duarte Coelho, built a chapel in 1521, in gratitude for miraculously surviving a Chinese naval attack at Canton. The chapel was later rebuilt and named **St Paul's Church**. Yet in most respects Melaka proved a disappointment for the Portuguese, as indeed it would later for the Dutch. Neither power was able to gain undisputed mastery of the Straits of Malacca and trade only flourished intermittently. By the time of the British Empire, Melaka had become a backwater, not just in comparison with the mighty trading centre of Singapore, but also with Penang.

The Europeans discovered that Melaka had major disadvantages. The soil was generally poor and much of the land was low-lying and swampy, ideal conditions for mosquitoes and malaria. There was always a high mortality rate among the Europeans living in the town. A glimpse of their suffering is revealed by the memorial tablets in Christ Church in Dutch Square and the inscriptions on the large, elaborately carved, granite gravestones which line the walls of St Paul's Church. Probably the saddest refers to the death of the wife of an English army captain, who was followed to her grave by all three of her children within a fortnight, the victims of diptheria. The Dutch in fact ran out of gravestones and had to resort to turning the Portuguese ones back to front.

The best known grave in Melaka is now empty. St Francis Xavier died in 1552 and was buried in the chancel of St Paul's Church. Six months later his body was exhumed and taken to Goa in India. The so-called 'Apostle of the Indies', St Francis had first arrived in Melaka in 1545, using the town as a base for his extensive travels throughout the Far East. An inspired

missionary, he was also famed for his miraculous deeds. On one of his visits to Melaka, he brought back to life a young girl who had been dead for several days.

In truth he never liked Melaka, finding its Portuguese masters arrogant and crude. When he left Melaka for what turned out to be the last time, the governor denied his mission to China official backing and, adding insult to injury, forced him to wade out to his ship at low tide. St Francis was soon covered in mud and, on reaching the sanctuary of a prominent rock, he was heard to curse the governor, while shaking the offending material from his clothes. Not long afterwards the governor died of leprosy. The rock was never again covered by the sea, even at high tide. The Portuguese later built a large cross on it, which can be seen in various drawings of 17th-century Melaka. A replica has been erected on the same spot in front of St Paul's Hill, now reclaimed land, by the Melaka Historical Society.

The most famous story current in Melaka about St Francis is in fact a posthumous one. Some sixty years after his burial, when the Vatican was considering the case for his canonization, the Pope ordered that his right arm should be severed from his body in Goa and sent to Rome. Blood is said to have gushed from the arm when it was removed. In Melaka a marble statue of St Francis was erected on St Paul's Hill in 1953, four hundred years after his temporary burial there. Not long afterwards, on a totally calm night, a giant casuarina tree toppled over and smashed on to the statue. When the tree was removed, the statue was found to be intact, except for the right hand which had snapped off.

The Portuguese left little impression upon Melaka. Their abiding interest was always trade, rather than territorial expansion or spreading Christianity. The most enduring legacy of their rule is the community they left behind. Unlike the other

colonial powers, the Portuguese encouraged intermarriage between their soldiers and local women. Young women were also brought from Portugal to marry local Malays. The result was the creation of a unique community, fusing the hot-blooded Latin temperament with the grace and charm of the East. Their descendants remain staunch Roman Catholics, speak *Christao,* an archaic form of Portuguese, and proudly bear names such as De Silva, Fernandez and Pereira.

In 1930 a settlement was founded specifically for the Portuguese Eurasian community, to help ensure that their identity and culture were preserved. Located some 3 km from the centre of Melaka, along the seafront, the settlement's major attraction is Medan Portugis, or **Portuguese Square**. Based upon the central square in Lisbon, Portuguese

Opposite: *Dutch Square, the heart of historic Melaka.* ***Above:*** *The distinctive strawberry coloured Christ Church in Dutch Square.*

Square is justifiably popular for its restaurants, which serve up delicious seafood dishes, such as fragrantly spiced baked fish wrapped in banana leaves. Every Saturday evening cultural performances are held in the Square and, as the dancers twirl around in their traditional costumes, it is only too easy to imagine that you are dining out in Portugal.

The principal occupation of the Portuguese community has always been fishing, a tradition celebrated by the Festa San Pedro, held every June in honour of St Peter, the patron saint of fishermen. The parish priest says mass and blesses the fishing boats, which are brightly decorated for the occasion. The rest of the day is taken up with dancing, singing and other forms of entertainment. Most of the community are parishioners of **St Peter's Church**, situated in the centre of town. Built in 1710 after the Dutch restored freedom of worship to Melaka's Roman Catholics, St Peter's is the oldest functioning Christian church in Malaysia. Its design is a striking mixture of east and west. The highlight of the Christian year at St Peter's is the Good Friday celebrations, which are unique in Malaysia. The churchyard becomes a mass of flickering flames, as hundreds of people, many of them non-Christians, participate in a candlelight procession headed by a life-size alabaster effigy of Christ. Swathed in purple robes and crowned in thorns, Christ lies on a golden bier, borne aloft by solemn black-caped men. More bearers follow with a statue of the Virgin Mary, her eyes cast up to heaven as she mourns the loss of her son.

One of the most charismatic members of the Portuguese community is to be found on St Paul's Hill, the home of his ancestors. A self-taught painter, Abensha specializes in oils and watercolours, painting scenes of Melakan life. The hill is his studio and his inspiration. He sits among the gnarled roots of an old tree, using his knee as an easel, with Melaka spread out before him. A tall striking man, with a mane of jet-black hair, thick drooping moustache, and infectious roguish smile,

Abensha has become something of a tourist attraction in his own right. He is difficult to miss in his enormous sombrero-style hat, fashioned out of *papier mâché,* which he made to protect himself from the sun.

The centre of Dutch influence in Melaka is also to be found in a square, the famous, brightly painted **Dutch Square**. The **Stadthuys**, or town hall, with its thick, salmon-pink walls and heavy wooden doors, is believed to be the first building erected by the Dutch, probably in the 1650s. It was from here that the officials of the Dutch East India Company, usually referred to as the VOC (Vereenigde Oostindische Compagnie), governed Melaka and tried to revive its former greatness. The Stadthuys is now home to the Melaka History Museum, which contains many interesting artefacts from the past, in addition to a series of colourful paintings depicting the major events in the history of the town. Across the square is another fine piece of Dutch architecture, the striking strawberry coloured **Christ Church**. It was built in 1753. Each of the huge rafters in the nave was carved from a single tree trunk, while the handmade wooden pews are the originals from the middle of the 18th century.

Dutch Square is a popular gathering place for trishaws and their riders, in effect an unofficial trishaw rank. These bicycle-drawn carriages are not just a tourist novelty, they are a popular mode of transport among the locals and seem to be waiting for weary pedestrians on almost every street corner. Their horns and bells are used less as a means of negotiating traffic, than as a way of attracting the attention of potential customers. The more enterprising offer guided tours, while others seek to increase their appeal by installing radios and flashing lights. Some are simply shabby. Trishaw riders are a breed of their own, wiry, well-worn looking characters, with an air of lethargic irreverence. They seem to spend as much time sleeping as they do peddling, and can often be seen sprawled out in the back of their buggies, enjoying forty winks and oblivious to the noise all around; but there again cycling a heavily laden trishaw is extremely hard work, especially in the midday heat.

The vulnerability of the Dutch during their years in Melaka is evident among the other historic sites of the town. They incorporated St Paul's Church, now a roofless ruin, into the defences of the town, turning the altar into a gun emplacement. To the east of Melaka is **St John's Fort**, built by the Dutch in the second half of the 18th century on the site of a Portuguese chapel. It is not really surprising that Melaka never regained its former glories during Dutch

Opposite: *Abensha, a tourist attraction in his own right as he sits and paints on St Paul's Hill.* ***Below:*** *Porta de Santiago, the only part of A Famosa to survive the demolition by Captain Farquhar and the British.*

times. The Dutch were great traders but, in their eyes, the town was always of secondary importance to the port of Batavia, now the Indonesian capital of Jakarta.

The story of the Dutch in Melaka and the rest of the Malay Peninsula is probably best told in their meticulous trading accounts. They reveal that the V.OC was losing more money than it ever made in Melaka and, after the British took over in 1795, the Company went bankrupt. All of the wages paid were carefully logged, as were the monthly allowances of rice and wine. The governor received twenty pots of wine, the chief merchant seventeen pots as well as 120 pounds of rice. The school master was, as far as the Dutch were concerned, a very lowly person, for he was given only three dollars a month, forty pounds of rice and no wine at all. Even the executioner got more!

The British came to Melaka not through force of arms, but by agreement with the Dutch, their allies in the Napoleonic Wars in Europe, and took over the town in 1795. They later handed it back temporarily in 1818, but by then the British had already implemented their greatest change in Melaka: the destruction of A Famosa and the town defences. Reluctant to return a well-fortified Melaka to their Dutch 'allies' and possibly endanger the future prosperity of their new colony in Penang, the British authorities ordered Captain William Farquhar to dismantle the fortifications.

A graphic account of the demolition of A Famosa has been left in the *Hikayat Abdullah,* a highly entertaining autobiography written by Munshi Abdullah, a noted teacher of Malay who, as scribe to Sir Stamford Raffles, the founder of Singapore, travelled extensively around the Malay Peninsula in the early 19th century. As the locals had foreseen, Farquhar's task did not prove easy. In retrospect this was hardly surprising. The Dutch alone had succeeded in taking A Famosa in 1641, and only then through the ravages of starvation on the garrison, rather than by a direct assault. In the 130 years of Portuguese rule the fortress had successfully

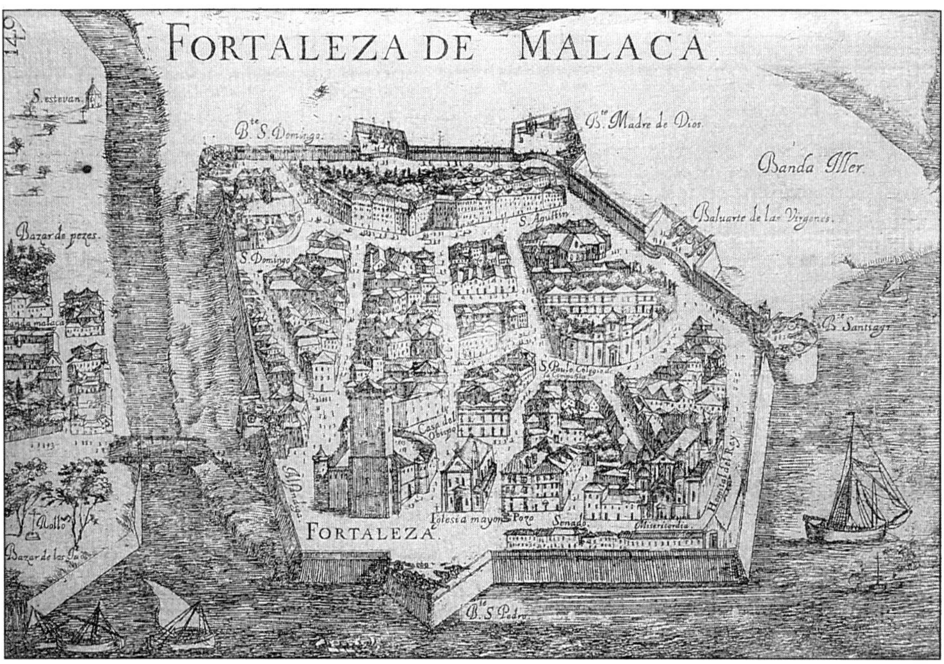

ANTIQUES OF THE ORIENT

withstood twenty sieges. Hundreds of labourers now set about the walls on the eastern side with picks, hammers and shovels, but they made little impression on the mighty walls. Even the prospect of double pay had no effect.

After three months of minimal progress, Farquhar resorted to dynamiting the walls. The effect was startling. The peace of Melaka was shattered by explosion after explosion and 'pieces of the fort as large as elephants, and even some as large as houses, were blown into the air and cascaded into the sea'. The town itself did not escape unscathed. More than a few houses were destroyed in the rain of debris. Nothing would have been left of the defences if Raffles had not happened on the scene and secured a halt to the destruction. The **Porta de Santiago** was saved for posterity. The gateway still conveys something of the massive strength of A Famosa, while the arms of the VOC are visible above the arch. At the same time there is a tinge of sadness about Porta de Santiago, for so little has survived of the once mighty fortress. Munshi Abdullah, only too aware of the great damage inflicted upon the town, wrote, 'the fort was the pride of Melaka and after its destruction the place lost its glory, like a woman bereaved of her husband'. Today much of the glory has returned to Melaka, not just in the splendid historical and cultural attractions that have survived and been restored, but also in the vibrancy of its everyday life.

Part of Melaka's charm lies in its narrow, meandering river which winds through the heart of the old town. Once a bustling channel and the mirror of bloody battles, the river is today quietly reflective. Simple fishing boats are moored along its banks, a far cry from the glorious Babylonian days when galleons, schooners and junks put into Melaka, their valuable and exotic cargoes being brought ashore to

the *godowns,* or warehouses, by hundreds of sweating coolies. There is a dramatic reminder of these past glories near the mouth of the river. The masts from a replica of a 16th-century Portuguese galleon rise high above the surrounding buildings. Boat trips are also available up the river for those who want to enjoy Melaka at a more leisurely pace.

Across the river from Dutch Square, the modern equivalent of Melaka's colourful merchant past is to be found in the **antique shops** of Jalan Hang Jebat, formerly Jonkers Street. Here visitors can hunt for their own little piece of Melakan history. Originally junk stores, most of the shops have been modernised, but one that has been untouched by the passage of time is **Kuttys**, now run by the son of the original proprietor who died in 1988 at the ripe old age of ninety. The shop is a delight to browse around, rather like rummaging through an old attic. The owner proudly insists that everything he sells is 'junk'.

Among the street's antique shops is a shoemakers selling what look like exquisitely brocaded baby shoes, only the feet these tiny shoes were once crafted for belonged to adult women. They are a remnant of the old Chinese practice of

Opposite: *A drawing of A Famosa published in 1552.* ***Above:*** *A 16th-century Portuguese galleon depicted on one of the gravestones in St Paul's Church.*

feet-binding, established as law during the Manchu Dynasty (1644-1912). Young girls of noble birth had their feet tightly bandaged to prevent growth. The resulting restriction in movement was thought to give the girls a more graceful gait, while also assuring that their feet would not be exposed at court. The ideal size of bound feet was an unbelievable three inches. Although not of noble lineage, Chinese immigrants who made their fortunes in the Malay Peninsula brought the custom with them. Feet-binding continued to be practised until the end of the Manchu Dynasty. Today there are only a handful of women left in Malaysia with feet small enough to fit the shoes made by Mr Yeo, the owner of the **Wah Aik Shoemaker Shop.** Fashioned out of Shanghai Hang Chong silk, the shoes are now mostly sold as souvenirs to tourists.

This area of Melaka has always been favoured by the Chinese inhabitants of the town, and in Jalan Tun Tan Cheng Lock is the famous **Baba Nyonya Heritage Museum**, a beautifully preserved townhouse which provides a rare look into the lifestyle of a Straits-born Chinese or *Peranakan* family. Called *Babas* (men) and *Nyonyas* (women), they are descendants of the Chinese merchants who settled in Melaka during its great days as a trading centre, marrying local Malay brides. As with the Portuguese settlers, this process of intermarriage produced a unique community. While retaining many of their Chinese customs and beliefs, such as ancestral worship, the *Peranakan* Chinese embraced important aspects of Malay culture. For instance, they eat with their fingers rather than with chopsticks, and speak Malay liberally sprinkled with Chinese words and phrases. The women have adopted Malay dress and developed their own *Nyonya* cuisine. A principal characteristic of many of their dishes is the very spicy taste, created through the use of coconut milk, *belacan* or shrimp paste, and various chillies and spices. Their brightly coloured cakes are popular throughout the country, proving a great favourite for the breaking of fast during Ramadan.

The townhouse was originally built in 1896 by the millionaire rubber planter, Chang Cheng Siew, and he, like other wealthy *Babas,* filled his house with the finest furniture and chinaware. *Peranakan* ancestral homes in Melaka are deceptively large. While they have narrow fronts, due to the Dutch practice of assessing taxation by the width of a house, they are very deep, incorporating inner courtyards which bring light to the windowless central rooms. The front room on the first floor is the bridal chamber, scene of some rather unusual marriage rituals. Traditional *Peranakan* weddings are very elaborate affairs, lasting twelve days and requiring much preparation. Two or three days before the wedding, the bridal chamber is blessed. A young boy, born at an astrologically favourable time, rolls over the bed three times, in the hope that the couple's first child will be a son. To see whether the boy's antics have done the trick, another ceremony is held at the close of the wedding festivities to predict the sex of the first born. A rooster and a hen are placed under the bed. *Padi* is put before them on the floor and the one which emerges first to eat the grains is believed to represent the sex of the child. Sadly, such rituals are rarely seen today, as most couples opt for more modern wedding ceremonies.

While most of the state's historic sites are to be found in Melaka town, it is worth exploring further afield. The state is renowned for its traditional Malay homes, with their distinctive, colourfully tiled front steps. The finest example of a Melaka house is to be found in the village of **Merlimau**, about 23 km south of Melaka. Built in 1894 for the *penghulu,* or headman,

COURTESY OF MUZIUM NEGARA

of Merlimau, the exterior is visually stunning. Art nouveau floral tiles, imported from China and Italy, adorn the front staircase, which leads to a spacious verandah embellished with carved balustrades, pillars and eaves. The *penghulu's* granddaughter now lives in the house. Visitors are welcome to look around in return for a small donation which goes towards maintaining the property. Just outside Merlimau is the **Makam Tun Teja**, the grave of Tun Teja, the wife of Sultan Mahmud, while at **Ayer Keroh**, some 10 km to the north of Melaka town, visitors can see replicas of the traditional houses of all thirteen Malaysian states. There is also a recreational park and lake, a golf course, a zoo and snake and crocodile farms.

Melaka's history and legendary past extend beyond its shores to a small group of islands. The largest island, **Pulau Besar**, was until recently home to just a few *kampung* houses, a handful of fishermen and a generous sprinkling of superstitions and curses. One popular belief is that you should not eat pork within 48 hours of visiting the island, otherwise you will fall ill, or worse your boat will sink. Today the island boasts a luxury hotel, the Tapa-Nyai Island Resort. Its name was inspired by Gunung Ledang's legendary princess, reputed to be the first person to set foot on the island. Strange tales surround the island's more recent past. When a livestock farm opened there in the 1960s, the cows became depressed and stopped mooing or grazing. Many died. When horses were later brought to the island, they suffered a similar fate. Mysterious circumstances also surrounded the failure of a tin mining venture on the island. Some locals believe the development of the new resort cast a curse over the whole state, causing Melaka's disastrous water shortage in early 1991. On neighbouring **Pulau Jawa** are the ruins of an early 17th-century Portuguese fort. The island is earmarked for development and there has been talk of mooring a floating restaurant in the shape

Above: *Baba Nyonya newly-weds in their bridal robes in the early 20th century.*

of a Portuguese galleon just offshore.

Much further out in the Straits of Malacca, the wreck of an authentic Portuguese galleon has recently been discovered. The *Flor de la Mar* sank on 26th January 1512, probably in a storm, while returning to India laden with booty taken by the Portuguese from Melaka. The ship was large, being capable of carrying up to 600 men, but she was evidently in very poor condition. During the attack on Melaka no Portuguese captain had been prepared to sail her and Albuquerque himself had taken command. In the event the ship saw no action, due to leaking like a sieve. The *Flor de la Mar* now lies on the seabed in Indonesian waters and it is hoped that one day she will be raised. The hold is believed to contain a vast hoard of treasure, tentatively valued at anything from RM2.5 billion to RM20 billion.

Melaka will always be primarily associated with the Malay Sultanate of the 15th century. Another great hero of those days in Melaka was Tun Perak, the *bendahara* saved in the streets of the town by Hang Tuah. His feats, if less famous, were the equal of those of Hang Tuah. On one occasion Tun Perak defeated a far larger Siamese fleet with an ingenious ruse. He landed a hundred men in the mangrove swamps along the Melakan coast, where they tied torches to the topmost branches of the trees. When night fell, the men lit the torches. The Siamese fleet sailed up during the hours of darkness, to be confronted by the lights from the few Melakan vessels and the string of lights along the line of the coast. As Tun Perak had hoped, the Siamese thought these lights came from hundreds of Melakan ships, lying in wait close into the shore, and in terror they fled to the south.

Tun Perak also experienced tragic setbacks, the greatest being the death of his son Tun Besar. One day Tun Besar and his friends were playing *sepak raga,* a game similar to volleyball but using the feet rather than the hands. As they played, Sultan Mansur's eldest son, Raja Muhammad, rode up with his own friends. The two groups had never got on. In one of those moments when events take an unfortunate and fateful course, Tun Besar kicked the rattan ball. To his horror, he sliced it, knocking off Raja Muhammad's headwear. Several of Tun Besar's friends began laughing, whereupon the furious Raja drew his *kris* and fatally stabbed Tun Besar.

Many Melakans expected Tun Perak to wreak terrible vengeance on the royal family, but his revenge was limited only to Muhammad. He declared to his fellow citizens, 'This prince cannot be - never shall be - our ruler at any time in the future!' Mansur duly exiled his eldest son to Pahang. Further than that Tun Perak would not go. Like his friend Hang Tuah, Tun Perak could never be disloyal to the sultan. Loyalty to the ruler was an essential element in the success of Melaka in the 15th century, laying the foundations for the achievements of Mansur and the other great sultans. Mansur himself fully understood this, declaring at Tun Perak's funeral, 'the name of Tun Perak will go down in history as the perfect model of loyalty. I pray to God that the men and women of Melaka will always follow his example.' Troubled times unfortunately lay ahead for the Melakans, but the tradition of absolute loyalty to the ruler was passed from Melaka to all the other Malay kingdoms. The Malay Sultanate in Melaka has in fact been the inspiration for nearly all aspects of royal life and etiquette in the Malay Peninsula, many of which are still in use today. It is therefore somewhat ironic that modern Melaka is one of the four Malaysian states without a sultan.

Opposite: *Two young Malay brothers waiting for the bus at their kampung.*

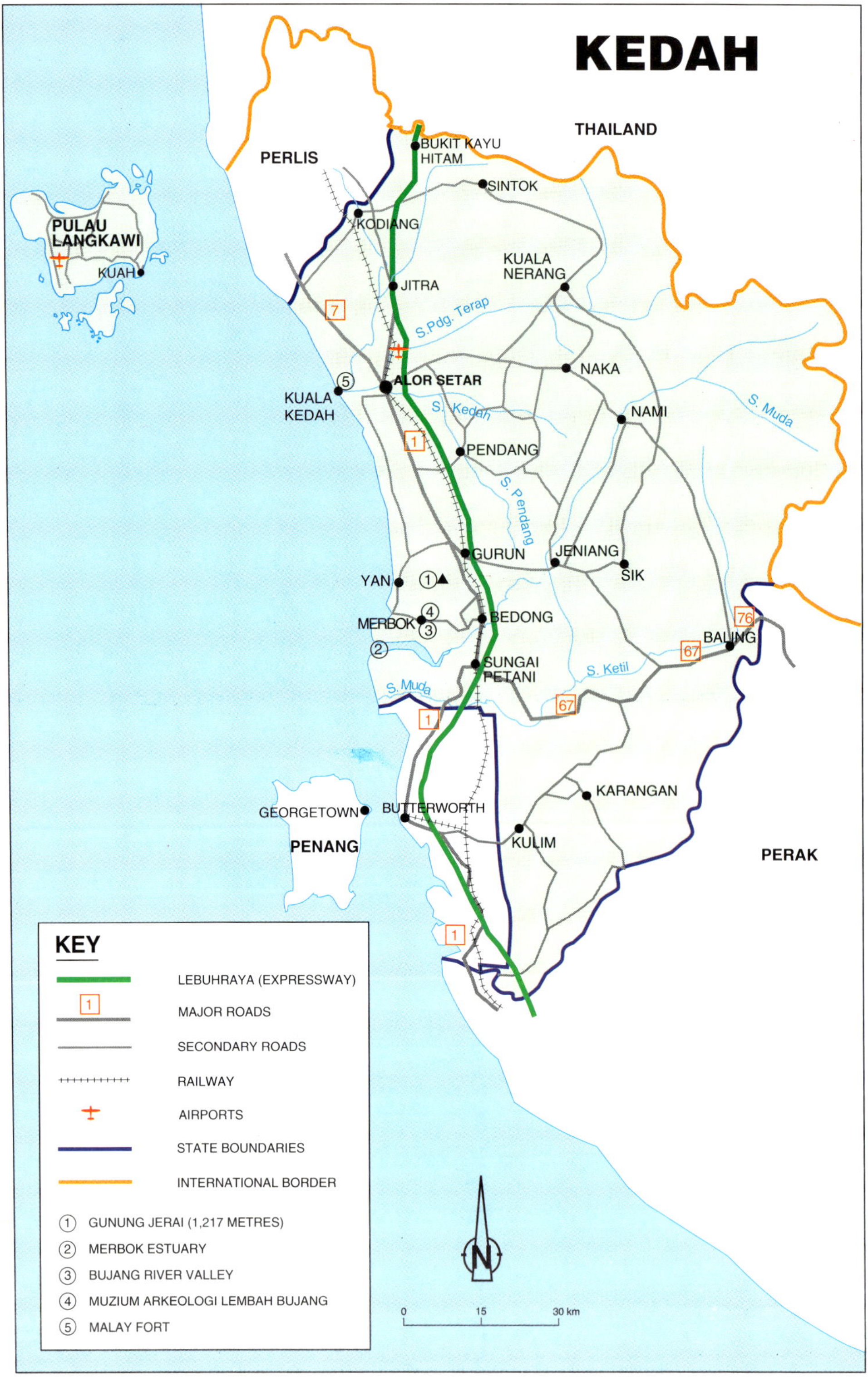
KEDAH
THAILAND
PERLIS
PULAU LANGKAWI
KUAH
BUKIT KAYU HITAM
SINTOK
KODIANG
JITRA
KUALA NERANG
S.Pdg. Terap
7
NAKA
ALOR SETAR
KUALA KEDAH
5
S. Kedah
NAMI
S. Muda
1
PENDANG
S. Pendang
GURUN
JENIANG
SIK
YAN
1
4
MERBOK
3
BEDONG
2
76
BALING
67
SUNGAI PETANI
S. Ketil
S. Muda
67
1
KARANGAN
GEORGETOWN
BUTTERWORTH
PENANG
KULIM
PERAK
1
KEY
LEBUHRAYA (EXPRESSWAY)
MAJOR ROADS
SECONDARY ROADS
RAILWAY
AIRPORTS
STATE BOUNDARIES
INTERNATIONAL BORDER
1 GUNUNG JERAI (1,217 METRES)
2 MERBOK ESTUARY
3 BUJANG RIVER VALLEY
4 MUZIUM ARKEOLOGI LEMBAH BUJANG
5 MALAY FORT
N
0
15
30 km

KEDAH AND PERLIS

Early Kingdoms of the Golden Khersonese

Many Malays believe that their history effectively began with the Melaka Sultanate in the 15th century. Melaka has a very rich and formative history, establishing many of the cultural foundations for modern Malaysia, but it was not the beginning. To the north, in the states of Kedah and Perlis, can be found traces of an earlier and equally fascinating Malay world.

Today's visitors to Kedah and Perlis will be confronted by fields of *padi* stretching as far as the eye can see, for this is Malaysia's 'Rice Bowl'. Farm workers can often be seen ploughing, planting or picking the rice stalks, while water buffaloes indulge themselves in messy mud baths to escape the searing heat of the midday sun. To the north and east the plains give way to undulating hills and valleys, the dramatic limestone mountains of northern Kedah and Perlis, and finally the border with Thailand. Offshore lie the legendary islands of the Langkawi archipelago, a favoured haven for tourists from all over the world. Fifteen hundred years ago, if not earlier, this land was a haven of another sort, for the historic importance of Kedah derived from its position as a sanctuary from the dangers of dark age sea travel.

The massive outcrop of **Gunung Jerai**, or Kedah Peak, rises to some 1,200 metres (3,992 feet) above the surrounding plains and is visible for miles around. A winding road leads to a mountain resort near the top. Watch out for your car engine overheating. The more cautious traveller might take one of the government land rovers which also ply the route. From the resort there are sweeping views across the coastal plain and out to sea, while the surrounding forest provides some challenging jungle trails and the chance to see a wide variety of orchids, rhododendrons, shrubs and ferns, perhaps even a mousedeer. For dark age travellers the peak was an obvious landmark, being easily identifiable from far out to sea. Moreover, to the south of Gunung Jerai the Merbok estuary provided a safe, natural landfall for shipping from India. The fertile plains merely added to the attractions of the area for these dark age visitors and inhabitants.

The early history of Kedah, like that of Melaka, is infused with heroic tales and feats. Such legends are an integral part of Malay culture, preserved for posterity in the *hikayat,* the most popular form of historical literature in Malaysia. The finest example of the hikayat is undoubtedly the *Sejarah Melayu,* but there are many others, ranging in time from the 16th to the 19th centuries and the work of Munshi Abdullah. They were meant to be recited aloud and the effect on the audience was always of paramount importance. This accounts for the repetition of words and phrases, which gives an almost lyrical effect, if read out aloud. Fiction was always liberally mixed with fact, with the writers drawing their tales from any available sources, such as Arabic and Persian legends, Indian stories or epics from Java. The latter were the inspiration for many of the feats of Hang Tuah. The content of the *hikayats* is in itself a reflection of the many cultural influences which have affected the

***State crests:** The wreaths of padi dominating both crests represent the importance of the crop to Kedah and Perlis, which are together known as Malaysia's 'Rice Bowl'.*

Malay Peninsula.

Various conventions dictated the treatment of certain subjects. For instance, the ideal ruler is depicted in a specific fashion. He is firstly identified through his illustrious pedigree, the greatest being able to trace their descent back to the legendary princes, who appeared on the sacred Bukit Si Guntang in Palembang and became the first Malay kings. The sultans of Melaka claimed descent from these princes and, through them, back to Alexander the Great. The ruler also possesses a sense of majesty, is wise, just in his actions and suitably pious. His kingdom prospers through trade, earning him the gratitude of his loyal subjects. He goes on to marry a beautiful princess with an equally prestigious lineage, and builds a magnificent palace, the like of which has never been seen before. The account of the reign of Sultan Mansur of Melaka in the *Sejarah Melayu* is an obvious case in point, but there are many other examples in Malay history.

The work dealing with the origins of Kedah is the *Hikayat Marong Mahawangsa,* more commonly known as the Kedah Annals. The hero of the tale is Raja Marong Mahawangsa, an ambassador from the fabled kingdom of Rum in Turkey, as well as a famed seaman and warrior, and a man wise in the art of magic. He would need all these skills, if he was to fulfil his mission of sailing to China with a young prince who was to marry the emperor's daughter. A sizeable fleet was raised and all went well until the ships reached Ceylon. There they encountered Garuda, the mighty eagle of the Hindu God Vishnu. Garuda had decided to prevent the marriage and had told King Solomon as much. Famed for his wisdom, Solomon had warned the headstrong eagle, 'you can do what you like in the matter, but you must always remember that God is the ultimate power that is All-Powerful, and anyone who disregards this absolute truth,...is doomed to disillusionment and discomfiture'.

Garuda chose to ignore Solomon's advice. He first kidnapped the intended bride and then sent a series of violent storms to destroy the fleet. Several of the ships were sunk, but Mahawangsa and his men kept their nerve, replying in kind by shooting magic arrows at the giant eagle. Garuda resorted to hurling giant boulders at the ships and one of them at last sank the prince's vessel. The eagle flew away victorious, leaving Mahawangsa and the remnants of the fleet in peace, but they could find no trace of the prince. He had in fact been washed up on the shores of Pulau Langkawi. The exact spot is thought to be the beach at **Gua Cerita**, or the Cave of Stories, an idyllic hideaway on the northern tip of the island. There are actually two caves, one on top of the other and connected by a rickety ladder. Some of the rock formations resemble the sort of furniture used by Fred Flintstone and his friends. Perhaps the Chinese princess slept on what looks like a stone bed and ate from a stone table, because, by extraordinary coincidence, Gua Cerita was the place where Garuda had hidden her.

While walking along the beach one morning, the princess found the prince lying unconscious in the shallows. She dragged him to the cave, where she nursed him back to health. The princess had already fallen in love with him by the time she discovered that he was her intended husband. They were later rescued from the island and taken to China where they married. Garuda had failed because, as King Solomon had known, God had willed the marriage and no one could challenge his authority.

Meanwhile, Marong Mahawangsa sailed on to the mainland, dropping anchor in the shadow of Gunung Jerai. Somewhat fearful, he and his men went ashore, only to be greeted by a friendly people. They duly asked Mahawangsa to be their king, a proposal he was more than happy to accept. So he and his men settled there, and thus founded the kingdom of Kedah.

Tales and fables abound in this part of Malaysia, not least on the hundred or so islands that make up the **Langkawi archipelago**. The islands present a stunning visual spectacle, whether viewed from the air or a boat. Flying into the airport on Pulau Langkawi, the largest and most developed island, some of the smaller islands appear as little more than rocky outcrops in the ocean. Others loom large, covered in luxuriant jungle vegetation and fringed with steep cliffs falling dramatically into the sea. Several of the islands have small fishing settlements, but most are uninhabited. The Langkawi archipelago is, as the guidebooks promise, a romantic and largely unspoilt retreat.

Pulau Langkawi is crowned with majestic marbled mountains, which look down on picturesque *padi* fields and rural *kampung* scenes. The coastline is composed of mile after mile of white sandy beaches, interspersed by secret caves and secluded coves. The island is a quiet uncomplicated place, where, until recently, it was said that the water buffaloes far outnumbered the local population. The capital, **Kuah**, is a long, straggling town, built around a bay. At one end of the town, past the golden domed Moorish mosque, is the jetty, where ferries arrive from the mainland and Penang, and boat trips around the islands begin. Kuah has been given a recent face-lift, as part of the Malaysian government's attempt to promote Langkawi as a tourist destination. In 1987 duty-free status was conferred upon the island and numerous duty-free shops have opened in Kuah. Many new hotels and chalets have been built, with prices to suit every pocket. There is some accommodation in Kuah, but most of the hotels are

Opposite: *A woman working in the padi fields.* ***Below:*** *Room service is a little different at the Pelangi Beach Resort on Pulau Langkawi.*

located along Pulau Langkawi's beautiful beaches. A good road runs around the island. There are plenty of taxis, a bus service and, for those who want to explore the sites at their own leisure, bicycles, motorbikes or cars can be hired.

Pulau Langkawi is steeped in legends. Almost every site has a tale to tell. The origins of the mountains which form the backbone of the island, as well as several of the place-names, go back to an ancient family feud. **Gunung Raya**, the highest peak on Pulau Langkawi, stands facing **Gunung Mat Cincang**, while in between lies the hill of **Bukit Sawar**. According to legend, all three were originally humans. Mat Raya had a son who fell in love with the daughter of Mat Cincang and began to court her. Unfortunately, Mat Cincang did not consider the boy a good enough match for his daughter and forbade any talk of marriage. The boy was heartbroken, while his father was furious at the insult to the family. A bitter feud ensued, which culminated in a furious fight. Both families

flung pots, pans, indeed anything that came to hand, at each other. A large pot containing gravy smashed to the ground at a place later known as **Belanga Pecah**, or broken pot, while the spot where the gravy spilt became Kuah, the Malay word for gravy. A cauldron of boiling water was also thrown, hot springs gushing into the air where it landed. These springs are said to be those at **Telaga Air Hangat**. The fight was eventually stopped by Mat Sawar, a friend of both families. Mat Sawar and the two family heads were then turned into mountains.

If another local tale is to be believed, the same mountain range was once inhabited by an enormous boa constrictor. The snake had agreed to protect the land of Kedah and only devour the hated Siamese, so long as each sultan sacrificed a daughter on his accession to the throne or when the kingdom went to war. True to its word, the snake performed heroically, on one occasion stretching its full length across a harbour entrance and preventing the Siamese fleet from attacking.

All went well until one sultan failed to pay the time-honoured tribute. The snake went berserk and began killing all the people and livestock it could find on Pulau Langkawi. At this rather opportune moment, a holy man arrived on the island and announced that he would save the inhabitants. He placed a mat on the ground and began to pray. Suddenly, the boa constrictor appeared, trapped the holy man in its coils and squeezed tight, before swallowing him whole. Yet this was no ordinary meal for the snake. The boa constrictor began to shake uncontrollably and, with an agonising hiss, slid at great speed back to the mountains, never to be seen again, although there is a postscript to the tale. Prospectors searching for tin in the area later reported discovering the bones of a huge snake in a narrow valley.

The most famous of all the Langkawi

legends is the Curse of Mahsuri. As with most popular folk tales, the story has undergone changes through the telling, being subjected to the whims and fancies of successive narrators, though the tragic ending remains the same. Mahsuri lived on the island some two hundred years ago and was renowned for her charm and beauty. She fell in love with the brother of the island chief, and married him. They had a child, but Mahsuri and her husband were soon parted, as he had to go and fight the Siamese. Meanwhile, a penniless poet chanced upon the *kampung* in which Mahsuri lived. Always a charitable soul, she took pity on the poet, and offered him food and a place to stay, which he gratefully accepted.

The chief's wife had always been jealous of Mahsuri and now she saw her chance. She told her husband that Mahsuri and the poet were having an affair. Without even investigating the allegations, the chief ordered Mahsuri to be put to death for adultery. Executions were public affairs in those days and, when the executioner plunged the *kris* into Mahsuri's body, there was a gasp from the spectators. White blood spurted from the fatal wound, signifying her innocence. Worse was to follow for the horrified onlookers. In her death throes, Mahsuri put a curse on the island, crying out, 'For this act of injustice, Langkawi will not prosper nor enjoy peace for seven generations!'

Many locals believe that the curse brought difficult times for Langkawi. Soon afterwards the island was overrun by the Siamese. The chief ordered the rice stored in the granary to be burned, in order to prevent it falling into Siamese hands. What are thought to be the remnants of the burnt rice can be seen today at the spot where the original granary stood, now known as the **Field of Burnt Rice**. A few charred grains sometimes appear, usually following a heavy storm. They are highly sought after, being valued as a cure for stomach pains

Opposite: *One of the waterfalls at Seven Wells.* ***Above:*** *The end of another day on Pulau Langkawi.*

and fever. The curse continued to cast a shadow over Langkawi during the years of colonial rule. Several British entrepreneurs tried to start businesses on the island, all to no avail. One man opened a fish factory, only for all the fish to swim away! The period of seven generations finally lapsed in the 1980s with the birth of Aishah Nawawi, a direct descendant of Mahsuri, who lives in Thailand. Since then there has been a spate of development projects on Pulau Langkawi, bringing in their wake the boom in tourism. All this has added credibility to the local belief that the curse has now been lifted.

Mahsuri was buried in the south of the island. The grave at **Makam Mahsuri** is encased in white marble, brought down from the slopes of the mountains, and surrounded by white walls, a poignant reminder of her innocence. Nearby is a well which she used from an early age until her untimely death. Photographs of some of Mahsuri's descendants are displayed on a board next to her grave. At the top is one of Aishah, supposedly responsible for the ending of the curse.

The beaches are the main attraction for most visitors to Pulau Langkawi. The most popular is **Pantai Cenang**, a 2 km stretch of sun-drenched white sand in the south-western corner of the island, and home to the luxurious Pelangi Beach Resort. In the early evenings local boys play volleyball on the sand, while the less energetic come out for a stroll and to watch the stunning sunsets, for which the beach is deservedly famous. Nearby is the island of **Pulau Rebak Kecil**, which the local people have dubbed 'Fantasy Island' after an American television series. A sand bar appears at low tide, and on occasions it is possible to walk across to the island. Much less populated, but no less attractive, is the beach at **Tanjung Rhu**, on the northern coast of Pulau Langkawi, the point from which boats can be hired for a trip to the legendary caves of Gua Cerita.

While most of the principal tourist sites are on Pulau Langkawi, other parts of the archipelago are well worth exploring. The islands have been sculpted by the elements into a wonderful assortment of shapes and sizes, with some lying very close together and separated by gorge-like passages. Island-hopping trips make a good day out. The local boatmen will point out that one of the islands, when viewed from a particular angle, resembles a reclining pregnant woman. This is **Pulau Dayang Bunting**, or the Island of the Pregnant Maiden. Nestling amidst the jungle which covers the island, is an emerald green lake of the same name, so-called because of a sad local tale.

A beautiful genie called Mambang Sari is said to have once lived on the island. One day she was spotted by a male genie, Mat Taja, who promptly fell in love with her. He was very shy and found it impossible to reveal his true feelings to her. So he sought the help of a wise old man, who told him that the way to Mambang Sari's heart was to catch the tears of a mermaid and wipe his face with them. The path of true love has been easier, but Mat Taja was a resourceful genie.

He went in search of a mermaid, found one and collected her tears in a bamboo container. He then rubbed the tears on to his face. As the old man had predicted, Mambang Sari fell in love with him. Unfortunately, this is not a tale with a happy ending. When Mambang Sari became pregnant, she went to the lake for the birth. A baby boy was born, but he died a week later. In her anguish she threw the body into the lake. A white crocodile, the spirit of the dead baby, is said to guard the lake. The waters of the lake are also believed to possess the power to make barren women pregnant. Local people tell the story of a woman who was unable to conceive a child for nineteen years. Soon after taking a drink from the lake, she became pregnant.

To the west of Pulau Dayang Bunting is **Pulau Singa Besar**, or Big Lion Island. There are no lions here, but the wildlife sanctuary on the island contains numerous

Above: *Boys playing in the emerald green waters of the lake on Pulau Dayang Bunting.*

S.K. CHONG

exotic birds and animals. Visitors can also enjoy a spot of snorkelling in the surrounding waters, although the best coral in the archipelago is to be found in the marine park surrounding **Pulau Payar**, a three hour boat trip from Kuah.

If the islands of Langkawi are one of Malaysia's great natural treasures, then in the shadow of Gunung Jerai stand some of Malaysia's greatest historical finds, providing an invaluable insight into the dark age past of Kedah. Here lies the reality behind the legend of Marong Mahawangsa. The first voyagers to the Malay Peninsula came from India, possibly as long as two thousand years ago. Blown by the westerly winds, they made landfall on the shores of Kedah. They initially came in search of gold and spices, the Malay Peninsula being called the 'Golden Khersonese' by Ptolemy and the other early Greek geographers in the 2nd century. Once started, trade grew rapidly. Local ports flourished as vessels, sailing from India on the south-west monsoon, had to wait for several months before they could return home with the north-easterly winds at the end of the year.

A further impetus to trade came in the 5th century with the opening of the sea routes to China. Two hundred years later a Chinese pilgrim visited a kingdom in the Malay Peninsula named *Chieh-ch'a*. Historians now believe that this kingdom was Kedah. It was centred on the valley of the Bujang River, a tributary of the Merbok. Archaeological excavations in the valley have unearthed some remarkable finds. Over fifty individual temple sites have been excavated and to date nine of them have been painstakingly reconstructed. A fitting climax to the decades of work came with the opening of the **Muzium Arkeologi Lembah Bujang** near Merbok in 1980.

The most famous 'exhibit' at the museum is the **Candi Bukit Batu Pahat**, rebuilt on the summit of the small hill behind the main building. In common with all the Hindu temples, it comprises two principal parts: the *vimana* or sanctuary, and the *mandapa* or hall. Constructed of sandstone bricks, the temple is believed to date from the 12th century or later and is remarkable for its combination of styles. The cults of Vishnu, the Hindu God Siva and Mahayana Buddhism are incorporated, providing one of the earliest examples of the Malay people adapting ideas from outside for their own use. A similar temple may well have existed on the very top of Gunung Jerai, where today the radio station stands. A small Hindu shrine probably marks the spot.

From the archaeological discoveries, it has been possible to piece together some of the dark age history of the Bujang valley. By the 7th century a successful port had grown up, and in the wake of the Indian merchants came Indian beliefs. Buddhism quickly took a hold on the local people. One of the finds dating from this period is a terracotta image of the Buddhist Goddess, Hariti, carrying a child. The port continued to flourish, with finds, dated to the 8th and 9th centuries, ranging from Chinese pottery to glass and beads from the Middle East. By the early 10th century the settlement had moved up the Bujang valley and become centred on the village of Pengkalan Bujang. During the next hundred years Hinduism came to be practised throughout the area. Hindu temples dating from this period are everywhere, often just metres away from earlier Buddhist ones, as for instance at Kampung Pendiat. The wealth of Pengkalan Bujang is illustrated by the variety and nature of the ceramics and glassware discovered on the site, while

Opposite: *Burau Bay on the west coast of Pulau Langkawi. The mountain in the background is Gunung Mat Cincang which forms the perfect profile of a human face.*

the temples bear testimony to the skills of the local craftsmen in design and construction.

On a few occasions the excavations in the area of the Bujang valley have even born out some of the tales to be found in the *Hikayat Marong Mahawangsa.* More legends probably surround the figure of Raja Bersiong than any other character in the history of Kedah. Reputed to be a cannibal, a trait he was said to have inherited from his mother, Bersiong also sported a fine pair of tusks. He is said to have built a fort at Bukit Penjara, a small hill overlooking the mouth of the Merbok River. Archaeologists have unearthed evidence of habitation here from as early as the 11th century, while a group of workmen discovered a cave which may have formed part of the fort.

The greatest kingdom to emerge in the Malay Peninsula during the dark ages was Srivijaya, the maritime empire centred on Palembang in Sumatra. Here is the true predecessor to Melaka as the great South East Asian *entrepôt.* There is much that remains very shadowy about Srivijaya, but it is clear that the settlements in the Bujang valley formed a key part of the empire. From the 7th century until possibly the late 13th century, Srivijaya dominated the Straits of Malacca, its rulers exercising authority over the surrounding lands, including Sumatra and much of the Malay Peninsula. One kingdom to fall under its sway was Melayu, thought to have been located on the Jambi River to the north of Palembang and from which the peninsula took its name and language. Malay became the language of Srivijayan trade and spread throughout the area. The centuries of Srivijayan dominance also saw the start of a long lasting migration of people from Sumatra to the Malay Peninsula.

At the heart of Srivijaya was trade, the empire in effect being one mighty commercial enterprise, handling goods from India, Western Asia and China, as well as those from its own lands and vassal states around the Straits of Malacca. The Srivijayans were in no doubt of the debt

they owed to the sea, if the action of one ruler is anything to go by. Every day he would hurl a gold bar into the sea to appease the gods of the oceans. The basis of Srivijayan control of the sea was the relationship between the rulers and the *orang laut,* or sea people. For countless decades the *orang laut,* with their unrivalled knowledge of local sea and weather conditions, had created havoc along the shipping lanes through piracy, a practice all too common in the waters of South East Asia. The Srivijayans quickly realised the obvious advantages of hiring the *orang laut* to keep open the empire's trading routes. Later generations of *orang laut* would perform a similar task for the Malay Sultanate in Melaka. Hang Tuah is believed to have come from an *orang laut* background.

Srivijaya went into a rapid decline in the 14th century. The *orang laut* became increasingly difficult to control, trade went elsewhere, and there were growing threats from Java and India. The end came when the Javanese overran the empire. One refugee from Palembang was Parameswara, the founder of the Malay Sultanate in Melaka. The kingdom in Kedah did not benefit at all from the fall of Srivijaya, and also went into decline. Thailand was a growing threat to the north and trade plummeted. The merchants moved away, ultimately to Melaka, and the economy of Kedah became dependent upon agriculture and the growing of rice.

The modern states of Kedah and Perlis account for nearly half of Malaysia's rice production. During the growing season the countryside becomes an unending sea of bright green shoots. Then, in the weeks before harvest, the *padi* ripens to a golden hue. Men and women are often to be seen working in the fields, particularly in the early morning when the sun is still bearable. For many visitors to the region, *padi* farming might seem a perfect escape from the pressures of modern life, but

Opposite: *The grave of Mahsuri.*
Below: *Candi Bukit Batu Pahat.*

appearances can be deceptive. *Padi* farming is an extremely arduous and, all too often, unrewarding occupation, and poverty has been a frequent problem in the past among the rural communities of Kedah and Perlis.

For years many of the farmers clung stubbornly to the old methods and beliefs. For instance, they always thought that the *padi* grain possessed a *semangat,* or spirit of life, which was prone to take fright and flee. This was certainly the case if a sickle or other heavy instrument was used to cut the grain at harvest time. The farmers believed that the loss of the *semangat* would lead to a poor harvest in the following year. The traditional method was to use a *tuai,* or reaping knife, which the farmer held in a way where the stalks could not 'see' the blade until the last moment, when the cut was made. As a result the *semangat* did not take fright and all would be well with the next crop. The problem was that, using the *tuai,* only a few stalks could be cut at a time, so harvesting was a laborious and prolonged affair.

Only recently have standards of living begun to rise significantly in the rural areas of Kedah and Perlis. The government has invested large sums in the construction of irrigation channels, so that the farmers no longer have to rely solely on the weather. New strains of high-yielding *padi* have been introduced, while mechanisation has improved methods of cultivation and harvesting. *Padi* farming has thus been dragged into the modern world. Roads now criss-cross the countryside, where earlier there were simply tracks and paths. Only in one respect has there been a negative side to this development. The improvement in communications and standards of education has been accompanied by a marked movement of young people to the towns, in search of better-paid jobs. Far too many *padi* farmers are the wrong side of fifty.

It was the ancestors of these farmers who, for generation after generation, perpetuated most of the myths and legends of Kedah. Storytelling was a way of life in the villages in the days before the arrival of

radio and television. During times of leisure, particularly after harvesting, the traditions of the *hikayat* were kept alive by skilled storytellers, many of whom came from Perlis. One of the most enduring myths, originating from the *Hikayat Marong Mahawangsa,* is that Kedah was once the legendary kingdom of Langkasuka. This seems unlikely as Langkasuka was probably located in the vicinity of Patani, on the east coast of Thailand. Nevertheless, there remains a widespread belief amongst Malays that this once great kingdom stretched across northern Malaysia and, for this reason, Langkasuka was mooted as a possible name for the country following independence.

According to Malay legend, Langkasuka was a rather strange place, being inhabited by the 'little people' and wild goats from the hills, while the ruler was a fairy princess. One tradition that Langkasuka passed on to Melaka and the other Malay kingdoms was that of the *nobat,* the orchestra of nine instruments which played at all major royal occasions, such as coronations and weddings. The instruments of the royal orchestra of Kedah were originally gifts from Sultan Mahmud of Melaka and are housed in the **Balai Nobat** in the state capital, Alor Setar. The Kedah *nobat* is today one of only four left in Malaysia, the others being in the kingdoms of Johor, Selangor and Terengganu. The various instruments were played for centuries by members of the same families, the privilege being passed on from father to son. Unfortunately, the lure of modern well-paid employment in recent years has undermined this hereditary tradition, as it has several other Malay customs.

Alor Setar has often been dubbed the 'Gateway to the North', but the town is much more than just a gateway to the northern parts of Malaysia and the border with Thailand. The town is well worth a visit and is also a good base from which to

Opposite: *Water buffaloes in the padi fields of Kedah.* ***Below:*** *Ducks hanging out to entice customers into a restaurant. Roast duck is a popular Chinese dish.*

explore the rest of Kedah. Alor Setar has a relaxed charm about it, the hallmark of all Malaysia's northern towns. The pace of life is slower and the 20th century seems less obtrusive. The principal attractions of the town are all grouped together, along Jalan Pekan Melayu, taking much of the slog out of sightseeing. The distinctive three-tiered octagonal tower is the Balai Nobat, housing the instruments of the royal orchestra.

On the same side of the road is the **Muzium Di Raja**. Built in the early 18th century, the building was originally the sultan's palace. The museum contains various displays and exhibits from Kedah's royal past and present, including the bridal chamber and the royal thrones. Next door is the intricately carved **Balai Besar**, or great hall, where the sultan used to sit in state and listen to the grievances of his subjects. The first building was destroyed by Bugis forces from Selangor in 1770 and the present structure, incorporating Thai architectural influences, dates from the end of the 19th century. Across the road is the

Masjid Zahir, the impressive Moorish state mosque. The elegant domes contrast sharply with the nearby modern concrete fountain, a popular meeting place for local people, young and old alike.

On the edge of Alor Setar is the **State Museum**, reminiscent in design of the Balai Besar. Also on the outskirts of town is the atap-roofed house where Malaysia's current Prime Minister, Dr Mahathir, was born and brought up. The house has been restored and is now open to the public. Alor Setar would seem to be an ideal breeding ground for prime ministers, as Tunku Abdul Rahman also came from Kedah, being a member of the royal family.

Along with the sea, the northern border with Thailand has proved the greatest influence on Kedah and the state of Perlis. The Siamese in fact brought about the separation of Kedah and Perlis in 1839, following an unsuccessful rebellion against their overlordship in Kedah. Before then Perlis had simply been a part of the kingdom of Kedah. The new state was ruled by Syed Sapee, a member of an influential Arab merchant family, who had married into the Kedah royal house. He was later given the title of Raja, but he was in effect little more than a local Malay chief, his position being ultimately dependent upon the Siamese. Independence for both Perlis and Kedah from Thailand came with the Treaty of Bangkok in 1909, which exchanged Siamese control for that of the British.

Perlis was thus established as a separate entity, although economically it remained a rice growing state and dependent upon the much larger and more prosperous Kedah. Perlis is the smallest state in the country, covering an area of less than 800 sq km. The Raja of Perlis resides in the sleepy royal town of **Arau**, to the south-east of the capital **Kangar**. Perlis is renowned for its *laksa,* a dish of thick rice noodles served in a spicy fish soup. One of the best places to sample it is the port of **Kuala Perlis**, 11 km to the south-west of Kangar. A regular ferry service operates from the port to Pulau Langkawi, only forty minutes away. Wooden houses are built in a higgledy-piggledy fashion along the river banks, where the fishing boats are often moored two or three abreast. In the early evening the waterfront becomes a giant restaurant as local people gather to eat and relax at the open-air food stalls.

The Thai border has proved anything but a blessing for Kedah and Perlis in the past. There is no great physical divide between the northern Malay states and Thai territory, no mountain range or mighty river, so the division is essentially man-made and all too easy to cross. Today the border is peaceful, with local people going back and forth to visit relatives and friends, while the border towns attract tourists and shoppers with their duty-free goods. The eccentricities of a largely man-made border are only too apparent at **Padang Besar** in Perlis. Here the two countries literally merge in the town and the railway station has had to be enlarged to accommodate the Malaysian and Thai border officials.

The Malay-Thai frontier has historically been a source of trouble for the people on both sides of the divide. In that respect Malaysia's northern border can be compared with the ancient boundary between England and Scotland. Both borders were difficult to guard and administer effectively. The countryside was sparsely populated, with few roads and even fewer police stations. Crime was almost impossible to prevent, the hills providing an ideal lair for outlaws and thieves from both sides of the border.

Today the dramatic scenery of Perlis and northern Kedah, with its stark limestone outcrops, attracts tourists rather than criminals. One of the best places to view

Opposite: *The Balai Nobat.* ***Below:*** *The fountains in the centre of Alor Setar are a popular meeting place for locals. Behind is the Masjid Zahir.*

the countryside is from the top of **Gunung Medan**, over 300 metres high and located about 6 km south of Kangar. A particularly curious sight from the top is the large clump of trees, naturally forming the outline of a dinosaur, which, so the local people will tell you, has embarked on a never-ending journey to the hills.

The area is also famed for its caves. The most interesting to visit is **Gua Kelam**, or the Cave of Darkness, located at **Kaki Bukit**, about 13 km from Padang Besar. The cave is 370 metres long and forms a natural tunnel through to the valley on the other side of the hill. It was originally carved out of the rock by the subterranean river, the noise of which adds a dramatic, if somewhat eerie, effect to the cave. There is a suspended wooden walkway running the entire length of the cave. It was constructed in 1935 to transport tin ore from the nearby mines to the town of Kaki Bukit. Watch out for the motorcyclists who use it as a short cut between Kaki Bukit and the border town of Wang Keliang. At the far end of the cave, the gloom gives way to bright sunlight, and the green and pleasant valley of Wang Tangga. For a brief moment the experience evokes thoughts of the fictional world of Shangri La, but this area is no paradise for the locals. The mines closed in the 1980s when the price of tin collapsed and Kaki Bukit, once a bustling tin mining community, is in danger of becoming a ghost town, now that its lifeblood has gone. Rubber smallholdings have provided some employment for the ex-miners, but the younger generation has had to look elsewhere for work.

The caves and limestone hills of Perlis are a favourite haunt for a number of venomous snakes, and at **Sungai Batu Pahat** there is a snake farm. It is primarily a research centre for the development of serums to combat snake bites. An interesting range of snakes are on display: some of them preserved in jars; others, including the deadly king cobra, very much alive. Items on the menu at feeding time include mice, frogs and fish. The Visitors' Centre also has a series of informative display

boards on snakes and their bites.

In the 19th century the sultans of Kedah left the local chiefs to look after the turbulent border districts. Fortunately, the chiefs never became too powerful and Kedah largely escaped the civil strife which plagued the Malay states to the south. They in fact found it very difficult to maintain order and more than one resorted to agreements with the local criminal fraternity. Crime was almost a way of life for many people in Kedah and Perlis. The economy was dependent on rice cultivation, a tough existence at the best of times, but floods, drought, heavy taxation or the arrival of the Siamese army could spell disaster. Often the only recourse for many was crime, in a rather extreme form of 'self-help'. At the same time there were elements who took to crime more from personal choice than economic necessity. The Sam-Sams were, as a people, notorious for banditry and robbery. Their way of life was similar to that of the gypsies in Europe, and they were equally disliked. Siamese speaking, their origins are very obscure. They may have been Muslim Malays who adopted the Siamese language, or Siamese who became Muslims.

The most profitable activity for the Sam-Sams was cattle-rustling. Cattle were an expensive item and commanded a high ransom, which most owners were prepared to pay to get them back. The stolen cattle were invariably driven across the border, the rustlers often leaving an obvious trail for the aggrieved farmer to follow. When he finally caught up with the bandits, negotiations were opened, a price agreed and the farmer and his livestock were reunited, if facing a rather long, and somewhat poorer, walk home.

A few of the Sam-Sam and Malay bandits acquired great fame during their lifetimes. Indeed tales of one or two still

Opposite: *Tasik Melati, a man-made lake located to the north of Kangar. In the background are two of the limestone outcrops which dominate the countryside in Perlis.* ***Below:*** *Fishermen working on their boat in Kuala Perlis.*

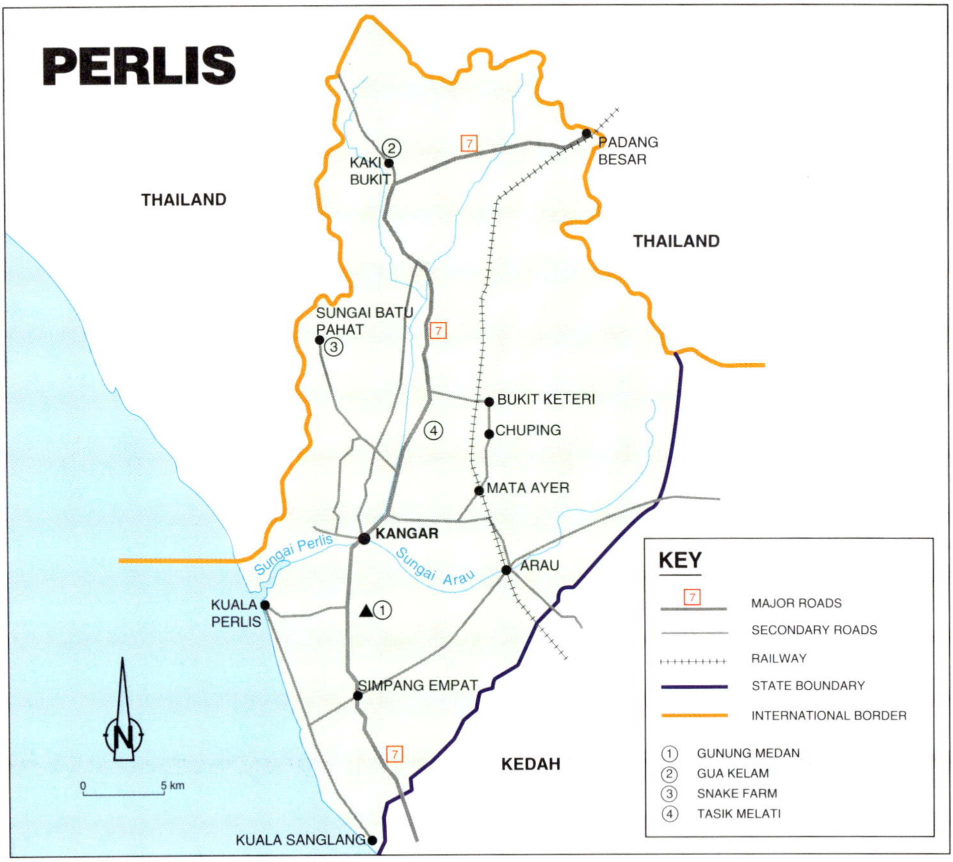

flourish today. Their renown was such that local people would often shelter them, believing that they possessed magical powers which made them invulnerable. One of the most famous was a Sam-Sam called Salleh Tui. Tunku Abdul Rahman once recalled, 'Salleh Tui was the greatest of Kedah's outlaws. He was also the terror of my boyhood days. Palace nursemaids would frighten us when we were playing late in the evening outside the house, by calling out 'Salleh Tui', saying he would be after us, and we would run indoors.'

In 1920 a reward of RM1,000 was offered for the capture of probably Kedah's most famous outlaw. He was described as follows: 'His age is approximately 30 years. His body is reddish, thin and tall. He has a slight moustache, and a dangling gold filling in one of his upper teeth. His hair is long over the forehead, and he is fond of wearing the *kopiah baldu* (a Muslim cap).' This was Nayan, the Malay Robin Hood, who robbed the rich to feed the poor. Highly skilled at the art of *silat,* he was also very adept with both *kris* and pistol. Nayan was always ready to defend any victim of injustice, whether at the hands of landlords, merchants or money-lenders; so the popular legends, told and retold on countless occasions, would have us believe.

The reality is rather different. Nayan started his life of crime as the right hand man in the dubious activities of a wealthy businessman, Sulaiman Kerekau. They fell out badly after Nayan, always a lady's man, had an affair with Sulaiman's wife. Only then did Nayan begin to acquire his more popular image.

Bent on revenge, Sulaiman tracked him down to the forests of Jeneri, and informed the police who set a trap. It was an ignominious end for the Malay Robin Hood. By now an opium addict, Nayan was easily lured into a village by promises of the drug. The village chief gave Nayan the opium and, when he was drowsy with the effects, attacked him. In the ensuing struggle Nayan was killed.

The kingdom of Kedah has always been vulnerable to attack, whether from across the Thai border or from the sea. At the fishing port of **Kuala Kedah**, some 12 km to the west of Alor Setar, there are the remains of a Malay fort, which for centuries protected the kingdom from naval attack. Reached by a short sampan ride across the river, the fort is one of the best preserved in the country, though time and the sea have taken their toll on the outer defences. Six cannons still rest on the crumbling walls, facing the river mouth. The fort was originally constructed against the Portuguese, only later to be attacked by both the Acehnese from Sumatra and the Bugis, before being rebuilt in 1771. Fifty years later a Siamese fleet arrived in the river. The local chief and his people thought the Siamese had come in peace, wishing only to purchase supplies of rice, prior to setting sail for Burma. It proved a costly mistake. The rice was brought to the quay as agreed but, without warning, the Siamese attacked, killing or taking prisoner all of the local inhabitants. The fort soon fell and in a short time Kedah had been overrun.

For twenty years Kedah was subjected to direct rule from Thailand and Sultan Ahmad (1803-1845) found himself without a kingdom. He was not restored until 1842. It was to prevent just such a disaster that Ahmad's father, Sultan Abdullah (1773-1798), had taken the momentous step of leasing the island of Penang to the British East India Company in return for military protection in 1786.

***Below:** Two of the remaining cannons overlooking the river from the fort at Kuala Kedah.*

FRANCIS LIGHT
FOUNDER OF PENANG
1786

PENANG

The Land of Light

Penang, the turtle-shaped island off the coast of Kedah, has a known history dating back to the early days of the Melaka Sultanate. It is even possible to see the first recorded footstep taken on the island, or so the local inhabitants will have you believe. A small shrine at **Batu Maung**, a fishing village not far from the airport, marks the footprint of Admiral Cheng Ho when he stepped ashore in 1405. He must have been a big man as the footprint is large enough to fit a giant's foot. The Admiral almost certainly did visit Penang as the island is first referred to on charts used by the early Chinese navigators.

In the following century Portuguese traders from India used Penang as a stopover point on their way to the spice islands further east. Guided to the island by Gunung Jerai, the Portuguese ships anchored just offshore on a small rocky islet, from where the crews rowed to the beach. There they replenished their water supplies and traded with the local people. In their honour, the locals named the islet Batu Feringgi, or Feringgi's Rock, the word *Feringgi* being an Indian term for Europeans. The name proved highly prophetic, not admittedly for the islet, now more popularly called Lovers Isle, but certainly with regard to the surrounding beach area, which also became known as **Batu Ferringi**. The name has stuck and today this stretch of beach is a major tourist destination, visited by large numbers of Europeans, indeed people from all over the world. This is where most of the island's luxury hotels are located.

The name Penang comes from the Malay word *pinang*, meaning betel-nut, the palm of which used to be a common sight all over the island. It is a name which will always be associated with the British and one man in particular, Francis Light. Born in Suffolk in 1740, Light served for several years in the Royal Navy and spent over two decades working as a merchant in the Far East, before he set sail for Penang in 1786 to establish a settlement on the island. He did not create a dynasty, as James Brooke would do in Sarawak, but he did put Penang firmly on the map, in the process laying the foundations for the modern state. Light is today a relatively obscure figure, and yet, in his own way, he was just as influential as Brooke was in the development of Sarawak, and indeed Stamford Raffles in the founding of Singapore.

Penang came into the hands of the British due to the plight of Sultan Abdullah of Kedah, who faced threats from the Siamese and the Bugis. In desperation he turned for help to the British East India Company (EIC) and Francis Light, who acted as their principal negotiator. The EIC had a long established monopoly on trade between Britain and the Far East, but was in urgent need of a base in South East Asia, both as an *entrepôt* for the growing Chinese market and as a refitting station for its ships. Penang was ideally suited for

State crest: *The pokok pinang, or betel-nut tree, gave the state its name. Underneath is a depiction of the Penang Bridge. The blue and white stripes represent the five Rukunegara, or guiding principles of the Malaysian people, and also the five administrative districts of the state. The state motto is 'united and loyal'.* ***Opposite:*** *The statue of Francis Light is given pride of place outside the Penang Museum.*

these requirements, and Light persuaded the Sultan to hand over the island in return for British military protection and financial compensation for the resultant loss of trade. The British had gained their first foothold on the Malay Peninsula. They would not leave for nearly two hundred years and, in the course of that time, would come to dominate all eleven states of Peninsular Malaysia.

Light arrived at Penang in August 1786 to take up his new post as chief administrator of the island, with the rather unflattering title of 'Superintendent'. He decided to christen the island Prince of Wales Island to honour the birthday of the heir to the British throne. The name was retained for official purposes for several years, but it never caught on, and Penang remained Penang for virtually everybody. So as not to offend the reigning British monarch, King George III, Light named the town he founded Georgetown. This time the name proved more enduring.

Light first set foot on the island at Point Penaga, now the **Esplanade** and the heart of historic Georgetown. It was here that he decided to start clearing the jungle for his new settlement. The trees were predominantly the jungle hardwood, *penaga*

KEY

1. PADANG
2. ESPLANADE
3. FORT CORNWALLIS
4. ST GEORGE' S CHURCH
5. COLONIAL OFFICES
6. PENANG MUSEUM
7. FRANCIS LIGHT'S GRAVE (PROTESTANT CEMETERY)
8. KOMTAR
9. CLOCK TOWER
10. CHEONG FATT TZE'S MANSION
11. KHOO KONGSI
12. GODDESS OF MERCY TEMPLE
13. KAPITAN KLING MOSQUE
14. ACHEEN STREET MOSQUE
15. CLAN PIERS
16. E&O HOTEL
17. TOURIST INFORMATION CENTRE
18. ISLAND BUS STATION
19. CITY BUS STATION

laut, and were very difficult to fell. In his diary Light complained, 'the wood is so exceedingly hard that the tools double like a piece of lead'. According to one of his officers, Light became so frustrated at the slow progress in clearing the jungle that he devised an ingenious method to motivate the woodcutters to greater efforts. He loaded a cannon with silver dollars and fired it into the trees. As Light had anticipated, this led to frenzied activity and the land was soon ready to be built upon.

A wooden stockade was hastily erected. This was the forerunner to **Fort Cornwallis**, named after the Governor General of the EIC and built on the same site. The fort, still an impressive sight today, was constructed in the early 19th century. Some of the original cannons still stand on the ramparts pointing out to sea, though no shot is believed to have ever been fired in anger. The most famous is **Seri Rambai**, popularly known as the travelling cannon, and it has certainly moved around. Cast in Holland in 1603 and still bearing the emblem of the VOC, the cannon was presented to the sultan of Johor by the Dutch three years later. Not long afterwards, the Acehnese captured it and, once more, Seri Rambai was on its travels, this time to Aceh in Sumatra. There it remained for nearly two hundred years, before the Acehnese took it to Selangor as a gift in their quest for an alliance with the Bugis. Seri Rambai was placed on the walls of the fort at Kuala Selangor, where the British found it in 1871. They brought the cannon to Penang. Many local people believe Seri Rambai possesses the power of fertility, and women can sometimes be seen placing flowers in its barrel and praying by its side.

The new colony grew rapidly as settlers flocked to the island from all over Asia and beyond. Roads were an immediate priority and Light himself marked out the square grid system between Lebuh Light, Lebuh Pantai, Lebuh Chulia and Jalan Masjid Kapitan Kling (formally Pitt Street), which remains virtually unchanged to the present day. Free grants of land were offered to attract settlers, a policy which proved popular, perhaps too popular. As Light wrote in his diary, 'our inhabitants increase very fast, Chulias, Chinese and Christians. They are already disputing the ground, everyone building as fast as he can.'

Rather surprisingly, the EIC showed a marked indifference at first towards the new settlement. Constant appeals from Light for more staff went largely unheeded. He had to do virtually everything himself. For instance, Penang's first judge and magistrate, John Dickens, uncle of the famous novelist, Charles Dickens, did not arrive until 1801, seven years after Light had died. To attract greater trade Light opened the port to all ships free of duties. Penang went on growing and, by the turn of the century, one of Light's successors claimed that there was 'not probably any part of the world, where in so small a space, so many different people are assembled together, and so great a variety of languages spoken'. For a time it seemed as though Light might have created a port as successful as Melaka in its heyday, but the commercial future and great riches were destined for Singapore, not Penang.

Light himself did not find Penang at all profitable during his first few months on the island. He admitted to a friend, 'this office of Superintending or Governing of this famous island is not a profitable one. My expenses (are) exceeding salary just as two to one.' Only in partnership with the shrewd Scottish merchant, James Scott, did Light begin to make any money. Penang seems to have held a peculiar attraction for the relatives of famous British authors, Scott coming from the same family as the novelist Sir Walter Scott.

Georgetown itself had serious drawbacks, not least the suitability of the site. To be fair to Light, he was a naval man and a trader, not a surveyor or a town planner, but the low-lying and swampy location of the town was far from ideal. Any second thoughts he may have had were overtaken by the rapid growth of the settlement. This only added to the shortcomings of the site. A major problem was the lack of drinking

water and yet, on some occasions, Georgetown suffered from a surfeit of water, being prone to floods. Even today certain areas of the city are susceptible to flash floods. Housing and sanitation were rudimentary in the extreme, most of the inhabitants experiencing conditions which one British official likened to those of the water buffalo.

The greatest threat to the British in Penang came in 1791 from the man who had ceded the island to them. Feeling betrayed by Light and the EIC, who had failed to provide the agreed military assistance and financial compensation, Sultan Abdullah set about retaking the island. He assembled an army at the mouth of the River Prai on the mainland. Light promptly despatched a force under Captain Andrew Glass which routed the Kedah army in a dawn attack. Abdullah had no choice but to accept the revised British terms for the cession of Penang. He was given a mere 6,000 Spanish dollars per annum. Another treaty of 'Peace, Friendship and Alliance' followed in 1800. Kedah now handed over to the EIC the strip of territory on the mainland between the Muda and Krian rivers, in return for which the annuity was raised to 10,000 Spanish dollars. The British believed that they had to control the mainland opposite Penang for strategic reasons. This new territory was named Province Wellesley, though for local Malays it was always **Seberang Prai**. Today Penang Island and Seberang Prai form the modern state of Penang, headed by a Governor appointed by the Yang di-Pertuan Agong. They are linked by a regular ferry service and the **Penang Bridge**, at 13.5 km the longest bridge in Asia. Since independence the Federal Government has continued to honour the British agreement, although the annuity is now paid in Malaysian ringgit rather than

Opposite: *The Clan Piers overlooked by Komtar, with Penang Hill in the distance.*
Above: *An engraving showing the raising of the Union Jack for the first time on the newly christened Prince of Wales Island in 1786.*

Spanish dollars.

Francis Light had already disappeared from the scene by the end of the 18th century. The incessant strain of 'superintending' undermined his health and he suffered repeated attacks of malaria. Towards the end, he confided in a letter to a friend in England, 'tho' I may linger a year or two, I conjecture I shall not have ye happiness to see you. As we cannot command our time in this world, the only thing to be done is to submit with patience.' A particularly severe attack of malaria resulted in his death in October 1794. He was buried in the **Protestant Cemetery** on Georgetown's Lebuh Farquhar. A stroll through the small cemetery will reveal the graves of many of Penang's earliest settlers, including that of Light's business partner James Scott. A copy of Light's will, together with other exhibits from the early days of the island, can be seen at the Penang Museum. At the entrance stands a bronze statue of Light, cast to commemorate the 150th anniversary of his founding of the settlement. As there is no known likeness of him, a degree of intelligent guesswork had to be used, the features being based on a portrait of his eldest son.

Only some years after Light's death did the EIC finally take the needs of Penang seriously and establish a sizeable administrative staff on the island. The EIC now went from one extreme to the other. Penang became so overstaffed that a visiting British dignitary quipped that he 'could not see what the island looked like for the number of cocked hats which shut out the view!' Across the ***Padang*** from Fort Cornwallis stand the majestic colonial offices, built later in the 19th century to house this 'army' of officials. **City Hall** remained the seat of local government until recently, when it moved to Komtar, the stark high-rise building which now dominates the city skyline. **Komtar**, sixty-five storeys high, also contains commercial offices, theatres, restaurants and shops. The viewing platform at the top offers stunning views of the eastern part of the island and the Penang Bridge.

Light left all his property to Martina Rozells, who had 'cohabited' with him since 1772, to use his own words. She is sadly a rather obscure figure and little is known about her. Some writers, of a decidedly fictional nature, have added romance to the story of Light and Penang by claiming that she was a princess from the Kedah royal family, and that the island was her dowry. They had five children. The eldest, William, was sent to England to be educated and never saw his father again. William was very much a chip off the old block. He entered the navy and, after a distinguished career afloat, went on to play a crucial role in the founding of Adelaide. It was only fitting that Adelaide and Georgetown should become twinned in 1973.

Light was always popular amongst the inhabitants of Penang. A simple tablet

erected to his memory can be seen in the small pavilion at the front of **St. George's Church**. It reads: 'In his capacity as Governor, the settlers and natives were greatly attached to him, and by his death had to mourn the loss of one who had watched over their interests as a father'. Light's greatest sadness was never returning to his beloved county of Suffolk in England. However, he did indulge himself in a sort of compromise by bringing a little bit of England to the tropics.

As early as 1787 a track had been cut to the top of **Penang Hill**. The temperate climate provided a welcome relief from the breathless heat of Georgetown. Light built a house there and planted strawberries, specially sent from Suffolk, in the garden. Strawberry Hill, which today houses the tea kiosk, is believed to be the original site. Penang Hill became a favourite retreat for officials, planters and their families. Hill stations were always an essential part of British life in the tropics, when a journey home took several weeks, and Penang Hill is one of a number to be found in Malaysia. Many imposing residences were built on Penang Hill during the course of the 19th century. One of these, an atap-roofed house surrounded by a rose garden, belonged to the wealthy Brown family. David Brown's principal residence was Glugor House on his estate between the Glugor and Kluang rivers, where he planted pepper, nutmeg and cloves. The estate no longer exists, the land having been developed as the Universiti Sains Malaysia and the Minden Hill residential area. Said to contain an 80 foot drawing room, complete with grand piano, Glugor House was sadly demolished in 1949 to make way for a modern villa. There is only one surviving relic of Brown's wealth in Penang: his bathtub. Made of Italian marble, it is lying outside the Penang Museum. Inside there is an early 19th-century painting of Glugor House by Captain Robert Smith. Brown's grave is also to be found in the

Opposite: *The Penang Hill railway.*
Above: *The old Crag Hotel on Penang Hill, with Gunung Jerai in the distance.*

Protestant Cemetery.

In the early days an ascent of Penang Hill had to be made by pony or a sedan chair carried by coolies, an experience once likened to riding a camel. The only alternative was to walk, and even today it remains a fairly exhausting climb. The hill path zigzags to the top from a starting point near the Botanical Gardens. The best way to enjoy the charm and beauty of the hill is to take the railway up and then have a leisurely walk down. The trails beneath the tall forest canopy are certainly well worth exploring.

The idea of a railway was first raised in 1897. A private company was formed to build it and construction began with a narrow gauge track and cable cars. Described at the time as an ingenious method of propulsion, a pelton wheel driven by water power was used as a cheap alternative to steam power. Unfortunately, it did not live up to expectations. After years of construction, the trial run was a total fiasco. The track could not be constructed in a straight line, due to the configuration of the hill, and the twisting nature of the route put too great a strain on the cable. A reporter from the Penang Gazette described the scene: 'Enthusiasm knew no bounds. The signal to start was given,...a cock crowed loudly on the station roof; the water power was turned on with a gentle hissing noise, the passengers waved their adieux to their less adventurous comrades on the platform and nothing happened.' Matters went from bad to worse when human propulsion was called upon. Everyone got out and pushed, at first with considerable good humour, then accompanied by much cursing and complaining. The empty car was eventually pushed two yards up the track, at which point manpower also gave out.

The British later revived the project and, utilising the technology from the funicular rail system in Switzerland, opened the present railway in 1932. Trains depart from the top and bottom of Penang Hill at thirty minute intervals. As the train makes its slow ascent, panoramic views of Georgetown appear below. Houses can be seen peeping out from the dense foliage on the hill, while others sit proudly on terraced slopes. One of the most imposing is the 'Great Wall', which, as its name suggests, is surrounded by a magnificent wall topped with stone ballustrades and flower pots. Penang Hill is in fact several peaks, with the railway coming to an end on Flagstaff Hill, so-called because the Union Jack used to be raised there to signal the arrival of the mail boat from Britain.

Probably the best time to visit Penang Hill is at dusk, when the view is quite spectacular. An ideal place to enjoy it from is the verandah of the **Bellevue Hotel**, once the residence of Penang's sheriff. The eye passes over the sweeping vistas of the coastal lowlands of the island to the narrow channel, dotted with ships, and beyond to the patchwork-paddied plains of the mainland and the distant dark shape of Gunung Jerai, sometimes quite distinct, sometimes a mere smudge on the horizon. The sky turns gold, tinted with pink, and then purple as the light fades and night slowly descends. The lights come on below, twinkling man-made stars, with those on the Penang Bridge providing the finale. The bridge looks almost mystical at night as it stretches out across the black void of the sea. The scene is the perfect tonic for a hectic day, the peace and serenity of the hill possessing an almost hypnotic effect.

The **Penang Museum** proudly displays one of the original wooden coaches from the railway and, for good measure, has a fine example of the railway's predecessor, a sedan chair. Housed in the old Penang Free School building on Lebuh Farquhar, the museum is well worth a visit. One local boy to attend the school was Cheah Chen Eok, who went on to amass a fortune. He never lost sight of his humble origins and donated the famous **clock tower** in the centre of Georgetown, to commemorate Queen Victoria's diamond jubilee. The tower is sixty feet high, symbolising the sixty years of her reign up to 1897.

Penang has never been short of millionaires. The most famous was probably Cheong Fatt Tze, an immensely wealthy man nicknamed 'China's Rockefeller' by the *New York Times*. Born into a poor Chinese family in 1840, Cheong left his homeland at the age of seventeen to seek his fortune in South East Asia. He took the region by storm, building up a commercial empire based on tin mining, agriculture, trading and opium. When asked the secret of his success, he answered: 'I exhausted the land's resources and observed the changing times; what others sold off I stored up and what they desired to buy I supplied, looking for the expensive place

Opposite: *The view from Penang Hill overlooking Georgetown and the narrow channel which separates the island from Seberang Prai. The high-rise building in the centre of the picture is Komtar.*
Above: *The famous clock tower in the heart of Georgetown.*

to sell something that was cheap.' Whether in life or death, Cheong never did anything by halves. He had seven wives and, after his death, his body lay in state in Penang, Singapore and Hong Kong. His impressive mansion in Penang can still be seen on Lebuh Leith. It has now been restored to its former grandeur and is due to open to the public.

The stately mansions on Jalan Sultan Ahmad Shah, popularly known as 'millionaires' row', provide further examples of the homes of Penang's fabulously rich. A walk along the shady tree-lined boulevard reveals elegant porticoed mansions with long driveways and manicured lawns. One of these mansions, 'Homestead', was so palatial that it was dubbed a mini Buckingham Palace. It was built in Penang's windfall years during the early 20th century, when great fortunes were made from the boom in rubber.

Jalan Sultan Ahmad Shah was originally called Northam Street. In common with other cities and towns in the country, the colonial street names of Georgetown have undergone a process of 'malayanisation'. In some instances the names have been changed completely; while in others they have simply been replaced by a Malay translation, for example, Beach Street has become Lebuh Pantai. Not only have official names changed, but some of the streets have also been given colloquial names by local inhabitants, reflecting their significance in days gone by. Lorong Prangin has the nickname *Goo Chiah Kay*, or Bullock Cart Street, because the area was the main producer of this early form of transport. Jalan Penang is also known as *Tiau Lang Kay*, or Hanging People Street, because convicted criminals used to be hanged at the point where the road meets Lebuh Chulia.

Many of Georgetown's streets evoke the past and there always seems to be something to surprise you round the next corner. The best way to explore the city is on foot. If you find it too exhausting, you can always hail the ubiquitous trishaw to give you a grand tour. Make sure you negotiate the fare up front. Well over half of Penang's population is Chinese and Georgetown is very much a Chinese city. If by chance you are feeling under the weather, try Lebuh Campbell, home to a number of Chinese chemists. There is nothing quite like these shops in the west. They are packed with all sorts of exotic items, each one designed to maintain the right balance between *yin* and *yang*, the passive and active forces, and hence ensure good health.

The Lebuh Penang-Lebuh Queen area of Georgetown is known as '**Little India**', as this is where the early Indian immigrants settled. Here you can brouse through textile stores selling *saris* and taste delicious spicy curries at the restaurants. Meals in south Indian restaurants are traditionally eaten off banana leaves rather than plates. Curries, vegetables and sauces are placed around a pile of rice or perhaps accompanied by a *roti canai,* Indian-style toast. When you have finished the meal, you fold the banana leaf in half. Most of the island's Malay population lives outside Georgetown and anyone prepared to venture away from the principal tourist sites of Penang will be rewarded with a glimpse of traditional *kampung* life. There are many fine examples of Malay houses, built on stilts, while along the coast attractive fishing villages compete for attention with long stretches of unspoilt, and usually deserted, beaches.

Penang is renowned for its temples. Near to the airport is the Temple of the Azure Cloud, more popularly known as the **Snake Temple**. Snakes have always been venerated by the Chinese, though the temple is in fact dedicated to a Buddhist priest, Chor Soo Kong, who was believed to possess remarkable powers of healing. According to local folklore, the snakes slithered out of the surrounding jungle and into the temple during the night following its completion, and have been there ever since. On entering the temple you do not see them at first, as your eyes take time to adjust to the light, then you notice one curled up on a candlestick holder, then another three on the altar, two more sleeping under a table and so on.

Dramatically located on a hilltop in Air Itam is the largest Buddhist temple in Malaysia, **Kek Lok Si Temple**. The temple is in the shadow of an enormous statue of Kuan Yin, the Goddess of Mercy, who looks out serenely over the surrounding hillsides. Kuan Yin is the most popular and loved of the Chinese deities, with a role similar to that of the Virgin Mary in the Christian faith. The crowning glory of the temple is the splendid seven-tiered 'Pagoda of Ten Thousand Buddhas', dedicated to all manifestations of the Buddha, hence its name. The pagoda is thirty metres high and incorporates a mixture of Chinese, Thai and Burmese architectural influences.

Further Thai architecture can be seen at **Wat Chayamangkalaram**, a colourful Buddhist temple just off Jalan Kelawei on the northern outskirts of Georgetown, which houses a massive gold-plated reclining Buddha. The oldest temple in Penang is the **Goddess of Mercy Temple**, located on Georgetown's Jalan Masjid Kapitan Kling and established by the first Chinese settlers on the island. The temple has a charm all of its own and is usually crowded. It is not just worshippers and visitors who flock to the place, as the ground in front of the entrance is a favourite haunt for hundreds of pigeons. Often shrouded in clouds of smoke escaping from the two giant burners at the entrance, the temple appears almost shabby in comparison with the nearby **Khoo Kongsi**, one of the most spectacular buildings on the island.

Opposite: *The 'Pagoda of Ten Thousand Buddhas' at the Kek Lok Si Temple.*
Above: *One of the beautiful butterflies at the Penang Butterfly Farm.*

Chinese immigrants arriving in Penang, indeed throughout Malaya, tended to stay together in their regional and dialect groupings; but within these various and distinctive communities, the family or the clan has always been the crucial element in social organisation. The importance of the family is an integral part of Confucianism, the set of Chinese beliefs and practices derived from the great philosopher, Confucius (551BC-479BC). *Kongsis,* or clan associations, are centres of ancestral worship, which encourage closer links between the members of the clan, who can all trace their ancestry back to the same great progenitor, and also provide them with social services and amenities.

The Khoo Kongsi is one of over a hundred such associations in Penang. At the end of the 19th century, the Khoo clan constructed a vast new temple on the scale of an imperial palace. Some members were uneasy at the size of the building, believing it might offend the Chinese emperor, even the gods. Perhaps they were right because, only a month after the temple was completed, it mysteriously caught fire and was destroyed. The clan opted for a more 'modest' replacement, the temple of today. Not that it is lacking in grandeur or opulence. The overall design is very striking, but it is the roof which makes the deepest impression. The crescent of the roof supports numerous carvings of dragons and other celestial animals, all exquisitely detailed and painted in a riot of colour. Inside the Khoo Kongsi richly ornamented beams, carved walls and attractive paintings depict legendary figures and events. On either side of the main hall, the thirty-six heavenly bodyguards, seated on their mythological steeds, adorn the walls; while, on the side walls of the ancestral hall, gilded wooden plaques honour distinguished past members of the clan.

The patron saint of the Khoo clan is the Great Duke, a legendary hero in Chinese history who achieved the improbable feat of successfully defending the country with only 8,000 troops against an invading army of one million men. A master of psychological warfare, the Duke hid his soldiers in the trees and undergrowth of a forest. When the enemy marched up, they imagined there were millions of eyes peering out at them from the forest, panicked and fled. The Duke's great triumph is immortalised in verses carved into the granite pillars of the Khoo Kongsi.

Another manifestation of the clan system is be found on the waterfront, near the jetty where the ferry boats arrive from Butterworth on the mainland. Here are the **Clan Piers**, rows of wooden houses built over the sea on stilts. The piers are divided between different clans. Most of the residents are boatmen or fishermen and do not object to visitors taking a walk through their wooden villages. That is as long as they are not from another clan!

An unwanted by-product of Chinese immigration into Penang and Malaya was the secret societies, which the settlers brought with them from China. Based on the various regional and dialect groupings, the societies were all too often fierce rivals of each other, rivalries which could quite easily lead to violence. In Penang the feuds reached a climax in the riots of 1867. The principal rivals were the Hokkien dominated Khian Teik and the Cantonese Ghee Hin, who were locked in a deadly struggle over control of the highly profitable opium trade. The Malays had their own societies and were also drawn into the feud. The initial spark for the riots was an almost unbelievably minor incident: a Malay threw a rambutan skin at a Khian Teik man who was peeping into his house.

The *Penang Gazette* reported the

Opposite: *Carvings on the roof of the Khoo Kongsi in Georgetown.*

ensuing events in all too graphic detail: 'the riot was a horrible scene of slaughter and violence. Every conceivable kind of weapon, from sticks and stones, to musket and cannon, were used. Bullets, cannon-balls, petards whizzed about in all directions, killing scores of secret society members. These members are tough people, fierce shrieks for blood and vengeance poured from their lips. Sweat gleamed on their faces caked with dust, and on their brown bodies as they faced their antagonists. Their voices rose above the thundering of guns, blazing muskets and booming cannon.' A cannonball, fired by the government in an attempt to end the disturbances, inflicted so much damage to the houses in one road that it was renamed Cannon Street. Only after nine days of fighting were the authorities able to restore order to the streets of Georgetown.

One of the principal figures behind the riots was the notorious Khoo Thean Teik, a member of the Khoo clan and leader of the Khian Teik society. His name translates into 'heavenly virtue' which, in view of his character, seemed decidedly misplaced. He was arrested and charged with having planned and instigated the riots, found guilty and sentenced to death. The British administration, with its small police force, soon had second thoughts, fearing Chinese retaliation, and commuted the sentence to life imprisonment. With good behaviour, Thean Teik was released after seven years and turned into an upright and law abiding citizen. He became a successful businessman and philanthropist, and died a respected figure of Penang society.

The **Acheen Street Mosque**, the oldest existing mosque in Penang, is still reputed to bear the scars of the riots, in the form of a round hole halfway up its octagonal, Arab-style minaret. The hole is believed to have been made by a cannonball. Whether it was fired from outside or inside is a matter of some dispute. One eyewitness claimed he heard cannon fire coming from the direction of the minaret. The mosque certainly did have its own cannon, which was fired to herald feast days and other important events. On one occasion the firing of the cannon led to trouble with the members of the nearby **Kapitan Kling Mosque**. The leader of the Acheen Street Mosque set the day for Hari Raya Puasa, to celebrate the end of Ramadan, as always for the next new moon, but the experts at Kapitan Kling Mosque disagreed with his lunar calculations. Furious at their behaviour, the Acheen Street leader had the cannon dragged to the Kapitan Kling Mosque and fired, to declare the start of Hari Raya Puasa. Undaunted, the Kapitan Kling faithful continued fasting. Fighting then broke out and one man was killed, before peace was restored. To help ensure future cooperation, the local authorities ordered the Muslim community in Georgetown to alternate between the two mosques for their Friday prayers, an arrangement which

continues to the present day.

Penang is one of the best places in Malaysia to sample the delights of the country's wide variety of food. Oliver Twist would have wanted thirds and fourths here! Local dishes include *laksa asam,* a rice noodle dish of *Nyonya* origin, and *rojak,* a type of Asian salad. *Nyonya* cuisine originated in the two former Straits Settlements of Penang and Melaka, and as in Melaka there is a *Baba Nyonya* community on the island. Penang cooking is so popular that, in Kuala Lumpur and other towns, there are stalls claiming to sell authentic Penang favourites, such as Penang Prawn Mee. Places to eat in Penang vary from inexpensive outdoor eating stalls and hawkerfare to plush restaurants and high priced cuisine. There is something to suit every palate and every pocket. **Gurney Drive** has some of the best hawker stalls to be found in Penang. Here, before your eyes, delicious dishes will be whipped up for you in minutes.

Penang is at its liveliest during festival time, particularly Chinese New Year, the most important event in the Chinese festive calendar. The Chinese base their year on the lunar system, which is about eleven days shorter than the solar year. They keep in step with the solar year by adding an extra month to their calendar every two or three years. Each year is assigned one of twelve animals which make up the Chinese zodiac. New Year's Day is celebrated on the first day of the new moon after the sun enters Aquarius, which always falls between 21st January and 20th February.

In the run-up to the big day, debts are settled, greeting cards are sent out, new clothes are purchased and houses are given a thorough spring-clean. The latter is both a spiritual and practical exercise, designed to drive away all evil influences. Scrolls

Opposite: *The lion dance is the most famous of all Chinese entertainments.*
Above: *Chinese opera is one of the favourite street entertainments in Penang during Chinese New Year. The performers wear striking make-up.*

and banners inscribed with lucky mottoes are often hung outside homes, so that visitors will carry the sentiments into the house with them. Offerings are also made to the Chinese deities, most importantly the Kitchen God. A week before New Year, the Kitchen God is believed to ascend to heaven to give an annual report on each family member to the Jade Emperor, the Supreme Head of the Taoist pantheon. Before he departs on his mission, the family honour the Kitchen God with a farewell dinner, usually consisting of sweet things, to induce him to deliver a favourable report; or if necessary something sticky, to prevent him from opening his mouth at all!

On New Year's Eve offices and shops in Georgetown close early, enabling families to hold reunion dinners. As New Year's Day begins, they again make offerings to the deities, particularly the God of Wealth. Until recently, families also ushered in the New Year by lighting firecrackers, and a tremendous barrage of sound would erupt on the stroke of midnight. As well as being part of the fun of New Year, the noise was designed to frighten away any evil spirits and, according to Chinese legend, was once used by terrified villagers to drive away a monster which was preying on them. The government has banned the use of firecrackers because of the dangers they pose, and the New Year now begins in relative silence.

On New Year's Day, children and unmarried adults receive *ang pows,* little red packets containing money, from their parents and other close relatives. A number of taboos are observed on this day. Black is not worn, because of its association with misfortune, and floors are not swept, in case any good luck brought into the house is swept out again. The same superstition has determined the basic design of traditional Chinese houses. Doorways at the front and back of the house are never placed in a straight line, as any good luck entering the house would then flow right out at the back. Chinese families also try not to use knives or other sharp instruments which may cut away 'the

ANTIQUES OF THE ORIENT

golden thread of wealth', and inauspicious words such as 'death' or 'accident' are avoided at all costs. Other more propitious words such as 'luck' and 'wealth' cannot be used often enough.

Lion dances are performed at various venues during the celebrations, adding to the festive atmosphere. They are believed to bring good luck and prosperity and are also held on other special occasions during the year, such as the opening of new business premises. Like the pantomime horse, the lion, which has a cloth body and elaborately decorated *papier mâché* head, consists of two performers, one forming the front part of the animal and the other bringing up the rear. The similarity ends there, as these creatures do not have four left feet, but move with great agility and grace. Equipped with fluttering eyelashes and flapping jaw, the half fierce, half humorous lion prances and twists in time to the beating of drums and gongs and the clashing of cymbals. In return for the good luck they bring to the houses and businesses they visit, the dancers are rewarded with *ang pows.* These may be suspended from a height so the lion has to perform a precarious balancing act to retrieve them, rearing up on its hind quarters and balancing on the backs of chairs. Sometimes the lion is led by a jester, a masked figure holding a fan. According to an old Chinese legend, the jester represents a monk who found a lion cub and tamed it by playing with it daily.

The festivities go on for fifteen days. The last day coincides with the first full moon of the New Year and is called Chap Goh Meh, the Hokkien term for the fifteenth night. In the days when Chinese maidens were sequestered, this was the one occasion when they appeared in public. In Georgetown they would converge on the Esplanade in the early evening, dressed in all their finery, and throw oranges into the sea, at the same time making a wish that they would find a good husband in the coming year. The ritual fulfilled a practical as well as symbolic role. The young men of the town could view the otherwise cloistered beauties and, if a girl caught their eye, an approach would be made to her parents. Although its traditional significance has gone in an age when men and women mix freely, the orange throwing ritual has been revived in recent years, adding to the fun of the last night of New Year. A stage is erected on the *Padang* and various acts entertain the crowds late into the evening.

Georgetown has come a long way since the malaria-ridden days under Francis Light, and is today one of the most attractive cities in Malaysia, an effective mix of the past and present, old narrow streets standing in the shadow of Komtar with all its modern amenities. The pace of life has quickened a great deal in recent

Opposite: *An early 19th-century painting of Georgetown. In the background is the coastline of Kedah.* ***Above:*** *The E & O Hotel.*

For Comfort, Cleanliness *and a* Health Resort

IN

PENANG

GO TO THE

Eastern and Oriental Hotel

Absolutely the Best in the Island

Charming Sea View   Beautiful Spot   Good Table   Every Home Comfort

The Hotel is to Undergo Thorough Alterations

TELEGRAMS: "SARKIES," PENANG

Cable Codes

for the use of Intended Visitors to Raffles Hotel, E. & O. Hotel and Strand Hotel

BUNCH: Wire if you have any vacant rooms and how many......
BUGBEAR: Reserve one single room for......
BUGGY: Reserve two single rooms for..
BUGLEHORN: Reserve three single rooms for......
BUGLER: Reserve four single rooms for
BUILDING: Reserve five single rooms for......
BULBOUS: Reserve six single rooms for......
BULGED: Reserve one double room for......
BULIMY: Reserve two double rooms for......
BULKINESS: Reserve three double rooms for......
BULLACE: Reserve four double rooms for......
BULLCALF: Reserve five double rooms for......
BULLDOG: Reserve six double rooms for......
BULLETIN: Reserve a single and a double room for......
BULLFINCH: Reserve two double and a single room for......
BULLFROG: Reserve three double and a single room for......
BULLIRAG: Reserve a double room with two beds for......
BULLOCK: Reserve two double rooms adjoining for......
BULLTROUT: Reserve two single rooms adjoining for......
BUMPER: Have a single horse and carriage waiting at the wharf for......
BUMKIN: Have a carriage and pair waiting at the wharf for...
BUMPTIOUS: Runner to look after Baggage.

SARKIES BROTHERS, Proprietors

years: everything is hustle and bustle, cars race past, and people are constantly rushing somewhere. Yet, barely a mile from Komtar, there is a place where it is possible to take a step back in time, admittedly not to the age of Light, that has gone forever, but to the days of a more palatial and elegant Penang. This is the **Eastern and Oriental Hotel**, more popularly known as the E & O and originally part of the famous Sarkies hotel empire, which included the Raffles in Singapore and the Strand in Rangoon.

Built during the age of parasols, tiffin and ballroom dances, the E & O celebrated its centenary in 1985. It advertises itself today as 'continuing a tradition of gracious living', and is full of pleasant reminders of its former grandeur. The hotel is deceptive from outside the main entrance. All the grandeur is inside and at the back, where the sea front garden, filled with frangipani and coconut trees, provides extensive views of the Kedah coastline. It is an ideal setting for afternoon tea, complete with cucumber sandwiches and fruit cake. In the lobby, photographs and newspaper clippings from the early 20th century adorn the walls, when guests included the likes of Somerset Maugham, Douglas Fairbanks, Rita Hayworth and Noel Coward. Maugham had a special suite on the ground floor, which has been left just as he liked it, all done out in white and appropriately named the White Room.

The E & O boasts a large ballroom complete with sprung dance floor, which was once the centre of social life in Georgetown. It is only too easy to imagine the leaders of the British community and their wives, during the days of empire, splendidly attired in dinner jackets and evening gowns, dancing and enjoying themselves into the early hours. The ballroom was built by Arshak Sarkies, who took over the running of the hotel from his elder brothers in 1891. Something of an extrovert, he was often to be seen waltzing around the dance floor, expertly balancing a tumbler of whisky and soda on his bald head. Arshak was renowned for his generosity and taste for the grandiose, and was considered the perfect host. During the rubber slump and depression of the late 1920s, he was known to write off the bill of many a businessman fallen on hard times, or simply to invite friends to stay free of charge at the hotel. Sadly, such qualities, combined with a passion for gambling, led to his own financial ruin. He died in 1931, an embittered recluse with a mountain of debts. His earlier generosity did not help his own family, who were evicted from their hotel living quarters. Fortunately, the E & O survived, although its days as the social hub of Penang were over.

In recent years the E & O has enjoyed something of a renaissance under the enthusiastic management of Don Chan. His passion is fishing, and mounted on the wall of the elegant 1885 Grill restaurant are the head and tail of a twelve foot long Marlin he caught off the island of Mauritius. Another permanant fixture in the restaurant is Mr Albert Yeoh and his band, who entertain diners every night with their wide repertoire of nostalgic songs. Albert has been playing his piano at the E & O for over forty years and remembers life at the hotel before independence, when he performed mostly for planters and tin miners. Cole Porter is his favourite songwriter and, when asked to play the song of his choice, the band strikes up with *I've Got You Under My Skin.* It is difficult not to leave the E & O, and indeed Penang as a whole, without feeling that way.

Opposite: *An advertisement from 1909 for the E & O with, as a sign of the times, an entertaining list of cable codes. The drawing depicts the esplanade and gardens at the back of the hotel.*

JOHOR
NEGERI SEMBILAN
PAHANG
MELAKA
S. Muar
SEGAMAT
LABIS
TANGKAK
KG. RAJA
PAGOH
MUAR
YONG PENG
AYER HITAM
BATU PAHAT
BENUT
PONTIAN KECIL
KUKUP
P. KUKUP
TANJUNG PIAI
JOHOR BAHRU
PASIR GUDANG PORT
SINGAPORE
KLUANG
KAHANG
KUALA JASIN
S. Endau
PADANG ENDAU
MERSING
JEMALUANG
TANJUNG LEMAN
S. Linggiu
KOTA TINGGI
S. Johor
JOHOR LAMA
DESARU
P. PEMANGGIL
P. RAWA
P. HUJUNG
P. TENGAH
P. BESAR
P. AUR
P. TINGGI
P. SIBU
KEY
LEBUHRAYA (EXPRESSWAY)
MAJOR ROADS
SECONDARY ROADS
RAILWAY
AIRPORT
STATE BOUNDARIES
INTERNATIONAL BORDER
1 GUNUNG LEDANG (1,276m)
2 AIR TERJUN LOMBONG
3 KAMPUNG MAKAM
4 ENDAU ROMPIN NATIONAL PARK
N
0 15 30 km

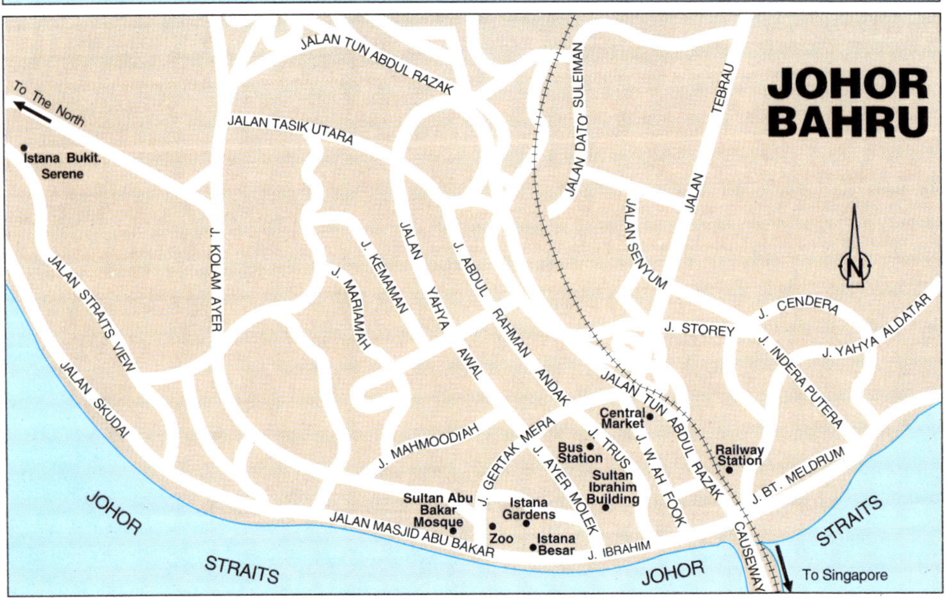
JOHOR BAHRU
To The North
Istana Bukit. Serene
JALAN TUN ABDUL RAZAK
JALAN TASIK UTARA
JALAN DATO' SULEIMAN
JALAN TEBRAU
J. KOLAM AYER
JALAN STRAITS VIEW
JALAN SKUDAI
J. MARIAMAH
J. KEMAMAN
JALAN YAHYA AWAL
J. ABDUL RAHMAN ANDAK
JALAN SENYUM
J. STOREY
J. CENDERA
J. YAHYA ALDATAR
J. INDERA PUTERA
JALAN TUN ABDUL RAZAK
J. MAHMOODIAH
J. GERTAK MERA
J. AYER MOLEK
J. TRUS
J. W. AH FOOK
Central Market
Bus Station
Sultan Ibrahim Building
Railway Station
J. BT. MELDRUM
Sultan Abu Bakar Mosque
Istana Gardens
Zoo
Istana Besar
JALAN MASJID ABU BAKAR
J. IBRAHIM
CAUSEWAY
JOHOR STRAITS
JOHOR
STRAITS
JOHOR
STRAITS
To Singapore
N

JOHOR

The Heir to Melaka.

The main road (Route 5) south from Melaka provides a very pleasant drive for visitors. Most of the heavy traffic has been drawn away by the *lebuhraya*, or expressway, while the road is lined with pretty *kampung* houses, many of them displaying the brightly coloured and distinctive Melakan steps. The road is also the modern link between Melaka and the state of Johor, the other great Malay kingdom of the past.

The historic ties between Melaka and Johor date back to the time of the Portuguese when, following the fall of Melaka in 1511, Sultan Mahmud took refuge in Johor. He had lost everything. Melaka was at the mercy of Albuquerque, while Tun Teja, his queen, had died during the headlong flight. As a leader Mahmud lacked sound judgement and was prone to bouts of lethargy, but he was now determined to do all in his power to regain Melaka. Unfortunately, he would never achieve it and neither would his successors, though their efforts were not all in vain. Despite numerous upheavals and setbacks, there arose from the ashes of Melaka the kingdom of Johor, stretching far and wide across the southern lands of the Malay Peninsula and the islands of the Riau and Lingga archipelagos. This kingdom, commonly known as 'Old Johor', was the true heir to Melaka, a thriving commercial state ruled by the descendants of the most prestigious of all Malay dynasties.

As he headed south Mahmud would have been confronted by a sight familiar to all motorists today as they drive into Johor from Melaka, the legendary **Gunung Ledang** (1,276 metres), or Mount Orphir. Did Mahmud's mind wander back to another setback earlier in his reign? According to legend, a beautiful princess inhabited the top of the mountain. Many believed she possessed the gift of immortality, in addition to the ability to change her appearance at will. Mahmud had become enthralled by the story and was determined to take the princess as his wife. He duly despatched Hang Tuah, together with two renowned warriors, Hang Setia and Tun Mamat, to Gunung Ledang with his offer of marriage to the princess.

So Hang Tuah set out to climb again the mountain where, as a boy, he had been taught many of his fighting skills by the Guru Adi Petra. The princess lived at the top, by repute in a fine house surrounded by an exotic garden. Visitors to the summit today will find a rather different scene: a rocky platform some 20 metres in width, with a variety of ferns providing virtually the only vegetation. Hang Tuah and his friends found the ascent extremely difficult due to high winds and poor visibility. When the path became dangerous, Tun Mamat volunteered to go on with two guides. They made it to the top, finding the garden, a paradise filled with multi-coloured flowers and echoing to the sound of bird song. Tun Mamat entered and was immediately confronted by an old woman - the princess in disguise - and four maidens. He told them of his mission and asked for

State crest: *The crown symbolises the sultan's sovereignty, while the tigers recall the time when wild animals roamed the state. The floral decorations beneath the shield represent gambier and black pepper, once Johor's main products. The state motto is 'in the hands of Allah'.*

an audience with the princess. The old woman listened in silence, before promising to pass on the message.

Shortly afterwards, the old woman returned and gave Tun Mamat an answer. The conditions for a marriage with the Sultan were extremely harsh. He had to build two bridges between Melaka and Gunung Ledang, one of gold and the other of silver, as well as provide seven trays filled with the hearts of mosquitoes, a similar amount of other insects' hearts, a vat of betel-nut juice, another vat of human tears, and finally two cups of human blood. Tun Mamat probably anticipated problems when the old woman informed him that one cup must come from the Sultan and the other from his son Ahmad. In the event Mahmud was prepared to try and meet all of the demands, save the last one. He would not harm his son. It was a different story after the flight to Johor when Mahmud had the unfortunate Ahmad, the hero of the defence of Melaka, put to death. Such were the twists and turns of politics at that time.

Isolated and majestic, Gunung Ledang stands as if guarding north-western Johor. Growing numbers of visitors come to make the ascent. A few are still drawn by tales of Adi Petra and the legend of the princess. In 1976 four youths returned from the summit to tell a remarkable story. They had run into the 'guardian of the secret of Gunung Ledang', described by the boys as a man in his forties, dressed entirely in black, with two *kris* thrust into his waistband. Could this have been Adi Petra? They joined the 'guardian' in a bout of *silat.* The boys had mastered the basics, but the expertise of the man in black was quite astonishing. He also showed them the grave of the legendary princess.

After entering Johor, Sultan Mahmud found his way to **Muar**. Also known today as Bandar Maharani, Muar was in Mahmud's time little more than a fishing village, but modern visitors will discover an attractive, if rather busy, town stretching along the southern bank of the River Muar. There is a peaceful air about the river, an obvious attraction for the anglers who can often be seen trying their luck along the banks. The heart of historic Muar is to be found in the riverside Jalan Petri, a tree-shaded road containing the palatial government offices from British times and, most impressive of all, the fine **Masjid Jamek**.

There are potent reminders of the days of Sultan Mahmud to the north-east of Muar. **Pagoh** was another refuge for the Sultan from the Portuguese. In a secluded spot at nearby **Kampung Raja** is the final resting place of Mahmud's father, the able and dedicated Sultan Alauddin of Melaka (1477-1488), whose promising reign ended with his premature death, probably by poisoning. He was only 26 years old. Mahmud eventually settled on the island of Bentan in the Riau archipelago. Bentan and the other islands were considered a friendly area, as well as being home to a large group of *orang laut*, whose help Mahmud enlisted against the Portuguese. More than once *orang laut* ships sailed to attack Melaka, but all to no avail. Portuguese revenge could be terrible. One of many places to suffer was Muar. The Portuguese overwhelmed the garrison and burned much of the settlement to the ground. Nor did they leave Mahmud in peace on Bentan, launching two unsuccessful attacks on the island before they overran the defences in 1526. Mahmud managed to get away, his feet badly cut and wrapped only in cloth. His plight became so desperate that his friends had to steal some rice and fish for him, before he found a ship going to Kampar on the east coast of Sumatra, where he died, a sad and lonely exile.

The wanderings of Mahmud were not an isolated event in the history of the old Johor kingdom. His successors were often little more than fugitive rulers, roaming across the wide reaches of their lands and islands, in search of sanctuary from the Portuguese and later the Acehnese. The capital of Johor shifted about twenty times between Mahmud's flight from Melaka and the end of the 17th century. Surprisingly, the modern capital, Johor Bahru, was not one of these earlier capitals and dates only from the middle of the 19th century. The town reflects the history and achievements of the 'new' kingdom, the Johor created by the dynasty of the *temenggongs*. The office of *temenggong* originated under the Malay Sultanate in the 15th century, when the holder was in overall charge of justice in Melaka, being responsible for the police, local defence and the collection of customs duties in the market.

By the beginning of the 19th century

Opposite: *An old man watching the world go by from the door of his kampung house. Dressed in the everyday kampung attire of a sarong and T-shirt, he is wearing a Muslim cap called a kopiah.* ***Below:*** *The Masjid Jamek at Muar, built by Sultan Ibrahim of Johor.*

the *temenggong* had become the key official in Johor and was in effect the ruler. Not that the state of Johor amounted to a great deal at the time. Riau and the southern islands had been torn away from Johor by European politicians acting thousands of miles away. The Anglo-Dutch Treaty, signed in London in 1824, had placed them in the Dutch sphere of influence, while Johor was consigned to the British, by then firmly entrenched in Singapore. At that time Johor was largely jungle. A party of Englishmen sailed along the Straits of Johor in 1825 and were far from impressed by what they saw, one of them writing, 'the country is one dreary forest without human habitation'. In less than a hundred years the party would have been confronted by a very different sight: Johor Bahru, created by the two greatest *temenggongs,* Ibrahim and his son Abu Bakar.

Temenggong Ibrahim was the true founder of modern Johor. In spite of being labelled a pirate, he won over the British and, in the long term, benefited enormously from their friendship. His principal objective was to develop Johor into a prosperous territorial base for his family. No Malay port could hope to rival the phenomenal growth of Singapore. The days of the great Malay *entrepôts* had sadly gone forever, but agriculture was a different matter. Ibrahim had to rely initially on the collection of jungle products, but fortune was on his side. In 1843 gutta-percha was discovered in the forests of Johor. A jungle resin similar to rubber, gutta-percha's importance rose dramatically when the British realized the potential of a material that could be moulded into any shape by heating, before hardening on cooling. The value of gutta-percha soared even further when it was discovered to be the only substance capable of protecting cables under water. Ibrahim immediately declared a personal monopoly on the collection of all gutta-percha in the forests of Johor, which he maintained by both fair means and foul. The merchants in Singapore were soon buying all of the gutta-percha he could supply and he quickly became an extremely wealthy man. This enabled him to begin the agricultural development of Johor. Pepper and gambier planters were authorized to settle in the state and so the first Chinese arrived in Johor.

COURTESY OF MUZIUM NEGARA

As the land clearances in Johor gathered momentum, Ibrahim built a hilltop factory at a place called Tanjung Putri, overlooking the Straits of Johor, in 1855. Such were the inauspicious beginnings of **Johor Bahru**. In the course of the next few years all the government offices moved to the new town, though Ibrahim himself preferred to stay in Singapore with his British friends. He was growing old and the key role in the government of Johor was increasingly being played by his son Abu Bakar.

No ruler has left a deeper imprint on modern Johor than Abu Bakar. He was 28 years old when his father died in 1862. Building on Ibrahim's achievements, Abu

Bakar established the modern state of Johor, in the process assuming the title of Sultan, and was probably the single most important Malay political figure of the 19th century. His reign witnessed some great achievements and much of Johor Bahru stands as a monument to the breadth of his vision.

Tanjung Putri had grown rapidly, and in 1866 Abu Bakar renamed the town Johor Bahru and turned it into his state capital. The nerve centre of his kingdom was the sumptuous **Istana Besar**, a magnificent sight on its low hill overlooking the Straits of Johor. There is an air of Versailles about the palace, particularly as the external style is predominantly European. The interior provides a fascinating glimpse into Malay royal life. Abu Bakar himself laid the foundation stone in 1864 and two years later the building was completed. The Throne Room and the domestic suites in the west wing are part of the original palace, but the east wing was demolished in 1912 and the Banqueting Hall rose in its place. The sheer scale of the hall, its many columns, the curving sweeps of the staircase and the splendid fittings and decoration, leave a lasting impression on the visitor.

The Istana Besar has recently been restored and opened to the public as the **Royal Abu Bakar Museum**, though it is very much a 'living' museum. The Throne Room has been the setting for the installation of every sultan since 1886 and is also the venue for the annual investiture ceremony to celebrate the sultan's birthday. The Banqueting Hall is still used for formal state occasions, such as banquets and the lying in state of members of the royal family. The palace contains a vast array of treasures, works of art, antiquities and furniture, most of which were collected by Abu Bakar and his son Sultan Ibrahim. The highlight is undoubtedly the Earl of Ellenborough centre-piece and dinner service, made in England in 1847 and

Opposite: *Sultan Abu Bakar of Johor.*
Above: *The Johor Bahru skyline overlooking the Causeway in the early evening.*

displayed at the Royal Exhibition four years later, before being purchased by Abu Bakar and brought to Johor.

Sultan Ibrahim (1895-1959) is perhaps more renowned for his contributions to the Hunting Room. An ace marksman, he once shot eight elephants in a single day. The room contains many of his trophies, harking back to an age when values were somewhat different to those of our own times. Hunters from Ibrahim's day did not necessarily emerge unscathed from their expeditions. Captain Harry Charles Syers, the British Commissioner of Police in Malaya, was another passionate hunter, but he met his match in a *seladang* in Pahang in 1897. The *seladang,* or wild buffalo, was considered the most dangerous animal to hunt in the Malay Peninsula, though Syers had seemingly mastered the art, having already shot thirteen of them. Number fourteen was to prove another matter. Syers and a planter friend first wounded the animal and then set off in pursuit after it fled. Suddenly, the *seladang* turned and charged at Syers. He shot at it, whereupon the animal swerved and went for the planter. More shots turned it again and, for a second time, it charged straight at Syers. He fired again and again, but this time the *seladang* kept on coming. Syers was knocked to the ground, where he was horribly gored before being tossed over twenty feet into the air. The planter desperately fired shot after shot into the *seladang,* and finally the animal went down. Fifteen bullets had been needed to kill the animal. It was far too late for Syers. He was barely alive and died on the following day.

The royal family now resides at the **Istana Bukit Serene**, built in the Swiss style on a hill to the west of Johor Bahru. The palace is set amidst extensive grounds, which contain the royal zoo. Occupying another imposing position overlooking the Straits of Johor is the **Sultan Abu Bakar Mosque**. Abu Bakar again laid the foundation stone, this time in 1892, but he never lived to see the project finished. Three years later he was dead, while the mosque was not completed until 1900. Yet, if he

could have seen the final result, he would undoubtedly have been pleased with the distinctive design.

Abu Bakar created an administration along western lines. He was advised by a council, two of whom were Chinese, and Johor was divided into administrative divisions. The Chinese representation on the royal council reflected their growing economic importance in the state. By the end of Abu Bakar's reign, their number had grown to over 100,000, but in stark contrast to the Chinese settlers in the states to the north, they were generally peaceful. This was largely due to the effectiveness of *kangchu* rule, a system of Chinese government unique to Johor. Each village, or *kangkar,* was governed by a semi-feudal headman, known as the *kangchu,* who was given a more or less free hand by the Malay authorities. In a very short time each *kangchu* had come to control all the lucrative forms of income in his village, notably the opium and gambling dens. The British later abolished the system when it became clear that the *kangchus* had become preoccupied with their profit-making activities, rather than their administrative duties. The state bureaucracy was constructed around an elite of able and loyal Malays, most of whom were descendants of the *orang kaya,* or nobility, from the old kingdom.

To the British Abu Bakar seemed thoroughly 'civilized', but for some of his fellow Malays, he was perhaps a little too 'civilized', if that meant pandering to the British. Abu Bakar always ruled Johor, not just in the interests of himself and his people, but like his father before him, with more than half an eye on the British in Singapore. In this way he gave them no reason to extend their control over the kingdom during his lifetime. At the same time Abu Bakar was an undoubted Anglophile. He could speak English and was always at home in British company,

Opposite: *The sumptuous Banqueting Hall at the Istana Besar.* ***Above:*** *The Sultan Ibrahim Building in Johor Bahru which houses the State Government offices.*

enjoying a game of billiards or cricket, and attending the horse races in Singapore. On his travels abroad, he visited Britain and was received by Queen Victoria. His close relationship with the British aroused Malay resentment, and there were some murmurings about his background when he became a sultan in 1885. Such criticisms were partly the result of jealousy, but they also raised, certainly not for the last time in Malay history, the question of the relationship between western influences and established local traditions and customs.

Some writers in the late 19th century expressed concern at the decline of Malay culture, especially among young people, and, for instance, urged Malays to preserve the purity of their language. Others were openly critical of those Malays who wore European or Chinese clothes. Similar sentiments are still being expressed in some quarters today, with the young again the principal target. If anything the threat would now seem to be even greater, with the influence of television, films, radio and

modern music. Yet many Malay traditions remain steadfast, none more so than Islam. In the 19th century there was the added concern for many Malay intellectuals that Islam appeared to be on the retreat everywhere before the advance of the Christian West. That would hardly seem to be the case today. The two religions coexist in most parts of the world, certainly in Malaysia, but of the two, Islam is the most vigorous. Christianity, in all of its many forms, would seem to be on the retreat, particularly in Europe and North America, and in urgent need of a reassessment of its role in western society. Islam is in contrast the rock upon which modern Malay society is built.

Johor Bahru is today one of the liveliest places in Malaysia. Discos, karaoke bars and hawker stalls abound, attracting Singaporeans in their thousands. The skyline is due for imminent change, with yet more hotels and office-cum-shopping complexes set to rise towards the clouds in the next few years. In front of the city stretches the **Causeway** across the Johor Straits to Singapore, the busiest border crossing in the world. A second crossing is being built to the south-west of Johor Bahru, which is due to open in 1997.

In the Straits can also be seen *kelongs,* as some people in Johor still make their living from the sea. Normally erected in water between 6 to 8 fathoms in depth, *kelongs* are large fish traps constructed of wood from the *nipah* palm, which is resistant to salt water. They are cleverly positioned to exploit local currents and tides, and guide shoals of fish into the trap where the nets await them. Women are never allowed on the *kelongs,* fishermen believing that they bring only bad luck and poor catches. The number of *kelongs* in the waters around Malaysia has declined in recent years due to the growth in deep sea fishing, particularly in the South China Sea. Now and again even stranger sights

might be seen in the waters off Johor. Not long ago an elephant swam across the Straits to one of the Singapore islands and had to be rescued with the help of two tame elephants, before being taken to the Endau Rompin National Park.

The presence of the Causeway gives Johor Bahru the sense of being at 'land's end', but the city is not in fact the most southerly tip of the Asian mainland. To discover the spot honoured by this geographical distinction, take Route 5 from Johor Bahru to Pontian Kecil, and then turn south to **Kukup**, a picturesque fishing village built on stilts and renowned for its seafood restaurants. They claim to serve the best fish in Johor. Just before the village take the road off to the left to Serkat, and from there the track down to **Tanjung Piai**. This is a far cry from Johor Bahru. Amidst dense mangrove swamps is a restaurant, with a boardwalk leading to a small pagoda at 'land's end'. There are fine views to the south and the seemingly unending succession of ships on the horizon heading to and from Singapore.

Johor still sits astride one of the world's vital trading routes, but the wealth of Abu Bakar's kingdom was never founded on commerce or shipping. Agriculture lay at the heart of the new Johor, though few plantations survive from the days of Abu Bakar. Where once there were pepper, gambier and later rubber estates, there are now oil palm plantations, the source of most of Malaysia's present day agricultural wealth. Take any road into the hinterland of Johor from Johor Bahru, whether Route 1, 3 or 5, and you will drive past acre after acre of oil palms, some young and rather squat, others more mature and rather taller, but all lined up in neat rows, like some vast army on a parade ground.

The growth in the oil palm industry is one of the success stories of Malaysia. The

Opposite: *An Indian cook making dosai in one of Johor Bahru's many restaurants. Made from rice flour, dosai are popular for breakfast, served with dhal curry or coconut chutney.* ***Above:*** *The Sultan Abu Bakar Mosque.*

palms dominate the landscape just as rubber trees did in the years of British rule. From almost nowhere prior to the 1960s, palm oil has emerged as a leader in the global market for oils and fats. In 1992 over six million tons were produced in Malaysia, a far cry from the position thirty years ago when the country could manage only 100,000 tons. The oil is capable of being refined to an extremely high quality and, significantly in our health conscious age, is very nutritious, containing both vitamins A and E. The palms have an economic life of thirty years and thrive in both poor soils and the very heavy rainfall of tropical Malaysia. Productivity is exceptional, with the yield per hectare being more than four times that of its principal competitors, such as soya bean or sunflower oils.

Johor Bahru and the oil palms reflect the success of the new kingdom of Johor, but what of the old Johor, the maritime power that followed in the wake of Melaka? As is often the case in the Malay Peninsula, the early settlements in Johor were to be found on the banks of a river: the Johor River in the east of the state. From Johor Bahru Route 3 runs to the headwaters of the river and the town of **Kota Tinggi**, one of the former capitals of the kingdom. Kota Tinggi is today a peaceful backwater, most visitors preferring to drive on to the beaches, resorts and islands of the east coast. The principal local attraction is the spectacular waterfalls at **Air Terjun Lombong**, some 15 km to the north.

At the end of the 17th century Kota Tinggi was the stage for an act of regicide that brought about the fall of the old kingdom of Johor. The kingdom had become centred on the Johor River in the early 1530s. The river was far from ideal for trade, being well off the beaten track, but it was easier to defend than the islands to the south. Nevertheless, the Portuguese were still a major threat. They repeatedly attacked the settlements along the Johor River. When the danger from the Portuguese receded, the Acehnese caused further havoc, carrying off two sultans into

captivity. Yet the rulers and people of Johor showed remarkable resilience and, in alliance with the Dutch, the kingdom recovered. The event that cemented the alliance was the siege of Melaka between August 1640 and January 1641. Although the forces of Johor did not play a leading role in the fighting, they gave the Dutch invaluable assistance by encircling Melaka on the landward side and preventing the Portuguese getting any reinforcements or supplies into the town.

The Johor sultans came to hold sway over the southern part of the Malay Peninsula, Singapore, the Riau and Lingga archipelagos, and Kampar and Siak in Sumatra. Trade flourished. Merchants and traders from India, China, the Middle East, Sumatra and Java flocked to the ports of Johor, attracted by the choice, quality and prices of the wares. Spaniards, Danes and a few Englishmen were also welcomed and evidently found the trade to their liking. Tolerance and profitability were the hallmarks of Johor in the years of its greatness. Here at last in the middle of the 17th century was a fitting successor to Melaka, an empire both prosperous and influential throughout the region, providing a much needed focus for all Malay loyalties.

Unfortunately, the greatness of Johor did not last. In the late 17th century the capital moved to Kota Tinggi. All seemed well until 1697 when the new ruler, Sultan Mahmud, took control of the kingdom. Matters soon began to get out of hand. Mahmud revealed himself to be a cruel and perverted tyrant. Foreign traders stayed away, while some of the *orang laut* returned to a life of piracy. Profits declined and the Johor *orang kaya* found themselves hard hit in the pocket.

Sultan Mahmud's taste for wanton violence went from bad to worse. On one occasion he was given a pair of pistols as a present and tried them out in the street

by shooting a passer-by in the shoulder. In 1699 he ordered the pregnant wife of Megat Sri Rama, the *laksamana,* to be disembowelled for eating a piece of jackfruit from his garden. The *orang kaya* rallied to the defence of Megat Sri Rama and began plotting against a ruler they now considered completely mad. They were understandably apprehensive about overthrowing Mahmud, as Malay royal tradition upheld the view that God alone could punish a sultan, whatever his misdeeds.

As Mahmud did not have a son, Johor's royal dynasty, descended from the Melaka Sultanate, came to an abrupt and brutal end in 1699. Just outside Kota Tinggi at **Kampung Makam** is the mausoleum of Sultan Mahmud. Set amidst peaceful surroundings, the tomb gives no indication of Mahmud's violent death. In a

Opposite: *A pleasure boat flying the Johor and Malaysian flags at Kukup, with a series of kelongs behind.* ***Above:*** *Ducklings for sale at the market in Johor Bahru.*

scene worthy of a Shakespearian drama, the Sultan was being carried by one of his servants to morning prayers at the mosque in Kota Tinggi. Along the way he passed through the market, where Megat Sri Rama emerged from the milling crowd and plunged a knife into him. Mahmud fell to the ground, whereupon the rest of the *orang kaya* rushed forward and began stabbing him repeatedly. The market was soon awash with royal blood as the Sultan lay dying. With his final breath, there passed away the legitimacy and greatness of Johor, the heir to Melaka.

Most Malays found it impossible to come to terms with the assassination, even allowing for Mahmud's appalling behaviour, and regarded the conspirators as traitors. According to one account, the Sultan had managed to wound Megat Sri Rama in the foot with his *kris* during the struggle. Due to *daulat,* the spiritual powers bestowed by kingship, grass began to grow in the wound and for four years Megat Sri Rama suffered excruciating pain before he died. The *bendahara* was proclaimed sultan, but the assassination left deep scars and the 18th century was to be one of turmoil for Johor.

The Johor River remains today a fairly inaccessible place, effectively protected by the unending oil palm plantations. The only way to explore the length and breadth of the river is by boat. Nevertheless, it is possible to reach several of the old settlements on the eastern bank of the river. This involves taking Route 92 south from Kota Tinggi, and then following the signposts along the laterite tracks which criss-cross the plantations. Batu Sawar and Pancor are former capitals of the old kingdom, but the most evocative and famous of the Johor River sites is **Johor Lama**. The original name of the settlement has disappeared from the pages of history and, for as long as people can remember, the place has been known simply as Johor Lama, or Old Johor. Reaching the village seems to take an eternity along the laterite tracks, although it is only 8 km from the main road. Always keep a look out for the bright blue kingfishers, which are often to be seen flying among the oil palms. At the village you might also see the inhabitants processing rubber latex from their smallholdings in the time-honoured fashion, with setting trays and mangles.

Sultan Alauddin (1528-1564) established his capital at Johor Lama in the 1540s. The *Sejarah Melayu* describe how the jungle was cleared to make way for the settlement, which was dominated by the royal palace, and included a fort, a mosque, and an audience hall. The earthen

***Above, left:** A young boy contemplating the water at Air Terjun Lombong near Kota Tinggi.* ***Above, right:** The earthen ramparts overlooking the Johor River are the only remains of the historic fort at Johor Lama.*

ramparts of the fort, overlooking the river, can still be viewed today. Visiting Johor Lama is like taking a step back in time. Cars are the exception rather than the rule and there is an all pervading air of solitude. It is difficult to imagine the violence and destruction that befell Johor Lama on more than one occasion.

The town never really recovered from the terrible sack by the Portuguese in 1587, even though it became the capital again in the late 17th century. The Portuguese ships successfully negotiated their way up the Johor River and then subjected the royal town to a fearful bombardment, causing untold damage. The Malays put up a furious resistance and repulsed the first Portuguese assault. After awaiting reinforcements from Melaka, the Portuguese tried again. This time they were more successful. A breach was made in the defences and the Portuguese swarmed into Johor Lama. Even then they had to take the town street by street and house by house. At last the valiant defenders gave way and fled into the jungle. The Portuguese ransacked the royal buildings and put the whole town to the torch.

One of the great strengths of the Johor kingdom was its ability to bounce back from adversity and such was the case after the destruction of Johor Lama in 1587. Unfortunately, there was to be no similar recovery after 1699. The old kingdom had gone forever. The authority of the new line of sultans was always in doubt. The divisions caused by Mahmud's assassination were exploited most dramatically by the Bugis. In a few years they had come to dominate the political life of Johor. Most Malays hated them, but were powerless to resist, not least because they saw the Bugis as God's punishment for the death of Mahmud. The *orang kaya* discovered that, unless they obeyed the Bugis leaders, they

Below: *Sultan Mahmud's mausoleum at Kampung Makam.* ***Overleaf:*** *The Sibu Island Cabanas resort on Pulau Sibu offers a stunning view of Pulau Tinggi, as well as directing visitors to all parts of the globe.*

WEST
SOUTH
NORTH
NORWAY 10105 KM.
SINGAPORE 135 KM.
SWEDEN
DENMARK 10013 KM.
AUSTRALIA 6168 KM.
U.KINGDOM 10895 KM.
SWITZERLAND 10422 KM.
CZECHOSLOVAKIA 9891 KM.
GERMANY 10406 KM.
KUALA LUMPUR 353 KM.
ITALY 10055 KM.
BELGIUM 10597 KM.
LUXEMBOURG 10486 KM.
AUSTRIA 9748 KM.
HOLLAND 10537 KM.
FRANCE 10772 KM.
SPAIN 11419 KM.
POLAND 9446 KM.
SIBU CABANAS

were squeezed out of the court. Probably the worst affected were those *orang laut* who had remained loyal to Johor. In virtually all of their roles they were superseded by the Bugis, no mean seamen themselves. A few swallowed their pride and served the Bugis, but the majority went their own way, some to follow other Malay rulers, but most back to piracy. It was a sad end for a famed group of seamen and warriors, who had played such a major role in shaping the history of the Malay Peninsula. By the end of the 18th century very few of them still survived, and those that did were described by one Malay writer as being filthy, repellent and little better than animals.

Islands have always played a vital part in the fortunes of Johor and on several occasions the sultans moved their capital to the Riau and Lingga archipelagos. Riau was the most important of the islands to the south and reached its height during the years of Bugis rule. An English merchant of the time called the port 'the key to the Straits', and ships sailed there from China, Cambodia, Thailand and all over South East Asia. There were all the usual goods for the Chinese market, such as forest products, pepper, gambier and tin from the west coast of the peninsula, which were traded for opium and cloth. It seemed like the good old days again, though there was one vital difference - Riau was not a Malay *entrepôt,* but a Bugis one. The port prospered for only a comparatively short period, much as its Bugis masters did in Johor. The rise of Singapore saw to that and, by the Treaty of London in 1824, Riau was consigned to the Indonesian world.

Johor might have been stripped of its southern islands, but the modern kingdom still possesses a string of beautiful and largely unspoilt islands lying off the east coast. The principal gateway to these islands and also Pulau Tioman, part of neighbouring Pahang, is **Mersing**. The town is an attractive place and is the venue every May for the festival of Air Papan, where visitors can see the *kuda kepang,* an ancient dance seldom seen outside Johor. It is performed by a group of nine to fifteen dancers, who 'ride' puppet horses to the rhythmic beat of the accompanying music. The horses are made of buffalo or goat skin stretched over a bamboo framework, and colourfully painted and decorated. During the performance one or more of the dancers will collapse on the floor, in a complete trance, and begin to emulate the actions of a horse, charging, kicking and gnashing their teeth. The 'spirit' of the horse is believed to have taken possession of them.

There are several versions as to the origins of the dance, though the most likely concerns the 15th-century mission of Wali Songo to spread the message of Islam in Java. Realising the villagers would be wary of strangers, he devised a dance on horseback to arouse their curiosity. From Java the dance spread to the Malay Peninsula. Live horses were replaced by puppets, and the dance was then passed down from

generation to generation. Very little would seem to have changed over the years. The dance is always accompanied by elaborate rituals and incantations before and after the performance. For instance, at the beginning of each dance, a *bomoh* will bless the dancers and musical instruments in an effort to prevent evil spirits from influencing the performance.

The Johor islands can be geographically divided into three groups. Pulau Besar, Pulau Hujung, Pulau Rawa and Pulau Tengah are the nearest to Mersing. Further south lie Pulau Sibu and Pulau Tinggi. Finally, there are two bigger islands further out in the South China Sea, Pulau Aur and Pulau Pemanggil. Besides these three groups, there are over fifty smaller islands where there are very few or no inhabitants. One of the most popular is **Pulau Sibu**, an island roughly 6 km in length and 1 km wide. It can be reached from Kampung Sedili Besar and Tanjung Leman, in addition to Mersing. One of the boats plying back and forth between Mersing and Sibu is the curiously named *Black Sausage,* which supplies a resort on the east coast of the island. Here Sibu faces the dramatic island of **Pulau Tinggi**, which rises like a mountain from the sea. Much of the accommodation on Sibu is fairly basic, but this merely adds to the sense of being a castaway on a tropical island. Sibu is largely unspoilt, with sparkling white beaches, rocky headlands and tracts of virgin rain forest. Virtually the only intrusion from the outside world is the sound of aircraft far overhead, on the flight path north from Singapore. It is in fact very difficult in modern Johor to get away from the influence of Singapore. Sultan Abu Bakar would undoubtedly have agreed.

Opposite: *A waterspout, or sea tornado, off the east coast of Johor. These occur when a rapidly gyrating vortex of wind descends from heavy storm clouds and whips up the sea, in the process sucking up a column of water which travels with the cloud.* ***Above:*** *The sound of aircraft is not the only intrusion from the modern world on Pulau Sibu.*

PERAK
THAILAND
PENANG
KEDAH
KELANTAN
PAHANG
SELANGOR
STRAITS OF MALACCA
KELIAN INTAN
GERIK
Tasik Temengor
S. Perak
SELAMA
LENGGONG
PARIT BUNTAR
BAGAN SERAI
Tasik Chenderoh
TAIPING
ENGGOR
S. SIPUT
KUALA SEPETANG
K. KANGSAR
CHEMOR
IPOH
BATU GAJAH
CAMERON HIGHLANDS
PARIT
KAMPAR
BOTA KANAN
S. Kinta
LUMUT
SITIAWAN
P. PANGKOR
P.PANGKOR LAUT
TAPAH
BIDOR
TELUK INTAN
S. Bernam
TG. MALIM
0 15 30 km
KEY
LEBUHRAYA (EXPRESSWAY)
MAJOR ROADS
SECONDARY ROADS
RAILWAY
AIRPORT / AIRSTRIP
STATE BOUNDARIES
INTERNATIONAL BORDER
1 SAYONG
2 BUKIT GANTANG
3 BUKIT LARUT (1,035 m)
4 PULAU BESAR
5 PASIR SALAK
6 KELLIE'S CASTLE
7 GOPENG
8 TAMBUN
9 GUNUNG RUNTUH (PERAK MAN)

PERAK

The Kingdom with the Silver Lining

There are nine sultanates in Malaysia today. Kedah is probably the oldest, but Perak may lie a very respectable second. The *Hikayat Marong Mahawangsa,* or Kedah Annals, certainly suggest as much, claiming that while Mahawangsa was the first sultan of Kedah, his son Raja Marong Mahapodisat founded Perak. As a young man Mahapodisat set off in search of new lands and adventure, just as his father had done before him. He came to the mouth of a river, which he sailed up, finally arriving at a large lake, in the middle of which lay four islands. Mahapodisat liked what he saw and took his famed bow, *Indra Sakti,* and fitted a silver arrow to it. He drew the bowstring back as far as his strength would allow and then let the arrow go. It flew like lightning into the heavens, before plunging to the ground on one of the islands, which was subsequently known as Pulau Indra Sakti. Mahapodisat founded his kingdom on the island, calling it Perak, after the silver arrow, the word *perak* meaning silver in Malay.

Disentangling historical fact from the tales and legends of the *hikayats* is never easy and, in this instance, matters are further complicated by local folklore which has another version of the founding of Perak. This is the Legend of the White Semang. A trusted courtier, Nakhodah Kassim, was despatched by the last ruler of Melaka, Sultan Mahmud, to find a new settlement in the north. He reached Perak where he encountered a group of *orang asli* of the Semang people. While he was trading with them, a young girl accidentally cut herself stripping a sugar cane. To everybody's amazement, white blood seeped from the wound.

Nakhodah was instantly smitten and a month later the couple were married. A daughter followed, if not in the usual fashion. The Perak River was always liable to flood during the monsoon and that year was no different, except in one way. When the river flooded, foam came floating downstream with all the other debris. This foam collected at the point on the bank where Nakhodah's wife went to bathe. When she moved part of it with a stick, she found a baby girl sitting peacefully in the middle. She took the infant home and she and Nakhodah adopted the girl, giving her the name Tun Puteh. The years passed by and the village, along with Nakhodah and his family, grew in wealth and importance.

When Nakhodah lay dying, he told Tun Puteh of his past and, with his last breath, ordered her to ask the Sultan of Melaka to send a ruler for Perak. Negotiations were promptly opened and Sultan Mahmud agreed to despatch his own son, Sultan Muzaffar (1528-1545), as the first ruler of the kingdom of Perak. The *Sejarah Melayu* have a slightly different story. Muzaffar had been passed over as heir to Melaka and decided to seek his fortune elsewhere, journeying first to Siak and then to Klang in Selangor, where he was noticed by a trader from Perak. Quickly sensing the possibilities, the trader befriended Muzaffar, took him to Perak and installed him as ruler. The voyage to Perak was not without its difficulties, if the

State crest: *At the top is the crest worn by the ruler on his tengkolok, or Malay head-dress, symbolising his sovereignty. The rice stalk represents the importance of padi farming in the state.*

Legend of the White Semang is to be believed. While off the Klang coast, one of Muzaffar's attendants pointed at some colourful fish in the water. Muzaffar leaned over the side of the boat to take a closer look and, as he did so, his crown slipped off into the sea and immediately sank. His attendants dived repeatedly to look for it, but with no luck. For this reason, Muzaffar and his descendants, who still rule in Perak today, have never had a crown.

The sultans of Perak possessed all of the other royal regalia, several items of which still feature in the coronation, the most famous being the sword of state, *Chura Si Manja Kini.* It is believed to have been the sword of Alexander the Great and, according to Perak tradition, was used in the installation of Parameswara as the first ruler of Melaka. Unfortunately, the sultans of Perak have needed such swords all too often in the past. The famous silver arrow of Raja Marong Mahapodisat had buried itself in a kingdom with a silver lining, not of the precious metal but of tin, the ore with the silvery lustre. Among the rock strata of Perak's mountainous central region lie rich veins of tin ore, which over the centuries have been revealed by erosion, and then washed by river and rain into the coastal plain below. Tin brought great wealth to Perak, but also defeats, disasters and domestic turmoil, as foreign and Malay powers sought to exploit and monopolise the trade. Perak was never one of the stronger states in the peninsula and, for much of the time, it was kicked back and forth like a football by the Portuguese and the Acehnese, or by the Acehnese and the Dutch, and later on by the Bugis and the Minangkabaus.

During the 18th and 19th centuries Perak was further weakened by a series of internal struggles over the succession to the throne and the profits from tin. The former was in part due to the uncertainties caused by Perak's succession system, which rotates among the various members of the royal family. This is not to deny the noble lineage of the Perak ruling dynasty. They are the only Malay kings to claim direct descent from the sultans of 15th-century Melaka and beyond them to the princes on Bukit Si Guntang. Yet such a prestigious background could not keep out the foreign powers. The troubles eventually brought in the British to protect their interests in the tin mines, but in earlier times it was the Dutch who were firmly entrenched in Perak.

The small fort on **Pulau Pangkor** is the most potent reminder of the Dutch presence in Perak. First occupied in 1670, the island was used by the Dutch as a storage depot for tin and, more importantly, as a base to combat repeated attacks on Dutch shipping by the local pirates. The fort, **Kota Belanda**, has been restored by the Muzium Negara and is little changed in appearance from a description made in 1689: 'built four square,...like a House: every square is about ten or twelve yards.

The Walls are of a good Thickness, made of Stone, and carried up to a good Height, of about thirty Foot, and covered over Head like a dwelling House.' Kota Belanda was never a success. The pirates continued to take a heavy toll on Dutch ships, while the fort was repeatedly attacked by local Malays, finally being overrun in 1690, forcing the Dutch to withdraw from the island.

The Dutch returned to Pangkor in 1743 and rebuilt the fort. This time they stayed for only five years. Close to the hapless little fort at Teluk Gedung is a giant granite boulder, known as **Batu Bersurat**. Carved on the face of the boulder is the year 1743, the initials VOC, the depiction of a tiger clutching a child in its paws and possibly the name of the inscriber, I.F.Cralo. This is a memorial to a young Dutch boy who disappeared one morning while playing on the beach near the rock. The Dutch believed he had been seized by a hungry tiger. Or was it wishful thinking to hide their shame? The locals insisted that the boy had been kidnapped by pirates. Mind you another version of events says that the boy was a girl and that the *orang laut* took her to the Sembilan Islands where she grew up and married the chief's son. Their descendants are said to live in Manong, near Kuala Kangsar.

Pangkor remained largely a backwater until present times and the growth of tourism. Where once Dutch soldiers patrolled along the beaches, holiday-makers now lie out on the white sands. One of the most attractive beaches is **Pantai Puteri Dewi**, or the Beach of the Fairy Princess, in the north-west of the island and owned by the Pan Pacific Resort. According to local legend, a young warrior from Sumatra fell in love with a beautiful princess and, to gain her favour, he sailed north to win his spurs in battle. When he failed to return after many months, the princess, distraught, set out and travelled

Opposite: *A sea eagle, with a fish held tight in its talons, heads for its nest on Pulau Pangkor.* ***Above:*** *The Dutch fort, Kota Belanda.*

far and wide in search of him. Only when she reached Pangkor did she discover the sad truth that he had died in battle and been buried on the island. The villagers showed her the grave, whereupon she rushed heart-broken to the cliff edge and threw herself onto the rocks below. The beach was duly named after her.

Huge armies of small crabs are a familiar sight on Pantai Puteri Dewi, moving across the sand with their curious sideways gait, or rapidly burrowing into it at the approach of danger, leaving the beach pock-marked with their diggings until the sea washes it smooth again. The hotel grounds are also a favourite haunt for hornbills, while sea eagles can often be seen soaring high above, searching for food.

Pangkor is an island of beauty and tranquillity, and in reality little changed from the time of the Dutch. The absence of a road bridge has seen to that. There is now an airstrip, but development is carefully controlled. The local economy remains dependent on fishing, as it has for centuries. Most of the fishing villages are on the eastern side of the island, facing the mainland, where the ferries also arrive from Lumut. In the past fishing was supplemented by piracy, whereas today it is bolstered by tourism. Travellers from Europe are now viewed in a rather different light by the locals!

To the south of the main island lies **Pulau Pangkor Laut**, reached by ferry from Pasir Bogak or the mainland. Once a leper colony, the island is now privately owned and the home of the Pangkor Laut Resort. Guests are welcomed at the jetty with garlands of flowers and cold drinks. A hilly jungle track crosses the island to the scenic horseshoe-shaped Emerald Bay, from where the British commando, Spencer Chapman, made his dramatic escape from Japanese occupied Malaya by submarine in 1944. Chapman had spent over three years fighting the Japanese, later writing *The Jungle is Neutral*, a vivid and much praised account of his time in the Malayan jungle. He reached the island hidden in a sampan and at night swam 45 metres out

into the bay where the submarine was waiting.

The Dutch might have failed on Pangkor, but they remained the key factor in the politics of Perak for another hundred years. A principal beneficiary of the Dutch alliance was Raja Iskandar of Perak (1752-1765), whose reign witnessed an unprecedented degree of peace in the kingdom, still being seen today as a *zaman mas,* or golden age. The Dutch alliance guaranteed protection from any enemies, such as the Acehnese, while strengthening the royal hand against rivals at home. Here was Malay kingship at its most effective. Iskandar chose an island at the meeting point of the Perak and Kinta rivers as his capital and named it Pulau Indra Sakti, after the place where the silver arrow had struck the ground. At the same time he travelled the kingdom as no ruler of Perak had done before him, appointing and supervising his officials, and showing himself off to his subjects. He inevitably commissioned a *hikayat* to record the story of his rule and so his cousin, Raja Chulan, wrote the informative *Misa Melayu.*

Unfortunately, the reign of a strong, forceful ruler is all too often followed by weakness and domestic strife, and such was the case after the death of Sultan Iskandar. Tin was the principal cause of the trouble. Local chiefs and officials became involved in the smuggling of tin, unthinkable in Iskandar's time, thus avoiding the royal duties, as well as the monopoly established by the Dutch. By the end of the 18th century, the Dutch were a spent force and brought no respite to Perak. The kingdom became a prey to other foreign powers and, in the early 19th century, Perak was attacked and occupied by forces from Selangor and Kedah, the latter acting as agents for the Siamese. Fortunately, the threat from the north disappeared in 1826 when, following lengthy talks with the

Opposite: *The beautiful secluded beach at Emerald Bay on Pulau Pangkor Laut.*
Above: *Sunset over Pantai Puteri Dewi on Pulau Pangkor. A cruise ship is anchored offshore.*

British, the Siamese agreed not to attack Perak or Selangor.

In the long term both Malay kingdoms had simply swapped one potential overlord for another. A British presence, in the shape of Captain James Low, was immediately apparent in Perak. He has left a vivid picture of Sultan Abdullah (1825-1830) and life at his court, which emphasises the closeness of the ruler and his people in an age when there was no real need for current levels of security. Low found Abdullah 'a very quiet person and very indulgent to his subjects,...he hears complaints and settles business early in the morning,...one day the Raja (Abdullah) gave a feast to his people, it being an anniversary. A long and slightly built shed was prepared as a kitchen. Here five or six huge iron pots were placed over fires. In each of these about thirty fowls were boiled....The Raja and his people dress in very ordinary garb except on occasions of ceremony....'

One of the leading figures at the Perak court was the *laksamana*, an office deriving from the Melaka Sultanate in the 15th century. The greatest of all *laksamanas* was undoubtedly Hang Tuah, who also had close connections with Perak. His famous *kris*, *Tameng Sari,* which he used in the duel with Hang Jebat, is part of the royal regalia. The dynasty of *laksamanas* in Perak during the 19th century was descended from a poor Pasai fisherman, Tok Kuala Bidor, who lived with his wife on the Perak River. The rise of Tok Bidor was sudden and unexpected, if local folklore is to be believed. He and his wife were said to be so poor that they had only one garment to share between them. When one went out, the other had to stay inside their hut. To make matters worse, Tok Bidor's fishtraps were being repeatedly robbed. One day he caught the thief, a genie. He grabbed the culprit, who cried out in alarm, 'Let me go and I will give you your heart's desire'. Having released the genie, Tok Bidor asked for an end to his life of poverty. The genie promised him that he would become the greatest

chief in Perak, but that his descendants would only prosper for seven generations. The prophesy did indeed come true. Tok Kuala Bidor became the *laksamana* of Perak, his daughter later marrying the sultan, but the family's fortunes would also take a decided turn for the worse after the seven generations had passed.

The simple life of the royal court and the people of Perak, be they fishermen or farmers, did not last. In the course of the 19th century Perak underwent dramatic and often violent change, which altered forever the social and political nature of the kingdom. The smuggling of tin and the petty rivalries between the Malay chiefs over the division of the revenues had continued apace, helped in no small part by the mining of new extensive deposits in Larut, reputedly discovered by an elephant. The animal was being used to haul heavy equipment, when it broke free and headed off into the jungle. The workers set off in pursuit. When they finally recaptured the elephant, they found it covered in mud, but mud rich in tin ore. Originally a desolate area of swamps stretching from the hills around Bukit Larut to the coast, the district was transformed by the discovery of tin. The inspiration behind much of this change was Long Jaafar, the son of a minor Perak chief, who settled in Kelian Pauh, now Taiping, where he established his first mines. When he arrived there were only three Chinese in the whole of Larut, but he now attracted them in their thousands to work the rapidly growing number of mines. As in Penang, they brought their secret societies and regional rivalries with them.

Long Jaafar died in 1857 and was buried at the fort he built at **Bukit Gantang**, near Taiping. The fort can still be visited today, a narrow trail leading from the Klinik Bidan to the overgrown remains. Long Jaafar's son, Ngah Ibrahim, built a new fort and residence at **Matang**,

The Lake Gardens at Taiping:
Opposite: *Reflections in one of the lakes.*
Below: *The magnificent rain trees overhanging the road.*

11 km to the west of Taiping. He was going to need it as Larut was a powder-keg just waiting to be touched off.

Today it is difficult to believe that the area around **Taiping** in Perak was the scene of a brutal civil war. Taiping itself is an attractive old town, overlooked by jungle-clad hills, the most famous of which is **Bukit Larut**, or Maxwell Hill as it was known in British times. There is a real charm in Bukit Larut's simplicity. It is a place to change down a gear or two, which is what the drivers of the government land rovers have to do on numerous occasions, as they negotiate the steep and twisting road to the summit. This is the only means of getting to the top, short of a tiring climb. The drive up is certainly exhilarating, something akin to a fairground ride, as you are flung from side to side, the driver skilfully negotiating seemingly endless hairpin bends (72 in all). In places the dense jungle gives way to glimpses of a plunging mountain stream or the land laid out below. Local people can also be seen, particularly in the late afternoon, taking their daily

'constitutional'. British habits seem to die hard. The summit itself offers fine views over Taiping and, on a clear day, west to the coastline, even occasionally as far as Penang.

The principal attraction in Taiping is the **Lake Gardens**, which incorporate a zoo and a 9-hole golf course. One of the most striking features of the Gardens is the huge, glorious rain trees, the branches and foliage of which form a spectacular, and sometimes very necessary, umbrella over the road, as Taiping has the heaviest annual rainfall in the Malay Peninsula. This is 'green' architecture in one of its earliest and most effective forms. Yet reminders of Taiping's violent past are never too far away. The mirrored lakes and lush landscaped gardens were created from an abandoned tin mine in the 1890s. The greatest change brought about by the fighting in the town was the replacement of the original name, Kelian Pauh, with Taiping, derived from the two Chinese words, *tai* and *peng*, which together mean 'everlasting peace'. Such were the sentiments of the Chinese leaders in the town after the bloodshed of well over a decade. Not that Taiping was much of a town in those days. The jungle was so close that, on one occasion, a rhinoceros appeared at the entrance to a ward in the hospital, walked through and disappeared out of the door at the back!

The fighting amongst the Chinese started in 1861 and gradually escalated, spreading first to Penang, before dragging in the local Malay chiefs. Their rivalries had simmered for years, but now burst into violence due to the succession dispute following the death of Sultan Ali (1865-1871). Perak was engulfed by civil war. In 1873 the British decided to intervene and restore order. The merchant community in Singapore had been urging such a course of action for years, the tin trade having been seriously disrupted. British priorities were thus clear from the outset. The Governor of the Straits Settlements, Sir Andrew Clarke, arranged a ceasefire and ordered the leading Malay chiefs from Perak to meet him on a steamship, the *Pluto,* anchored off Pangkor, to settle the succession issue. One of the claimants, Raja Abdullah, wrote to Clarke, inviting him to send a Resident to Perak in return for being recognised as Sultan. The scene was thus set for the famous Treaty of Pangkor (1874), by which the British took control of a Malay kingdom for the first time. Abdullah was made Sultan and a Resident was allotted to the kingdom. The British would stay for over eighty years, not as long as the Portuguese or the Dutch, but their influence would be far more pervasive. No wonder the name Pangkor is familiar to all Malaysian schoolchildren, for the treaty was a landmark in the history of the country.

The leader of Ngah Ibrahim's forces in the civil war, Captain T.C.S. Speedy, a colourful freebooter, was immediately installed as Assistant Resident. A rather dilapidated old house, which once belonged to Speedy, can still be seen today, next to the Kota Ngah Ibrahim in Matang. Another Briton to arrive in Perak was Frank Swettenham, a key figure in the shaping of colonial rule in Malaya in the last quarter of the 19th century. The most important official to come to the kingdom was also the most controversial: J.W.W. Birch, the first Resident in British Malaya. He was destined never to leave Perak, being murdered at Pasir Salak on 2nd November 1875.

Pasir Salak is located on the banks of the Perak River. This lower part of the river is rich in history. A road runs alongside it from Teluk Intan to Parit, through what is known as the **Valley of the Kings**. Where now motor cars carry travellers up and down the valley, so for hundreds of years the river itself provided the only

Opposite: *The tilting clock tower at Teluk Intan.* ***Below:*** *A boy takes the plunge into the Perak River at Pasir Salak, the spot where J.W.W. Birch was murdered in 1875.*

means of transport. The kingdom of Perak was to all intents and purposes the Perak River and its tributaries. At various intervals along the river are to be found the simple graves of past sultans, all marked by yellow signs. Sultan Muzaffar's grave is located at Teluk Bakong, 11 km south of Bota Kanan.

Teluk Intan is famous for its clock tower, Malaysia's answer to the leaning tower of Pisa. Built in 1885, the tilting tower is seen as proof that the town, situated at the confluence of the Perak and Bidor rivers, is slowly sinking. Near to Teluk Intan, by the side of the railway line, is a small plaque in memory of a wild bull elephant which fatally charged and derailed a train 'invading' its jungle territory in 1894. The skull of the elephant is on display at the Muzium Negara in Kuala Lumpur.

Yet it is to **Pasir Salak** and the fate of Birch that the visitor is drawn. Today a bridge spans the river from Kampung Gajah to Pasir Salak. Birch was attacked and killed by the men of Datuk Maharaja Lela, the local chief, while he was washing himself on a raft attached to the river bank. Maharaja Lela and the principal figures in the plot were later executed. Several others were exiled to the Seychelles, including Ngah Ibrahim and the *laksamana* Muhammad Amin. The children of the *laksamana* claimed that they were the seventh generation in direct descent from Tok Kuala Bidor, the founder of the family's fortunes. The genie's prophesy that the fisherman's descendants would prosper for only seven generations had been true.

COURTESY OF MUZIUM NEGARA

The historical complex at Pasir Salak features displays outlining the events surrounding Birch's death. Attractively landscaped on the banks of the river, the complex is centred on two *kutai,* or traditional Perak houses. An obelisk stands close to the spot where Birch died, while nearby is another memorial, in the form of a large metal *kris,* commemorating Maharaja Lela and his associates in the plot.

Though experienced in colonial government, having served in Ceylon, James Birch was wholly unsuited to the demands of being the first Resident in British Malaya. Aloof, arrogant and short-tempered, Birch lacked any real diplomatic skills and tried to bully the local chiefs, often giving them 'a good dressing down' in public. No one came to hate him more than Sultan Abdullah (1874-1876), who called on the spirits to have him removed. At a private seance attended by the Sultan, the Resident's spirit was produced in the form of a butterfly, which was then killed with a knife. Abdullah announced that Birch himself would be dead within a month. The British firmly believed in the Sultan's involvement in the murder and exiled him to the Seychelles.

Birch's posting to Perak was the start of what came to be known as the Residential system, the cornerstone of British rule in Malaya. The Treaty of Pangkor stated that the Resident's advice 'must be asked and acted upon on all

questions other than those touching Malay religion and custom'. The Malay chiefs probably believed that the British presence would be similar to that of the Dutch in the 18th century, but they were to be sadly mistaken. The British intended far more extensive powers for the Resident. Difficulties were therefore bound to lie ahead, making it essential that the first Resident in Perak was a man of patience, tact and, probably most important of all, with a good knowledge of the country, its customs and language. Birch possessed none of these qualities.

The British were determined to bring about far reaching changes in Malay society. Slavery had been abolished in the Empire and the British were intent upon stamping it out in Malaya. This was undoubtedly a laudable aim, but there were distinctions in the practice of slavery in the Malay kingdoms which the British tended to ignore. While there was slavery of the western form, largely involving the *orang asli,* many so-called slaves were in fact debt bondsmen. This involved a person 'mortgaging' himself in return for financial assistance from his creditor, usually his ruler or chief. In times of hardship, such as following a bad harvest, this was often the only way a peasant could raise funds. If he was subsequently unable to repay the debt, he was taken into his creditor's household until the outstanding sum was paid. At the same time the issue of slavery was fundamental to the prestige of the chiefs. In the Malay world the number of slaves held by a chief was as important to his status as his revenue.

To make matters worse, revenue was another source of friction between the British and the local chiefs in Perak, indeed throughout Malaya. The British wanted to centralise revenue collection and thus reverse the trend of the 19th century. This had seen the Malay chiefs ignoring royal orders and raising their own taxes, in

Opposite: *J.W.W. Birch, the first British Resident in Perak.* ***Above:*** *The golden domes and minarets of the Masjid Ubudiah in Kuala Kangsar.*

the process becoming financially independent. Not surprisingly, they were intensely hostile to the British plan of a central treasury which paid out salaries to them, subject of course to the Resident's control. When the Resident was someone like Birch, then such a proposal was abhorrent to the chiefs.

Wild rumours swept across Perak, adding to the growing unease. Birch was even thought to be plotting the overthrow of Sultan Abdullah. In November 1875 he made his final fateful journey to Pasir Salak, intending to post notices announcing British control of all taxation, but Maharaja Lela and his men were lying in wait. Birch's grave can be found at **Pulau Besar**, to the south of Kampung Gajah.

The changes which Maharaja Lela and the other conspirators had sought to prevent, came about, but the British also learned from the assassination of Birch. Arrogance and coercion were going to get them nowhere and, most importantly, would harm trade. A more subtle, indirect approach was required, which, in the famous words of Frank Swettenham in 1876, was 'to preserve the accepted customs and traditions of the country, to enlist the sympathies and interests of the people in our assistance, and to teach them the advantages of good government and enlightened policy'. Birch's successor as Resident in Perak, Hugh Low, was probably the greatest Resident of them all. He successfully pursued the aims set out by Swettenham and his achievements in Perak became the yardstick by which other Residents were measured. A principal factor in his success was fully compensating the sultan and the local chiefs for the revenue they had lost from the abolition of slavery and the creation of a central treasury. In time the Malay ruling classes, not just in Perak but throughout the British Federated States, became the staunchest supporters of colonial rule.

In Perak Sultan Idris (1887-1916) established a close working relationship with both Low and Swettenham, and during his reign **Kuala Kangsar**, higher up the Perak River, became the most important royal town in Malaya. In 1897 the first Conference of Malay Rulers was held there, while the Federal Council, the forerunner of Malaysia's Parliament, was also inaugurated there in 1909. During these years Idris was probably the closest friend the British had among the Malay sultans, certainly after the death of Sultan Abu Bakar of Johor in 1895. He is best remembered today as an educationalist, taking a close personal interest in the founding of the **Malay College** at Kuala Kangsar in January 1905. Known as the 'Eton of the East', the College provided aristocratic Malay boys with a British public school education, preparing most of them for careers in the Malay Administrative Service. Not surprisingly, the College soon acquired another nickname among the Malays: *Bab ud-Darajat,* or the 'Gateway to High Rank'. The College remains to this day a centre of academic excellence.

Kuala Kangsar is a very attractive, quiet town. Its crowning glory is the stunning **Masjid Ubudiah**. With its assortment of golden domes and minarets, the mosque is a magnificent sight and deserves all of the superlatives lavished upon it. Sultan Idris laid the foundation stone in 1913, but he did not live to see the mosque completed, dying in 1916, the year before it was opened. Nearby is the royal palace, the **Istana Iskandariah**, which is also topped with gleaming golden domes. Across the road is the delightful **Istana Kenangan**, meaning the Palace of Memories, a more than apt location for the Royal Museum. Constructed in traditional Malay style without a single nail or the use of plans, the palace is beautifully decorated with intricate wood carvings and yellow, black and white woven wall panels. The Istana Kenangan was used as a temporary residence by Sultan Iskandar (1918-1938) while the present palace was being built.

For a small fare, visitors can take a boat across the Perak River from Kuala Kangsar to **Sayong**, which is also accessible by road. Sayong is famous for its pottery, in particular the black gourd-shaped jars known locally as *labu*. A number of the *kampung* houses have their own workshops-cum-showrooms, where visitors can watch the villagers making the *labu*. Perak has the largest clay reserves in Malaysia and the craftsmen of Sayong obtain most of their supplies from the river bank. The clay is worked into the required shape on the potter's wheel and then left to dry. The external design is added to the jar, either by carving or stamping, before it is fired in a home-made kiln. The jar is then left to cool under a mound of *padi* husks, giving it the distinctive black colour. A few of the traditions are changing. Some of the villagers now use moulds and powdered clay, the latter being a much cleaner alternative to wading around in the river and

Opposite: *One of Sayong's potters making a labu pot in her kampung workshop.* ***Below:*** *The striking Istana Kenangan in Kuala Kangsar.*

digging it up. The craft centre at **Enggor** is another place where Sayong pottery is made. Women can also be seen working at *tekat,* the art of embroidering gold thread on velvet. *Tekatan* embroidery is used to decorate the bridal chamber in traditional Malay weddings, in addition to embellishing cushions, betel sets and shoes.

From Kuala Kangsar Route 76 runs north for just over 100 km to Gerik, the western gateway to the spectacular **East/West Highway** (Route 4) which crosses Malaysia's mountainous interior. Completed in 1982, at a cost of RM400 million, the highway took eleven years to construct and opened up Kelantan to motorists from Kedah and Penang, without the lengthy detour via Kuala Lumpur. Erosion by wind and rain remains a problem and there are frequent engineering works, but any inconvenience is more than offset by the splendid surrounding scenery. From Gerik the highway runs down to the River Perak Reservoir Bridge which leads to Pulau Banding in the middle of the man-made Tasik Temengor. The Highway then climbs to the top of the Titiwangsa Range at a height of 1031 metres, offering extensive views across the jungle-clad mountains to Thailand. After running parallel to the Thai border, the highway heads east and drops down into Kelantan.

Wherever the British went in the world they took their eccentrics with them. To **Gerik** they sent Hubert Berkeley as District Officer. He ruled upper Perak like an uncrowned king for almost twenty years. Tales about 'Tuan' Berkeley have become part of Perak folklore. Viewing himself as a curious combination of Malay chief and English squire, he invariably wore Malay clothes, while he drove around the district in a horse-drawn carriage. The accompanying servants dressed in the red and white livery of the Berkeley family. One day he was all set to go off on an elephant ride into the jungle, a favourite pastime of his, when the clerk of the district court came running up and told him that he had twenty-five cases to hear. Berkeley was angered until he discovered that the cases were all minor and that each

defendant had pleaded guilty. 'All right', he said, 'odd numbers discharged, even numbers fined five dollars!' Then he rode away on his elephant.

Berkeley had a novel way of settling boundary disputes. He would adjourn the court and summon the litigants and all their witnesses to join him at the site in question. Here he formed the opposing parties into two teams and held a tug of war contest, in a sort of trial by combat. The disputed land went to the winning team. The British have always had a taste for lavatorial humour and Berkeley was no exception. He was a firm believer in accompanying his house guests to the toilet. On the wall of his lavatory was a large photograph of Swettenham. Berkeley explained to his friends that a sight of the horrible chap made his bowels move in a more effective fashion, or words to that effect!

A contemporary of Hubert Berkeley was William Kellie Smith, whose enduring monument, a 20th-century 'castle', is located on Route A8 to the east of Batu

Opposite: *Kellie's Castle.* ***Above:*** *The statue of Kellie Smith on the roof of the Sri Mariamman Temple.* ***Below:*** *One of the few remaining tin dredgers in Perak.*

Gajah. This is no Tower of London or Windsor Castle, but **Kellie's Castle** is one of the most enduring symbols of British rule. It stands aloof and majestic on a small hill, complete with a four-storey square tower; glorious and yet superficial, with, as a sign of the times, a lift shaft. The castle was never completed and Kellie Smith never lived in it, not even for a single day. That is the tragedy of the place. Kellie Smith was both a romantic, wishing to evoke memories of the castles of his native Scotland, and something of an egotist, trying to outdo the homes of his fellow planters in Perak. According to one tale, he planned to build the tower high enough for him to see Ipoh, over 15 km away. Today an air of sadness pervades the large empty rooms, the peeling plasterwork, and the weathered masonry. Indeed, from a distance, it looks like the archetypal haunted house.

Kellie Smith was born in Dallas, Scotland, in 1870 and made his fortune from tin and rubber, the castle overlooking what was his rubber estate. Even today he is remembered by the locals as a generous and compassionate man. The son of one of his rubber tappers will happily recount the local tale of why 'Tuan' Kellie Smith built the nearby **Sri Mariamman Temple** for his estate workers and their families. Kellie Smith already had a daughter, but he despaired of ever having a son and heir. So he asked his workers to pray for a boy, promising them a new temple if the gods granted their request. Sure enough their prayers worked and Kellie Smith and his wife Helen had a son. He kept his word and the temple was built.

As is so often the case in Malaysia, there is another equally plausible explanation for the building of the temple. During the construction of the castle, many of Kellie Smith's estate workers were struck down by Spanish flu, and according to some accounts, he built the temple as an act of appeasement to the Hindu gods. When it was completed, the epidemic promptly came to an end. One thing is certain. Kellie Smith has been immortalized as a carved figure on the temple roof.

Surrounded by various gods, he is depicted wearing army uniform, his hand resting on a gun. The presence of the figure speaks volumes for Kellie Smith's standing amongst the estate workers. Unfortunately, there is a sad ending to the story of Kellie Smith. After the birth of his son, he went on a trip to Europe. While in Lisbon he fell ill and died of pneumonia in 1926.

Rubber and tin were the economic pillars of the British Empire in Malaya. The richest tin area in Perak was the Kinta valley, which by the early 20th century was the world's most productive tin field. The tin was easily mined, being located only 10 to 20 metres from the surface. It was initially worked in the 1880s and 1890s through opencast mining. By the early 20th century the industry was undergoing a process of change. The dominance of the Chinese mining companies, based on their supply of large cheap labour forces, was being undermined by the need for British technology and capital. With the more accessible tin deposits now exhausted, the opencast method was gradually replaced by hydraulic mining and dredging. The Kinta valley today still contains a few reminders of these glorious tin mining years. Deserted mining pools nestle amongst man-made dunes, built of spoil, while here and there the pools provide a resting-place for huge rusting, metal contraptions - the old tin dredgers. They stand forlornly, awaiting the fate of so many before them: to be sold as scrap metal.

A handful of tin dredgers continue to operate in Perak, but in their heyday there were well over a hundred working in Malaysian tin mines. They first appeared in the Kinta valley in 1913. A dredger is an extraordinary sight - a large metal shed, floating on a natural or artificial lake, and 'guided' by its chain of heavy buckets, searching out the tin like the antennae of some giant insect. The buckets scoop out

Opposite: *The drum section of the school band being put through its paces at St Michael's School in the centre of Ipoh.*
Above: *The Ipoh Railway Station.*

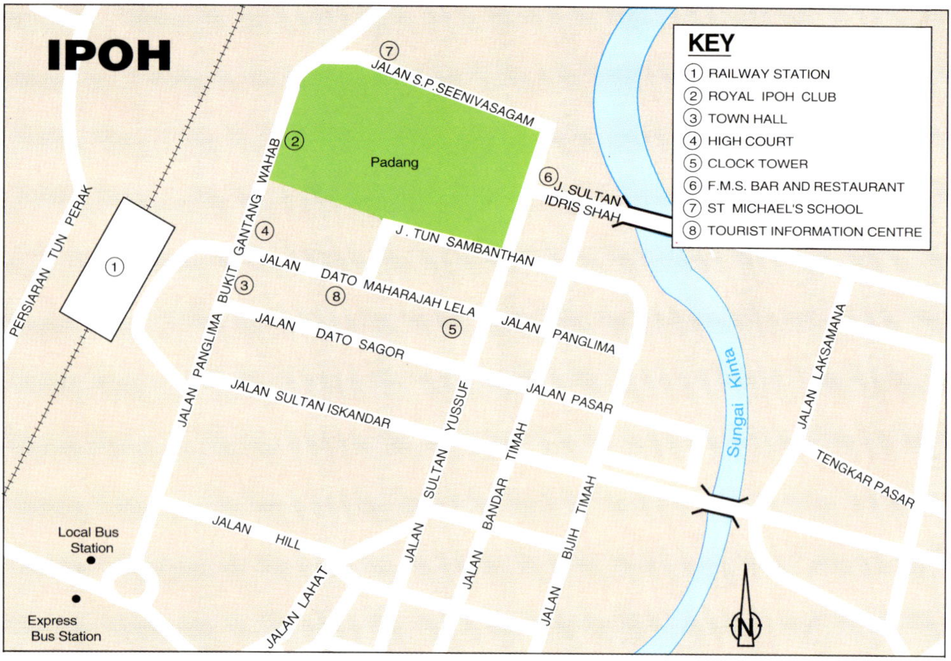

the tin bearing earth, transporting it into the heart of the dredger, where jets of water break up the material as it falls on to revolving screens. Large boulders and rubble are held by the screens, leaving the tin bearing soil to pass through to a primary separating plant. There the heavy particles of tin are recovered.

To exploit the tin deposits in Perak more effectively, the British tackled the transport problem by building roads and railways within the Kinta valley and the other mining areas. Malaya's first railway, between Taiping and Port Weld, now **Kuala Sepetang**, was opened in 1885. Ten years later work began on the first road linking Ipoh and Taiping with Kuala Lumpur.

All economic booms come to an end and tin was no exception. As recently as 1980 Malaysia was still the world's leading tin producer, but the following decade proved a disaster as the international price of tin plummeted. Tin in Perak is now described as a 'sunset industry' by veteran miners. Where once the State Government received RM30 million per annum in tin revenues, it now receives little or nothing. There are some who are optimistic about the future, believing the industry will pick up again, for tin deposits in Perak are far from exhausted, but the old days seem certain never to return.

Today the Kinta valley is dotted with towns which prospered in the heyday of tin: the capital Ipoh, Taiping, Batu Gajah, Gopeng, Papan and several others. Some, such as Ipoh, have obviously continued to grow, diversifying into other industries, some have declined, while a few, like Papan, have become little more than ghost towns. The irony is that Papan may still be sitting on top of a treasure trove. Perhaps every cloud does have a silver lining. Papan is believed to be built on rich tin deposits, indeed much of the town's land has already been bought up by a mining company. Whenever the tin price rises again, there is talk of relocating the remaining population and starting to mine the site.

Though never a mining town, **Ipoh**

still owes its existence to tin, originating as the smelting centre for the surrounding mines. In its early days, Ipoh was like any frontier town, with fortunes being made and lost. The name is believed to derive from the *ipuh* or *upas* tree, the poisonous sap of which the local *orang asli* used in their blowpipes. The trees were once abundant, but only two remain in Ipoh today, one being found in front of the railway station. Ipoh began as a landing stage on the Kinta River, beyond which the river was no longer navigable. A Chinese settlement rapidly developed on the site, which had formerly belonged to the local Malay chief, Datuk Panglima Kinta.

British and Chinese influences are only too apparent in Ipoh. The colonial past is seen in the neoclassical architecture. The Moorish-style **Ipoh Railway Station**, with its domes and arches, is reminiscent of the one at Kuala Lumpur. Ipoh also has the inevitable *padang,* reflecting the British passion for sports. It is surrounded by casuarina trees and overlooked by the mock Tudor **Royal Ipoh Club**. Opposite the railway station are the **Town Hall** and the **High Court**, both built in the same gracious style. Behind them stands the **clock tower**, undoubtedly one of the finest in the country. Erected in memory of Birch, the tower features colourful murals on all four sides, depicting various professions during different periods of history. At the junction of Jalan Sultan ldris Shah and Jalan Sultan Yussuf, close to the *Padang,* stands another relic of British times, the **F.M.S (Federated Malay States) Bar and Restaurant**. Once a favourite with colonial officials, planters and miners, the bar retains its distinctive 'frontier' atmosphere.

Yet it is the Chinese, rather than the British, who have left the greatest impression on Ipoh and the Kinta valley, this land where so many of the original immigrants and their descendants mined for tin. Ipoh is famed for its Chinese cuisine. Some Malaysians travel long distances to sample the delights of Ipoh cooking; others go dreamy-eyed when you mention Ipoh and

Above: *A colourful mural at Perak Tong.*

food in the same breath. The city serves up some excellent Chinese food at very reasonable prices. A favoured eating spot for the locals is the bustling **Woolley Food Centre**.

The Chinese have also left their mark in the dramatic limestone country around Ipoh, where several caves have been turned into places of worship. In a few instances elaborate frontages have been built to cover the cave mouths, making it look as if the limestone formed around the buildings, rather than vice versa. To the south of Ipoh on Route 1 is the **Sam Poh Tong**, with its hidden walled garden. Off to the east is the more recent **Kek Look Tong**, probably the most natural of the cave temples. **Perak Tong** is located 6 km to the north of Ipoh on Route 1. The walls are decorated with colourful murals based on Chinese legends and folklore. Beyond the main altar, steps lead to the upper reaches of the cave. A statue of a rotund laughing Buddha sits at the bottom. He is probably laughing for one very good reason: some four hundred steps later you reach the top! There are good views from the lookout point over the Kinta valley.

Also on Route 1 is the **Mekprasit Temple**, admittedly not a cave temple but no less interesting with its ready-made congregation. Row after row of Buddhist monks kneel in silent meditation facing a large reclining Buddha. They can give an unsuspecting visitor quite a start and more than one person has admitted to being momentarily fooled into thinking they were real people, rather than models.

These caves in and around Ipoh may well have been inhabited as long as two thousand years ago. A series of rock paintings dating from that period were discovered at **Tambun** by a British army patrol during the 'Emergency'. They are not easy to find, being down an unmarked track off the Ipoh to Tambun road. Some distance down the track, there are stone steps, partly obscured by vegetation. At the top of the steps is a rock wall, on which are displayed the very faded paintings. They depict various human and animal figures. Some are only in outline, while others are coloured with a reddish haematite pigment. They probably span several hundred years and are thought to have been done by *orang asli* from the Senoi people. The gibbon-like figure might well be Engku, the Supreme Deity of the Senoi. The cliff may have been an oracle site. Whenever a member of the tribe consulted the oracle, a new picture would have been painted on the rock face, in the hope that an answer would be forthcoming.

Perak has a past even earlier than the paintings at Tambun. The discovery of a human skeleton, known as Perak Man, at a cave in Gunung Runtuh, near **Lenggong**, situated to the north of Kuala Kangsar, has revealed that this area was home to Stone Age man. The bones have been dated to some ten thousand years ago, making them the oldest set of bones to be found in Peninsular Malaysia. Perak Man was 40 to 45 years old when he died, at a time when the average life expectancy was no more than 25 years. He was also deformed due to a severe back problem. As tribes of that period did not generally have many uses for old and handicapped people, experts have suggested that Perak Man may have been the 'wise old man' of his people.

Above: *One of the Senoi rock paintings at Tambun.*

SELANGOR

The Benevolent Realm

The modern state of Selangor, centred on the Klang river valley, is the heartland of Malaysian industry and commerce. Here is the country's 'Silicon Valley', the home of Proton, the national motor car, and the engine-room of the drive for 'Vision 2020'. The development of Selangor is perfectly illustrated by the rise of the new state capital, **Shah Alam**. The town skyline, indeed the country for miles around, is dominated by the shimmering blue aluminium dome of the **Masjid Negeri**, or State Mosque, one of the modern wonders of South East Asia. The design of the mosque incorporates a highly effective mix of traditional Islamic and local Malay styles, but it is probably the sheer size of the building which first strikes any visitor. Set amidst an attractive landscape of gardens, trees and lakes, the mosque can accommodate 20,000 people in the main prayer hall alone. The computer-designed dome rises 107 metres from the ground and is 52 metres in diameter, while the four minarets reach a height of just under 145 metres. Such figures are impressive, but they do little to convey the simplicity and innate beauty of the building. At prayer times the mosque comes alive. The main hall is packed with worshippers, all kneeling in the direction of Mecca, while the building and surrounding area echo to the sound of readings from the Koran.

State crest: *The spear and kris are part of the state regalia. The Jawi script expresses the state motto, 'under the protection of Allah'. Below is the broad sash worn around the waist by Selangor warriors in the past.* ***Below:*** *The Masjid Negeri at Shah Alam, the state capital of Selangor.*

SELANGOR
PERAK
PAHANG
NEGERI SEMBILAN
STRAITS OF MALACCA
SABAK
SUNGAI BESAR
SEKINCHAN
KUALA SELANGOR
K.KUBU BAHARU
RASA
RAWANG
KAPAR
KLANG
SHAH ALAM
AMPANG
CHERAS
KAJANG
BANGI
JENJARUM
BANTING
MORIB
SEPANG
S. Bernam
S. Tengi
S. Selangor
S. Klang
S. Langat
0
10
20 km
N
KEY
LEBUHRAYA (EXPRESSWAY)
MAJOR ROADS
SECONDARY ROADS
RAILWAY
STATE BOUNDARIES
KUALA LUMPUR
1 PETALING JAYA
2 MASJID NEGERI
3 PORT KLANG
4 INTERNATIONAL AIRPORT, SUBANG
5 MAH MERI VILLAGE, PULAU CAREY
6 ORANG ASLI MUSEUM, GOMBAK
7 TEMPLER PARK
8 BATU CAVES
9 ROYAL SELANGOR PEWTER FACTORY
10 RUBBER RESEARCH INSTITUTE, SUNGAI BULOH
11 JUGRA
12 BANDAR
13 BUKIT MELAWATI
14 KOTA RAJA MAHDI, GEDUNG RAJA ABDULLAH
15 DUSUN TUA
16 PROPOSED NEW AIRPORT

Selangor may well be 'the premier state', as it is often described, but over two hundred years ago it was a very different place. Rain forest stretched unbroken from the Main Range down to the coast. The population, probably no more than 20,000 people, lived in small villages along the principal rivers. All trade and communications between the coast and the interior passed up and down these rivers. The jungle remained the preserve of the *orang asli,* the aborigines of Peninsular Malaysia.

It is difficult, and perhaps inappropriate, to generalise about the *orang asli* in Malaysia today. *Orang asli* is a collective, generic term, covering a rather heterogeneous group of people. For administrative purposes they are divided into three main tribal groupings: the Senoi, Negritos and Proto-Malays. These groups can be further subdivided into eighteen distinct ethnic and linguistic communities. The estimated *orang asli* population in the country is some 82,000, with over half belonging to the Senoi group of tribes. They are distributed throughout the whole length of Peninsular Malaysia, with major concentrations in Pahang and Perak. Some *orang asli* still pursue a nomadic life in the forests of Malaysia, hunting and gathering fruits, while others practise a primitive form of shifting agriculture, cultivating crops in an area for a year or two until the soil is exhausted and then moving on.

Growing numbers of the *orang asli* have adapted to a more modern lifestyle. Among these are the Mah Meri, one of the Senoi tribes. While the words Mah Meri mean inland people or forest people, they in fact live in the coastal districts of Selangor. Several Mah Meri settlements are accessible by car, with the village on **Pulau Carey** being the easiest to visit since the building of a road bridge from the mainland. The Mah Meri on the island make a living from smallholdings of oil palm or working in local factories, but their most famous pursuit is wood carving. Made from the wood of the mangrove tree, *nyirih batu,* Mah Meri carvings are something of a collector's item. The most talented woodcarver is Pion anak Bumbun, whose work has been presented by the Prime Minister Dr Mahathir to leading foreign dignitaries.

The Mah Meri have a long tradition in woodcarving, originally crafting intricate wooden masks and statues to ward off evil spirits during illness. A mask which had to be made all too frequently in the past was that of Kala, a spirit associated with malaria. Like many of the *orang asli,* the Mah Meri are animists or nature worshippers, believing in the power of numerous spirits. Each *moyang,* or spirit, possesses a specific role and plays a vital part in the daily life of the individual, his

Below: *The Mah Meri villagers on Pulau Carey performing a traditional dance during their New Year celebrations. The man is wearing a spirit mask.*

family and village. Ill health is seen as the result of a disharmony or imbalance, brought about by the influence of one or more evil spirits.

When someone falls ill, the *bomoh* is traditionally called upon to cure them. He uses a mask of the evil spirit to show the patient what his tormentor looks like and thus paves the way for a cure. In more serious cases various offerings are made in an effort to coax the malevolent spirit from the body of the victim. These offerings are placed in a spirit tray or basket, into which the *bomoh* cajoles the evil spirit. Occasionally, an entire family, or even the whole village, is afflicted by disease or some other natural disaster. A spirit house or, in the most serious cases, a spirit boat is now built, containing many different carvings. If the villagers resort to a spirit boat, they carry it down to the water's edge, with all the spirits aboard, and then launch it on its journey across the seas, hopefully never to return. Freed from their desperate predicament, the villagers celebrate in time-honoured fashion with a feast.

Many of the Mah Meri no longer believe in such practices. Modern education and technology have seen to that. When a villager now falls ill, he or she consults the local doctor, rather than the *bomoh* and his masks. Pion anak Bumbun's wonderful carvings are today aimed at visitors and tourists, rather than Kala and the other evil spirits. Some of the old beliefs and practices do still persist among the more isolated tribes. The **Orang Asli Museum** at Gombak in Selangor gives a unique insight into these remarkable people, their culture and skills.

Selangor has always benefited from the abundance of resources to be found in the state, whether in its mineral deposits, the talents of its peoples or the richness of its land. Such resources have acted like a magnet to traders, settlers and other powers. Undoubtedly the most attractive of these resources has been tin. Just as in Perak, deposits of tin have been washed out of the hills into the rivers of Selangor. The town of Klang, located at the mouth of the Klang River, benefited from tin for a

very long period, possibly dating from the 11th century or even earlier. Four hundred years later, Melaka came to hold sway over Klang, sending Tun Perak there to serve his political apprenticeship as *penghulu.*

Yet the true founders of Selangor were not men from Melaka, or indeed from anywhere else in the Malay Peninisula, but from the island of Sulawesi far away to the east. In the 17th century Sulawesi was beset by wars and a shortage of farming land, forcing large numbers of Bugis to flee the island. They initially took sanctuary in Java and Sumatra, but following friction with the local people, many crossed the Straits of Malacca and settled in the sparsely populated lands around the Klang, Selangor and Linggi rivers. During the next hundred years or so, the Bugis, like many earlier settlers in the peninsula, were gradually assimilated into Malay society. In the meantime they made a major contribution to Malay history. Indeed the 18th century has been called the 'Age of the Bugis'.

The Bugis had much in common with the Vikings of early medieval Europe. Their naval prowess enabled then to range far and wide across the seas of South East Asia in their square-rigged, two-masted ships. Passionate traders, they also indulged themselves freely in fighting and looting, quickly acquiring a fearsome reputation. They must have been a splendid sight in their chain-mail armour, terrifying all their enemies with their war dances and chants, before setting about them with great courage and considerable success.

The fighting skills of the Bugis soon attracted a host of potential employers. Malay princes saw the hiring of Bugis mercenaries as an obvious way to gain a decisive advantage over their rivals. A succession dispute saw them fighting in Kedah in 1770. The ageing Sultan Muhammad Jiwa (c.1740-1773) had handed over the rule of the kingdom to the

Opposite: *The Mah Meri villagers being blessed by the bomoh during their New Year celebrations.* ***Below:*** *Some of the famous Mah Meri woodcarvings.*

future Sultan Abdullah, his only son by a slave wife, in the process angering a powerful faction at the court. They responded by hiring the legendary Bugis warrior, Raja Haji, at the price of a free hand to pillage the property of the Indian and Chinese merchants in Kedah. Raja Haji and his men descended on the northern kingdom and drove out Muhammed Jiwa, but then preyed on far more than the foreign traders. Alor Setar, Kuala Kedah and most of the other towns in the kingdom went up in flames, while everything of value was carried back to Selangor.

The Bugis in Selangor had nominally been under the overlordship of Johor, at least until the year 1766. In stark contrast to Johor, where Bugis influence caused untold resentment, Selangor saw the gradual integration of the Bugis and their practices into the Malay environment. This was never more apparent than when Raja Haji's brother, Raja Lumu, with the full support of the Bugis elders, or *orang tua,* asserted the independence of Selangor from Johor, by proclaiming himself sultan. He observed Malay tradition by sailing to Perak and being installed as the ruler of Selangor by Sultan Mahmud of Perak (1765-1773), taking the title of Sultan Salehuddin (1766-1782). Mahmud also presented him with that essential mark of Malay royalty, the *nobat.* Sultan Salehuddin was crowned on his return to Selangor, probably with a crown brought from Sulawesi.

Sultan Salehuddin and the Bugis in Selangor grew wealthy on the profits of tin mining. Their authority was mostly confined to the coastal districts of the kingdom, as the remote inland areas remained the preserve of the *orang asli.* **Kuala Selangor** is the final resting place of Salehuddin and his two successors. The strategic importance of the town at the mouth of the Selangor River is revealed by the existence of two hill forts, still standing guard over the river today. The larger and better preserved of the forts is built on **Bukit Melawati**, the ramparts of which provide sweeping views over the Straits of Malacca and the mangrove swamps of **Kuala Selangor Nature Park**. The fort was originally constructed early in the reign of Sultan Ibrahim (1782-1826), the second ruler of Selangor. The Dutch overran the defences in 1784, rebuilt the fortress and called it Fort Altingsburg, before Ibrahim recaptured the stronghold some ten years later.

Today the Dutch cannons have long since fallen quiet, though they still dominate the defences, maintaining a long and lonely vigil over the surrounding countryside. Above them rises the **Altingsburg Lighthouse**, performing yet another type of vigil for the numerous vessels passing along the coast. The quay in the town used to be connected to the fort by a hundred steps, a few of which have survived. Steps are in this context something of a misnomer, for they are in reality great granite slabs, forming a slippery walk through the dramatic rain trees which characterise this most attractive of forts.

The best view of Bukit Melawati is undoubtedly that from the other fort, which is located on **Bukit Tanjung Keramat**, some 2 km to the west. The fort is overgrown and something of a scramble to reach, but the outlines of the ramparts are unmistakable. In the lee of the fort lies a small, picturesque lake and the village of

Tanjung Keramat, the home of a shrine much venerated by the local people. The inhabitants tell the story of a very pious girl forced by her parents to marry a man she did not love. On her wedding day the girl ran away, later appearing before her parents in a dream. She told them never to look for her, saying that she had found an ideal place to spend the rest of her life. On the following day, against her wishes, the girl's parents went in search of her and discovered her clothes hanging on a tree by the lake. They decided to build a shrine there, dedicated to her memory. Over the years the shrine has proved popular with married couples wanting a child. The tree beside the shrine is often covered in ribbons, people tying them to the branches in the hope that their wish will come true.

Kuala Selangor is probably the nearest the modern visitor to Selangor can get to the world of Raja Haji. He was able to unite all the Bugis factions behind him. Brave, almost to the point of recklessness, he led his men by example, in the process becoming a legend. His end came at the siege of Melaka in 1784. For five months Raja Haji and his men battered away at the Dutch garrison. Melaka seemed certain to fall until the arrival of six Dutch ships with 2,000 men. Unaware of the Dutch reinforcements, Raja Haji awoke one morning to find his fleet being shelled and his camp under attack from fresh, well-armed troops. The issue was never in doubt. Raja Haji's men pleaded with him to save himself, but he had always stood his ground in battle and, with a dagger in one hand and the Koran in the other, he faced his enemies. A single shot rang out and Raja Haji fell dead, shot through the heart.

In the 19th century tin played as large a role in the development of Selangor as it did in Perak. Great wealth flooded into the kingdom, but at the price of civil war and eventual colonial control. Selangor was

Opposite: *The lake at Tanjung Keramat near Kuala Selangor.* ***Below:*** *The ramparts and cannons of Bukit Melawati in Kuala Selangor are a popular spot for visitors.*

COURTESY OF MUZIUM NEGARA

divided into five districts, Klang, Langat, Bernam, Lukut and Kuala Selangor, each based on a tin bearing river. All five districts were ruled by a Malay chief, who recognized the overall supremacy of the sultan. The chiefs received the bulk of the tin revenue from their individual areas, after giving the sultan his agreed share. This situation was made unstable by the differences in revenue between the districts, the greed of the chiefs and the weakness of Sultan Abdul Samad (1859-1893), who retired to a life of gardening and opium smoking in Langat. Elsewhere the Malay chiefs were left largely to their own devices. Raja Jumaat held Lukut in a firm grip, as did the Malay chief in Bernam, but matters were very different in the districts of Klang and Kuala Selangor, where most of the fighting in the civil war took place.

Klang was the major prize in the war, as any visitor to the town will discover today. Two of the principal protagonists, Raja Abdullah and Raja Mahdi, had residences in Klang. Raja Abdullah constructed the **Gedung Raja Abdullah** in 1857, making it the oldest surviving building in Selangor. The ground floor was used as a warehouse to store his tin, while he and his family lived on the first floor. When fighting broke out in Klang in 1867, Abdullah was forced to flee by paddle-steamer to Melaka. After the end of the civil war, the building was pressed into service as the district police station. In 1984 it was restored to its former glory, opening as the Klang Tin Museum eight years later. The museum features numerous tin artefacts, highly informative dioramas, documents and pictures, as well as models of the larger mining equipment, including dredgers. Also close to the river, if in a far more dramatic position, is the **Kota Raja Mahdi**, built by Abdullah's rival, Raja Mahdi, during the civil war. The main gate and the earthen ramparts are all that remain of the fort today.

The struggle for forts such as Kota Raja Mahdi dominated the war. Most were little more than wooden stockades, built at strategic points on the river banks or in clearings along the jungle trails. Yet

their defences should not be underestimated. The walls were made of sapling trunks, lashed together with rattan, and often surmounted by bamboo stakes. Some were further protected by an outer screen of banana stems, to prevent gunshot from penetrating. That perennial favourite of jungle warfare, the pit containing sharpened bamboo spikes, was also frequently used to prevent night attacks. The fighting was largely confined to attacks on these forts by armies of one to two thousand men, followed by long periods of relative inactivity. Except in the clearings or by the rivers, the rain forest presented an impenetrable barrier to all, save a single file of men laboriously hacking their way through the vegetation. The best means of a decisive victory was an ambush. Failing that the war dissolved into a series of sieges. An assault, using ladders and ropes, was thought the most effective way of capturing a fort, but there was a high risk of heavy casualties. The only realistic alternative was to cut off all supplies of food and water to the garrison, never an easy undertaking in a tropical environment.

Most of the soldiers were followers of the leading Malay protagonists or Chinese miners. They wore a shirt or tunic and shorts, all made of coarse cotton, and straw sandals on their feet. Many also possessed a cape of palm leaves for protection from the rain. The Chinese troops were usually armed with a long sword and a musket, a pouch of gunpowder hanging from their wrist. The Malay soldiers preferred a wider variety of weapons: a spear, one or two swords of differing lengths, a *kris,* as well as a musket. A leather jerkin or wooden shield provided some body protection, but the chief concern for the men on all sides was mobility in very difficult terrain.

The civil war was in the end settled by outside intervention. As in Perak the wealth of Selangor attracted the British. Raja Abdullah had died in Melaka, though his cause was upheld by his son, Raja Ismail, who found a willing ally in the Kedah prince, Tengku Kudin. A noted adventurer, Kudin had his eyes on Klang from the outset. He was to prove the greatest thorn in Raja Mahdi's side. Both protagonists looked for support from the other Malay kingdoms and the Chinese mining communities.

Kudin was also able to win financial backing from several prominent British businessmen in Singapore, including James Guthrie Davidson. His family was the driving force behind the merchant house of Guthries & Co. In March 1870 Kudin captured Klang, forcing Raja Mahdi to fall back on Kuala Selangor. With crucial help from his friends in Singapore, Kudin was able to convince the British that his rule in Klang would encourage trade. Reinforcements entered Selangor on Kudin's side and, by 1873, both the Klang and Selangor rivers were under his control. Inevitably there was a price. In the following year the British imposed a Resident on Sultan Abdul Samad. Davidson was duly appointed, with Swettenham as his assistant.

Swettenham was based at **Jugra** in the district of Langat, the centre of royal power in late 19th-century Selangor. The **Sri Jugra Lighthouse** stands proudly on the highest hill overlooking the River Langat and commands views of the area in

Pages 130-131: *Sultan Abdul Samad and his entourage in the 1870s. The small boy standing at his side is his grandson, Raja Suleiman, later sultan. The man on the right with the protruding head-dress is Syed Mashor, the famous warrior who fought for control of Kuala Lumpur in the civil war.* ***Opposite:*** *The famous iron chest which once belonged to Sultan Abdul Samad.*

all directions. Further down the hill are the remains of the district office. With its mangrove swamps and reputation for disease, Langat was never a popular posting amongst British officials. Swettenham said the mosquitoes in the district were the worst he ever encountered. Nearby, occupying another hilltop, is the **Mausoleum of Sultan Abdul Samad**. Set in suitably tranquil surroundings, the graveyard is one of the historic treasures of Selangor.

Jugra contains several other historical sites, one or two of which require advanced map reading skills to locate, as well as a robust vehicle to reach! Near the river, and just past the charcoal producing village, can be found the old post office, now fallen on decidedly hard times. The jungle has broken in, though the granite walls are still standing and provide a useful climbing frame for the abundant foliage and brambles. Equally under attack from nature is the **Istana Jugra**, now little more than a ruin, where Sultan Abdul Samad lived during his time in Langat. Finding the palace is in itself something of an achievement, as

there is little left to indicate the rich heritage of the building. The jungle has virtually reclaimed it.

The Istana Jugra was famous for its iron chest, which has had to be taken to a nearby house belonging to a descendant of Sultan Abdul Samad. The palace is just too unsafe. Made by the Bugis in Riau, the chest is a family heirloom and believed to possess mystical powers. Abdul Samad used to keep his money in it. Every day, when the schoolchildren went past, he would scoop out a handful of coins and toss them on the ground for the children to pick up. In this way he hoped to encourage them to study harder.

The chest's reputed powers were amply demonstrated in the 1960s when officials from the Muzium Negara decided to remove it from the crumbling palace, take it to Kuala Lumpur and put it on display in the museum. Locals warned them that the chest should not leave Jugra and that such a move would bring bad luck. The officials did not heed their advice, but soon wished they had. Strange noises came from inside the chest, which the officials could not open, even though they had a key specially made for the lock. They eventually resorted to a crowbar, only finding a few old papers inside the chest. Perhaps they had hoped to find some of Abdul Samad's coins. The services of a *bomoh* were called upon to help placate the spirits of the chest, but he did not get very far in his incantations before he fainted. Nearby objects started falling over and the curator began to have nightmares. After only a week the chest was on its way back to Jugra.

Just outside the town of Jugra, at **Bandar**, is the **Masjid Bandar** built by Sultan Alaeddin Suleiman (1893-1938), the successor to Sultan Abdul Samad. Nearby is the **Istana Bandar**, designed by Sultan Alaeddin himself. Wooden carvings are a major feature of the palace, many of them thought to be the Sultan's own work. He lived there for some thirty years before his death in 1938. The palace has recently been restored and there are plans to open it to the public as a museum.

In 1896 Selangor joined the British colonial states of Perak, Negeri Sembilan and Pahang to form the Federated Malay States, with the capital at Kuala Lumpur. Selangor, with Kuala Lumpur at its centre, became the heart of British Malaya, with no effort being spared to exploit the wealth of the kingdom. Here was indeed the 'benevolent realm'. In the major towns paved streets, lighting, sanitation and hospitals appeared, while roads were laid to the mining areas and the rubber estates. By the early 20th century, rubber rather than tin was generating the funds for the development of Selangor. However, tin is still closely associated with Selangor due to the international success of **Royal Selangor Pewter**. The factory is located just off Jalan Genting Kelang, on the north-eastern outskirts of Kuala Lumpur, and is open to visitors. Pewter is an alloy of tin, copper and antimony. The tin content in Royal Selangor Pewter is 97%. Outside the showroom at the factory is the world's largest tankard, officially recognised by the Guinness Book of Records. The pewter tankard can hold a staggering 2,796 litres or 615 gallons.

In the course of a few years, the planting of rubber trees transformed the Malayan countryside, to the point where rubber became synonymous with Malaya. Rubber trees still abound in Malaysia today, but they now share the countryside with other plantation crops, notably palm oil, and are in demand not only for their latex, but also their wood, which is used in the manufacture of furniture. There is an air of sadness about some of the remaining rubber estates. Many of the trees have come to the end of their productive life and are overgrown and neglected, their once proud trunks disappearing amidst a tangle

***Opposite:** The Istana Bandar. **Below:** The mausoleum of Sultan Abdul Samad at Jugra.*

of weeds and scrub, the old scars left by long gone tappers a last reminder of the past when 'king' rubber ruled Selangor and Malaya. The seemingly endless lines of rubber trees stretched the length and breadth of the peninsula, for it was the perfect crop for the country, the tree being hardy and disease resistant, and capable of growing in a variety of soils and conditions. The ultimate irony is that the product that did most to ensure the prosperity of British Malaya, in the end rendered it defenceless to invasion. After landing in Kelantan in December 1941, the Japanese forces were able to advance down the Malay Peninsula, moving from plantation to plantation, often on bicycles, and so bypass that most natural of all defences, the rain forest. Thus was the fate of Singapore sealed. When the British surrendered in February 1942, the sun was beginning to set on their empire in South East Asia.

The rubber tree is not indigenous to the Malay Peninsula and neither was it the first plantation crop to be introduced into Selangor. Coffee was successfully grown at the end of the 19th century, but within a decade most planters had turned to rubber. The first seedlings came to Malaya in 1876, by way of Kew in London from Brazil, which, until the end of the 19th century, accounted for nearly all of the world's production of natural rubber. In Brazil the rubber tree was called *caa o-chu,* which means 'the tree that weeps', while *latex* is the Spanish word for milk. The latex oozes out of the tree when it is wounded and, in drying, protects the scar. The name 'rubber' comes from the British scientist, Joseph Priestley, who was suitably impressed by the substance when he used some to rub out pencil markings in 1770. At that time rubber had only limited uses as a raw material, as Frederick the Great of Prussia discovered. A French scientist made some 'Wellington' boots for him, but they were never a success. In the summer the boots became hot and sticky, while they went brittle in the cold of the winter. These problems were overcome in 1839 when Charles Goodyear discovered the process of vulcanisation, enabling rubber to withstand large changes in temperature. The age of rubber had arrived.

The first seedlings sent to Malaya failed, but more followed. Nine of these were planted at the side of the British Residency at Kuala Kangsar in Perak. One of the trees can still be seen today. As yet there was little interest in rubber as a commercial product. That is until Henry Ridley arrived on the scene in November 1888 to become the Director of the Botanical Gardens in Singapore. For him the cause of rubber in Malaya became a crusade, earning him the nickname 'Rubber' Ridley. He discovered the most effective method of tapping the trees and urged planters to experiment with rubber, but there was minimal response. To the coffee planters he was known as 'Mad' Ridley. By 1897 only 140 hectares had been planted with rubber trees in the whole country.

Then, in a matter of a few years, the economic climate changed. Coffee prices plummeted and desperate planters turned to rubber, at the precise moment when the development of the motor car and pneumatic tyres brought a great surge in demand. By 1908 every state in Malaya had rubber estates, with some 109,000 hectares throughout the country being planted with rubber trees. Five years later the figure had risen to around 322,000 hectares and was still climbing rapidly. Although a rubber tree could not be tapped for seven years, it could initially be interplanted with more rapidly producing crops. Once a tree was ready to be tapped, it had a productive life of some thirty years, requiring relatively little care or upkeep.

Numerous small rubber planting companies were founded in the early years of the 20th century. They were backed by the great merchant houses of Singapore, such as Sime Darby, Harrisons and Crosfield, and Guthries. Investors far away in Europe were attracted to rubber by the involvement of these great financial institutions. The merchant houses developed the agency system in Malaya, in which a single agency was responsible for supervising a number of small planting companies and their estates. The agency appointed a manager and his staff to run each estate, while looking after all technical and financial business. The managers were of course British and so that famed colonial breed, the rubber planters, came to Malaya.

Guthries still own many estates in Selangor and their logo is a familiar sight at the side of roads passing through rubber and oil palm plantations. The company was founded by a Scot, Alexander Guthrie, in 1821. Like the other Singapore merchant houses, Guthries prospered in what was traditionally known as the 'jam and pickle' business, exporting what was available and importing whatever was needed. Guthries never lost sight of the origins of the company's founder and most of the employees in the early 20th century were from Scotland. In contrast, one of their great rivals, Bousteads, tended to go for that British obsession, men of the right school tie.

Whatever their origins, the planters had an unenviable reputation, which still persists today. Immortalized in works by Somerset Maugham, the planters were seen as indolent and promiscuous drunkards. Many were the 'black sheep' of their family, some having to leave Britain in a hurry. Yet the overall picture is rather different. Alcohol was cheap and easily available in Malaya at that time, and few planters would have denied that they did drink a large amount, but many regarded it as the only way of getting through an arduous, monotonous and, on occasions, insecure existence. In later years Guthries sought to employ men with degrees in agriculture from Scottish universities, but the essential prerequisite for success as a planter was the ability to control the Indian workforce. The estate manager and his assistants, if he had any, had to be up at 5.30 am every day for the muster of tappers and labourers. Only when it was raining could the manager or his assistants miss the muster.

Food and drink were never far from the thoughts of the planters. During the morning there was 'brunch', usually consisting of porridge (only the British could eat porridge in a tropical climate!), eggs, bacon, toast and marmalade. Then it was off to the plantations to supervise the tappers. Various methods of tapping the trees were used, but the crucial point was to ensure that the trees were not harmed. If the tapper cut too deep into the bark, then its renewal would be damaged, thus affecting the productivity of the tree. The tappers

Above: *A rubber tapper at work.*

started work after the 5.30 am muster, returning some five hours later to collect the latex from the cups, by which time they had cut some 500 to 600 trees. The latex had to be weighed and checked for its dry rubber content, usually about 3 lb of dry rubber to the gallon. A coagulant was next added to harden the latex and produce a spongy 'cheese' which, on the next day, was compressed in a mangle to form sheets. These were hung on racks and smoked, before being packed in bales or boxes and exported.

By the middle of the afternoon the work of the rubber estate was largely over and the planters were left to their own devices. For many this meant visiting the club, some of the larger estates even having their own, where sports dominated all other activities. Golf and tennis were to the fore, though team games, such as soccer, rugby and cricket were also played at the more established clubs. Sporting prowess was often a distinct advantage in becoming a planter. Guthries had a reputation for hiring international rugby players, with half an eye on strengthening the company team. Then there was the club bar, that preserve of male society. In his famous work, *The Soul of Malaya*, Henri Fauconnier described a scene familiar to all planters: 'we were all standing round the bar,....the boy never stopped pouring out whisky; bottles of soda-water opened with a rhythmic hiss like ripples in the sand'. On occasions the drinking did get out of hand, but generally it provided a much needed tonic to a narrow existence. The planters had an answer for the resultant hangover: a prairie oyster, containing raw eggs and Worcester sauce. The early morning sun did the rest and by 'brunch' time the effects had disappeared.

Planting was a hard life. Added to the monotony of the work and, for many, the loneliness, there was the ever present threat of disease. Typhus and dysentery were common, but the greatest threat remained malaria. Knowledge of the disease was growing. The role of the mosquito in spreading malaria was discovered in central America in 1899, a year before Dr Malcolm Watson came to Malaya as Chief Medical Officer. Watson immediately set about restricting the natural habitat of the mosquito by draining and spraying swamps, and improving the flow of water in streams. Such methods soon became commonplace and, with the growing use of quinine, malaria outbreaks declined to manageable proportions.

Perhaps even greater insecurity came from the dramatic fluctuations in the price of rubber. The boom in the first decade of the 20th century was more than offset by the terrible depressions of the 1920s and 1930s. Many smallholders went bankrupt, but the big companies also suffered, having to lay off large numbers of their employees or put them on reduced salaries. Yet the rubber industry survived and, if you get up early enough, Indian tappers can still be seen working their way around the rubber estates, just as their parents and grandparents did before them. It is one of the great sights of Malaysia, but it should not hide the difficulties these Indian labourers have experienced over the years. Slumps in the rubber industry meant, at worst, unemployment for the planters, but for the Indian labourers and their families, they caused untold poverty, even starvation. These immigrants, mostly from the Tamil areas of southern India, were the answer to the labour shortages which afflicted the first rubber plantations.

There was a general belief among the British that the Malays were unsuited to the rigours of estate work. This did not deter Bill Bangs, one of the more remarkable estate managers. Bangs was appointed manager of an estate in Kelantan, which he could only reach by jungle track and canoe. The place was run-down and alive with mosquitoes, and within weeks he was fighting for his life, suffering not from malaria but typhus. At one point he was measured for his coffin, but he survived. Turning his attentions to the estate, he decided to recruit a wholly Malay workforce, causing consternation amongst his fellow planters. Bangs found that, if he treated the Malays fairly and they liked him, all the work got done and the estate prospered. He respected all the Malay feasts, such as Hari Raya Puasa, killing a buffalo or a bullock for a communal banquet and laying on traditional Malay dances and entertainment. Bangs fell in love with the country and its people, becoming a Muslim and Malayan citizen in 1948.

Everywhere else in Malaya the rubber estates relied on the Tamils, who came in their thousands from southern India. The British brought them to Malaya as an unashamed source of cheap, indeed very cheap, labour. Some efforts were made by the British authorities to improve living conditions on the estates, only for most planters to block any reforms if they involved extra expense. While the Tamils were undoubtedly better off than in their villages in India, they still hovered just above the poverty line, all too often plunging below it when the price of rubber fell.

The museum at the **Rubber Research Institute** in Sungai Buloh goes a long way towards recreating the atmosphere of the great days of rubber. Opened in 1992, the museum is situated on a 1,300 hectare plantation, where, if visitors give sufficient notice (2-3 days) to the Institute, they can try their hand at tapping a tree. It is certainly not as easy as it looks. On the walls are photographs from the early days of rubber in Malaya, while among the displays are examples of the equipment used for tapping and processing the latex. The Brazilians never forgave the British for taking the rubber seedlings to Malaya but, in an act of considerable generosity, a

Below: *The rolling fairways of the golf course at Templer Park, with the limestone outcrop of Bukit Takun behind.*

COURTESY OF THE MTPB

professor at the University of Sao Paulo donated two latex balls to the museum. They date from ancient times and were used in games by the Paresis tribe from the Mato Grosso in Brazil.

While agriculture in most of Selangor is dominated by rubber and oil palm plantations, the district of **Ulu Langat**, particularly around Dusun Tua, is one of the leading areas in the country for durians, the so-called 'king of fruits'. There are two seasons in the year for durians: the main one being from June to August, with another between November and February. During these months the rickety, palm-thatched stalls which dot most roadsides in the country, are piled high with the large, greenish, spiky fruit.

The durian is a controversial fruit with an overwhelming, pungent odour. So strong is the smell, that it is banned from the larger hotels, as well as some public places. Signs sometimes warn of a fine if the smell is detected in hotel rooms. One writer, in a famous description, likened the 'durian experience' to eating custard in a public lavatory. It is difficult to sit on the fence where durians are concerned. You either love them or hate them. Most Malaysians love them and gorge themselves on the fruit during the seasons. A good durian, such as the D24, commands a high price and one farmer was recently offered RM150 for his prize specimen. He could not bring himself to part with the fruit and instead shared it amongst his family.

The taste of the durian almost defies description, though a few visitors have made a valiant effort to capture the distinctive flavour in words. The naturalist Alfred Wallace definitely fell into the durian addict category, admitting that 'the more you eat, the less you feel inclined to stop'. He felt that almonds gave the best general idea of the flavour of the 'rich, butter-like custard' flesh. Intermingled with this were the flavours of 'cream cheese, onion sauce, brown sherry and other incongruities'. To the 'incongruities' might be added the essence of coffee, one of the principal characteristics of the rich, creamy D24 variety. Some enthusiasts claim that the durian is an aphrodisiac and there is an old Malay saying, 'when the durian falls, the sarong will fall!'

Confronted by a vast pile of durians at one of these stalls, what should a visitor look for when he or she selects the 'right' one? Always go for a durian that has a mild smell because a strong odour will indicate overripeness, in addition to probably putting you off for life! There must be no broken skin, and the stalk should look fresh and not shrivelled. The final test is to shake the fruit gently, while all the time looking knowledgeable. If there are small knocking sounds, then the flesh is ripe enough to have separated from the skin and should be just right. Having selected the fruit, the time has come for the serious business of haggling.

The leading town in Ulu Langat is **Kajang**, 26 km to the south-east of Kuala Lumpur along Route 1. Kajang is famed for its *satay,* probably the best known of all Malaysia's dishes. Marinated pieces of beef, chicken or mutton are barbecued on skewers over a charcoal fire, and served with slices of onion and cucumber, a peanut chilli sauce and *ketupat,* or rice cakes steamed in coconut leaves. What makes Kajang *satay* so tasty is the local recipe for the sauce. The town's *satay* stalls are located at the intersection of Jalan Besar and Jalan Sulaiman, and are still run by the descendants of Haji Tasmin, who first established Kajang's reputation for *satay* in the early 20th century. Some 5 km from Kajang on the road to the expressway is one of the more curious sights in Malaysia, a very large tree growing out of the side of a three-storey house! At the moment it is difficult to say whether the tree or the house is getting the better of the struggle, though the tree certainly has the advantage of height.

The **Batu Caves**, located 13 km to the north of Kuala Lumpur in the district of Gombak, are the most popular tourist site in Selangor. The caves are also the leading Hindu shrine in Malaysia and the scene every year of the festival of Thaipusam, honouring the deity Lord Murugan, son of Siva. For centuries the jungle hid the existence of the caves, before the American naturalist, William Hornaby, discovered them on a hunting trip with H.C. Syers in 1878. The caves became a popular destination for picnic parties during colonial days, the guests making the journey by elephant. The Hindu population began making pilgrimages to the caves for Thaipusam in the 1890s, turning them into a shrine to Lord Murugan. At first the worshippers had to scale the steep, jagged face of the limestone outcrop to reach the shrine, but today there are 272 steps up to the Temple Cave. At the bottom another cave has been turned into an art gallery containing colourful statues and wall paintings depicting characters and scenes from Hindu mythology.

Thaipusam is celebrated at the end of January or the beginning of February, and signifies the day when Lord Murugan received from Siva the *vel,* a spear-like weapon which he used in his fight against evil. The festivities take place in a number of Malaysian cities and towns, but those at the Batu Caves always attract the largest crowds. Thaipusam is a time for performing penance for past sins and giving thanks for answered prayers. It is also a chance for devotees to reaffirm their strength of faith. The celebrations last for three days, beginning with a predawn procession from the **Sri Maha Mariamman Temple** in Kuala Lumpur, when a silver chariot carrying a statue of Lord Murugan is pulled by two garlanded oxen, sporting brightly painted horns, to the Batu Caves. Thousands of Hindus follow the procession, while others turn out to watch it pass by, breaking coconuts on the ground in front of the chariot, as offerings to the deity.

The Batu Caves take on a chaotic, almost carnival air during Thaipusam, with as many as 800,000 people attending the festivities. Some devotees make the ascent to the Temple Cave on the first day, but most go up on the following day. In

Opposite: *Satay, Malaysia's answer to the shish kebab.* ***Below:*** *A range of Royal Selangor Pewter ware.*

COURTESY OF ROYAL SELANGOR PEWTER

the weeks before Thaipusam they prepare themselves by purifying their bodies and minds. They follow a strictly vegetarian diet, refrain from smoking and drinking alcohol, and focus their thoughts on God, while as far as possible observing *mounam,* or silence. As if this is not enough, they are also encouraged to endure acts of personal hardship, such as sleeping on bare floors.

When Thaipusam arrives, the devotees fulfill their vows to Lord Murugan in a variety of ways. They begin by carrying out a ritual bathing ceremony at a nearby river. Some then pierce their cheeks and tongue with a spear-like skewer, a representation of the *vel.* Others carry a large *kavadi,* an elaborately decorated metal frame attached to the body by hooks. The *kavadi* is often adorned with peacock feathers as, according to the Hindu scriptures, Lord Murugan chose this magnificent bird as his mode of transport. The centre-piece of the *kavadi* is a statue or photograph of Lord Murugan. Instead of a frame, some devotees have the hooks attached to their backs by thin ropes, pulled tight by a relative or friend like the reins on a horse, or attached to a small chariot construction. In other instances, limes are attached to the hooks. Such acts could be mistaken by an outsider for some sort of masochistic ritual - fascinating, mesmerising, a little intimidating and not for the squeamish. It is difficult to believe, but the devotees, like the proverbial man on a bed of nails, feel no pain. They are in a deep spiritual trance. The women opt for less extreme methods of fulfilling their vows, many of them carrying a pot of milk on their heads as an offering to Lord Murugan. Some children have their heads shaved, while babies are carried up to the temple by their parents in a cradle. A devotee once brought a five-legged cow as an offering, which understandably caused quite a sensation. The beast has been immortalised with a statue in the temple grounds.

Stalls line the route to the temple steps which become a seething mass of pilgrims and onlookers. The air is filled with the smell of incense, the rhythmic beating of drums and the incessant chanting of '*vel! vel!*' Sometimes barefoot devotees stop and begin a trance dance, twirling round and round in spiritual abandon, seeming to look straight through the spectators with their wild, unblinking eyes. Occasionally, onlookers find the atmosphere overpowering and fall into a trance themselves. Dehydrated and drenched in sweat, the devotees are often in a state of near collapse as they stagger up the steps. A medical team stands by to help anyone who faints. When they enter the cave, the devotees remove their *kavadis,* skewers and hooks. Priests rub holy ash into the wounds. Miraculously, the wounds rarely bleed and there are very few marks left on the skin. This is seen by Hindus as the work of God.

On the third day the chariot carries

the statue of Lord Murugan back to the Sri Maha Mariamman Temple. The Hindu scriptures contain no justification for piercing the skin with hooks or skewers. Such acts of faith developed as a result of social pressures, rather than religious ones, being seen as a demonstration of manhood. Concern has recently been expressed that some of the devotees are bordering on exhibitionism. Religious leaders are now encouraging the devotees to fulfill their vows in more traditional ways, such as carrying pots of milk. They advise them that inner feeling is more important than outer practice, so there is no significant difference between carrying a milk pot and pulling a chariot. Such acts are not only unnecessary, but threaten to turn Thaipusam into a spectator sport.

A rich and diverse kingdom, Selangor is the arrival point for most of Malaysia's foreign tourists, with the current international airport being located at **Subang**, about 22 km from Kuala Lumpur. A new international airport, due to open in time for the Commonwealth Games in 1998, is being built at **Sepang** in the south of Selangor. From Subang, or later Sepang, most visitors will head straight for Kuala Lumpur, entering the Federal Territory by way of the **Kota Darul Ehsan**, the imposing ceremonial arch on Route 2. It is in fact very difficult to divorce the history of Selangor from that of Kuala Lumpur, for many years the state capital, though there are some significant differences, notably the role of the Chinese and one man in particular, the remarkable Yap Ah Loy.

Opposite: *The devotees going up the steps to the Temple Cave during Thaipusam.* ***Above, left and right:*** *Devotees fulfilling their vows to Lord Murugan. The red powder smeared on their bodies is Kunggumum. Made from uncooked rice, it is traditionally used for the red mark, or pottu, which married Hindu women put on their foreheads. The limes are used to remove and ward off any evil spirits. The limes on the end of the vel also serve a practical purpose, protecting spectators from the sharp points.*

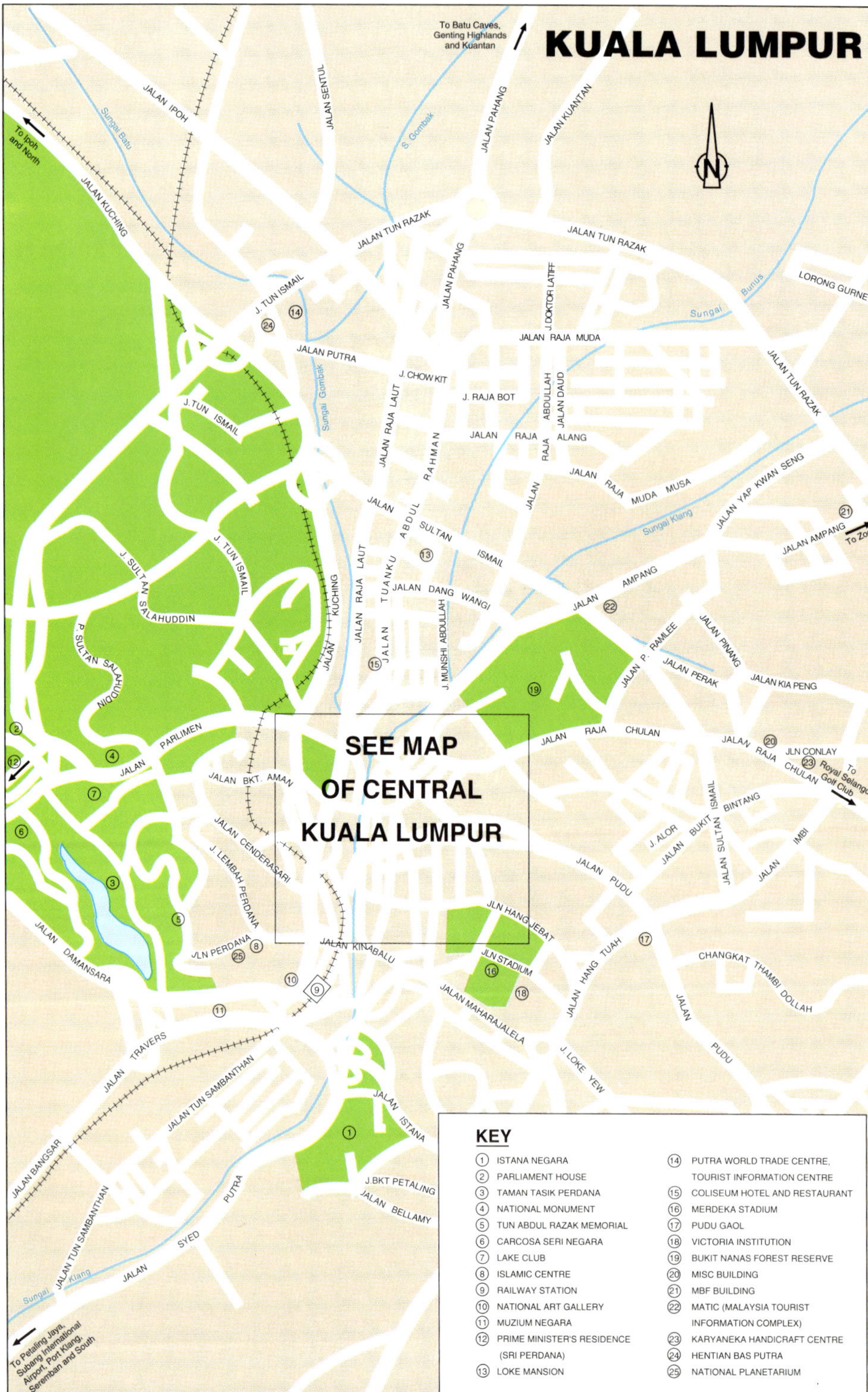
KUALA LUMPUR
To Batu Caves, Genting Highlands and Kuantan
To Ipoh and North
To Zoo
To Royal Selangor Golf Club
To Petaling Jaya, Subang International Airport, Port Klang, Seremban and South
SEE MAP OF CENTRAL KUALA LUMPUR
JALAN IPOH
JALAN SENTUL
JALAN PAHANG
JALAN KUANTAN
JALAN KUCHING
JALAN TUN RAZAK
LORONG GURNEY
J. TUN ISMAIL
JALAN PUTRA
J. DOKTOR LATIFF
JALAN RAJA MUDA
J. CHOW KIT
J. RAJA BOT
JALAN RAJA LAUT
ABDULLAH
JALAN DAUD
JALAN RAJA ALANG
JALAN RAJA MUDA MUSA
JALAN YAP KWAN SENG
JALAN SULTAN ISMAIL
JALAN TUANKU ABDUL RAHMAN
JALAN DANG WANGI
J. MUNSHI ABDULLAH
JALAN AMPANG
J. SULTAN SALAHUDDIN
P. SULTAN SALAHUDDIN
JALAN PARLIMEN
JALAN P. RAMLEE
JALAN PINANG
JALAN PERAK
JALAN KIA PENG
JALAN RAJA CHULAN
JLN CONLAY
JALAN BKT. AMAN
JALAN CENDERASARI
J. LEMBAH PERDANA
JLN PERDANA
JALAN SULTAN ISMAIL
JALAN BUKIT BINTANG
J. ALOR
JALAN IMBI
JALAN PUDU
JLN HANG JEBAT
JLN STADIUM
JALAN KINABALU
JALAN HANG TUAH
CHANGKAT THAMBI DOLLAH
JALAN DAMANSARA
JALAN MAHARAJALELA
J. LOKE YEW
JALAN TRAVERS
JALAN TUN SAMBANTHAN
JALAN BANGSAR
JALAN ISTANA
J.BKT PETALING
JALAN BELLAMY
JALAN SYED PUTRA
Sungai Batu
S. Gombak
Sungai Gombak
Sungai Bunus
Sungai Klang
KEY
1 ISTANA NEGARA
2 PARLIAMENT HOUSE
3 TAMAN TASIK PERDANA
4 NATIONAL MONUMENT
5 TUN ABDUL RAZAK MEMORIAL
6 CARCOSA SERI NEGARA
7 LAKE CLUB
8 ISLAMIC CENTRE
9 RAILWAY STATION
10 NATIONAL ART GALLERY
11 MUZIUM NEGARA
12 PRIME MINISTER'S RESIDENCE (SRI PERDANA)
13 LOKE MANSION
14 PUTRA WORLD TRADE CENTRE, TOURIST INFORMATION CENTRE
15 COLISEUM HOTEL AND RESTAURANT
16 MERDEKA STADIUM
17 PUDU GAOL
18 VICTORIA INSTITUTION
19 BUKIT NANAS FOREST RESERVE
20 MISC BUILDING
21 MBF BUILDING
22 MATIC (MALAYSIA TOURIST INFORMATION COMPLEX)
23 KARYANEKA HANDICRAFT CENTRE
24 HENTIAN BAS PUTRA
25 NATIONAL PLANETARIUM

KUALA LUMPUR

The Heartbeat of the Nation

Few capital cities in the world have as short a past as Kuala Lumpur, or have had as rapid a growth. One hundred and fifty years ago the 'city' was just a 'muddy river junction', the meaning of the name Kuala Lumpur, where deep in the jungle the Gombak flowed into the Klang. It was a place of no consequence until tin deposits were discovered in and around the rivers. The subsequent growth of Kuala Lumpur has been phenomenal. In 1887 the town became the capital of Selangor, and nine years later, the capital of the nation. When Malaya achieved independence on 31st August 1957, the national flag was raised for the first time in Merdeka Square. In 1972 Kuala Lumpur was proclaimed a city, and two years later was also designated a Federal Territory.

Kuala Lumpur is today one of the busiest cities in South East Asia. During the day it is an international centre for commerce and finance, as well as the political heart of the nation, while at night the city lights come on and the streets throng with people of all ages out to enjoy themselves. Many of the prominent buildings of the city are illuminated, among them the **Masjid Negara**, or National Mosque, on Jalan Perdana, built in 1965. The main dome is in the form of an eighteen pointed star, representing the thirteen states of Malaysia and the Five Pillars of Islam. The eye is inevitably drawn though to the high-rise buildings of the so-called 'golden triangle', the commercial, hotel and shopping centre of the city, bounded by Jalan Ampang, Jalan Tun Razak and Jalan Imbi. At the time of independence this part of Kuala Lumpur was still mostly jungle. Now it has a skyline to match that of any western city.

Nightlife in Kuala Lumpur revolves around Chinatown, the *pasar malam* or night markets, and the shopping complexes. Kuala Lumpur has over twenty shopping complexes and is beginning to rival Singapore and Hong Kong as the region's premier shopping city. They provide convenience shopping at its best: a wide range of shops and goods, with plenty of scope for refreshment and a sit-down, all under a single roof and of course air-conditioned. The shopping complexes are open every day of the week from 10 am to 10 pm.

There is a wide choice of food available in the shopping complexes, as indeed there is throughout the city. Malaysians love to eat out and Kuala Lumpur provides them with innumerable restaurants, *kedai kopi* or coffee shops, and hawkers stalls. At lunchtime and in the early evening, street corners and small alleys throughout the city are taken over by street vendors, selling any number of hot and cold dishes, plus a

National crest: *The star and crescent symbolise Islam, with the fourteen points on the star representing the country's thirteen states and their unity with the Federal Government. The four central panels and the five kris represent the former Federated and unfederated Malay states respectively. Around them are representations of the other four states. The national flower, the hibiscus, is depicted at the bottom of the shield. The yellow scroll represents the royal colour of the rulers. The national motto is 'quality through unity'.*
Pages 144-145: *The 'muddy river junction' at the heart of Kuala Lumpur where the Gombak (on the left) joins the Klang. The Masjid Jamek in the centre of the picture stands on the site of the original Malay burial ground.*

variety of drinks, all at bargain prices. One piece of advice: if you eat too much hot, spicy Malay food, then, according to Malay folklore, you should turn your plate several times and the sting will instantly disappear.

The modern city of Kuala Lumpur is a far cry from the tragic settlement of 1857. Virtually the only similarity is that the two rivers remain very muddy to the present day. The first miners to arrive were 87 Chinese coolies. They settled at Ampang, some 4 km to the east of the confluence of the two rivers, where tin was known to exist. The jungle was cleared, but then malaria struck. Each day more men went down with the disease, lying delirious for a day or two in their beds, before dying. Within a month only 18 of the original party were still alive. The attempt to exploit the tin of Ampang seemed at an end, but the lure of great wealth proved too strong. Another 150 miners made the arduous journey, first by boat up the Klang River and then on foot to Ampang. This time they were more successful. The ravages of malaria declined and the first tin was exported downriver in 1859. More mines were opened and profits began to grow.

There are still a few reminders of Ampang's early days. Old women can sometimes be seen panning for tin in the river, while the squatter settlements give the area the semblance of a frontier town. Though illegal, many of the squatter homes have acquired a degree of permanence, some even being connected to water and electricity supplies. The government has tried to ease the squatter problem by providing cheap, modern flats in the area.

Once it became clear that the mines at Ampang were going to be successful, traders followed in the hope of making a profit from supplying the mining communities. The first to settle in the area were two Chinese, Hiu Siew and his friend Ah Sze, nicknamed 'Sweet Potato' because of his gentle personality. They set up their shop at the meeting point of the two rivers. A space was cleared in the jungle and a few huts erected. This was the true beginning of Kuala Lumpur. The site proved a good one and the two friends were soon doing excellent business, importing supplies for the miners and exporting tin.

The success of Hiu Siew and Ah Sze attracted others and, by the early 1860s, Kuala Lumpur had grown into a large and flourishing village. Boats were loaded and unloaded on the east bank of the Klang, just below the junction with the Gombak. On the slopes above the river bank were the shops and houses of the Chinese traders. There were no bridges across the river and the western bank was only accessible by boat. The area now occupied by Merdeka Square was no more than a jungle clearing used by vegetable growers. Surrounding the small, vulnerable settlement were jungle and swamps, the latter being ideal breeding grounds for malaria-carrying mosquitoes.

Precisely when the settlement

acquired the name Kuala Lumpur is unknown, though it was in local use in Selangor from the early 1870s. The name itself is something of a puzzle. 'Muddy river junction' is the meaning of Kuala Lumpur but, while an apt description of the site, the name runs counter to traditional Malay usage. *Kuala* is the Malay word for the mouth of a river, either where it flows into the sea or a larger river. As the River Gombak joins the Klang at this point, the settlement should technically speaking have been called *Kuala Gombak,* but there are no contemporary references to such a name. Was there perhaps a River Lumpur? At least one old map has the lower reaches of the Gombak named the 'Sungai Lumpur'. In the early days the settlement was overwhelmingly Chinese and this may provide another possible explanation for the name. The first Chinese called the place *Klang Lam-Pa* to distinguish it from Klang, *Lam-Pa* meaning flooded jungle or swampy land. As the years passed, the name perhaps stuck and was malayanised to Kuala Lumpur.

Kuala Lumpur was in every respect a frontier town in the early days. Having been paid, the miners descended on the settlement, frequenting the opium dens and brothels. The greatest attraction was gambling, which was organised in a large shed. The secret societies were as influential in Kuala Lumpur as they were in Penang and Perak, providing an effective substitute for family and village ties in a strange and threatening environment. The societies were quite ruthless in the mining areas, often resorting to violence in the struggle for the richest deposits. The *towkays,* or heads of the societies, came to monopolise the supply of essentials, such as food, liquor and opium, as well as controlling the brothels and gambling outlets. These leaders were usually thrown up in this anarchic society through personal bravery, or cruelty, and force of character, in addition to possessing a healthy supply of money. In Kuala Lumpur the main society was the Hai San, whose leaders came principally from the Hakka dialect group. They were bitterly opposed by the Ghee Hin, based a few miles to the north around Kanching in Selangor.

The Malay traders of Kuala Lumpur did business with the Chinese, but lived apart from them. Their settlement was upstream, just above the junction of the two rivers, being centred on the present Jalan Tun Perak, originally called Java Street. This ran into the aptly named Malay Street, or Jalan Melayu as it is today. The Malay burial ground was situated in the triangle of land between the two rivers, where today the Masjid Jamek stands as a fitting monument to the first Malay settlement in

Opposite: *The art of making teh tarik, or pulled tea, the Malaysian answer to milk shake.* ***Above:*** *The distinctive Petronas Tower at the Dayabumi Complex, over looking some of the colonial buildings on Jalan Raja.*

Kuala Lumpur. Gradually, the Malays began to move out of town and settle in the villages to the north and south. The Malay chiefs of Selangor preferred to keep well away from Kuala Lumpur, dealing with the Chinese mining communities through the overall headman, or *Kapitan China.* It was in fact the Malays who conferred this title on the Chinese leader.

The greatest *Kapitan China* in Kuala Lumpur was Yap Ah Loy, who held the position from 1868 until his death in 1885. A fascinating character, Yap Ah Loy was destined to play a pivotal and immensely profitable role in the rise of Kuala Lumpur. Born in 1837 in the Kwangtung province of southern China, he was a Hakka from the Fei Chew clan. At the age of seventeen he left China for Malaya, working in a tin mine and a shop, before deciding to return home. Yap never made it. Getting as far as Singapore, he lost all his money and possessions in a gambling den. He returned to Malaya and ended up at Lukut. Three years later he was still there, working as a cook, but his fortunes had begun to change. He had saved sufficient capital to set up as a pig dealer and drove a herd of pigs around the mining communities, selling them for tin. At the same time he began to cultivate his links with other Fei Chew Hakka and their society, the Hai San.

Yap Ah Loy rose quickly, becoming the *Kapitan China* of Sungai Ujung, but he stayed there for only about a year. In 1862 he moved to Kuala Lumpur, opened two mines of his own and soon became very wealthy. Six years later Yap reached the pinnacle of the Chinese community in Kuala Lumpur and became the *Kapitan China.* From the outset he ruled with an iron fist, as crime had become all too common in the town. Stringent new laws were introduced. For robbery, a first offence led to the thief being dragged through the streets with the stolen property tied to his back. A second offence resulted in an ear being cut off, while for a third, and final one, the thief was executed. Not surprisingly, the crime of theft almost disappeared. Yap tried to keep Kuala Lumpur out of the Selangor Civil War, but as the tin revenues were a principal cause of the struggle, this proved an impossibility. One of the first victims was 'Sweet Potato' Ah Sze who was murdered in 1869 by members of the Ghee Hin society, the great rivals of the Fei Chew Hakka. Yap's men took revenge early in the following year, massacring large numbers of the Ghee Hin at Kanching. The two societies were thus dragged into the war: Yap and his Fei Chews on the side of Tengku Kudin and the Ghee Hin with Raja Mahdi.

Kuala Lumpur was a key factor in the

Opposite: *Once the home of a wealthy tin miner, this elegant mansion along Jalan Ampang now houses the Malaysia Tourist Information Complex. Drawn by Syed Noah, one of the artists at Central Market.* ***Below:*** *Yap Ah Loy.*

COURTESY OF ARKIB NEGARA

struggle and Syed Mashor, a supporter of Raja Mahdi, was determined to take it from Yap Ah Loy and the Fei Chew. A famed warrior of the day, Mashor came from Borneo and claimed to be descended from the Prophet Muhammad, hence the title Syed. His first attack on Kuala Lumpur came in September 1870, but he and his men were driven off after the Fei Chew won a resounding victory at Ampang. Mashor returned in the following year and this time laid siege to the town. For two months the defenders survived on supplies ferried in by boat from Klang. Most of the women and children, including Yap's family, were able to escape in the opposite direction. Yet there was no disguising the fact that the position of Kuala Lumpur was becoming critical. By July the town was completely cut off from all outside aid. In a last desperate gamble Yap tried to fight his way out of the town. The result was a bloody battle near where the airport at Subang now stands. Many of the Chinese miners were killed, but Yap managed to escape into the jungle and eventually reached Klang, wearing, so we are told, only his underwear. Kuala Lumpur fell to Syed Mashor in the following month.

All seemed lost for Yap Ah Loy, but the war in the rest of Selangor was favouring his ally, Tengku Kudin. By early 1873 Yap was in a position to recapture Kuala Lumpur. The final battle for the town was bitter and destructive. A special feature of Yap's successful assault was the use of rockets. According to Chinese folklore, God appeared to Yap in a dream and told him of the presence in his army of a man expert in the use of rockets. More likely, Yap brought the man from China. The rockets were made of large pieces of bamboo, with gunpowder inserted at the bottom, and dammar rammed down on top. When they were fired, the burning mass of dammar shot into the air, setting alight everything on which it fell. In March 1873 Yap retook Kuala Lumpur.

The biggest problem facing Yap Ah Loy on his return to Kuala Lumpur was the state of the mines. Many were flooded and therefore incapable of producing much

KEY

1. MERDEKA SQUARE
2. SULTAN ABDUL SAMAD BUILDING
3. ROYAL SELANGOR CLUB
4. ST MARY'S CATHEDRAL
5. MASJID JAMEK
6. HONGKONG AND SHANGHAI BANK (SITE OF YAP AH LOY'S HOUSE)
7. MEDAN PASAR
8. TZE YA TEMPLE
9. CENTRAL MARKET
10. DAYABUMI COMPLEX
11. MASJID NEGARA
12. SRI MAHA MARIAMMAN TEMPLE
13. WAH HING'S FUNERAL STORE
14. STADIUM NEGARA
15. MAYBANK TOWER
16. PUDURAYA BUS STATION
17. KLANG BUS STATION
18. TOURIST INFORMATION CENTRE

needed finance. Indeed he had to raise extensive loans in Singapore to get them started again. In the town itself most of the buildings had been destroyed. Yap's rockets had worked only too well. A large number of the Chinese wanted to give up and go elsewhere, believing the place was afflicted by evil spirits, but Yap would have none of it. He bullied most into staying and set about rebuilding the town. At the same time, he did all he could to encourage the Malays living in the surrounding districts to grow rice and other foodstuffs, reducing Kuala Lumpur's costly dependence on imported supplies. Yap himself planted tapioca, a pursuit that is still commemorated in *Shu Chong Kai,* or Tapioca Factory Street, the Chinese name for Jalan Petaling.

Yap's position remained precarious

Opposite: *Some familiar landmarks in Kuala Lumpur have disappeared as the city continues to grow. This was the Selangor Turf Club before the site was developed in 1993.*

until tin prices doubled in the middle of 1879. In a matter of months he had paid off all his debts and amassed a fortune. He became in every sense 'Mr Kuala Lumpur', diversifying into virtually every activity in the town. He kept law and order, or at least his police force of six officers did, administered justice, maintained a primitive hospital and inevitably controlled the gambling dens, brothels and the sale of opium and liquor. His house was to be found on the southern side of Market Street, now Lebuh Pasar Besar, facing the market, in the centre of Kuala Lumpur. The site is today occupied by the Hongkong and Shanghai Bank. Across the road is the **Medan Pasar**, a small open square, but during Yap's time the location of his principal gambling den.

Kuala Lumpur was an extremely unhygienic place to live in during these years. When Frank Swettenham visited the town, he complained: 'the refuse of the drains is simply removed therefrom and laid on the side of the road....smallpox, cholera and fever break out here very often'. Unpleasant odours invaded even Yap's house, a visitor once noting that it took a strong stomach to eat there. Perhaps this was why Yap greeted all his guests with a glass of champagne. The biggest danger to Kuala Lumpur was fire. The houses were built mostly of wood and palm-thatch and any fire would spread rapidly, not just from house to house but also across the narrow alleys. Fire precautions were rudimentary: each house-owner had to have a bucket of water ready. The great fire duly came on 4th January 1881. Starting when an oil lamp overturned in an opium shop, the fire spread with astonishing speed and destroyed the entire town. Rebuilding commenced almost immediately, though this time the houses were constructed in brick or adobe with tile roofs. Needless to say, Yap supplied all the necessary materials.

Yap Ah Loy's 'rule' in Kuala

Below: *The Padang, now the heart of Merdeka Square, overlooked by the Royal Selangor Club.*

Lumpur was in fact drawing to a close. As the town prospered, so the population grew in leaps and bounds, in the face of which Yap's decidedly basic administration just could not cope. The future lay with the British, who had sent their first official to the town in 1879. They immediately curbed the more unacceptable aspects of Yap's business empire. While Kuala Lumpur went from strength to strength, Klang, at the mouth of the river and hitherto the capital of Selangor, declined; reports telling of 'deserted houses, overgrown roads and fields'. In 1880 the Selangor government made the inevitable move to Kuala Lumpur. Sultan Abdul Samad of Selangor had already undertaken the first royal visit to Kuala Lumpur in the previous year. He travelled by river launch from Klang to Damansara, from where he was carried in a sedan chair over the bumpy and hilly track to the town. The heat was intense and the poor Chinese coolies, sweating and cursing, complained incessantly about the burden. On the outskirts of Kuala Lumpur, the Sultan was met by the leading Malay citizens, who escorted him into the town where he was given a twenty-one gun salute and greeted by Yap Ah Loy.

The first British Resident to take up office in Kuala Lumpur was Captain Bloomfield Douglas. An arrogant and generally disagreeable man, Douglas had very firm ideas about the nature of his residence in the town. He chose the site, the hill above the River Gombak, now occupied by **Sri Perdana**, the official residence of the Prime Minister, and planned to build a personal fortress there, from which he could bombard the town at will if the need arose! Much to the Captain's fury, the funds could

Below, left: *Many of the city's leading hotels feature special dinner buffets during Ramadan. The tradition at the Pan Pacific Hotel is for a drum to be banged to signal the breaking of fast.* ***Below:*** *A paper model of a servant. The Chinese practice is to burn such models at funerals, so that the person or object they represent can accompany the dead soul into the next life.*

not be found for the fortress and he had to make do with dismantling the existing residence at Klang, along with all the other government buildings, and bringing them upriver to be reassembled in Kuala Lumpur. There was in every sense a transfer of power from Klang to Kuala Lumpur. Douglas did not stay in Kuala Lumpur for long, resigning in 1882 to avoid an investigation into financial irregularities.

The buildings from Klang were erected overlooking the swampy and uneven land on the west bank of the Klang River. This land was immediately drained and levelled to provide the police with a place to drill on. The site of the *Padang* was thus initially called the Parade Ground. From 1884 the central part of the Parade Ground was used for cricket and sport gradually took over the whole area, enabling the Acting Resident, Sir Ernest Birch, an accomplished cricketer, to supervise the creation of the *Padang* of today. Immediately behind the *Padang* was Barrack Road, now Jalan Raja, where there was accommodation for the police officers. The Police Headquarters, known as 'The Fort', were situated in Bluff Road, now Jalan Bukit Aman.

The driving force behind the rebuilding of Kuala Lumpur after the fire was Swettenham, who became Resident in 1882. His building programme lasted some five years. To the south of the Railway Station, Brickfields Road, now Jalan Tun Sambanthan, derived its name from the number of brick and lime kilns located there during the construction period. The layout of the area around the old market was retained, although the streets were made wider. Each shophouse was set back from the road to allow space for a covered pavement, Swettenham's so-called 'five-foot-ways', designed to protect pedestrians from the sun and rain. These walkways are today a feature of many Malaysian towns.

The basic street plan in the centre of Kuala Lumpur is little changed, though a large number of the buildings, including many shophouses, have disappeared and been replaced by modern concrete and glass edifices. One of the most distinctive

is the **Maybank Tower**, situated on Jalan Pudu opposite **Puduraya Bus Station**. Several of the more recent skyscrapers in Kuala Lumpur are known as 'intelligent' buildings, because the lighting and air-conditioning in every room are regulated automatically, according to the number of people present. The resultant savings in electricity have been considerable.

Some fine shophouses have survived in the streets of **Chinatown**. At the heart of Chinatown is **Jalan Petaling**, described in the 1880s as being 'lined on each side by stalls; crowded in every conceivable nook and cranny by Chinese; (with) two continuous lines of carriages, gharries and rickshaws ....and a strong odour of cooking floating around'. Jalan Petaling appears much the same today, particularly during the evening, which is the best time to visit Chinatown. Part of the road is closed to vehicles and transformed into a bustling, brightly lit night market. The market stalls offer items of every description and quality, from local handicrafts to fake Gucci leather goods and the inevitable 'Rolex' watches.

Chinatown attracts many people to its streets: locals enjoying a night out, backpackers searching for a cheap meal and accommodation, and visitors on the look out for a present to take home. All blend happily into the lively atmosphere. There is no better place in Kuala Lumpur to enjoy seafood delicacies, such as abalone with mushrooms, shark's fin soup, chilli crabs, or sweet and sour prawns, while indulging in that favourite human pastime, people watching. Waiters stand outside their restaurants enthusiastically vying for custom. Who indeed can resist their calls of 'cold Anchor beer!', 'food very good here, very cheap!', or 'time for a Tiger?'

Yap Ah Loy died in April 1885.

Opposite: *Alfro Wong, the Asian limbo dancing champion, performing at Central Market. The top of the bottle represents his lowest limbo height.* ***Above:*** *A traditional Sikh dance, called Bhangra, being performed at Central Market by a troupe of Punjabi dancers.*

Today it is very difficult to imagine the town of his time. For instance, Yap knew Jalan Tun H.S. Lee, now a road of banks, shops and restaurants, as the High Street and the location of his mining workshop, smelting shed, cattle yards and abattoir. Yet reminders of his day do still exist. Behind Jalan Hang Kasturi, through one of the narrow covered alley markets, is the **Tze Ya Temple**. Built in 1883 on land donated by Yap, the temple is small and at first seems rather cluttered, but it possesses an attractive intimacy. This is perhaps the nearest a modern visitor can get to Yap and fittingly his portrait is to be found at the back of the temple. Effigies of the Lord Buddha are everywhere, while any evil spirits are kept firmly outside by two extremely intimidating Chinese warriors painted on the front doors.

The area between Jalan Hang Kasturi and the Klang River was poorly drained in Yap's time and he kept his pigs there. Today it is the site of **Central Market**, one of the major tourist attractions in Kuala Lumpur. The art deco building, with its distinctive pink and pale blue facade, dates from 1936 and originally housed Kuala Lumpur's 'wet' market. In the mid-1980s the building seemed doomed. Plans were drawn up to demolish the market and replace it with another skyscraper. Then one far-sighted developer stepped in, purchased the building and converted it into the cultural and shopping centre of today. Modelled on Covent Garden in London, Central Market contains over two hundred shops, stalls and restaurants. There is a wide range of Malaysian arts and crafts for sale, including *batik*, Royal Selangor Pewter and *orang asli* handicrafts. Artists are only too keen to paint your portrait, while on the first floor you can have your palm read by Master Chan, a renowned local fortune-teller. There are also some very popular eating houses, none more so than *Hameeds,* a sort of Malaysian fast food establishment, renowned for its fish head curry. Waiters are always on hand, and the food and drinks arrive in record time.

Outside Central Market is the

riverside promenade, a popular place to relax and enjoy a beer. Cultural performances are held at weekends on the open-air stage overlooking the river. There are both contemporary and traditional shows, including *wayang kulit,* or shadow play productions. The audience sits on woven mats on the ground, just as Malays did in the past. This stretch of the Klang, from Central Market upstream to the confluence with the Gombak and the Masjid Jamek, is the most attractive part of the river. Modern development has in several places played its part in enhancing the appearance of the river, perhaps not in the essential measures to control flooding, but certainly in the **Dayabumi Complex.** Reached from Central Market by the Malacca Steps and the footbridge over the river, the Complex is dominated by the distinctive tower, which houses the headquarters of Petronas, the national oil and gas corporation.

First opened in 1909 on the site of the original Malay burial ground, the **Masjid Jamek,** or Jamek Mosque, is just a short stroll along the riverside promenade from Central Market. Due to the open-plan design of the mosque, this is an excellent place for visitors to observe Friday prayers. The striking red brick and marble building is typical of north Indian Islamic architecture and was designed by the British engineer, A .B. Hubbock, who served in India before being posted to Malaya. In recent years the mosque has had its fair share of misfortune. In 1992 land subsidence caused part of the Gombak embankment at the side of the mosque to fall into the river. Worse was to come in the following year when the main dome collapsed during a particularly severe thunderstorm. The mosque will always be among the great attractions of Kuala Lumpur, not least because of the fascinating character who welcomes visitors at the entrance. His name is Matahari, a gently spoken man, always smiling and always dressed from head to foot in green. He

describes himself as a servant of God and has worked unpaid at the mosque since 1987. After several years of leading what he describes as a 'bad life', Matahari underwent a profound transformation, devoting himself to Islam.

Yap Ah Loy was not the only Chinese entrepreneur who made a valuable contribution to the growth of Kuala Lumpur. **Loke Mansion** on Jalan Medan Tuanku, now an art centre, is connected with two such figures. Chow Ah Yoke first built a mansion on the site in the early 1880s, which Loke Yew acquired in 1892. Over the next twelve years he rebuilt the place, infusing it with an effective blend of eastern and western styles. His mansion also had the distinction of being the first in Kuala Lumpur to be lit by electricity. Loke made his fortune from tin mining,

Opposite: *Jalan Parlimen is one of the principal routes into the centre of Kuala Lumpur.* ***Above:*** *The famous clock tower which crowns the Sultan Abdul Samad Building on Jalan Raja.*

becoming the richest and most influential Chinese businessman in Selangor. Yet he never lost sight of his peasant origins. The land was always dear to him and he became one of the great pioneers in rubber. He was a workaholic and scorned any thought of retirement. On one occasion, his wife became so incensed by his absence from dinner that she drove to the estate he was working on, and found him out in the rain showing a labourer how to dig a hole. He was still working at the age of seventy, when an attack of malaria killed him in 1917.

The Chinese have always had a very practical attitude to the inconvenience of death. They believe that everybody will be judged in the afterlife, but also think of the heavens as a mirror of earth. Therefore they try to give the soul as good a start as possible in the next life. Just as the ancient Egyptians sent the pharaohs on their way to the next world in the pyramids with all their worldly goods, so the Chinese provide their dead with paper money and paper models of houses, cars and many other material items. These are burned at the funeral, so that the objects they symbolise accompany the soul on its journey. There are inevitably many sceptics of this practice, but the Chinese are quick to point out that none of us know the basic requirements, spiritual or material, of the next world. **Wah Hing's Funeral Store** on Jalan Petaling sells a wide range of these paper models. Every effort is made to keep up with the times. Paper credit cards and mobile telephones are currently proving very popular. This part of Jalan Petaling could almost be called 'death street', since there are several coffin shops nearby.

Even among the more modern areas of the city there are reminders that Kuala Lumpur was initially a Chinese town. One of the many office blocks lining Jalan Ampang in the 'golden triangle' is the **MBF Building**, located at the junction with Pesiaran Hampshire. A close examination of the building will reveal that the ground floor doors are all set at angles to the principal walls. None of them looks out directly on to the road. Mirrored glass

is everywhere. This is all the influence of an expert in Chinese geomancy, or *feng-shui*, brought in at great expense by the owners to advise on the design of the building. The Chinese believe that heaven and earth are living forces driven by currents of energy, some positive, some negative. The positive currents, those carrying good *chih,* or life force, are known as dragon lines. They are thought to follow the flow of underground water and the direction of magnetic fields beneath the earth's surface. Hence the use of the term *feng-shui,* which means 'wind and water'. The *feng-shui* expert, armed with his magnetic compass, ensures that a building, even an individual room or a door, is aligned to a dragon line and protected from any negative currents. If not then the Chinese believe bad luck and trouble will ensue.

At the end of the 19th century, progress, in the form of modern transport, rapidly removed many of the old barriers to travel within the Malay Peninsula. From the outset Kuala Lumpur was at the heart of this growing network of communications. The railway between Kuala Lumpur and Klang was opened in 1886. The guest of honour on the inaugural journey was Sultan Abdul Samad, then aged 81, who remarked that it was the best bullock cart he had ever travelled in! The Sultan later gave his name to probably the finest example of Moorish architecture in Kuala Lumpur, the government building on the eastern side of Merdeka Square. Constructed in the mid-1890s, the copper domed **Sultan Abdul Samad Building** now houses the Supreme Court and is one of the city's most famous landmarks. Yet it could have been so different. The original British plan was for a Renaissance style of building. Fortunately, more sensitive voices were raised in favour of a facade in keeping with the Muslim traditions of the country and so the British architect, A.C.

Opposite: *An express train to Singapore leaving the Kuala Lumpur Railway Station.* ***Above:*** *Friday prayers at the Masjid Jamek. Perhaps not everybody is totally attentive.*

Norman, utilising his knowledge of northern Indian styles, was commissioned to produce the distinctive design of today. Norman and Hubbock, the designer of the Masjid Jamek, were together responsible for many of the famous colonial buildings in the centre of Kuala Lumpur.

At first there was only a single railway track between Kuala Lumpur and Klang. The unthinkable, a head-on collision, happened in August 1893, with one person losing his life. Kuala Lumpur's original station was simply a shed with a corrugated iron roof, located in Jalan Cheng Lock. The extra width of the road today is explained by the fact that the track used to run down the middle. The station in Jalan Cheng Lock lasted little more than ten years, its replacement being one of the great railway stations of the world. The British at first disapproved of the design for failing to comply with their specifications for stations at home. It seems Hubbock had forgotten to make allowance in his plans for heavy snow!

Common sense prevailed and the **Kuala Lumpur Railway Station** was approved and built by 1911. Hubbock's ornate design of graceful colonnaded arches and domed minarets make it one of the great sights in the capital. In the 1930s one humorous European traveller described the architecture of the building as belonging to 'the late Marzipan period'. The station was rather fortunate to survive the Second World War. American aircraft tried to destroy it in March 1945, but the bombs missed and instead flattened the Selangor Museum. Kuala Lumpur was the centre of an expanding rail network. Other routes followed in Selangor and the first railways were laid in Perak and Negeri Sembilan. The three systems were then linked and extended to provide the west coast line from Singapore to Penang and on to Bangkok.

Two old British steam locomotives, which between them saw over eighty years of service on Malayan railways, have pride of place outside the nearby **Muzium Negara**, or National Museum, on Jalan Damansara. Officially opened on 31st August 1963, the museum occupies the site

COURTESY OF MUZIUM NEGARA

of the ill-fated Selangor Museum. The building incorporates traditional Malay and modern styles of architecture. The wall at the front is decorated with two large murals depicting the history and peoples of Malaysia. Among the host of exhibits there is a fine replica on the ground floor of the last royal circumcision procession, which took place in Kelantan in 1933. The young prince is shown seated on a giant mythical bird. When he arrived at the palace, the prince was escorted to the chamber where the *tok mudin,* or circumcisor, awaited. Behind the *tok mudin* stood two palace guards, with their swords drawn, ready to execute him if he bungled his surgery! Another, perhaps more famous, item on display is the British amok catcher. Resembling a pitch fork with sharp jagged edges on the inside of the prongs, the idea was to trap the man who had run amok around the neck and force him into submission. If he struggled too much, he would cut his own throat. Such was British ingenuity!

After the railway came the motor car. Today it is hard to conceive of a Kuala Lumpur without cars, buses and motor cycles. Around almost every corner there seems to be that scourge of modern cities, a traffic jam. Getting across Kuala Lumpur, whether by car, taxi or bus, can prove as time consuming as the old 19th-century forms of transport. Motor vehicles first arrived in the country in 1902, leading to the construction of more and better roads between the main towns. By 1928 there were trunk roads linking Kuala Lumpur with Ipoh and Alor Setar in the north, and Johor Bahru to the south.

Since the days of Yap Ah Loy, Kuala Lumpur had been subjected to serious flooding during the wet season, but the events of December 1926 were on a completely different scale. Record levels of rainfall caused the Klang to burst its banks,

Opposite: *A cricket match being played on the Padang during British times, with the Sultan Abdul Samad Building in the background.* ***Below:*** *British officials inspecting the streets of Kuala Lumpur during the flood of December 1926.*

COURTESY OF MUZIUM NEGARA

flooding the town to a depth of three feet. Boats and rafts became a familiar sight in the streets. The staff of the Post Office showed commendable dedication by travelling to work by sampan and climbing in through the windows. The Chartered Bank, then located in the fine old building on Jalan Raja overlooking the *Padang,* had its underground strongroom sealed with cement, but the water still found a way in. When the flood subsided and the strongroom was opened, the staff found banknotes, worth millions of dollars, completely soaked. The manager ordered his staff to take the notes to the *Padang* and lay them out in the sunshine to dry, under armed guard of course. There can have been few more extraordinary sights in the history of Kuala Lumpur. The overall lesson was not lost on the government. A new and straighter channel was cut for the Klang, with flood retention walls on both sides of the river. This was only a beginning and today both the Klang and Gombak look rather artificial, encased in concrete and perhaps a little too straight.

Probably the most enduring symbol of British rule in Kuala Lumpur is the **Royal Selangor Club**, popularly known since the days of the Empire as the 'Spotted Dog' or simply the 'Dog'. From modest beginnings in 1884 in a little plank building with an atap roof, the Club has grown into the mock Tudor complex of wooden bungalows and verandahs that overlooks the green finery of the *Padang*. Its rise was not without mishap. The first salaried secretary disappeared, leaving an unexplained deficit of RM1,100 in the accounts. There are several conflicting stories as to how the Club acquired the nickname the 'Spotted Dog'. It may have resulted from the fact that the Club did not practise race or class restrictions. There are a few other possibilities. The Club's first emblem was a poorly drawn tiger which was subsequently ridiculed as a 'spotted dog'; or the name might have derived from one of several stories involving black and white dalmatians being walked on the *Padang*.

For many of the district officials and planters, the 'Spotted Dog' was almost like a second home, where they could escape from the drudgery of their work, have a long leisurely lunch - nothing has changed there today - and sink into one of those great long chairs with leg rests and a hole in the side which handily accommodated their 'gin-sling' or *stengah* (whisky soda). There was always something going on, as the British set about entertaining themselves, possibly watching a play put on by the drama group or attending a dance. The Club is today far more luxurious than in the time of the British, but not far away in Jalan Tuanku Abdul Rahman is the **Coliseum Hotel and Restaurant**, which is little changed from those days. Once described as being 'halfway between an English pub and the sort of place John Wayne used to smash up in the movies', the Coliseum does indeed have a feel of the wild west about it. The decor is spartan in the extreme and there are saloon-style swing doors at the entrance. The speciality of the restaurant is sizzling steak, for which guests don large white bibs to protect their clothes, while the bar has a good selection of beers and spirits. The Coliseum remains as popular as it was in the days of the British, when it was reputed to be a favourite haunt of Somerset Maugham.

In the small and tightly-knit British colonial community, sexual entanglements were almost inevitable. The most notorious in Malaya was the Ethel Proudlock affair, later adapted by Maugham into his famous short story, *The letter*. One evening in April 1911, Ethel, wife of the acting headmaster of the Victoria Institution, Kuala Lumpur's leading secondary school, fired six shots at William Steward, fatally wounding him. At the murder trial she said that Steward had come uninvited to her house, while her husband was away, and tried to rape her. She killed him in self-defence. What went against her was the fact that, after she had put two bullets into Steward, he tried to escape and she shot him a further four times. The prosecution never established that Steward was Ethel's lover, though she did admit that they had met on the previous evening, when she had suggested he visit her and her husband in the future. Ethel was found guilty and sentenced to death, causing an uproar amongst the British community. The sultan later granted a pardon and Ethel returned to England. In the Maugham version, the wife is acquitted and an incriminating letter, summoning her lover to the house, is destroyed. Hollywood later turned the story into a film starring Bette Davis.

Sport was the preferred pastime for most of the British during their time in Malaya. The presence of a *padang* in nearly all the principal towns under their control is testimony to the British passion for sports. None really compares with the *Padang* in Kuala Lumpur, whether in the quality of the ground or the setting. As at home the sporting calendar was divided into 'seasons'. Football and cricket were played from March through to the end of August, while in the rest of the year there was rugby and hockey. Weather played no part in this, it was just a matter of convenience. Probably the most famous cricket match played on the *Padang* was that

***Opposite:** The Lake Gardens, Kuala Lumpur's green lung.* ***Below:** Parliament House.*

between Malaya and Australia in June 1927. The Australian team included five experienced Test players but, in one of the great upsets of all time, Malaya won by 39 runs. One astonished writer reacted to events with a flow of hyperbole: 'No one except the actual spectators could believe the news. It was against the order of nature. It was as if Queen Victoria had been amused....or as if the Nelson Column of Trafalgar Square had been stolen by a Scots nationalist. It couldn't have happened.'

The Scots among the British community were the driving force behind the introduction of golf to Malaya. A 9-hole course was opened on Bukit Petaling in 1893, which included the site of an old Chinese graveyard. The members were told that the bodies had been disinterred and transported back to China for reburial, but many an errant shot into the rough is supposed to have unearthed a bone or even a skull. The government later acquired the site for a public park and the **Royal Selangor Golf Club**, as it became, moved to its present home in Jalan Kelab Golf in 1921. Cricket has never really caught on with the local population. Golf is quite popular, particularly among the more affluent, but football is another matter. Boys can often be seen playing on any available piece of ground. There are highly competitive local and state leagues, while crowds flock to the various grounds around the country to support their teams in the Malaysia Cup and leagues.

Today the lush green grass of the *Padang* is more for show than action, complimenting the ornamental fountains and gardens that form the heart of **Merdeka Square**. Erected in 1989 and rising some 100 metres above Merdeka Square is the tallest flag-pole in the world, with the Malaysian flag fluttering proudly from the top. The design of the flag is highly symbolic. There are fourteen red and white stripes signifying the equal status in the Federation of the thirteen constituent states and the Federal Government. The blue represents the unity of the Malaysian people, yellow is the royal colour, while the star

and crescent symbolise Islam. The star has fourteen points representing the unity of the Federation. In the north-western corner of Merdeka Square is **St Mary's Cathedral**, the principal Anglican church in Kuala Lumpur. The gallery and organ screen were erected in memory of the British High Commissioner, Sir Henry Gurney, assassinated by the Communists during the 'Emergency' (1948-1960). Each year on Merdeka Day, 31st August, Malaysian independence is celebrated with a march past along Jalan Raja, on the eastern side of Merdeka Square.

The seat of the Malaysian government lies elsewhere in Kuala Lumpur, much of it in the hills overlooking the city from the west. This area is also the home of **Taman Tasik Perdana**, another creation of the British Empire, or more precisely Alfred Venning, truly an eccentric but also a man of vision. In 1888 Venning proposed to Swettenham that a botanical garden should be made out of a long ravine in the hills. Swettenham went and had a look, spending several mornings scrambling through the ravine with Venning, before giving the go ahead. Over the next ten years Venning cleared and laid out an area covering over 170 acres. He created a lake by damming a small river and planted hundreds of trees and shrubs. The subsequent growth of Kuala Lumpur has reduced the size of Venning's garden, but it remains a favourite escape from the city for visitors and locals alike.

Located on high ground within Taman Tasik Perdana is **Parliament House**, built in the early 1960s. The Malaysian Parliament consists of two houses: the *Dewan Rakyat,* or the House of Representatives, directly elected by universal suffrage, and the *Dewan Negara,* or Senate, representing the state assemblies and special interest groups. Nearby is the **National Monument**, a great bronze sculpture erected to commemorate the soldiers who died in the triumph over the Communists in the 'Emergency'. Seven men from the Malaysian Armed Forces are portrayed, each symbolising one of seven qualities: leadership, unity, strength, vigilance, suffering, courage and sacrifice. In the years since nationhood the political leaders of the country have had to show many of these qualities in their approach to national and international problems.

Taman Tasik Perdana also contains a memorial to one of these leaders, Malaysia's second Prime Minister Tun Abdul Razak. He came to power in 1970 at an extremely difficult time for the country, with the racial troubles of the previous year all too fresh in the mind. Through strong leadership, he was able to bring much needed unity and direction to Malaysia. Within walking distance of Taman Tasik Perdana is the **Istana Negara**, the palace of Malaysia's Head of

***Opposite:** The 1st tee at the Royal Selangor Golf Club.* ***Above:** The National Monument.*

State, the Yang di-Pertuan Agong. Set amidst extensive and highly manicured lawns and gardens, the royal palace with its golden domes is an impressive sight.

The greatest testimony to the success of Malaysia's post independence leaders is Kuala Lumpur itself. The city continues to grow, upwards as well as outwards. More hotels and office blocks are set to rise towards the clouds, and yet Kuala Lumpur retains its essential character. At a time when the streets of several leading cities in the world are deemed too dangerous for pedestrians, Kuala Lumpur is a fascinating and safe place just to wander around at will. Many visitors start off at the **Malaysia Tourist Information Complex** (MATIC), housed in an imposing mansion along Jalan Ampang. This is one of the most exclusive parts of Kuala Lumpur, with numerous embassies and highly desirable residences.

Also in the 'golden triangle' is the **Karyaneka Handicraft Centre** on Jalan Raja Chulan, which has a showroom selling a range of Malaysian arts and crafts. Nearby in Jalan Conlay is the **MISC Building**, the headquarters of the Malaysian International Shipping Corporation. From its inception in 1968, MISC has been a commercial success and now has over fifty vessels. Most of the ships have been given the names of Malaysian flowers, the first being the *Bunga Raya*, or hibiscus, which is the national flower. MISC vessels travel to all parts of the world, so it is rather apt that, in the Maritime Museum on the ground floor of the building, there is a memorial to the greatest of Malay voyagers. Everybody has heard of Ferdinand Magellan, but only a few know of his servant and friend Enrique of Melaka, possibly the first man to circumnavigate the globe.

Enrique was a Malay who, according to one contemporary source, originated from the Philippines. He was captured by the Portuguese at Melaka in 1511. Magellan had taken part in the siege and, as a reward for his services, was given the choice of a slave by Albuquerque. He chose a boy of thirteen, naming him Enrigue of Melaka, and took him home to Portugal, by way of the Indian Ocean and the Cape of Good Hope. Over the years Enrique became less of a slave and more a friend and confidant to Magellan. He was presented to Charles I of Spain when Magellan turned his back on his fellow countrymen in Portugal and took service with the Spanish.

Magellan set off on his epic voyage around the world in 1519. The ever-faithful Enrique went with him. Magellan sailed across the Atlantic Ocean, down the coast of South America, round Cape Horn and into the Pacific. In a journey bedevilled by mutiny and desertion, Enrique was one of the few men Magellan could trust completely. He was particularly useful as an interpreter when the fleet reached the Philippines, after crossing the Pacific Ocean. Had Enrique returned to his native land and become the first man to sail around the world? Unfortunately, we will probably never know for certain.

Tragedy struck on the island of Mactan where Magellan was killed by the local people. Enrique was wounded and evidently blamed Magellan's death on the Spanish, who had refused to come to the aid of their Portuguese captain. His temper was not improved by the refusal of the new leaders of the expedition to honour Magellan's will and give him his freedom. Enrique managed to escape and stayed in the Philippines, disappearing from the pages of history, but he had already earned his place among the legendary figures of Malaysia, a man fit to stand alongside Hang Tuah or Yap Ah Loy.

Opposite: *Reflections: Kuala Lumpur old and new.*

NEGERI SEMBILAN
SELANGOR
PAHANG
JOHOR
MELAKA
STRAITS OF MALACCA
DURIAN TIPUS
TITI
KUALA KELAWANG
SIMPANG PERTANG
AYER HITAM
MANTIN
NILAI
BAHAU
LABU
SEREMBAN
RAHANG
TERACHI
KUALA PILAH
SRI MENANTI
ROMPIN
S. Muar
MAMBAU
DANGI
PEDAS
REMBAU
CHUAH
LUKUT
RANTAU
CHENGKAU
JOHOL
GEMAS
PORT DICKSON
KOTA
TAMPIN
LINGGI
PASIR PANJANG
LUBOK CHINA
CAPE RACHADO
S. Linggi
9
10
86
11
1
13
51
5
53
KEY
LEBUHRAYA (EXPRESSWAY)
MAJOR ROADS
SECONDARY ROADS
RAILWAY
STATE BOUNDARIES
1 PENGKALAN KEMPAS
2 LIGHTHOUSE
3 ISTANA LAMA
4 KOTA LUKUT
5 LAKE GARDENS, CULTURAL HANDICRAFT COMPLEX
N
0
10
20 km

NEGERI SEMBILAN

The Land of the Buffalo People

Sandwiched between Selangor and Melaka on the west coast of Peninsular Malaysia, Negeri Sembilan is less well-known than its neighbours, yet it possesses an equally fascinating past and a very distinctive culture. The name Negeri Sembilan means nine states in Malay, and refers to the fact that these lands were once a loose coalition of nine districts ruled over by local Malay chiefs. The first steps at integration were made in the late 18th century, but it was not until the arrival of the British a hundred years later that the process was completed, and the modern state of Negeri Sembilan was formed. Its landscape rests easily on the eye, ranging from gently undulating hills in the north-east to a fertile coastal plain, fringed by some of the best beaches on the west coast.

The recorded history of the lands of Negeri Sembilan began inevitably in the 15th century during the great days of Melaka. Yet there is a past much earlier than this, if one shrouded in mystery, and still evident today in the form of stone megaliths found in various parts of the state. These tall, irregularly shaped stones are known as the *batu hidup,* or living stones, as the local inhabitants once believed that they were actually growing. Fearful of the supernatural and the unknown, the people prayed to the spirits of the stones for protection and turned them into shrines. Some thought the stones

State crest: *The nine sheaves of rice and the nine-pointed star represent the nine districts which united to form Negeri Sembilan. The sword and sheath symbolise justice.* ***Below:*** *A Minangkabau couple on their wedding day.*

marked the graves of famous warriors or their early forefathers. Whatever their significance, the stones are still revered by many of the local inhabitants. Indeed a few remain convinced that the stones are growing.

A large number of these megaliths can be seen around Kuala Pilah and Tampin, but the most famous stones are to be found near **Pengkalan Kempas**, a small village on Route 5 between Melaka and Port Dickson. Here stand three carved granite monoliths, popularly known as the 'sword', the 'spoon', and the 'rudder', due to their shapes. They are the only stones which are carved, adding to the mystery surrounding their past. They are thought to date from the 2nd or 3rd century, though they are evidently related in some way to the adjacent grave of Sheikh Ahmad Majnun, who died in the 15th century. According to local legend, the 'sword' represents the sword worn by the Sheikh. The 'sword' does seem to have a special significance as it is the only stone fully carved on the facade. The presence of the word 'Allah' adds to the intrigue, particularly as the carvings are mostly animistic in content. Were the stones perhaps brought from another site, and erected there in an effort to glorify the Sheikh's grave? Or was the site already considered to be a sacred place, and chosen as the Sheikh's burial ground because of the presence of the ancient stones? The carving of 'Allah' might have been added to distinguish it as an Islamic shrine. The truth will probably never be known.

The tomb of Sheikh Ahmad Majnun is one of the oldest Islamic graves in Malaysia. The inscriptions, carved on a pillar in front of the grave, date it to the years 1467-1468. After that the inscriptions are as confusing as virtually everything else at Pengkalan Kempas. One section of the inscriptions calls the Sheikh a holy man, while another condemns him as a traitor. Sheikh Ahmad Majnun was an Islamic missionary, who probably fell out with Sultan Mansur of Melaka, and he seems to have been killed in a skirmish with Melakan troops. His surviving followers erected the memorial at Pengkalan Kempas. The Sultan's men were the likely source of the inscription calling him a traitor. The pillar is known locally as the 'ordeal stone', because of the circular hole below the inscriptions which, according to popular belief, is an ancient lie detector. The suspect puts his arm through the hole and, if he lies, the stone is said to tighten around it.

From Pengkalan Kempas, Route 5 winds its way west to the coast, where a narrow track leads to the hilltop lighthouse of **Cape Rachado**, also known as Tanjung Tuan. Rachado is thought to have been the name of a Portuguese sea captain, though the lighthouse dates from British times. Permission to visit the lighthouse must be obtained from the Harbour Master's Office in Melaka. Armed with a permit, any visitor will find the staff at Cape Rachado more than happy to conduct an impromptu guided tour. A narrow spiralling stone staircase leads to the mirror room at the top of the tower, with its intricate and beautifully maintained machinery. From here you can climb out on to the parapet, which commands spectacular views over the Straits of Malacca. Sailing ships have now mostly gone, but their modern, rather ugly, equivalents - tankers and container ships - can clearly be seen plying up and down the Straits. Occasionally, the past is evoked, as an Indonesian *perahu,* with its graceful lines, sails into view.

The thickly wooded cape is home to a variety of birds, and hawks and eagles can sometimes be seen soaring above the tree tops, on the look out for their next meal. A steep jungle path leads from the lighthouse down to a secluded beach, where Hang Tuah is believed to have come to meditate. It might be said that he made a lasting 'impression'. About 50 metres off to the right of the path is a boulder with a

footprint embedded in it, said to have been made by the great man himself.

Cape Rachado is less than 40 km away from the coast of Sumatra and, on a clear day, its outline can be seen against the canvas of blue sea and sky. Sumatra is the original homeland of the Minangkabau people, many of whom decided in days gone by to cross the Straits of Malacca and make a new life for themselves in Negeri Sembilan. They began migrating to *tanah seberang,* or the opposite land, as they called the Malay Peninsula, in the 15th century, lured by the wealth and fame of Melaka. Leaving the Padang Highlands of Sumatra, they paddled down the Siak and Kampar rivers to the coast, where they boarded ships bound for the peninsula. They settled in the hilly regions of Negeri Sembilan. The attractions were obvious.

Opposite, left: *The 'ordeal stone' at Pengkalan Kempas.* ***Opposite, right:*** *The ancient stones popularly known as the 'sword', the 'spoon' and the 'rudder'.* ***Above:*** *The lighthouse at Cape Rachado.*

The terrain was similar to that in Sumatra, while the soil and weather conditions were well-suited to their traditional mixed farming. These areas were already in the possession of Malay chiefs, but as land was then in plentiful supply, the Minangkabau settlers paid only token gifts for large tracts of the countryside.

At first a trickle, the numbers of immigrants gradually increased, reaching a peak in the second half of the 17th century. The Minangkabaus have given Negeri Sembilan a distinctive character, most obvious today in the elegant style of architecture. Minangkabau buildings are topped with upswept roofs, a stylised representation of buffalo horns. Such roofs are the trade mark of Negeri Sembilan. One of the best places to see houses built in this style is along Route 51 from Seremban to Kuala Pilah, an attractive road in its own right as it climbs up and down a series of hills. The buffalo horn motif is also used for the head-dress worn by Minangkabau women on festive occasions. Their association with the buffalo is more than decorative, accounting for their very name. This is attributed to an old Minangkabau legend in which cunning rather than brute strength defeated the Javanese.

In the past wars were only too common between the peoples of Java and Sumatra, and long ago a vast Javanese army invaded the land of the Minangkabaus, after the king of Java had been spurned by a beautiful Minangkabau princess. His army was said to be so large that all the troops, honing their swords together on the side of a mighty rock, had turned it into a gorge. Despite the size of the Javanese army, the outcome was years of indecisive fighting until both sides agreed to settle the issue by a single buffalo fight. The Javanese scoured the countryside and chose as their champion the largest and strongest buffalo they could find, while the clever Minangkabaus separated a young suckling from its mother and filed its immature horns into razor-sharp points. The duel was brief but decisive. Having been deprived of its mother's milk, the calf instinctively nuzzled under its opponent's belly, in the process fatally piercing the mighty Javanese buffalo with its sharpened horns. In celebration of their victory, the people took the name Minangkabau, from the words *menang kerbau,* meaning victorious buffalo.

The Minangkabau settlers shared a common ethnical, linguistic and religious background with the peninsular Malays, and like the Bugis in Selangor, were gradually assimilated into the local Malay community. However, they differed from them in one important respect: their customary laws. These laws, known as *Adat Perpatih,* revolve around a matrilineal kinship system and are still practised in Negeri Sembilan today. Ancestry is traced through the female line and inheritance is passed from mother to daughter. Whereas in some societies daughters are seen as a burden, it is vital under *Adat Perpatih* that a woman has a daughter, if she is to keep her inheritance within her immediate family. When a deceased woman has no daughters, her land and property pass to other female relatives.

Matrilineal customs are practised among other races, but what makes them so interesting in Malaysia is their co-existence with Islam, where the emphasis is on the role of the man. The Minangkabau people have to some extent adapted their customary laws to fit in with their Islamic beliefs, but such a compromise can only go so far and some important differences remain. For example, in *Adat Perpatih* all the family inheritance passes to the daughter or daughters, while under Islamic law they receive only a third, the remainder going to their brothers.

Adat Perpatih covers all aspects of Minangkabau life and has been likened to an unwritten constitution. Its rules and regulations are enshrined in a series of adages, known as *teromba,* which have been passed down from generation to generation by word of mouth. The system was surprisingly devised by a man, a Minangkabau chief called Datuk Perpatih, in recognition of the bravery of a young woman. The Minangkabau people are divided into *sukus,* or clans, whose members can trace their lineage back to the same great ancestress. Each *suku* is led by a *lembaga.* Like the Chinese clans, the *sukus* help members who have fallen on hard times and expect to share in the good fortune of those who prosper. This caring, sharing philosophy is summed up by the *Adat* saying: 'What we drop is common loss; What we gain is common profit'.

There are twelve sukus in Negeri Sembilan and marriage between members of the same *suku* is forbidden. Such a union is regarded as incestuous. Although Islam permits a man to have up to four wives, monogamy is the general rule, as

Opposite: *A water buffalo enjoying a mud bath. The shape of the horns is the inspiration for Minangkabau architecture.*
Below: *The preparations begin for the feast at a Minangkabau wedding.*

indeed it is for Muslims throughout the country. The husband lives in his wife's home, as a 'guest' in her *suku,* and the couple's children are brought up as members of her *suku.* The husband's position is not an easy one. He is looked upon as something of an asset by the other members of the *suku,* and is expected to heed their wishes, as the following verses from the *teromba* illustrate:

'If he is strong, he shall be our champion;
If a fool, he will be ordered here and there;
Clever, and we will invite his council;
Learned, and we will ask his prayers;
Rich, and we will use his gold....
Follow the customs of your wife's family.
When you tread the soil of a country and live beneath its sky,
Follow the customs of that country.
A bridegroom among his wife's relations
Is like a soft cucumber against thorny durian fruit;
If he rolls against them, he is hurt,
And he is hurt if they roll against him.'

Adat Perpatih is not designed to oppress men. Although gender relationships are tilted in favour of women, men are treated with respect and play an integral part in *suku* life.

The Minangkabau people have always enjoyed an excuse for a good party. All their major festivities are traditionally spread over several days and involve the whole community, thus ensuring that everyone enjoys themselves to the full. According to Minangkabau folklore, it was during one of their more protracted celebrations that the song and dance routine, the *rentak kuda,* was conceived. After nearly a week of festivities, some of the guests had begun to lose their party spirit and showed signs of exhaustion, if not a desire to go home. Suddenly, a beautiful woman appeared before them, singing and dancing with almost manic enthusiasm. Flagging spirits were instantly raised. Soon everybody was joining in, moving their hands and feet to the rhythm, similar in tempo to that of a galloping horse. Hence the name *rentak kuda,* or the beat of the horse. The dance is still used as a 'pick-me-up' today during important

ceremonies and feasts.

Another dance which the Minangkabaus brought with them from Sumatra is the *tarian lilin,* or candle dance, often performed in semi-darkness for added effect. Each dancer, dressed in traditional Minangkabau costume, places a lighted candle in the middle of a saucer. Wearing a ring on the tip of their middle finger, they tap the saucer in rhythm to the music. The dance was inspired by the tale of a beautiful woman whose betrothed went on *merantau,* or wanderings, as many young Minangkabau men once did. He promised to return when he had made his fortune. While he was away, she lost her engagement ring. Distraught at the loss of her most treasured possession, she began a thorough search for the ring. When darkness fell, she continued the search with the light from a candle placed on a saucer. We do not know whether she found her ring, or if her betrothed ever made his fortune and returned to marry her, but the graceful movements of her body as she looked for the ring are imitated during the dance. The *tarian lilin* has now spread far beyond Negeri Sembilan, and is performed throughout Malaysia.

The Minangkabaus accepted the authority of the local Malay chiefs who already ruled over the districts in which they had settled. They were also happy to acknowledge Melaka and later Johor as their ultimate overlord. In time the Malay chiefs themselves adopted *Adat Perpatih.* There were no formal links between the Minangkabaus in the various districts of Negeri Sembilan, though each group was organised along the same social and

Opposite: *The bride waits in the bridal chamber for the groom and his entourage to arrive for the exchange of rings ceremony. The bed cover, made specially for the wedding, is a beautiful example of tekatan embroidery.* ***Above:*** *The bersanding, one of the highlights of the marriage ceremony, when guests come up to the bridal dais to bless the couple. Each guest is given a bunga telur, a decorated hard-boiled egg. The eggs symbolise fertility.*

political lines.

In the 18th century this state of affairs began to change. The troubles in Johor following the assassination of Sultan Mahmud in 1699 left the Minangkabaus without an effective overlord. They eventually asked the Sultan of Johor for permission to appoint their own ruler and a Sumatran prince, Raja Melewar, was made the first Yang di-Pertuan Besar of Negeri Sembilan by the chiefs of four of the districts: Sungai Ujung, Rembau, Jelebu and Johol. The traditional date for his installation is 1773, though there are references to Raja Melewar being present in Negeri Sembilan earlier in the century.

Raja Melewar set up his royal capital at **Sri Menanti**. He was accorded the usual ceremonial privileges of Malay rulers, such as the use of the royal colour yellow, but he possessed little real power. He was not allowed to raise taxes and had to rely on *mas manah,* or gifts, from his leading subjects for the upkeep of his court. The British destroyed the original royal palace in 1875, but its replacement, constructed at the turn of the century and in royal service until 1931, can still be seen today. Built entirely of wood and nestling in the picturesque and peaceful valley of Sri Menanti, surrounded by forested hills, the **Istana Lama** is one of Malaysia's most charming royal residences. The palace was designed by two well-known Malay carpenters, Kahar and Taib, and may have been partly inspired by descriptions of Sultan Mansur's famous palace in Melaka. There are certainly some similarities between its design and that of the Melaka Sultanate Palace.

Adorned with intricate wood carvings, the palace has four storeys, and incorporates 99 pillars, all made from *penak,* the local name for the hardwood *cengal.* These pillars represent famous warriors from the various *sukus.* In the centre of the building is a tower known as the Tingkat Gunung. The roof is topped with a distinctive open-scissors motif which was later adopted for the roof of the Muzium Negara in Kuala Lumpur. When the palace was in use, the basic distribution of rooms was

similar to those in Melaka. The sultan received his subjects on the first floor, the royal family occupied the second floor, while the third floor was the sole domain of the ruler. The royal treasures were housed in the Tingkat Gunung, which also served as a lookout post. What was once a turfed square in front of the palace, used for royal sporting events, has been turned into an attractively landscaped garden. In the 1930s the royal family moved to the nearby and much larger **Istana Besar**. A modern stone building with whitewashed walls and a blue tiled roof, it resembles its namesake in Johor. The Istana Lama was opened to the public in 1992 as the royal museum.

On the outskirts of Sri Menanti is the **Royal Mausoleum**, the final resting place of Raja Melewar. He died in 1795, whereupon a new prince was sent from the Minangkabau homeland and appointed his successor. This practice of importing the Yang di-Pertuan Besar from Sumatra continued until the early 19th century. The present ruling family is descended from Raja Lenggang Laut (1809-1824), the fourth Yang di-Pertuan Besar, though the dynasty had to survive a series of succession disputes later in the century. By the time of Raja Lenggang Laut a distinct royal class known as the *anak raja* had appeared, composed of the offspring of the earlier rulers. They showed themselves more than capable of claiming the throne for themselves, if the opportunity arose. In one respect the succession system in Negeri Sembilan has remained different from those practised in the other Malay kingdoms. The four chiefs of Sungai Ujung, Rembau, Jelebu and Johol have retained the right to elect each new ruler, though in recent times the election has become something of a formality.

Conflict was not confined to the

Opposite: *The bride and groom meeting their guests. The couple change their costumes several times during the wedding festivities.* ***Below:*** *The Istana Lama at Sri Menanti.*

royal family during the turbulent decades of the 19th century. The rivers of Negeri Sembilan were, like those to the north, blessed with extensive tin deposits. They brought great wealth to the kingdom, but also the inevitable disorder, as the local chiefs fought for control of the profits. As in Perak and Selangor, these rivalries led ultimately to the intervention of the British, with the first Resident being appointed for Sungai Ujung, the largest of the nine districts, in 1874. It was colonial rule which brought about the historic union of all the districts to form the modern state of Negeri Sembilan in 1895. A single Resident was then appointed for the whole of the kingdom.

The small town of **Lukut**, some 7 km from the seaside town of Port Dickson, was an important tin mining area during the 19th century. This was where Yap Ah Loy worked as a cook before going to Kuala Lumpur. Lukut belonged to neighbouring Selangor until the 1870s, when it was forfeited to Negeri Sembilan during negotiations between the two kingdoms to settle outstanding boundary disputes. On a hill above the town is a fort, built in 1847 by the local ruler, Raja Jumaat, to provide a secure base from which to control the tin trade. He did not want to suffer the fate of one of his predecessors, who was killed with all his family in a clash with a Chinese secret society. **Kota Lukut** is one of the best preserved Bugis strongholds in the country. The fort is situated in a very strong position, and was defended by large muzzle-loading guns. It is doubtful if Raja Jumaat really needed such a powerful fort. His wise and firm rule maintained law and order and attracted many new settlers to the area. For much of the time, the sultan of Selangor left Raja Jumaat to his own devices and all the profits from the local tin trade.

The turning for Kota Lukut lies just outside the town on Route 5, with a laterite track leading up the hill to the fort. It is advisable to wear a protective 'armour' of insect repellent, as the fort is a favourite haunt for mosquitoes. They seem to be particularly aggressive and persistent at Kota Lukut. The first garrison of twenty-two men would have been hard-pressed to put up such an effective 'defence'. As the hordes of mosquitoes plunge into the fray, curious thoughts spring to mind. Are these insects somehow possessed of the spirits of the original Bugis defenders? Why do visitors ever come here? Yet Kota Lukut is well worth 'penetrating'. The ramparts are still an imposing sight today, dominating the Lukut river valley, while the size of the fort bears witness to the engineering skills of the Bugis. Almost a square in design, the fort is some 200 metres by 180 metres, with the remains of a two-storey building in the centre, no doubt the hub of the original defences.

The capital of Negeri Sembilan, **Seremban**, is another Malaysian town which grew up in the wake of the tin boom. The original settlement was little more than two rows of shophouses. Today Seremban is a bustling and burgeoning town, with an increasingly modern skyline. Situated only forty-five minutes from Kuala Lumpur via the expressway, Seremban is part of the Malaysian capital's growing commuter belt. The links between Negeri Sembilan and the Minangkabau homeland in Sumatra were reinforced in 1986, when Seremban was twinned with the West Sumatran town of Bukittinggi.

Seremban is a good place to sample some Minangkabau food, renowned for being hot and spicy. Among the most popular dishes is *rendang,* tender chunks of spicy beef cooked in coconut milk. *Rendang* is popular throughout Malaysia, particularly for festive occasions such as Hari Raya Puasa, and is often eaten with another speciality of the region, *lemang,* glutinous rice cooked in bamboo. Banana leaves are used to line the inside of a piece of bamboo, which is then filled with rice and coconut milk. The bamboo is cooked over a low and steady flame for a period of four hours. If you like your food really hot, there is the chicken dish *masak lemak cili padi.* The *cili padi* is the hottest of all the chillies, its fiery taste earning it the nickname *cili api,* literally meaning fire chillies. You have been warned!

At the heart of Seremban are the attractively landscaped **Lake Gardens**, the town's main recreational area. The Gardens incorporate two lakes, forming a popular circuit for joggers, and include a mini bird park. Among the tropical flora are some eye-catching examples of topiary, with bushes fashioned in the shapes of various animals, a cannon and a *kris.* Overlooking one of the lakes is the modern **Masjid Negeri**, or State Mosque, constructed around nine pillars, symbolising the original nine districts of Negeri Sembilan. The building is almost unrecognisable as a mosque, save for the crescent and star motif adorning each pillar which symbolises enlightenment for Muslims. Although very different from traditional Minangkabau buildings, the design incorporates an interesting variation on the upswept roof theme. Close to the mosque is the striking Minangkabau-style

Opposite: *The entrance to the Bugis fort at Kota Lukut.* ***Below:*** *Women from Negeri Sembilan wearing the traditional Minangkabau head-dress, a stylised representation of buffalo horns, at the Merdeka Day march past along Jalan Raja in Kuala Lumpur.*

State Secretariat, which sports several pairs of pointed buffalo horns in its roof structure. Across the road is the old State Secretariat, an elegant colonial building which now houses the **State Library**. The palace of the Yang di-Pertuan Besar, the **Istana Hinggap**, is also situated in the Lake Gardens.

The other main attraction for visitors to Seremban is the **Taman Seni Budaya**, or Cultural Handicraft Complex, situated along Jalan Labu on the outskirts of the town. The main building in the Complex, known as the **Teratak Perpatih**, is perhaps the most stunning example of the state's Minangkabau architecture. Made of wood, it is crowned with an almost bewildering array of buffalo horns. The building was originally constructed as the venue for the International Koran Reading Competition, held in Seremban in 1984. It was later reassembled on its present site and contains displays of local handicrafts and historical items.

The grounds contain two more buildings, both dating from the 19th century and also relocated from other sites. The first is the small State Museum which was originally a royal residence, the **Istana Ampang Tinggi**, built in 1861 by Negeri Sembilan's fifth ruler as a gift for his daughter. The palace was used until the 1930s, after which it fell into disrepair. The building was salvaged in 1953 and transported, piece by piece, from Kuala Pilah to the Lake Gardens, later being moved again and reconstructed at the Complex. For a palace, it is a very modest building, of much simpler Minangkabau design than the Teratak Perpatih, with only a very gentle roof curvature. The museum houses collections of weapons, brass and silverware.

Next to the Istana Ampang Tinggi is another wooden house constructed in the same simple longhouse style, so characteristic of many Minangkabau buildings. The locals call it the **Rumah Berhantu**, or the Haunted House, though nobody seems to know why or who is supposed to do the haunting. Constructed in 1898, the house has been beautifully preserved and features a wooden shingled roof and ornate wood carvings, including verses from the Koran. Originally located at Kampung Anak Air Garam in Mambau, it was dismantled in 1924 and shipped to Britain as an example of Malay architecture for an exhibition at Wembley. For those who are unable to visit the famous megaliths at Pengkalan Kempas, replicas of the three ancient stones have been erected in the gardens of the Complex. There is also a covered stage for the performance of cultural shows and demonstrations of traditional pastimes in Negeri Sembilan.

Seremban is 33 km from the coast and Negeri Sembilan's beaches, which stretch south of Port Dickson for some 18 km to the **Blue Lagoon**, virtually in the shadow of Cape Rachado. **Port Dickson**, popularly known as 'P.D.', is one of the few places in Malaysia to have retained its British name. The town is named after Sir Frederick Dickson, a leading official in the Straits Settlements. He identified the area in the late 1880s as a potential deep water port for the export of tin from the Sungai Ujung mines, as well as a possible 'playground' for British officials and planters. Before Sir Frederick came on the scene, it was the site of the small village of Arang, which took its name from the principal occupation of the inhabitants, the making of *arang,* or charcoal. Success as a port proved elusive and Port Dickson was never in a position to rival the larger ports to the north. As a 'playground' the town has been far more successful, becoming one of the most popular beach resorts on the west coast. It is primarily a Malaysian haunt, as foreign tourists tend to head for Penang and Langkawi. With easy access from Kuala Lumpur, Port Dickson's beaches

attract large numbers of city dwellers every weekend. Hotels, holiday homes and restaurants are dotted along the coastal road.

Life has changed dramatically for many people in Negeri Sembilan during recent times and *Adat Perpatih* faces an uncertain future. Matrilineal society is rooted in an agrarian economy and, until recently, most men in Negeri Sembilan were farmers. Many worked on their wife's ancestral land and lived in her house, but growing numbers of men are now leaving the land for the towns and more lucrative employment in Malaysia's expanding industrial and service sectors. This has fundamentally changed gender relationships, with men no longer being economically dependent upon their wives. The husband can assert more authority in the home. He is no longer 'a soft cucumber against thorny durian fruit'.

It is not only men's prospects which have changed. As standards of education have risen, there has also been a growing trend for women to enter paid employment. Some ancestral lands, particularly *padi* fields, have fallen into disuse, their importance in the matrilineal system of inheritance becoming purely symbolic. Migration has further weakened *Adat Perpatih,* as the previously tight-knit *sukus* become dispersed. In addition to these socio-economic changes, the hold of orthodox Islam has strengthened, raising further doubts about the ability of *Adat Perpatih* to survive in Negeri Sembilan. Some Muslims have preferred to abandon customs which contradict Islamic law.

It would be a great shame if *Adat Perpatih* was to become a casualty of progress, as the variety of cultures which coexist in Malaysia make the country such a fascinating place to visit. Perhaps *Adat Perpatih* can adapt itself to the changing times and survive in a diluted form, but it is unlikely ever again to play the central role it once did in Negeri Sembilan.

Above: *The Teratak Perpatih at the Taman Seni Budaya in Seremban, with its stunning Minangkabau-style roof.*

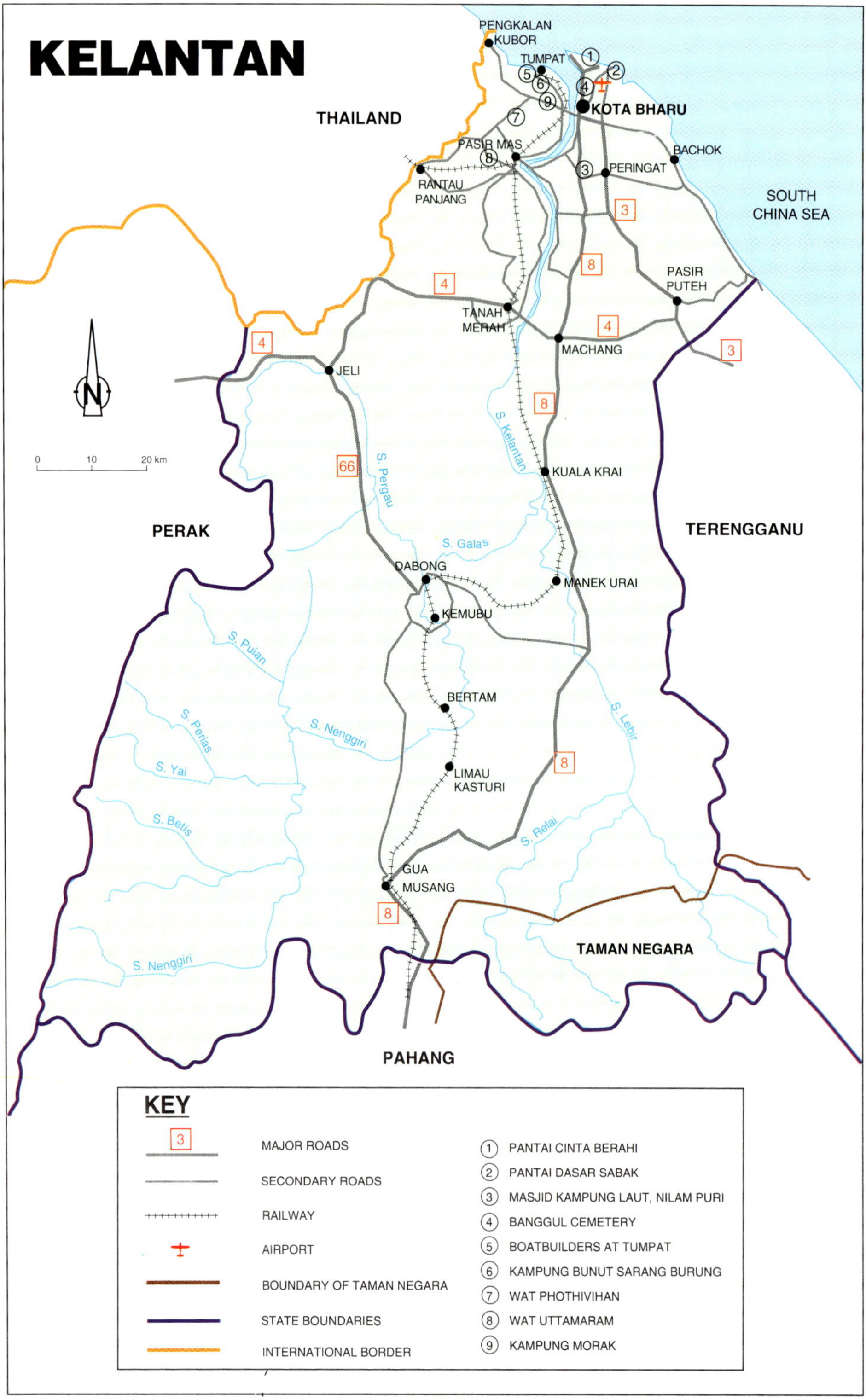
KELANTAN
THAILAND
PENGKALAN KUBOR
TUMPAT
KOTA BHARU
PASIR MAS
RANTAU PANJANG
BACHOK
PERINGAT
SOUTH CHINA SEA
PASIR PUTEH
TANAH MERAH
MACHANG
JELI
S. Kelantan
S. Pergau
KUALA KRAI
PERAK
TERENGGANU
S. Galas
DABONG
MANEK URAI
KEMUBU
S. Puian
S. Perias
S. Nenggiri
BERTAM
S. Lebir
S. Yai
LIMAU KASTURI
S. Betis
S. Relai
GUA MUSANG
TAMAN NEGARA
S. Nenggiri
PAHANG
0 10 20 km
N
KEY
MAJOR ROADS
SECONDARY ROADS
RAILWAY
AIRPORT
BOUNDARY OF TAMAN NEGARA
STATE BOUNDARIES
INTERNATIONAL BORDER
1 PANTAI CINTA BERAHI
2 PANTAI DASAR SABAK
3 MASJID KAMPUNG LAUT, NILAM PURI
4 BANGGUL CEMETERY
5 BOATBUILDERS AT TUMPAT
6 KAMPUNG BUNUT SARANG BURUNG
7 WAT PHOTHIVIHAN
8 WAT UTTAMARAM
9 KAMPUNG MORAK

KELANTAN

The Cultural Capital of Malaysia

If Kuala Lumpur is the heartbeat of Malaysia, with its road and rail network stretching like arteries to every corner, then the east coast must surely be the soul of the country. This is a land of unsophisticated charm. Picture-postcard fishing villages nestle in sheltered estuary mouths, deserted beaches shimmer in the hot sun, while offshore lie idyllic tropical islands fringed with coral gardens.

For much of its past the east coast has been left alone, isolated by the peninsula's Main Range. Until the 20th century the three kingdoms of Kelantan, Terengganu and Pahang had few, if any roads. Transport along the coast was by boat, a form of travel only available for part of the year. In the monsoon season the sea was often closed to shipping for several months. Jungle tracks, and above all, rivers were the only feasible means of moving around the countryside. Not until the last twenty or thirty years has an effective road system been developed. Before that roads were more like lanes and the numerous rivers, each requiring a ferry crossing, were a constant inconvenience. The older taxi drivers can still remember those days, when they always thought twice about taking a long distance fare up or down the east coast. All that changed with the opening of Route 3, the highway along the east coast, Route 2 from Kuala Lumpur to Kuantan and, the greatest feat of all, the East/West Highway (Route 4) from Perak to Kelantan. Ferries and long tortuous journeys became a thing of the past as the east coast was opened up for commerce and tourism.

Yet the region has remained much as it has always done. Kelantan and Terengganu in particular, with their predominantly Malay populations, have kept their traditional character and appeal. Kelantan has always been the most isolated of all the states in Peninsular Malaysia, tucked away in the north-eastern corner of the country. Visitors ignore it at their peril as Kelantan boasts a rich and fascinating cultural heritage. For many Malays, Kelantan is the cultural capital of Malaysia.

A great deal of the Malay past has centred on the exploits of kings and warriors, but the early history of Kelantan revolves around the deeds of two women, Cik Siti Wan Kembang and her adopted daughter Puteri Saadong. The legacy of these two remarkable ladies is still evident today in the streets of Kota Bharu, the capital of Kelantan, where women dominate life in the markets and hawker centres. The lives of Cik Siti and Puteri Saadong are shrouded in mystery, adding to the legends which surround them. Both of them were said to possess spiritual and magical powers. Cik Siti was installed as ruler of Kelantan at **Kuala Krai** in the early 17th century. She was very fond of animals. Her favourite pet was reputed to be a deer and, in memory of this, the animal has been given pride of place in the state crest of Kelantan. Like most, if not all women, Cik Siti had a passion for gold. Her pet deer was said to be golden in colour. One

State crest: *The deer are a reminder of the days when Cik Siti Wan Kembang ruled the state. The kris represent the power of Kelantanese Malays, while the cannons signify that the state is ever ready to defend itself. The state motto is 'obedience to Allah, loyalty to the Kelantan Government'.*

of her prized possessions was a golden *kris* and she is even rumoured to have meditated in caves decorated with gold. Cik Siti also liked to wear the colour in the form of *kain songket,* richly coloured silk fabric woven with gold thread. In her day *kain songket* was only worn by royalty. This is no longer the case, though it is still considered a special attire and is favoured for formal occasions, such as weddings.

Cik Siti passed on to Puteri Saadong all her female wiles and powers, preparing the young girl for the inevitable trials ahead. Puteri Saadong grew into a beautiful woman. The first sadness in her life came with the death of Cik Siti, whose grave is thought to be at **Banggul Cemetery** on Jalan Pantai Cinta Berahi, some 6 km from Kota Bharu. The cemetery is very large, and the tomb is not easy to locate, despite recently being restored.

In the 17th century Kelantan was constantly threatened from the north by the Siamese. Puteri Saadong married Raja Abdullah, the son of the ruler of Jembal, but the Thai king had heard stories of her beauty and wanted her for himself. What the Thai king wanted he usually got, and so it proved on this occasion. Puteri Saadong agreed to go to Thailand, in order to save Kelantan from invasion, but only on the condition that the king kept his hands to himself. Before she left for Bangkok, she received a promise from Abdullah that he would not take another wife.

If legend is to be believed, Puteri Saadong had an interesting time in Thailand, where her magical powers proved invaluable. The Thai king showed himself to be totally lacking in any honour and immediately grabbed her. She pushed the king off and warned him of a terrible fate, if he persisted in trying to touch her. 'I will spit on you and turn you into a toad', she told him. The king ignored the warning and made another lunge for her, whereupon Puteri Saadong spat on him and sure enough the king of Thailand turned into a toad. The Siamese were furious and wanted to kill her, but Puteri Saadong, sensing a chance to go home, calmed them by promising to turn the toad back into the

king, if she could return to Kelantan. With no other options at hand, the Siamese agreed to the proposal. Puteri Saadong asked for a bowl of water and put her foot into it, before encouraging the toad to take a drink. In an instant the toad was transformed into a very relieved Thai king. This time he honoured the agreement.

When Puteri Saadong returned to Kelantan, she discovered that Raja Abdullah had broken his promise and taken a lady from the court as his wife. A terrible quarrel broke out and, losing her temper, she fatally stabbed him with her hair pin. His tomb can still be seen today at Kampung Padang Halban, about 20 km south of Kota Bharu. Distraught, Puteri Saadong withdrew to the south and the legendary Bukit Marak, where Cik Siti had brought her up as a young girl.

The Kelantanese are a warm, friendly people and, in common with Malays throughout the country, they are courteous by nature and possess an innate grace, perhaps the result of their long tradition of court life and etiquette. As probably the most staunchly Islamic state in the country, many visitors think Kelantan will be dull and repressive, with little to offer them. This is not the case. **Kota Bharu** is a bustling, colourful place, with a good deal to see. There are two lively markets. **Central Market** must be one of the most photographed markets in Malaysia. Women arrive early each morning to set up their fruit and vegetable displays in the central courtyard. Many transport their produce to the market in huge baskets balanced on their heads. Others employ the services of trishaw riders, and it is not uncommon to see trishaws being peddled to the market crammed full of produce such as durians, watermelons and bunches of green beans, to the point where you wonder if the odd one might not topple over.

Everything at the market is neatly laid

Opposite: *The fruit and vegetable displays at Central Market in Kota Bharu.*
Below: *Kelantanese schoolboys relaxing after a hard game of football.*

out on mats, in a stunning symmetrical pattern. The translucent market roof bathes the whole area in light, heightening the varied colours of the produce on display. The upper floors look down on the courtyard and provide a perfect vantage point from which to take in the busy, colourful scene below. The vast majority of the traders are women, their menfolk being mostly fishermen who are either at sea or at home

mending their nets. The women sit proudly behind their displays of fruit and vegetables, chatting and laughing among themselves. It is almost a shame to purchase anything and upset their beautifully laid out wares. Not that they seem to mind and none are keen to allow you to pass without opening your wallet or purse.

One of the liveliest places in Kota Bharu during the evening is the **Pasar Makan Malam**, near Central Market in Jalan Padang Garong, which sells delicious Kelantanese fare such as the popular rice dishes *nasi dagang* (rice with tuna-fish) and *nasi kerabu* (rice with herbs). The Kelantanese are renowned for their sweet tooth and the market also offers a tempting array of local cakes. During the day the square is a rather barren place, but as night falls, it quickly fills up with hawker stalls and tantalising smells begin to waft through the air. The night market is always popular with the locals, who come here with their families and friends to enjoy the cheap and tasty cuisine on offer. Tables and chairs are provided in part of the square and, once you have chosen your food, you can sit down, order something to quench your thirst from one of the surrounding drinks stalls, and tuck in, while taking in the atmosphere.

Every year the streets of Kota Bharu are hung with ornate decorations as *Puja Umur,* or the Sultan's Birthday, draws near. This is a leading event in the Kelantan festive calendar. A variety of activities are organised, including cultural shows, concerts, fêtes and a regatta on the Kelantan River. On the day of the boat races, crowds throng the banks of the usually quiet river, many perched precariously in an attempt to find the best vantage point. The highlight of the day is undoubtedly the longboat races. The longboats, six per race, are propelled at tremendous speed up the course by teams of extremely fit and muscular young paddlers, against a backdrop of wildly cheering crowds. The finish

Above: *The traditional way to travel short distances in Malaysia is by trishaw, although at times it does get a little crowded!*

is in front of the royal boathouse, where all the crews, winners and losers alike, collapse exhausted.

Kota Bharu is also the centre for the arts and crafts of Kelantan, pursuits which have earned the kingdom the description of 'the haven of Malay culture'. No one in Kelantan would ever claim a monopoly of Malay culture, but the kingdom is the birthplace of many of the country's traditional art forms. The skills of the people have been handed down from generation to generation until the present day. Working in the fields has always been arduous and all too often unrewarding, but during periods of leisure, particularly after harvesting the *padi,* the Kelantanese have for centuries relaxed by indulging themselves in a wide range of activities, such as bird-singing competitions, playing the *rebana* drums, *gasing* contests and various crafts. The fishermen have likewise used their spare time during the monsoon season, when the rough seas keep their boats at home, to develop their own skills at these traditional pursuits.

The Malays have always been fond of birds, which are often seen in elaborately carved birdcages hanging outside *kampung* houses. In Kelantan, as elsewhere, bird-singing competitions between doves have proved very popular. The birds compete in cages suspended from 8 metre poles. The doves are apparently most relaxed at this height, feeling they are in a tree, and sing their best. It is not just the villagers of Kelantan who have shown a passion for birds and their singing. At the other end of the social scale, a queen from the neighbouring Malay kingdom of Patani developed a deep affection for a particular bird, named Asyik, which led to the creation of a famous Malay dance. The bird is said to have possessed a very sweet voice, but one day it flew away, never to return. The queen was inconsolable. The court jester decided he had better do something to cheer her up, so he gathered together the ladies-in-waiting and choreographed a dance for them, in which their movements resembled those of a bird. The dance, aptly named the *tarian asyik,* did

the trick, enchanting the queen. Kelantan has always had close ties with Patani and the dance soon became popular at the royal court in Kota Bharu.

The principal venue in Kota Bharu for Kelantan's wide range of traditional pastimes is the **Gelanggang Seni**, or Kelantan Cultural Centre, just off Jalan Mahmood. Regular performances are held on set afternoons and evenings each week, except during the monsoon season and Ramadan. The evening performances include the staging of traditional dances and theatre in the main hall. In the afternoon a two hour programme is offered, with the various events being performed outside under wooden shelters. A cacophony of sound greets the audience for the start of the afternoon proceedings, as the orchestra tunes up for its accompaniment to the *silat* display later in the programme. In a far corner men prepare for a game of *gasing*.

The show begins with the thunderous roar of the *rebana* drums, giant drums made from hollowed out logs and covered with buffalo hide. The drums are beaten using either bare hands or padded drumsticks, and the performance is a very energetic and exhausting affair. The drummers put all their efforts into it, building up to a frenetic climax. The history of this king of drums goes back several hundred years, when it was used as a mode of communication between villages, a sort of primitive forerunner to the Morse code. The drummers devised an ingenious variety of rhythmic beats to convey messages, ranging from warnings of war to wedding invitations. It is easy to understand how effective this jungle morse must have been when you hear the drums today. The sound instantly evokes memories of Tarzan films, when African villagers beat their drum messages across the jungle and Tarzan responded with his mighty warble cry, before swinging into action. Every year,

Opposite: *The rebana drums being played at the Gelanggang Seni in Kota Bharu.* ***Below:*** *The art of gasing is nowhere near as easy as it looks.*

once the harvest is completed, the Festival of Drums is held, in which teams of twelve men from each village, two to a drum, demonstrate their skills in a light-hearted competition; though to judge from the partisan cheers of their supporters, perhaps it is not that light-hearted!

Silat is the Malay art of self-defence. Its most famous exponent was Hang Tuah. He honed his skills in the heat of battle, but *silat* now usually takes the form of a dance in which two men mimic a duel, much in the fashion of shadow boxing. The performers wear fixed smiles of concentration on their faces, as they slowly twist and turn, rarely touching each other with their hand chops and leg kicks. The dance is a study in masculine elegance. The performers are perfectly balanced and their movements graceful. The dance ends with a mock struggle in which one man emerges the victor.

Gasing, or top spinning, is another popular pastime. The *gasing* is a disc-shaped piece of hardwood with a steel spike through the centre. The game requires strength, considerable dexterity and very precise timing. A length of cord is wrapped tightly around the disc, which is used to launch it, rather like a yoyo, but in this case the disc does not come back. The player aims his disc at a specially built 'landing pad', in the form of a low, flat-topped mound, where his partner waits to scoop the spinning *gasing* off the ground with a thin wooden bat. This part of the game can be quite dangerous, as the top is thrown at great speed and does not always land on the target. Spectators are kept back to avoid injury from the ones that get away. The top is then mounted on a small wooden post and left to spin away. An expert top spinner can make a *gasing* spin for up to two hours. Local tales tell of tops spinning for as long as twenty-four hours, even longer if a spirit enters it, but that is hardly fair play! In addition to the spinning contest, where the top that out-spins the others is the winner, there is the striking match, a more aggressive encounter, in which each team tries to strike and topple the spinning tops of the opposition. The *orang asli* have their own mystical beliefs about *gasing*. They think that dead *bomohs* enjoy the odd game or two in heaven. Lightning is said to be the flashes of the cords as they set the tops spinning, while the sound of them spinning reaches human ears as thunder.

The skills of the Kelantanese are not just confined to musical and sporting pursuits. The kingdom also boasts many highly skilled craftsmen producing a wide variety of wares, from *batik* and leather puppets to kites and silver trinkets. Silver, along with gold, has played a recurrent and symbolic role in the history of Kelantan. The Siamese were a thorn in the side of the kingdom for a great deal longer than the lifetime of Puteri Saadong. Kelantan came to acknowledge the overall authority of Thailand and every three years sent a famous tribute, the *bunga mas dan perak,* or 'the gold and silver flowers', to Bangkok as a token of the kingdom's vassal status. The *bunga mas* consisted of two small trees, about a metre high and fashioned out of gold and silver. These works of art required meticulous craftsmanship and took at least six months to complete. According to one eyewitness, each *bunga mas* was a faithful replica of the real thing, even including birds perched in the branches of the trees. The leaves were fashioned out of sheets of thinly beaten gold and silver foil, and then punched with a vein-like pattern.

The techniques used in the fashioning of the *bunga mas* can still be seen today in Kelantan's exquisite silverware. This is one of several cottage industries to be found in the state. The most popular outlets for the purchase of silver goods, including tea sets, trays, bowls, ashtrays, cutlery and jewellery, are the **silversmiths** along Jalan Sultanah Zainab in Kota Bharu. These shops are supplied by a dwindling number of craftsmen working at home. There are also some in-house workers and no visit to the shops is complete without watching them display their skills, although the workshops hardly inspire confidence. There is no air-conditioning and plenty of heat and dust, while the tools and machinery look as though they date from before the industrial revolution. Yet the craftsmen make light of any difficulties and create masterpieces of design and intricacy. It is sad to reflect that these gifted men are among the last of a dying breed. Too many are getting on in years and they are not being replaced. Just as young Malays are turning their backs on the countryside, so they also show little interest in these ancient crafts, preferring to work for the government or in a factory .

A fine replica of the *bunga mas* can be seen on display at the **State Museum**, located on Jalan Hospital in Kota Bharu.

Opposite: *The replica of the bunga mas on display at the State Museum in Kota Bharu.* ***Below:*** *The traditional Kelantanese gates and pillars at the heart of the Cultural Zone in Kota Bharu.*

The origins of this unique form of tribute and its precise significance are far from clear. The practice continued until the British assumed control of Kelantan, Terengganu and Kedah under the terms of the Treaty of Bangkok in 1909. The *bunga mas* was sent for the last time in that year, though the recipient was not the Thai king in Bangkok but the British monarch, Edward VII. The British failed in 1909 to bring all the northern Malay kingdoms under their colonial umbrella. The Siamese steadfastly refused to give up Patani, which has remained part of Thailand to the present day. One of the most important Malay kingdoms was thus severed from the Malay world.

Kelantan's rich and varied past is commemorated in the **Cultural Zone** which has recently been created in the centre of Kota Bharu. This project, aimed at enhancing the tourist and educational facilities available in Kelantan, would not have been possible without the active involvement of the current ruler, Sultan Ismail Petra, who donated the two palaces now housing royal museums. Both palaces were originally built as wedding gifts, and it is fair to say that a touch of romanticism pervades the whole enterprise. The square in front of the Istana Balai Besar has taken on the appearance of a small fort, with the construction of an imposing pair of gates, built in traditional Kelantanese style, and five individual pillars all surmounted by replicas of the Koran, emphasising the role of Islam in the kingdom.

The northern side of the square is overlooked by the **Istana Jahar**, now restored to its original state and containing the Museum of Royal Traditions and Ceremonies. There are some interesting exhibits on childbirth and weddings, but it is the building itself which draws the attention of the visitor. Pride of place must go to the two ornate spiral staircases. There are also several beautifully carved wooden panels, while the first floor balcony is an excellent place to view the square and the **Istana Balai Besar**, constructed by Sultan Muhammad II (1837-1886) and used for investiture ceremonies and other formal functions. The Istana Jahar was built in 1887 during the reign of Sultan Ahmad (1886-1889) for his son, Long Kudin, who succeeded him as sultan. In front of the entrance is a large *jahar* tree, meaning 'flame of the forest', from which the palace takes its name.

Originally a brick extension to the Istana Jahar, the **Istana Batu** was built by Sultan Ismail (1920-1944) in 1939, as a wedding gift for his nephew, the future Sultan Yahya Petra (1960-1979). In 1969 it became the official residence of the Crown Prince, now Sultan Ismail Petra. He was the first to have the Blue Room decorated in blue. Opened to the public in 1991 as the Royal Museum, the Istana Batu is small and intimate, with a cosy, lived in feel to it. Whether in the Blue Room, the Yellow Room or the fine dining room, the Istana Batu brings the visitor as close as

possible to royal family life. Nearby in Jalan Hilir Kota is the **Handicraft Village and Craft Museum**. Constructed entirely in wood, the village resembles a typical Malay *kampung* and sells a range of handicrafts.

Kota Bharu became the capital in the reign of Sultan Muhammad II due to the frequency with which the Kelantan River broke its banks at Pulau Saba, the former capital. Flooding remains a threat today and a boat trip along the river will reveal mile after mile of heavy boulders protecting the *kampungs* which line the southern bank. In the late 18th century a Chinese merchant, Hsieh Ching-kao, left a vivid account of life at the court of Long Yunus (1763-1798), the founder of the present royal dynasty. He was particularly fascinated by the various ordeals carried out at the Kelantanese court, which have some similarities with the trials endured by witches in Europe at that time. If a case was difficult to decide, the king ordered an ordeal by water. Both sides in the dispute found a young boy and brought him to the river. The two boys grasped the end of a bamboo pole and sank beneath the surface. The one that stayed under the longest was judged to represent the successful party in the case. For more serious matters, a long piece of iron was put in a cauldron of boiling oil. The plaintiff and defendant were then ordered by the king to pull it out. The innocent party would supposedly retrieve the bar without injury, while the guilty one was scarred for life. With some relief, Hsieh reported that most cases were usually settled long before matters came to the ordeal by boiling oil.

Much to Hsieh's surprise, the Kelantanese did not eat with chopsticks, but used their right hands. This is a common practice amongst the Malays and Indians throughout Malaysia. Hsieh also noted that to offer food to guests with the left hand was a sign of extreme disrespect. The left hand is never used for eating,

Opposite: *A typical wakaf in the Kelantanese countryside.* ***Above:*** *The dining room in the Istana Batu.*

though the explanation for this is less to do with etiquette and more to do with the basic aspects of life!

A chief concern for Long Yunus and all his successors up to 1909 was the relationship with Thailand. The days of the *bunga mas* now seem a long time ago, but the historic links are preserved by the presence of a small Thai population living in Kelantan. They are mainly to be found in and around **Tumpat**, a town famed for its boatbuilders. Tumpat is not far from the border crossing at **Pengkalan Kubor**, where a ferry service takes passengers across the river to Thailand. This is a good place simply to stand and watch the busy river scene. Long-tailed speedboats zip back and forth, dodging in and out of the fishing and cargo boats. It might not be the Causeway at Johor Bahru, but it is no less interesting and a great deal more frenzied.

The roads from Kota Bharu to the border wind through verdant *padi* and tobacco fields. Along the way wooden shelters dot the countryside. These are *wakafs*, or public shelters, which provide local villagers and travellers with a place to meet and rest. There is often a nearby well for drinking and washing. Some *wakafs* are simple ramshackle affairs, while others are quite smart, incorporating a tiered roof structure, thought to have been inspired by the architecture of Siamese temples. The *wakaf* probably originated from Patani over a hundred years ago. The oldest in Malaysia is believed to be the **Wakaf Tok Haji Latif** at the village of Kampung Bunut Sarang Burung, near Tumpat.

Most of the Thais living in Kelantan have remained Buddhists, as is shown by the number of Thai temples in the area. Two very beautiful, if very different, temples deserve a visit. **Wat Phothivihan** near Cabang Empat is the better known of the two temples, with its huge reclining Buddha, the largest in the country, measuring some forty metres in length. Around the base is a series of colourful reliefs depicting the life of the Lord Buddha, or the 'Enlightened One' as the title means. Wat Phothivihan has a delightful setting,

providing a perfect place for prayer and meditation.

Wat Uttamaram is more off the beaten track, being located down a narrow lane, not far from Repek. The temple is decorated, indeed covered, in animals, most in the form of statues and paintings, though a few of the real variety are also to be found. Cattle graze in the open space in front of temple, and from time to time wander into the grounds. For a moment you do a 'double take', as a bemused 'real' cow stands next to a statue in its own image. Fearsome naga serpents stare out from the foot of the stairways leading up to the temple, while green dragons wrap themselves around the pillars at the top. Just for good measure snarling tigers, each exhibiting an impressive set of fangs, protect the stairs themselves. Stone they may be, but they still look intimidating.The temple also shows Hindu influences, one gateway being adorned with Garuda, the mighty eagle of Vishnu.

The centuries of contact between the Siamese and Malaysia's northern kingdoms led to the emergence of a distinctive Malay culture, particularly in Kelantan. The Thai contribution can be seen in the local dialect and several art forms. The Kelantanese dialect is quite different from that heard in the south, or even in the centre of the country. People from Kuala Lumpur tell you that they sometimes find it hard to understand the dialect, so you can imagine the uphill struggle for visitors armed with a simple tourist's guide to the national language. Fortunately, English is spoken in the main towns and it is amazing what sign language can achieve.

The noted 19th-century traveller Munshi Abdullah visited Kelantan, and found some of the traditional forms of entertainment very different from those performed elsewhere in the Malay Peninsula. *Menora* is the Siamese name

Opposite: *The reclining Buddha surrounded by the reliefs depicting the life of the Lord Buddha at Wat Phothivihan.*

Below: *Some of the statues and paintings which adorn Wat Uttamaram.*

for an ancient form of drama found only in southern Thailand and Kelantan, and thought to have been first performed in the kingdom in the 19th century. Men play the female parts and, on both sides of the border, the performers are usually Thais, with the dialogue in Malay. The characters often wear grotesque masks to act out the drama, which usually revolves around tales of princely adventures. *Menora* bears a superficial similarity to the dance drama of *mak yong,* which originated in Cambodia, and was later introduced into the Malay court of Patani, from where it spread southwards into Kelantan. *Mak yong* was at first a royal entertainment, performed by palace staff, with most of the characters being played by women. There is a recognised story line to follow, but no written text, so each performance is slightly different. Performers have the chance to show off their skills at improvisation, coming up with their own spontaneous dialogue.

Kelantan is probably best known for *wayang kulit,* or the shadow play. This ancient art form employs the principles of light and shadow to bring its characters to life. The history of *wayang kulit* is as shadowy as its puppets and there has been considerable dispute over the play's origins, though most believe they lie in Java. The basic techniques were known in China as early as the 3rd century, when a monk projected the image of the emperor's favourite concubine on to a cloth screen. *Wayang kulit* probably came to Kelantan from Patani and was certainly known in the time of Long Yunus. All the tales and most of the characters depicted in *wayang kulit* are from the great Hindu epic, the *Ramayana.* This centres on the heroic, or not so heroic, figure of Prince Rama, as each *tok dalang,* the master of the play, presents his own distinctive version. Prince Rama is often portrayed as a petulant, amorous, even effeminate figure, but in the end he always emerges triumphant, overcoming the various villains of the piece. Over the years Malay audiences have also become accustomed to the introduction of local characters, such as the comic duo Pak

Dogol and Wak Long.

Pak Dogol is a rustic character, but an important one, possessing considerable influence in the countryside. He has a closely shaven head, a prominent high-bridged nose, a long upper lip and a small, firm chin. Above the waist he is naked, his large belly flopping over the long, baggy trousers which he wears. He carries a *parang,* or woodcutter's knife. His boon companion and foil is the grotesque duck-nosed Wak Long, a mischievous busybody who knows all the local gossip.

Behind the scenes, the *tok dalang* performs a truly awesome juggling act. *Wayang kulit* is really the ultimate in one man shows and the *tok dalang,* the master of numerous theatrical trades, its star. His skilful hands move the many puppets around the screen, while at the same time he acts out all the parts from memory, using different voices to bring the characters to life, in addition to directing the accompanying orchestra. The puppets are usually crafted from dried cow hide or goat skin and, although they appear as black shadows on the stage, they are intricately detailed, painted in oils, and fashioned in a grotesque style. The Thai influence can be seen in the upturned, curved fingers, the costumes and the pinnacled head-dresses. The shadows of these other world figures are cast on a white cotton screen using a lamp. The setting of the theatre is designed to add to the mystique of the play. The *tok dalang* and the orchestra are hidden behind the screen and, in the darkness, the eye is drawn to the light source in the middle of the screen and the heroes and villains gliding gracefully across it.

Wayang kulit has been delighting audiences throughout the Malay Peninsula

Opposite: *Dark and threatening storm clouds can appear as if from nowhere along the east coast.* ***Below:*** *Some of the characters, including Pak Dogol and Wak Long (both on the right), in wayang kulit, or the shadow play, one of the great Kelantanese art forms.*

for well over a hundred years, but times have changed. Unrelenting competition from television and the cinema has taken away much of the audience for *wayang kulit* and the other traditional forms of entertainment, leaving them largely dependent on tourism for their future. The position of *menora* and *mak yong* looks particularly bleak, as the ruling Pan Malaysian Islamic Party (PAS) in Kelantan has banned performances of both dance dramas on religious grounds. The PAS government also disapproves of certain features of *wayang kulit,* and only allows performances in the state for tourists. Perhaps an even greater problem facing *wayang kulit* and the dance dramas is the familiar one for many traditional arts and crafts throughout the country. Malay youngsters show little interest in learning these ancient skills and the number of performers is declining rapidly.

Islam has undoubtedly had a profound influence on Kelantan. A hundred years ago, small-scale sea and river fishing and *padi* farming continued to dominate the economic life of Kelantan, at a time when other states in the Malay Peninsula were experiencing far reaching changes due to the tin and rubber industries. Kelantan remains much the same today, but progress in this part of the country is measured less by economic development than by the standards of an Islamic state, where faith, self-discipline and learning count for so much. For instance, in the field of education, the *pondok* schools in Kelantan have always provided a powerful forum for the spread of Islamic and Malay values. *Pondok,* or hut, schools were originally boarding schools with a difference. Wishing to study under a particular religious teacher, the pupils would go to wherever the teacher happened to be based, erect their own huts and start attending his classes.

One of the most famous Kelantanese religious teachers was Tok Kenali. Born in a village near Kota Bharu in 1868, he went to study in Mecca, returning to Kelantan in 1908 when he began to teach. He quickly established a reputation as a gifted teacher

and at one time had as many as three hundred pupils. He also taught at the **Masjid Muhammadi** overlooking Merdeka Square in the centre of Kota Bharu, adding to the fame of the mosque as a centre of Islamic studies. It became known as the *Serambi Mekah,* or the Verandah of Mecca.

Kelantan is also home to what is thought to be the oldest mosque in Malaysia. The **Masjid Kampung Laut** was originally built some two miles downstream from Kota Bharu but, during the great flood of 1966, the Kelantan River rose to the level of the roof and left the mosque very badly damaged. Four years later the remains were moved to the current site at Nilam Puri, where the mosque was reconstructed, using the original materials wherever possible. The mosque is thought to have been originally built by a group of Muslim missionaries, who landed in Kelantan on their way to Java.

Kota Bharu is an excellent base for exploring the surrounding countryside. There are now opportunities for visitors to stay two or three nights in a Malay *kampung,* experiencing the simple lifestyle of a family in a village like **Kampung Morak**. Here they might stay with *'Pakcik',* or 'Uncle', Yusof Mamad, famed local *wayang kulit* puppet maker, *silat* instructor and musician. He has lived all his life in the village and says of his new charges, 'I treat my guests as if they were my own children and am always pleased to have them in my own house. They sample all of the local customs.'

Many visitors to Kelantan head for the beaches. The most famous is **Pantai Cinta Berahi**, or the Beach of Passionate Love, some 10 km along Route D1 from Kota Bharu. The road passes through several *kampungs* en route to the beach. Along the way there are a number of local cottage industries. One of these is housed in an imposing white Spanish-style building,

Opposite: *The tok dalang is the master of all ceremonies in wayang kulit.* ***Below:*** *Haji Ismail Jusoh and his spectacular kites.*

complete with ornate balconies overflowing with flowers. This is where the late Che Minah Haji Osman used to produce her intricate and beautiful *kain songket* designs. A renowned expert, she learned the craft from her mother and aunt. The family tradition has been maintained by her daughter. The showroom sells a range of silk and cotton *kain songket* designs. Although Cik Siti Wan Kembang favoured *kain songket* woven with gold threads, silver is now a popular alternative. The intricate designs are woven in the workroom by women sitting at traditional two-paddle floor looms.

Along the same road is the business of another famed Kelantanese craftsman, Haji Ismail Jusoh. His skill lies in kite making. He has built up a reputation as Kelantan's best and enjoys royal patronage. Kite flying is a long established pastime found in many parts of the world. A hundred years ago kite flying was popular all over the Malay Peninsula, but today it is largely confined to Kelantan and Terengganu, where competitions are held after the *padi* harvest. A fascinating assortment of shapes and designs exist. The most popular shape is the *wau bulan,* or moon kite, so named because the tailpiece resembles a crescent. This has been adopted by Malaysian Airline Systems (MAS) as its logo. The ornamental kites are very large, even taller than the men who fly them, measuring approximately 1.8 metres (6 ft) across the wing and 2.1 metres (7 ft) from top to tail. The frame is made from bamboo, which is strong, light and flexible. The kites are beautifully decorated with brightly coloured paper. The weight and balance must be carefully calculated, as a wrong measurement will prevent the giant kites from ever leaving the ground. A *mengkuang* string is often stretched across the frame, which when airborne, emits a humming noise as it vibrates in the wind.

Another popular spot on the coast of Kelantan is **Pantai Dasar Sabak**, a quiet stretch of beach fringed with casuarina trees. A solitary pillbox, which children happily clamber over today, is the only reminder of the beach's more sinister past.

It was here that the Japanese first landed in British Malaya at 12.25 am on the night of 8th December 1941, signalling the start of the Second World War in the Far East. The Japanese attack on the American Pacific Fleet at Pearl Harbor began 95 minutes later at 8 am on 7th December. The discrepancy in the times and dates is of course explained by the 18 hour time difference between Malaysia and Hawaii. Japanese veterans of the campaign in Kelantan donated the funds for the **clock tower** in Kota Bharu, to symbolise their hopes for continued peace in the region.

A little further along the coast from Pantai Dasar Sabak is the fishing village of **Kampung Sabak**. At dawn the local fishermen go out to sea in their boats, returning later the same day. They use the traditional brightly painted *bangau* boats. *Bangau* is the Malay name for the snow-white egret, a frequent sight in these parts, often perched cheekily on the backs of water buffalo grazing in the *padi* fields. The name was adopted for this type of fishing boat because the *bangau* was the inspiration for the carved, colourfully painted figurehead forming the spar holder attached to the bow of the vessel. In fact *bangaus* rarely fly over the sea, though they do have a liking for fish. As the boats come in at Kampung Sabak with the daily catch, the local children gather round excitedly. The boats are hauled out of the water by their brawny crews and are met on the beach by the women and the older men whose fishing days have passed. Once the catch is landed, the women take over. The fish are sorted out and fish sales start there and then with some lively haggling. Cik Siti Wan Kembang and Puteri Saadong would have been proud of them.

Opposite: *The Masjid Kampung Laut at Nilam Puri.* ***Above:*** *The colourfully painted bangau boats pulled up on the beach at Kampung Sabak.*

TERENGGANU
SOUTH CHINA SEA
P. PERHENTIAN KECIL
P. PERHENTIAN BESAR
PULAU REDANG
P. PINANG
KUALA BESUT
KG. RAJA
84
JERTIH
KG. BETING LINTANG
3
S. Besut
KG. PENAREK
KG. KERUAK
KG. BULOH
KG. MERANG
3
3
KUALA TERENGGANU
PULAU KAPAS
MARANG
S. Terengganu
WAKAF TAPAI
AJIL
Tasik Kenyir
14
3
KELANTAN
TAMAN NEGARA
S. Berang
RANTAU ABANG
DUNGUN
S. Paka
PAKA
KERTEH
PAHANG
14
KEMASIK
S. Kemaman
KIJAL
3
KG. AYER PUTEH
KG. K. KEMAMAN
CHUKAI
S. Cherul
KEY
3
MAJOR ROADS
SECONDARY ROADS
AIRPORT
STATE BOUNDARIES
BOUNDARY OF TAMAN NEGARA
1 KAMPUNG BULOH
2 EMPANGAN KENYIR
3 SEKAYU WATERFALLS
4 LEATHERBACK TURTLES
N
0
10
20 km

TERENGGANU

A Garden of Eden

Situated in the heart of the east coast, Terengganu is a state of unspoilt natural beauty. The stunning coastline, stretching for over 200 km, is famous for its long sandy beaches, framed by swaying palm trees and washed by the crystal clear warm waters of the South China Sea. In the picturesque fishing villages which dot the coastline, life carries on at an unhurried, relaxed pace. It is little wonder that the magnificent leatherback turtle, the world's largest turtle, has chosen this idyllic setting as one of its few nesting sites.

For centuries Terengganu saw little change. The economy, like that of Kelantan to the north, was dependent upon fishing and *padi* farming until offshore deposits of oil and gas were discovered in the 1970s. Almost overnight, the state capital of Kuala Terengganu was transformed from a sleepy fishing port into a busy modern town, with the appearance of high-rise buildings, smart new bridges and modern roads. The centre of the oil industry is in fact to be found to the south at **Kerteh**, over 100 km down Route 3, past Dungun and the charming fishing village of **Paka** with its blue domed mosque. The Petronas Refinery Complex comes as a rude awakening to any unsuspecting motorist enjoying the scenic beauty of the coastline, but it is confined to a relatively small area. Oil is now Malaysia's major export earner and, due to its low sulphur content, is in great demand from pollution conscious nations. As early as 1980 oil exports had outstripped those of the long dominant rubber industry.

The riches of the South China Sea have always been a vital element in the livelihood of the people of Terengganu. Chinese sources show that, from at least the 5th century, tortoiseshell and cowries were being exported from these shores, and as the markets in China developed, other sea products also found their way north. These included sea slugs, which were used as an ingredient in Chinese soups and medicines. The *orang laut* made their living by collecting these shells and small creatures from the seabed. Their diving skills and intimate knowledge of the local waters won them many admirers, including one 12th-century Chinese writer who referred to the Malays as that 'variety of wild men from near the sea who can live in water without closing their eyes'.

Some of the old skills are still used today in Terengganu by the local fishermen. Possibly the most scenic, and certainly the most photographed, of the many fishing villages is **Marang**, only 15 km to the south of Kuala Terengganu, but a world away in terms of atmosphere and lifestyle. Its palm-fringed lagoon faces Pulau Kapas, Terengganu's most accessible island, just thirty minutes away from Marang by boat. Most people see Marang during the day, but for those prepared to brave an early morning call, dawn at around 7 am is an experience in itself, as the sun rises in all its glory behind the island.

A major part of the village's livelihood comes from catching *sotong*, or

State crest: *The sword, kris and mace symbolise the authority of the state. The book on the right represents the Koran, while the one on the left is a book of law. The yellow stole symbolises Malay royalty.*

Pages 204-205: *Dawn over a Terengganu fishing village.*

squid. Successive generations of Marang men have gone squid fishing in the waters around Pulau Kapas, though in recent times there have been major changes in their boats and equipment. They originally put to sea in traditional fishing boats, similar to those still used at Kampung Sabak in Kelantan, but these have now given way to modern, broad-beamed vessels, powered by diesel engines. Squid fishing is a nocturnal activity and during the squid season, which lasts from April to September, a string of lights, twinkling like some new constellation of stars, can be seen around Pulau Kapas. These lights are the key to squid fishing. Powered by large generators, the lights are hung out over the side of the boats, simulating daylight to the unsuspecting squid below. In minutes they are swarming up in their hundreds from the depths. A simple multi-hooked fishing line does the job of catching them. Each hook has a few strands of thread attached to it, which sparkle in the bright light, attracting the squid.

Many other fish are caught in the waters off Terengganu, including *aya* (tunny fish), *belanak* (mullet), *kerisi* (sea bream) and *pari* (skate). The fishing grounds are divided into *unjangs*, or fish houses. These can be identified by bamboo poles sticking out of the water. Below the surface clusters of coconut fronds are attached to the poles, which are designed to attract passing shoals of fish. In that respect the *unjang* really is a fish house. The fish appear to be attracted by the plankton and other small marine creatures which gather there. Each fish house is owned by an individual fisherman, although fishing at another *unjang* is a common occurrence. There is an enviable spirit of cooperation between the local fishermen, if one laced with the sense of competition that is part and parcel of fishing everywhere. The approach amongst Marang men is fairly simple. If your fish house is not producing decent catches, then try somebody else's! The traditional method of gauging the number of fish in the *unjang* is for a member of the crew to dive over the side and 'listen' for the sound of the fish at a depth of some two to three metres. While previous generations of fishermen believed implicitly in this human form of sonar, their counterparts of today often employ modern technology to do the job for them.

Many of the old fishing superstitions in Terengganu have sadly disappeared. The wearing of shoes on board used to be strictly forbidden, the fishermen believing that it brought bad luck, poor catches, or even worse. Today the young fishermen seem to wear anything from sports trainers to flip-flops. Hindu spirits were once invoked before a fishing trip, usually by readings or chants, in order to bring good luck, but the practice has now largely ceased. This was perhaps inevitable, given the fact that most of the fishermen in Terengganu are Muslims.

It is always a busy and exciting time

as the fish are landed, graded and weighed. Most of the catch in Terengganu is destined for Kuala Lumpur and Singapore. The latter was the major market for fish from these waters as early as 1895 when the British official Hugh Clifford visited the state. Today the bulk of the fish are refrigerated and transported by road, but in Clifford's day the catch was laid out to dry in the sun before being taken south by cart or boat. Some squid are still found drying on racks in and around Marang. Early in the morning women can be seen by the jetty cutting off the heads and tentacles of the squid and removing the ink sacs. Their young sons then wash the squid in the harbour and lay them out on the racks. It is easy to see why Clifford thought the local people in Terengganu 'among the most industrious Malays in the peninsula'.

Marang is a tight-knit community, where everybody knows everybody else. The men are tough, fishing being a far from easy occupation, but they always seem to be laughing and joking. The old-timers sadly tell you that it is a job for young men and the crews on the boats testify to this. Despite the advances in marine technology, the fishermen of Marang still rely on some of the old *orang laut* skills. They know intimately the local sand bars and currents, and can read weather with remarkable accuracy. This is essential as the weather can change with startling speed on the east coast. Tropical storms, unleashing gale-force winds, torrential rain and mountainous seas, often appear with little or no warning...that is to the layman. The locals can detect a storm well before the tell-tale heavy clouds close in, from the appearance of the sea and the murmur and feel of the wind. Their advice in such a situation is simple and to the point. Get into port as quickly as possible.

Any visitor to Marang will quickly come to appreciate the principal features of life on Malaysia's east coast: the strength

Opposite: *Part of the Petronas Oil Refinery at Kerteh.* ***Below:*** *Fishing boats in the palm-fringed lagoon at Marang.*

of family ties, the industry of the people, their friendly, generous nature and, above all, the guiding light of Islam. This is never more apparent than during the fasting month of Ramadan, when Muslims abstain from drinking, eating and smoking during daylight hours. This display of self-discipline, which the Prophet Muhammad observed, is particularly testing in Malaysia's humid climate. Offices and shops tend to close early during the month, and the Malays adopt a relaxed and sensible approach to the day.

The climax of the day during Ramadan is *buka puasa,* or the breaking of fast, usually at around 7.20 pm, by which time the Malays have been without food and drink for over thirteen hours. The spirit of 'open house' prevails throughout the month, with friends and neighbours breaking fast and going to the mosque together. Most Malays end the daily fast by drinking or eating something sweet, to get their blood sugar level back up again. Special *buka puasa* buffets are laid on by the top hotels and restaurants throughout the country during the fasting month. For anyone with a sweet tooth they are a must. In Terengganu quiet descends at the time of breaking fast. Hardly anyone is about, and even Route 3 falls silent. Everybody is somewhere else eating and drinking.

The end of Ramadan is a time for festivities following the draining weeks of fasting. Towns and villages throughout the country are gaily decorated for Hari Raya Puasa, the celebration marking the completion of the fasting month and the first day of *Syawal,* the tenth month of the Muslim calendar. Like the Chinese calendar, the Muslim year is based on the lunar system. Unlike the Chinese, the Muslims do not compensate for the fact that the lunar year is eleven days shorter than the solar year by adding in an extra month every few years. Therefore Hari Raya Puasa, also known as Hari Raya Aidil Fitri, slips back every year and coincides with Chinese New Year about once every thirty years.

Hari Raya Puasa, like Ramadan, lasts for a month, although most of the festivities

are held in the first week. Malaysia is one of the few remaining Muslim countries which does not fix the date beforehand for the start of Hari Raya Puasa. Religious elders watch for the new moon from several vantage points around the country, and declare Hari Raya Puasa for the day following their first sighting of the thin silver crescent of the new moon - the symbol of Islam - in the night sky. The Keeper of the Royal Seal then makes the official announcement on television and radio. As there is always a degree of uncertainty about the date on which Hari Raya Puasa will start, invitations to the celebrations have to be worded somewhat vaguely.

Hari Raya Puasa is the time of the year when many Malays return to their villages, or *balik kampung,* to visit their families. Mothers and grandmothers in the villages take great pains to prepare the favourite dishes and delicacies for this annual family reunion. Early on the morning of Hari Raya Puasa the men attend prayers at the mosque, while the women stay behind to get ready for the visitors later in the day. The whole family gathers for a grand breakfast. The children ask for forgiveness from their parents and are given presents of money. The growing trend is to put the money in green packets, similar to the *ang pows* given during Chinese New Year. Many Malays also make a visit to the cemetery, where they pray for the souls of departed loved ones and sprinkle scented leaves and flowers on the graves as a mark of respect.

The highlight of Hari Raya Puasa for Malays throughout the country is 'open house', when they invite friends from all races and religions to their homes, to join in the celebrations and tuck into the delicious range of dishes specially prepared for the festivities. The most lavish are undoubtedly those hosted by the sultans at their *istanas*, and by the Prime Minister at

Opposite: *One of the more basic methods of catching fish in the waters around Malaysia is by casting a net in the shallows.* ***Below:*** *Sotong being laid out to dry near Marang.*

his official residence in Kuala Lumpur which always attracts a huge crowd. Anyone is welcome to come and a list of times and dates is published in the newspapers. Hari Raya Puasa is a time for eating and many Malays quickly regain the pounds they lost during Ramadan. If you are invited to several homes for 'open house', you need to pace yourself, as you are expected to eat and drink something at each.

The practice of 'open house' was first introduced by Tunku Abdul Rahman, who opened his house to the public during Hari Raya Puasa. Not only VIPs came to greet him '*Selamat Hari Raya*', but also ordinary people in large numbers. This uniquely Malaysian form of celebration quickly became established amongst all the ethnic groups in the country. The Chinese, Indian and European communities now hold 'open house' when they celebrate Chinese New Year, Deepavali and Christmas.

Ramadan is a purifying process for Muslims. The stomach is emptied so that the human spirit may be filled with piety and righteousness. They are also seeking to rise above earthly desires, loosen their worldly attachment and move closer to God. Patience and perseverance are developed and Muslims receive a valuable experience in adapting to difficult circumstances. The fasting month is one of the Five Pillars of Islam, the others being the profession of faith, the performance of prayers five times a day, the payment of an annual tithe to help the poor and undertaking the *Haj*. This is the pilgrimage to Mecca, which Muslims are expected to make at least once during their lifetime. For many this may be the only trip they ever take abroad.

Muslims are exposed to the faith from the day they are born. The first words a baby hears are the call to prayer and the profession of faith, the cornerstone of Islam: 'There is no God but Allah and Muhammad is the messenger of Allah'. All Muslims must obey the will of Allah, which was communicated to the Prophet Muhammad by the Angel Gabriel, and

written down in the Koran. A true book of wisdom, the Koran covers not just teachings on religious, spiritual and ethical matters, but also includes the disciplines of history, politics, law, economics and sociology. It describes Muslims as 'the nation of the middle course' and favours democratic decision-making.

Visitors to Malaysia will soon discover the five daily prayer times. The first is before daybreak when the voice of the *muazin* carries across the stillness of early morning from the local mosque's minaret, calling the faithful to prayer. Friday is the Muslim holy day and many Malaysian towns become congested at lunchtime as Malays hurry to their mosque for midday prayers. In Terengganu, Kelantan and Kedah, Thursday and Friday form the weekend, while the other states follow western convention, with Saturday and Sunday being the rest days.

Islamic teaching has laid down certain rules regarding dress. These relate to the *aurat*, parts of the body which should not be exposed in public. Women should cover all parts of the body except their face and hands, while men have to cover themselves between the navel and knees. Many Malay women, particularly in Terengganu and the other east coast states, wear the *baju kurung*, which consists of a full-length skirt and a coordinating long-sleeved overblouse. A head-dress called a mini-*telekung* is usually worn which leaves only the face exposed. This style of dress can be very elegant, particularly as Malay women tend to opt for bright vibrant colours.

The earliest evidence for the presence of Islam in the Malay Peninsula was literally unearthed in Terengganu just over a hundred years ago. The **Terengganu Stone** is the most famous treasure in the state and is the highlight of the exhibits at the **State Museum**, situated on Bukit Losong on the western outskirts of Kuala

Terengganu. The Stone dates from the year 702H of the Islamic calendar, or 1303. The Islamic calendar began in 622, the year of the *Hijrah*, when the Prophet Muhammad fled from Mecca to Medina. The fact that there are less than 622 years between 702H and 1303 is explained by the shorter period of the Islamic year.

Written in Arabic script, the inscriptions on the Terengganu Stone set out Muslim laws relating to debauchery, immorality and false witness, with a scale of punishment for the various offences. The Stone was discovered after heavy flooding in 1887, lying half buried on the banks of the River Tara just outside **Kampung Buloh**, near the town of Kuala Berang. A monument surmounted by a replica of the Stone has been erected at the spot where the original was discovered. It stands in a picturesque rural setting, surrounded by tobacco farms. Women can

Opposite: *Lightning strikes over the South China Sea off Kuala Terengganu.*
Above: *The Terengganu Stone.*

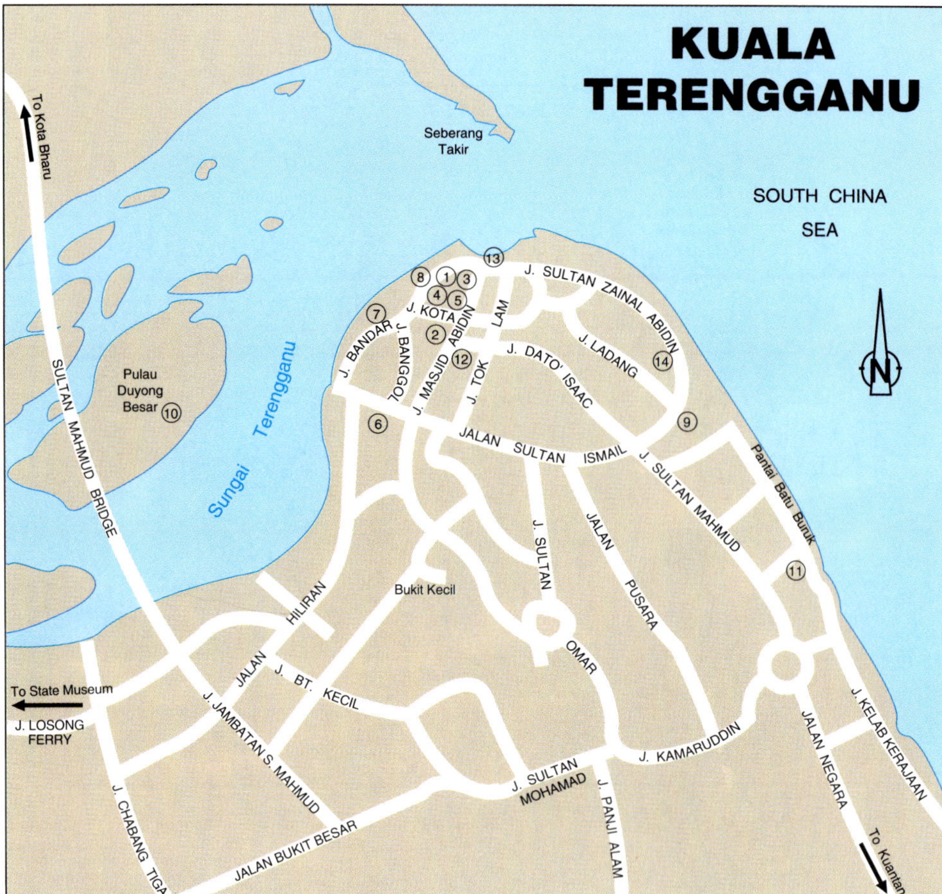

KEY

1. BUKIT PUTERI
2. MASJID ABIDIN
3. ISTANA MAZIAH
4. ISTANA KECIL
5. RUMAH TENGKU BENTARA RAJA
6. BUKIT KLEDANG
7. KAMPUNG CHINA
8. CENTRAL MARKET
9. KAMPUNG LADANG (BRASSWARE WORKSHOPS)
10. BOATBUILDERS
11. PANGKALAN BUDAYA (CULTURAL CENTRE)
12. LOCAL BUS STATION
13. EXPRESS BUS STATION
14. TOURIST INFORMATION CENTRE

often be seen returning from the fields balancing huge woven baskets of the crop on their heads. At the beginning of the 20th century, a local merchant found the Stone being used as a footstep at the mosque in Kampung Buloh. Given the importance of the Stone, it was later moved to the Muzium Negara in Kuala Lumpur, finally returning home to Kuala Terengganu in 1991.

Located at the mouth of the Terengganu River, **Kuala Terengganu** has retained much of its old charm, despite the recent development. The main centre of activity in the town is the bustling waterfront. There are frequent ferries across the river to Pulau Duyong Besar and the fishing village of **Seberang Takir**, which is well-known for its dried fish and prawn crackers. The village offers excellent views of the waterfront at Kuala Terengganu, with the old Chinese shophouses of

Kampung China built out on stilts over the river. **Pulau Duyong Besar** is famous for its boatbuilders, who work entirely from memory without using any plans. Their sturdy boats are renowned for being seaworthy, an essential quality in these waters. Most of the Marang fishing fleet was constructed by the highly skilled craftsmen at Pulau Duyong Besar.

Overlooking the waterfront is the town's **Central Market**. A lively atmosphere prevails in the wet market with all the fish laid out on stone slabs. Outside the wet market there is more animated haggling between traders and customers over the wide variety of fruit and vegetables on sale. Across the road is **Bukit Puteri**, or the Hill of the Princess. According to legend, the hill is named after a princess who lived there many centuries ago. She was of a generous disposition and happily lent her belongings, particularly her crockery, to the local people. Unfortunately, they abused her generosity. Bowls and plates were either not returned or given back damaged. The princess became so angry with the local people that she decided to have nothing more to do with them and moved to Besut.

Perched on the top of Bukit Puteri is a small fort, dating from the early 19th century and the days of Sultan Baginda Omar (1839-1876). In 1839 Baginda (the Conqueror) Omar overthrew his cousin Sultan Muhammad (1836-1839), by taking the fort at the third attempt. He was now sultan of Terengganu, as had been predicted when he was a boy. An astrologer had told him that he was destined to rule the kingdom, pointing to a mole on his chest as proof. There were plenty of rivals, and a few days later one of his elder brothers bit the mole off! Baginda Omar had no intention of being overthrown himself. He had the fort on Bukit Puteri rebuilt and lived there during the first years of his reign. The fort has a number of cannons and a large bell, used in the past to alert the inhabitants

Above: *The cannons are now purely for show on Bukit Puteri in Kuala Terengganu.*

of the town to major disturbances, such as an enemy attack, a fire or someone running amok. Probably the worst example in Terengganu of a man running amok came one dark night in 1886. Tok Kaya Bija Diraja killed his wife and most of his household, wounding the rest, before setting fire to his home. The fire quickly spread to the surrounding houses and, as the inhabitants rushed into the street, Tok Kaya set about them. By the time he was killed, he had murdered thirty people, while the fire accounted for over fifty houses.

After a few years Baginda Omar built himself a splendid palace, the Istana Hijau. Unfortunately, it was destroyed by fire in 1882. Baginda Omar also built the **Masjid Abidin**, named after Sultan Zainal Abidin II (1793-1808) who had constructed the first mosque on the site. Baginda Omar was a larger than life character. He made frequent tours of Kuala Terengganu and always carried sackfuls of coins which he distributed to the poor. In his later years he is reputed to have used a six foot iron cannon as a walking stick to help him from the palace steps to his royal litter. He is buried in the Masjid Abidin, his coffin being carried there in 1876 beneath four white umbrellas and to the accompaniment of a sixteen gun salute.

The grave of another famous figure in Terengganu history lies in far less auspicious surroundings on the top of **Bukit Kledang**, which overlooks Jalan Sultan Ismail in Kuala Terengganu. It belongs to Zainal Abidin I (c.1721-1733), the first sultan of Terengganu. According to tradition, he was placed on the throne by Nang Chayam, the queen of Patani, who had adopted him as her own son. Zainal Abidin later married Nang Chayam's cousin who lies beside him on the hill.

On the outskirts of Kuala Terengganu is the town's popular beach, **Pantai Batu Buruk**, which has fine views to the south and Pulau Kapas. In the early evening boys gather there to play football, while horses are often put through their paces along the beach. The hawker stalls on the esplanade add to the festive atmosphere.

Pantai Batu Buruk is also the location of the **Pangkalan Budaya**, Terengganu's cultural centre, which stages traditional games, dances and dramas during the weekend. At the northern end of the beach is Kuala Terengganu's top hotel, the Pantai Primula. Virtually in the shadow of the hotel is **Kampung Ladang**, the site of several brassware workshops. The trade is believed to have been brought to Terengganu by Chinese artisans from Funan. A splendid example of local craftsmanship can be seen at the State Museum in the form of a giant brass incense burner made in 1940.

Pantai Batu Buruk is at its liveliest during the Pantai Pesta in August. This beach festival was originally part of the celebrations held at the end of the *padi* harvesting season. There are various exhibitions, cultural performances, competitions and a food fest. One of the dances staged, the *ulik mayang,* originated in Terengganu and has been performed for generations in the local fishing villages. The dance centres on the attempts of a village *bomoh* to revive a fisherman who has nearly drowned during a storm at sea. The *bomoh* initially fails in his efforts and enlists the help of the seven princesses of the *mayang pinang* spirit. Their beauty has the desired effect and the fisherman finally comes round.

In northern Terengganu the winding country lanes reveal typical rustic *padi* scenes, with water buffaloes cooling themselves contentedly in their mud baths. Here visitors may come across women harvesting *pandanus* leaves. These are then cut into strips, dyed and woven with skilful hands into mats, hats and other colourful objects. There are two types of *pandanus* leaves. The *pandan* has a finer weave than the *mengkuang* and is more expensive. Conical-shaped *pandanus* hats are a frequent sight in the *padi* fields, giving the

Opposite: *The Chinese shophouses of Kampung China with the modern skyline of Kuala Terengganu behind.* ***Below:*** *A craftsman at work in one of the brassware workshops in Kuala Terengganu.*

wearer vital protection from the glaring heat of the sun.

Another cottage industry in Terengganu is *batik* production, and rows of brightly coloured *batik* cloth can sometimes be seen hanging out to dry in the rural areas. *Batik* is now produced throughout Malaysia, but the greatest experts are to be found in the *kampungs* of Terengganu. *Batik* involves the application of wax on cloth, usually silk or cotton. This is done in one of two ways, either by the block method or *canting*. In the block method strips of metal are fashioned into the required design and attached to hand blocks. These are then covered in molten wax, which is stamped on to the cloth. The waxed parts of the cloth do not take the colour when the fabric is immersed in a bath of the required dye. The wax is then removed by boiling the cloth. The process may be repeated several times to achieve the desired pattern and colour combination. In the *canting* method, a special wax applicator is used for the much finer art of drawing freehand designs and images. The colours are then added with a paint brush. The results can be quite startling in terms of colour, intricacy and design, and *batik* paintings have become a popular art form.

The production of *batik* in Malaysia is a relatively recent industry, certainly when compared to other arts and crafts practised in the country. It is thought to have been first produced in Indonesia, and was adopted by Malay craftsmen on the east coast early in the 20th century. An imaginative range of items is produced today using *batik,* including attractive vases and lampstands. Terengganu is most closely associated with the colourful *batik* sarong, popular for everyday wear amongst the local population and, more recently, worn as beachwear by growing numbers of tourists. The father of Terengganu *batik* is the late Haji Ali Ismail. Many of the craftsmen in the state acquired their skills from him, either directly, or indirectly through someone who had worked under him as an apprentice.

Terengganu also has several popular inland scenic attractions. The **Sekayu Waterfalls** on Route T115 in the west of the state are a favourite hideaway for locals and visitors alike, but pride of place must go to the freshwater **Tasik Kenyir**. An easy day trip from Kuala Terengganu, Tasik Kenyir is also to be found in the west of the state, lying 15 km from Kuala Berang at the end of Route T134. The lake is man-made, being part of a major hydroelectric project, completed in 1987 and covering an area of some 369 sq km. A Visitors' Centre is located on top of the massive rock-filled dam wall at **Empangan Kenyir**. From here there are fine views of the flooded valleys and the surrounding hills. Tasik Kenyir is a paradise for anglers, with large numbers of *toman* (murrel), *baung* (catfish), *sebarau* (carp) and many other fish thriving in its waters. Visitors can stay overnight on a houseboat and there are also facilities for canoeing and jungle trekking.

During the construction of Tasik Kenyir, the water level rose faster than anticipated due to heavy monsoon rains. The lower levels were quickly submerged and in some areas wildlife became trapped on the higher ground. Among the beleaguered animals was a group of wild elephants. A rescue mission, aptly named 'Operation Jumbo', was launched to save them. The elephants were tranquillized and taken by raft, with the help of tame elephants, to Taman Negara. The two week rescue operation was captured on film and can be seen at the park headquarters in Kuala Tahan. It is now possible to follow the elephants and enter Taman Negara from Terengganu.

Terengganu is probably best known for its stunning tropical islands, blessed with fine white sand, secluded rocky coves, crystal clear waters and beautiful coral gardens. It is the islands' abundant and brightly coloured coral reefs, teeming with marine life, which attract most visitors, whether for a rather leisurely spot of snorkelling or the more serious business of scuba diving. The main islands have been classified as marine parks in an effort to preserve their natural beauty.

Each island has its own individual characteristics. **Pulau Kapas** is the easiest to reach from the coast of Terengganu and has the most accessible coral. A five minute boat trip from the main island is **Pulau Gemia**, where the coral supports a vibrant fish life and lies a matter of feet from the water's edge. **Kuala Besut** in the north of Terengganu is the gateway to the **Perhentian Islands**, which are simply distinguished by the addition of the name Besar (big) for the larger one, and Kecil (small) for the other. The word *perhentian* means stopover and, according to the local inhabitants, the islands were

Opposite: *A batik worker plunges the batik cloth into the dye at a kampung workshop on the east coast.* ***Below:*** *The finished product.*

so-named because seafarers used to stop there for fresh water and a rest. Today visitors come for their own 'stopover', to swim, snorkel and dive, as well as trek through the islands' rain forests. Pulau Perhentian Kecil is home to an attractive fishing village, while most of the accommodation is across the narrow channel on Pulau Perhentian Besar.

The jewel in the coral crown off Terengganu's coast is undoubtedly **Pulau Redang** and its associated islets. The Redang archipelago is largely unspoilt, and more than lives up to the tourist literature. The white sand is so powder-fine and airy that it stays cool even in the heat of the day. The warm and inviting, beautifully clear aquamarine waters offer excellent visibility and perfect conditions for diving. In shallow areas, where the light casts patterns in the sand, you can even view the coral from the comfort of your boat.

A coral reef is a tropical shallow water ecosystem, requiring bright light, stable high salinities and temperatures between 22°C and 29°C for its establishment and growth. The reef supports many plants and animals, including the coral itself. Hard corals are the external limestone skeletons of tiny organisms called polyps. Over thousands of years the skeletons of innumerable polyps have built up into coral reefs, the largest in the world being the Great Barrier Reef in Australia. Besides the hard coral, a reef also contains soft coral. This has the external appearance of hard coral, but is soft to the touch. Soft coral is found in exposed parts of the reef, the flexible structure being ideally suited to withstanding wave action during storms and monsoons.

Redang and the other islands off the coast of Terengganu have an abundance of both hard and soft coral, presenting a multitude of colours. The richest and the most diverse coral at Redang is located in the reefs along the eastern side of the main island and around the eight smaller islets. The corals thrive on the oxygen, nitrogen and nutrients swept in by the waves of the South China Sea. Among the many attractions for divers are two large dome-shaped

DANIEL D'ORVILLE

colonies of coral called *porites*, which lie off the northern coast of Pulau Ling. The biggest is 10 metres in height.

Sadly, in some places there are beds of dead coral, which present a stark reminder of how fragile an ecosystem the coral reefs are. This is partly the result of blast fishing and damage from anchors before the area was given protected status. In the 1970s the coral was attacked by the deadly crown-of-thorns starfish, a voracious eater which feeds on the live coral polyps, leaving behind only the white skeletal remains. More recently, fresh water run-off and increased siltation resulting from development schemes have also adversely affected a number of the reefs.

Redang's reefs are home to thousands upon thousands of sponges, crustaceans, molluscs and fish. Brightly coloured butterfly fish, angel fish and parrot fish swim among the coral, while lobsters and crabs are often on view, crawling into any available nook and cranny. Sea anemones thrive, their tentacles waving in the current. Diving in and out of the poisonous tentacles are the clownfish, so-called because of the white markings across their face which resemble a clown's make-up. A chemical in the skin of the fish protects it from the sting of the tentacles. Where the bottom is sandy, sea slugs and cucumbers abound. Elsewhere among the coral lie the deadly giant clams, their jaw-like mantles, blue-tinted and beckoning, waiting for the next unsuspecting victim. The richness of life on the coral reefs draws a variety of predators. From deeper waters come fish such as snapper, grouper, barracuda and sharks. A few lucky divers have also encountered giant manta rays and the rare whale shark. It is huge but totally harmless, being attracted to Redang by the plankton-rich waters. Divers sometimes also come across a hawksbill turtle or a green turtle

Opposite: *Sunset over Pulau Perhentian Kecil.* ***Above:*** *The waters off the east coast are renowned for their colourful coral reefs and abundant fish life.*

on its way to the island's shores to nest.

The most famous turtles to visit Terengganu are those which come ashore on the beach at **Rantau Abang**, 56 km south of Kuala Terengganu. From May until September Rantau Abang is one of the handful of sites in the world where the leatherback turtle chooses to lay its eggs. An old Malay legend tells of a submerged rock resembling a turtle, which lies just offshore from the beach and is said to be the reason they are attracted here. A more likely explanation is that the beach has a deep water approach and heavy surf, enabling the turtles to crawl a shorter distance to nest.

Like all sea turtles, the leatherbacks have a history dating back to the age of the dinosaurs. They have not changed much since their prehistoric days, and still bear a very close resemblance to their 'distant' ancestors. As the name suggests, the leatherback has a smooth leathery shell, or carapace, rather than a hard bony one. This is marked by seven longitudinal ridges. They feed mainly on jellyfish. A nesting female can have a length of up to 2 metres and might easily weigh half a ton. The largest leatherback on record is an adult male that drowned off the coast of Wales after becoming entangled in a fishing net. This giant among giants weighed in at just under a ton and was 2.9 metres long. Although this is a hefty weight to carry around on land, the leatherbacks move with ease in the sea, their shape enabling them to travel rapidly across vast distances. The streamlined shell reduces water friction and the long flippers have good muscles to power them along. With these swimming aids, leatherbacks have been known to reach speeds of 10 km an hour, while studies of their migratory habits have reported turtles from Rantau Abang turning up as far away as Hawaii. The longest leatherback migration on record is 5,900 km. This long distance travel is related to their search for jellyfish, which drift with the ocean currents.

Tourists flock to Rantau Abang to see these huge reptiles, so graceful in the water, lumber slowly up the beach to find a nesting site. Only the females make this laborious excursion, laying their eggs along the same stretch of beach on which they began their life, and to which their offspring will one day return. Once the males go to sea, they never return to shore. Each female nests between five and nine times during the season and the peak months are June and July. After she has laid her last clutch of the season, she will not return to nest again for another two or three years.

Nesting usually takes place at night. As soon as darkness falls, the daily vigil begins as the locals scan the beach for turtles and the tell-tale flipper tracks. Tourists soon start arriving and settle down for what could be a long wait for a turtle to emerge from the blackness of the sea. Those staying at the nearby Tanjung Jara Hotel can

skip the wait by registering at reception. They will be called in their rooms as soon as a leatherback has been spotted. Word quickly gets around once a turtle is sighted. Watching the nesting process is one of nature's great spectacles. The turtle hauls herself up the beach to select a suitable site above the high tide mark. She digs a large depression in the sand with her back flippers, in which she lays her soft-shelled, cue-ball sized eggs. These usually number between 50 and 140. She then covers them with sand and returns to the South China Sea. The **Turtle Information Centre** at Rantau Abang has displays and a film show about these gentle giants and their brief sojourn on the beach to nest.

Turtles are extremely sensitive to noise and light. Observers are therefore asked to remain quiet, not to get too close to the turtles and not to use torches or flash photography. In the past these simple rules have all too often been ignored, turning the nesting process into a nightmare for the defenceless turtle. Chan Eng Heng and Liew Hock Chark are Malaysia's leading authorities on the leatherback. Based at the Fisheries and Marine Science Centre of Universiti Pertanian Malaysia, they have spearheaded a campaign to protect the leatherback and educate the public about the 'dos and don'ts' of turtle watching. They stress that turtles and tourists can coexist providing the rules are followed. Disturbing or harming the turtles is now a criminal offence, and enforcement officers from the Fisheries Department are mobilised on the beaches during the nesting season to ensure the rules are followed.

It is not only watching the turtles which has proved a problem in the past. Ever since people acquired a taste for turtle eggs, locals have been collecting them from the nest sites to sell. They are in demand for their alleged aphrodisiac and beautifying properties, although there is no scientific proof for either claim and their

Opposite: *A white-faced gibbon at the Sekayu Waterfalls.* ***Above:*** *The beautiful aquamarine waters around Pulau Redang.*

nutritional value is less than that of a chicken egg. This has undoubtedly been a major factor in the decline of Rantau Abang's leatherback population. In the 1950s there were around 11,000 nestings at Rantau Abang each year. Given their multiple nesting habits, this meant that some 2,000 leatherbacks visited the beach annually. By 1992 the number of nesting turtles recorded had dwindled to less than fifty. The leatherbacks also face threats at sea. Sometimes they get caught in fishing nets and drown because they cannot surface for air. Sea pollution is another obvious killer.

Fortunately, the eggs collected at Rantau Abang no longer end up on somebody's plate. The sale of eggs for consumption became illegal in 1988. A hatchery project has been established on the beach to help reverse the decline in leatherback numbers. The beach is divided into lots which are tendered to licensed egg collectors. The Fisheries Department buys the eggs from the licensees for the hatchery. With this system of management, the locals' livelihood does not suffer as a result of the conservation measures. The licensees are also authorised to collect a small entrance fee from visitors for watching the turtles nest on their beach lots. After being removed from the nest site, the eggs are labelled and reburied in the hatchery, an open-air and fenced-off area. Fifty to sixty days later, the baby giants start to emerge from the sand. After being counted, they are released close to the sea.

For those who are not fortunate enough to see the real thing at Rantau Abang, there is a concrete specimen of a fully grown leatherback mounted on one of the main roundabouts in Kuala Terengganu. Seasoned leatherback watchers have pointed out that the artist responsible for the replica did not carry out his research properly. He has endowed his creation with nine longitudinal carapace ridges, rather than nature's seven!

Below: *Terengganu is justifiably famous for its beautiful and deserted beaches, just waiting to be discovered.*

PAHANG

The Kingdom of Dreams

In December 1969 an old man suddenly appeared before the congregation at the mosque in Kampung Pulau Tawar near Jerantut, and claimed to be Mat Kilau, the legendary Malay warrior who had fought the British in Pahang at the end of the 19th century. Since the rebellion he said that he had lived the life of a fugitive in southern Thailand, Kelantan and Terengganu, only returning to his native Pahang in 1926. He had remained quiet about his identity until 1969, due to a vow he had taken before Sultan Abdullah of Pahang (1917-1932). It was a startling revelation which initially aroused little but scepticism. The Pahang Government set up a board of inquiry and, after extensive examinations, the old man's claims were upheld. Mat Kilau, probably the greatest Malay patriot, had returned from the grave.

Regarding his 'death', supposedly at the hands of Siamese soldiers, Mat Kilau explained that he had been seriously wounded. With a keen sense for his own survival, he had promptly played dead, apparently fooling the soldiers. They had later handed his 'body' to Sultan Muhammad IV of Kelantan (1890-1920) for burial. The Sultan had no personal grievance against him, but did not wish to antagonise the Siamese or the British. Therefore it was preferable for all concerned if Mat Kilau simply disappeared. The Sultan allowed him to escape, on the condition that he never revealed his identity. The same considerations led to Sultan Abdullah securing a similar promise from Mat Kilau in the 1920s. To allay any suspicions the Siamese or the British might have had, Sultan Muhammad arranged a burial for Mat Kilau at Bunut Payong in Kelantan, the coffin being weighted with the trunk of a banana tree.

The reappearance of Mat Kilau is a tale that is larger than life, and yet only too typical of the kingdom of Pahang. This is the big country. Pahang is the largest state in Peninsular Malaysia, contains the peninsula's highest mountain, Gunung Tahan, and has its longest river, the Pahang River. Tales of the beauty and wealth of Pahang

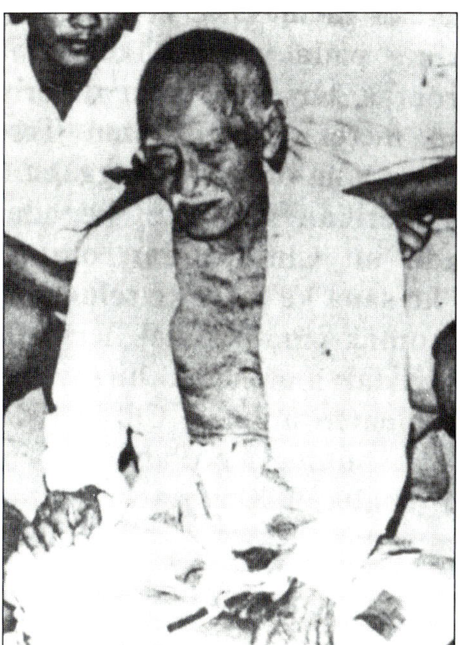

COURTESY OF MUZIUM NEGARA

State crest: *The head of the spear symbolises the ruler's sovereignty, and is in the shape of a coffee leaf in memory of Sultan Ahmad, who plotted the capture of Pekan over a cup of coffee. The crossed elephant tusks signify the authority of the sultan, and are a reminder of the close association in the past between Malay rulers and elephants, in particular their use as a royal mode of transport.* ***Left:*** *Mat Kilau in 1969.*

PAHANG
KELANTAN
G. TAHAN
(2,187 m)
TAMAN NEGARA
TERENGGANU
CAMERON HIGHLANDS
59
8
S.Tembeling
KUALA LIPIS
S. Jelai
KUALA TEMBELING
KAMPUNG CHERATING
14
3
BENTA
64
S. Lipis
PERAK
JERANTUT
8
S. Kuantan
BESERAH
98
KUANTAN
RAUB
FRASER'S HILL
S.Pahang
64
2
8
83
62
12
3
SOUTH CHINA SEA
BENTONG
2
2
MENTAKAB
TEMERLOH
S. Pahang
PEKAN
82
GENTING HIGHLANDS
2
Tasik Chini
SELANGOR
9
10
12
3
63
Tasik Bera
PULAU TIOMAN
11
S.Rompin
NEGERI SEMBILAN
KUALA ROMPIN
3
GUNUNG BESAR
(1,036 m)
S. Endau
JOHOR
N
0
20
40 km
KEY
2
MAJOR ROADS
SECONDARY ROADS
RAILWAY
AIRPORT / AIRSTRIP
BOUNDARY OF TAMAN NEGARA
STATE BOUNDARIES
1 KAMPUNG PULAU TAWAR
2 BIRTHPLACE OF TUN ABDUL RAZAK
3 TELUK CHEMPEDAK
4 ISTANA ABU BAKAR, SULTAN ABU BAKAR MUSEUM
5 PAHANG SILK WEAVING CENTRE, PULAU KELADI
6 SUNGAI LEMBING
7 GUA CHARAH
8 SUNGAI PANDAN WATERFALL
9 KAMPUNG TEMAI
10 KUALA TAHAN
11 KOTA GELANGGI
12 BUDU
13 ENDAU ROMPIN NATIONAL PARK

have been luring people for many centuries. Indeed one of the kingdom's natural resources is generally believed to be the origin of the name Pahang, which means tin in the Khmer language. Malay folklore tells a different story, attributing the name of the state and the Pahang River to a legendary *mahang* tree, which stood at the river's confluence with the River Pahang Tua.

The Pahang River runs through the heart of the kingdom. It is formed from two tributaries, the Jelai and Tembeling, flowing south to the area of Temerloh, where it swings eastwards in a great loop, before entering the South China Sea at Kuala Pahang. Powerful legends have been woven around the river, many of them saying that it led to a land full of gold. In the 16th century the Portuguese writer, d'Eredia, recounted the tale of a Pahang king who sent a piece of gold-stone, measuring some two and a half yards in length, to the Portuguese governor in Melaka. There has never been anything more attractive to man than gold and, over the centuries, dreams of untold wealth have sent men to every corner of the world in search of this most precious of metals. Unfortunately, Pahang's gold deposits around **Raub**, near the border with Selangor, were always limited and difficult to mine.

The tales of great riches were sustained by Pahang's remoteness. The Main Range, stretching north to south like a great wall, made land communications from the west coast states a very uncertain venture, but the lure of gold induced many to attempt the journey. In January 1827 a British merchant, Charles Grey, set out from Melaka in the hope of trading opium for gold. His timing was deliberate: the north-east monsoon would leave the rivers in flood and therefore easier to negotiate by boat. After a journey of seventeen days, involving the back-breaking work of hauling the boat and goods through the jungle and hour after interminable hour of paddling, Grey and his men finally reached the

Above: *The rain forest canopy.*

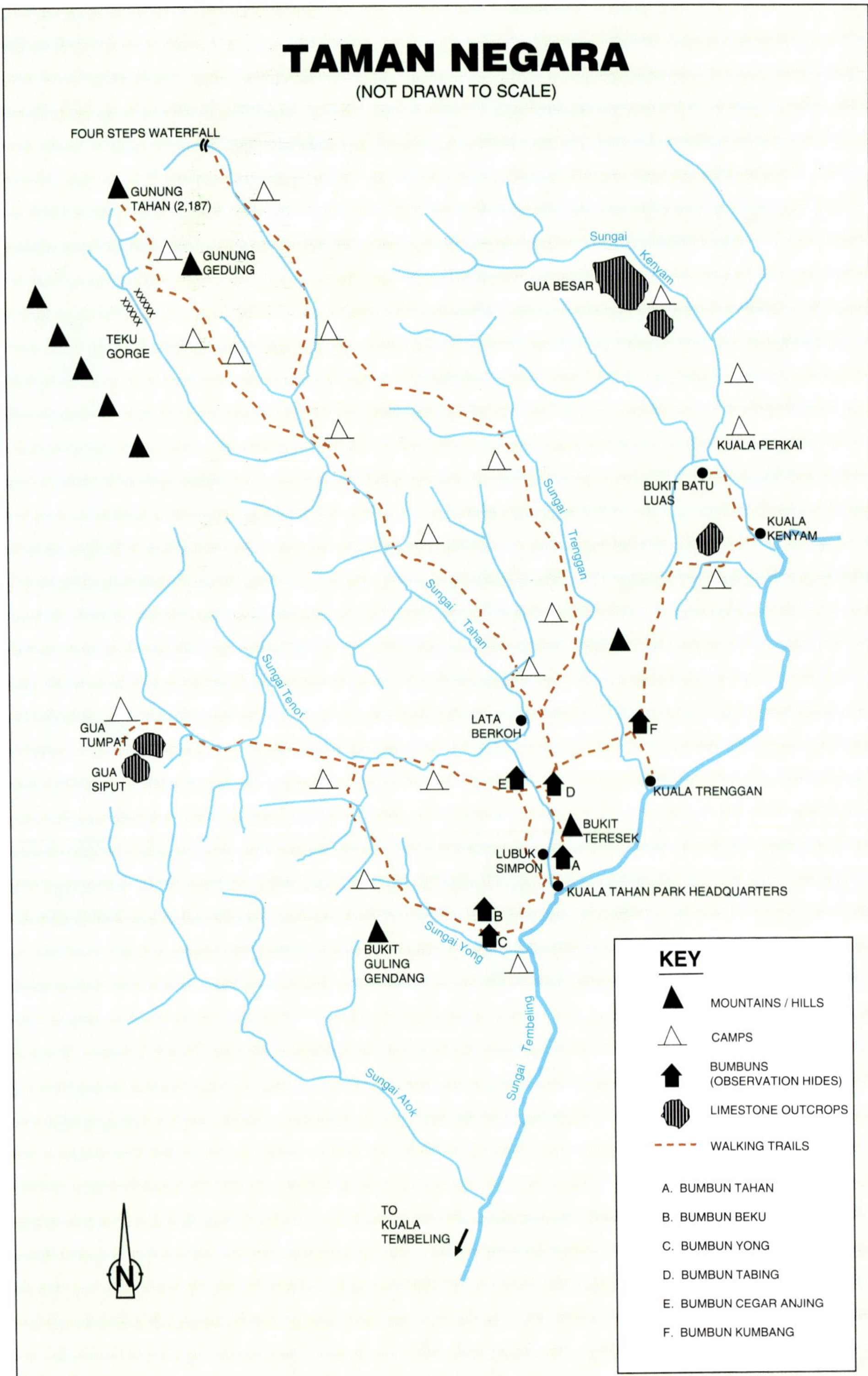
TAMAN NEGARA
(NOT DRAWN TO SCALE)
FOUR STEPS WATERFALL
GUNUNG TAHAN (2,187)
GUNUNG GEDUNG
TEKU GORGE
Sungai Kenyam
GUA BESAR
KUALA PERKAI
BUKIT BATU LUAS
KUALA KENYAM
Sungai Trenggan
Sungai Tahan
Sungai Tenor
GUA TUMPAT
GUA SIPUT
LATA BERKOH
E
D
F
KUALA TRENGGAN
BUKIT TERESEK
LUBUK SIMPON
A
KUALA TAHAN PARK HEADQUARTERS
B
C
Sungai Yong
BUKIT GULING GENDANG
Sungai Tembeling
Sungai Atok
TO KUALA TEMBELING
N
KEY
MOUNTAINS / HILLS
CAMPS
BUMBUNS (OBSERVATION HIDES)
LIMESTONE OUTCROPS
WALKING TRAILS
A. BUMBUN TAHAN
B. BUMBUN BEKU
C. BUMBUN YONG
D. BUMBUN TABING
E. BUMBUN CEGAR ANJING
F. BUMBUN KUMBANG

Pahang River.

That was as far as Grey got. The locals would not allow him to go any further, due to the distance to the gold mines, which they told him were another forty days paddling away, and the dangers for Europeans of travelling in that part of the country. Grey's hopes for Pahang had proved little more than a pipe-dream, though he was able to sell five chests of opium before setting off for home. Retracing their steps, Grey and his intrepid band battled against strong river currents and incessant rain. The journey took another three weeks, only to end in tragedy. Ten days after emerging from the jungle, Grey was dead from malaria.

Today there are two main roads, Routes 2 and 64, across the Main Range into Pahang. Route 64 leads to **Jerantut**, the stepping-off point for **Taman Negara**, Malaysia's oldest and largest national park, which covers over 4,000 sq km of the sort of country the ill-fated Grey and his men had to battle through. Appropriately enough, visitors can only reach the park headquarters at Kuala Tahan by river, though engines have now replaced paddle-power. The boats depart from the jetty at Kuala Tembeling, 16 km to the north of Jerantut, and take three to four hours to reach Kuala Tahan. Along the way water buffaloes are a common sight, enjoying a cooling dip in the river. Bright blue kingfishers can sometimes be seen perched on branches overhanging the river banks. Occasionally, an otter might even be spotted. If you happen to see what looks like a crocodile on the banks of the river, don't panic! These reptiles are in fact water monitor lizards, which grow up to two metres in length. Visitors can also fly to Taman Negara, though they still have to negotiate the last few kilometres to Kuala Tahan by boat.

Established in the late 1930s, Taman Negara includes land from three states, Pahang, Terengganu and Kelantan, with just over half lying in Pahang. The park contains both virgin lowland rain forest and mountain forest, and has fourteen river systems within its boundaries. Taman Negara is also home to the Batek people, one of the Negrito groups of the *orang asli*. They continue to lead a nomadic life, hunting and gathering food in the jungle, and their makeshift palm-thatched shelters can sometimes be seen by the rivers and along the forest trails.

The lowland rainforest is characterised by huge trees soaring to a height of over 70 metres, their crowns forming a leafy canopy which blocks out most of the sunlight. In the twilight world beneath, the trees support a variety of ferns, creepers, lianas and rattans. In some instances the trees have fallen victim to strangling figs. As the name suggests, the fig slowly strangles the host tree by forming a lattice-work of stems around the trunk. Due to the poor

Above: *One of the mighty rain forest trees in Taman Negara.*

light at ground level, the undergrowth in a lowland rain forest is not the impenetrable jungle often imagined. Dense undergrowth is usually the result of logging. Once the land is exposed to light, vines and other fast growing species spring up from the forest floor.

The park headquarters at **Kuala Tahan** is the starting-off point for all the activities in the park, and is also the site of the Taman Negara Resort, which offers a range of accommodation from a spot at the campsite to attractive wooden chalets. The activities include exploring the jungle trails, fishing, swimming, shooting rapids, mountain climbing and spending a night in one of the *bumbuns*, or observation hides. The *bumbuns* are small huts built on stilts. Five of the six *bumbuns* around Kuala Tahan overlook salt-licks in the lowland forest. These salt-licks occur naturally at places in the jungle where mineral salts are found on the surface. Animals, particularly the herbivores, visit the licks to supplement their mineral intake. The closest hide to Kuala Tahan is **Bumbun Tahan**, only a five minute walk away. Wild pigs and sambar and barking deer are frequent visitors here. Indeed the odd deer can sometimes be spotted outside the self-service restaurant at park headquarters on the look out for an easy meal.

All of the park's other *bumbuns* are equipped with beds and a toilet for overnight stays, as it is under cover of darkness that many of the animals visit the salt-licks. Providing there are several people staying at the *bumbun*, a rota system can be organised to ensure that someone is always on watch and everyone gets some sleep. If you are lucky, you may see a Malayan tapir, an unusual looking creature with a long nose and a black and white body. Elephants and *seladang* are occasionally spotted. Indeed one visitor at **Bumbun Kumbang** encountered an elephant rather unexpectedly, while on her way to the toilet! However, the closest most visitors are likely to get to such big game is their tracks or droppings.

One forest inhabitant which is only too keen to make your acquaintance is that infamous jungle vampire, the leech. Long trousers, together with insect repellent applied on shoes and socks, or better still jungle boots, will help keep these 'affectionate' creatures at bay. If one of the little suckers does get you, then salt or that old jungle movie favourite, a lighted cigarette, should get it off. The alternative is to let the leech drink its fill. Once it is bloated, it will happily drop off. It is worth remembering that although leeches have a rather gruesome reputation, their bites are not harmful.

One of the most popular, and shortest, jungle trails is to the top of **Bukit Teresek**, about an hour's walk from Kuala Tahan. The main lookout point offers panoramic views to the north and the lowland forests of the upper Tahan valley, stretching away in the distance to the range of mountains near the border with

Kelantan. On a clear day the table-topped summit of **Gunung Tahan** (2,187 metres), the highest mountain in Peninsular Malaysia, is visible. The view from Bukit Teresek is rather deceptive, as Gunung Tahan appears to be smaller than the surrounding mountains. Treks to Gunung Tahan can be arranged at the park headquarters. This is not a journey for the faint-hearted. The trail is over 60 km long and involves climbs totalling nearly 4,000 metres, several river crossings, some of them hazardous, and unending insects and leeches. At the same time the scenery is quite breathtaking and there is no more remote location in Peninsular Malaysia. The return trip takes eight or nine days, with another two added on if you wish to see the spectacular **Four Steps Waterfalls**, where the headwaters of the River Tahan plunge down the eastern side of the mountain.

Before this century the sea route to Pahang was far less risky than crossing the Main Range. Unfortunately, this left the country vulnerable to attack from the South China Sea. The early part of the 17th century was a particularly sad time for Pahang. The Acehnese from northern Sumatra overran the country, killing large numbers of the population and taking many of the survivors back to Aceh in chains. The Pahang river valley was laid waste and became the haunt of pirates. The ultimate beneficiary of the Acehnese onslaught was Johor, as Pahang became little more than a province of its powerful southern neighbour.

The relationship between Pahang and Johor waxed and waned over the centuries. It is perhaps best symbolised today by the **Endau Rompin National Park**, which straddles the border between the two states. Founded in 1989, the park covers an area of 800 sq km and consists of rugged low hills, covered by rain forest, and the River Endau and several of its tributaries. The highest point is Gunung Besar (1,036 metres).

Opposite: *A Batek man fishing on the Tembeling River in Taman Negara.*
Above: *A family of palm civet-cats.*

Accessible only from Johor, the park is difficult to reach and a four-wheel drive vehicle is essential. Some 5 km to the east of Kahang on Route 50, a laterite road heads north to the Bukit Cantik palm oil plant. After that logging tracks lead to Kampung Peta, an *orang asli* village, where boats can be hired for the trip up the River Endau to Kuala Jasin and the park.

While under the authority of Johor, Pahang became the special preserve of the *bendaharas*, who, as the years passed, became increasingly independent, gradually assuming all the authority of kingship. For instance, they exercised the power of capital punishment, when in principle only a sultan could order the shedding of blood. The *bendaharas* got round this little problem in a clever way. When they ordered an execution, the *kris* was plunged into the victim's heart through a piece of cotton wool, so preventing any blood dripping to the ground. Among the Pahang state regalia is the long execution *kris* used during the rule of the *bendaharas*.

Executions held in the former state capital of Pekan conformed to a basic pattern. On the three days before the event, the executioner marched around the town, banging a drum and proclaiming the victim's fate. When the day of the execution arrived, the prisoner was taken to Pulau Limin, a small island in the Pahang River, which has now disappeared. A chain was placed around his neck, his hands were bound and he was stabbed with the *kris*. The executioner then made another tour of Pekan and collected three *tampang*, Pahang's tin currency, from each shopkeeper for the expense of burying the body.

In the first half of the 19th century Pahang was ruled by Bendahara Tun Ali (1806-1857), the most successful of the *bendaharas* and the direct ancestor of the current sultan. A kindly and benevolent man, Bendahara Tun Ali was loved by his subjects and his 'reign' was largely trouble free. Peace brought stability to the country and virtual independence from Johor. Bendahara Tun Ali certainly saw himself as a free spirit and his son, Ahmad, went on to assume the title of Sultan in 1881. The new royal house was legitimised and glorified in traditional Malay fashion by the writing of the *Hikayat Pahang*.

In 1838 Munshi Abdullah journeyed through Pahang, leaving a vivid picture of what he saw. While finding Pahang a fertile country, he was surprised by the lack of shops and roads. He thought the atap-roofed houses were built without any method or thought, and was shocked by the level of dirt. The currency was another of his bugbears. In Pahang ancient Malayan *tampang* survived as the currency until a hundred years ago. The original *tampang* were solid ingots of tin, valued by their tin content. These were later replaced by the hollow, inscribed pieces of Munshi Abdullah's time, where the intrinsic value bore little relationship to the nominal

wealth.

Munshi Abdullah wrote, with masterly understatement, 'the system of currency in Pahang is, to my mind, inconvenient'. He went on to explain, 'sixteen *tampang* are equivalent to one dollar. A *tampang* cannot be divided, for instance, into three-quarters, or a half, or a quarter. If it is desired to buy anything, however trifling, a *tampang* must be paid for it.' Munshi Abdullah asked Tengku Sulaiman, Bendahara Tun Ali's son-in-law, whether this outdated form of currency could be changed. Tengku Sulaiman burst out laughing and answered, 'I often wished to change it but man-eating tigers came along and fierce crocodiles were seen in the rivers, and for that reason no change was made!'

Munshi Abdullah journeyed to Pahang by ship, disembarking at the royal town of **Pekan** on the southern bank of the Pahang River, where he was greeted by hundreds of Malays and Chinese, all armed to the teeth. Today Pekan is a rather more peaceful place. From its beginnings the settlement has in effect been two towns: Pekan Lama, the home of the Malay royalty and nobility; and Pekan Bharu, where the Chinese merchants and shopkeepers live and work. The royal town is dominated by the **Istana Abu Bakar**, which is set amidst extensive grounds, with a large area being turned over to the royal family's passion for sports. The football pitch would be the envy of many professional clubs, but most impressive of all is the polo field. Even this has a dual purpose, being used as a golf course between polo tournaments, as the tell-tale tees and greens reveal. There is no more fitting venue for polo outside of Windsor Great Park in England, indeed Prince Philip has played a chukka or two at Pekan. The royal stables are conveniently located just behind the main pavilion, but pride of place must go to the marvellous old steam locomotive, aptly named *Pekan* and on display at the side of the polo field.

Before Sultan Abu Bakar (1932-1974) moved to his new palace, he resided at the building which now houses the **Sultan Abu Bakar Museum**. The fine double-storey brick building was built by the British in 1929, replacing an earlier

Opposite: *Colourful fungus formations along one of the forest trails.* ***Above:*** *A Malayan water monitor lizard.* ***Below:*** *The stink horn fungus, so-called because of the unpleasant smell it emits. The odour attracts insects which help disperse the spores.*

wooden mansion. The museum was opened in 1976 and contains many interesting artefacts relating to the history and culture of Pahang, ranging from a small houseboat, originally belonging to the sultan, to a collection of *tampang*. The old wooden mansion was the residence of J.R. Rodger, the first British Resident of Pahang, until the state capital was moved to Kuala Lipis in 1898. The building was then used by the Resident whenever business brought him back to Pekan.

The site of the museum dates from the 15th century, when it was the location of Kota Beram, the palace of Pahang's early sultans. The palace derived its name from Beman Chengkobat, the favourite elephant of Sultan Abdul Jamal (1494-1512). Pahang's most famous princess, Tun Teja, was already betrothed to Sultan Abdul Jamal when Hang Tuah's son-in-law, Hang Nadim, abducted her and took her to Melaka as a bride for Sultan Mahmud. According to the *Sejarah Melayu*, Sultan Abdul Jamal was so furious that he mounted Beman Chengkobat and charged straight into the pillars of the palace, threatening to do the same to the Sultanate Palace in Melaka. It proved to be an empty threat. Sultan Mahmud later had Beman Chengkobat kidnapped and taken to Melaka as well! Elephants have remained closely associated with Pahang, crossed elephant tusks forming part of the state crest.

Just outside Pekan at Pulau Keladi on Route 82 is the **Pahang Silk Weaving Centre**. Here local women can be seen spinning the silk thread before weaving it on large wooden looms. They produce a variety of colourful products, including sarongs and scarfs, which are on sale to visitors. The art of weaving is believed to have been brought to Pahang by a Bugis lord, Keraing Aji, in 1722, and then passed down from generation to generation. Less than a kilometre further along Route 82 is the birthplace of Tun Abdul Razak, the country's second Prime Minister. The small, attractive house is a reconstruction of the original. From these humble origins Tun Abdul Razak, the son of the local

District Officer, set out on a glittering career, firstly as a young lawyer, then serving in the famous Force 136 during the Second World War, and finally as an international statesman.

To the north of Pekan, Route 3 leads to Kuantan, the modern capital of Pahang, though a quieter and more scenic route is provided by the road which runs along the coast. Here your fellow road users are just as likely to be herds of cattle as cars. They block your way and no end of hooting the horn will move them until they are good and ready. Off to the right there are frequent glimpses of long, sandy beaches, clearly visible through the slender palm trees, with not a soul in sight. Always in the distance is the seemingly motionless South China Sea. Now and again there is a solitary wooden home, or even a small *kampung*, but the traditional Malay architecture enriches rather than ruins the landscape. Virtually the only sign of human activity is the occasional fishing boat dotting the far horizon.

The British established the town of **Kuantan**, situated at the mouth of the River Kuantan, during the heyday of Pahang's tin mining industry. The biggest attraction is **Teluk Chempedak**, the beach located some 5 km from the town centre and the site of Kuantan's luxury hotels. Teluk Chempedak is at its liveliest during the weekend when the locals come to take a stroll or a swim. A small esplanade, with good seafood restaurants and a handicraft centre, runs along part of the beach. Higher up the Kuantan valley is the centre of Pahang's now dormant tin mining industry. **Sungai Lembing** is an old mining town and the site of Malaysia's only underground mine, in its day one of the deepest

Opposite: *Some of the shophouses in Kuantan, built during the colonial days. The split bamboo blinds, known as bidai, are a distinctive feature of many shops throughout the country. They are used to shut out the glaring sun and advertise the shop's merchandise.* ***Below:*** *A buffalo cart laden with basketfuls of fish makes its way up the beach at Beserah, near Kuantan.*

in the world. The mine closed when tin prices collapsed in the 1980s and is unlikely to reopen due to flooding. The countryside around Sungai Lembing is dominated by a limestone hill, which contains a series of caves known as **Gua Charah**. A steep climb leads up to the caves, one of which contains a nine metre reclining Buddha. Other shrines dot the caves and paintings adorn the walls. Not far from Gua Charah is the spectacular **Sungai Pandan Waterfall**, which drops over a hundred metres into a refreshingly cool natural pool.

From Kuantan north to the Terengganu border is one of the most attractive coastlines in Malaysia. Near the border is **Kampung Cherating**, a popular destination for backpackers, with a range of rustic beachfront accommodation and a relaxed, friendly atmosphere. The fishing village at **Beserah**, 9 km from Kuantan, is situated on a seemingly endless stretch of beach, and is well-known for its salted fish, which can usually be seen lying out to dry on raised platforms. The principal attraction for visitors is the landing of the daily catch. Unique to the village is the practice of using water buffaloes to transport the fish from the boats to the *kampung*. Everything starts to happen at around 2 pm. The water buffaloes are reluctantly hauled out of the small estuary, where they happily wallow for most of the day, and harnessed to open carts by their masters. They then lumber down to the sea and into the shallows. Here they stand in a thoroughly disinterested fashion while the fishermen load the carts with baskets of fish. When the carts are full, there comes the moment of truth for the buffaloes. The beach shelves quite steeply so they have to charge up the slope at a fair rate of knots to get to the top with their heavy load. All make it, though some need the encouragement of a whip on their thick hides.

If you are lucky you might see another animal at work along this part of the coast, but one far more nimble and athletic than the water buffaloes of Beserah. These are the monkeys trained by their masters to 'work' the coconut palms. The

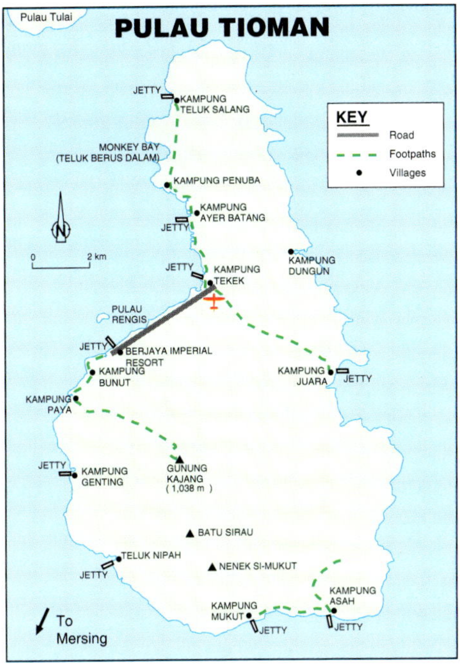

monkey is sent up the tree on a long chain, an ascent made at remarkable speed. After selecting its target, a nice ripe coconut, the monkey proceeds to twist it off with all four limbs. Watch out! The coconut can land anywhere and always hits the ground with quite a thump. The monkey then comes scampering down the tree, looking for its reward.

Lying some 30 km off the south-east coast of Pahang is **Pulau Tioman**, one of Malaysia's most enchanting islands and the setting for the Hollywood musical *South Pacific*. According to local legend, Pulau Tioman derives its name from a pet *tiong*, or mynah bird, which belonged to one of the island's early inhabitants. The island has a long history, its rugged terrain, dominated by the spectacular twin peaks of Batu Sirau and Nenek Si-Mukut, having served as an important landmark for navigators during the days of sailing ships. An abundant source of fresh water also attracted passing ships and, from the 11th to the 19th centuries, the island was an important trading centre astride the sea route to China.

Pulau Tioman remains a relatively unspoilt tropical island, with beautiful beaches and colourful coral gardens. Most of the accommodation is on the west coast of the island. For those who want to be pampered, there is the luxurious Berjaya Imperial Resort, with its scenic golf course. Pulau Tioman is also the perfect retreat for budget travellers, with plenty of beachfront chalets and A-frame huts to choose from. The most popular spots for snorkelling and diving are off Salang beach, Monkey Bay, and around the nearby islets of Pulau Rengis and Pulau Tulai. The only road on the island is the short stretch of tarmac between the airstrip at Kampung Tekek, the main village on the island, and the Berjaya Imperial Resort. The other villages are accessible by paths and trails, and the 'Sea Bus' service which operates around the island.

Opposite: *One of Pulau Tioman's beautiful bays.* ***Below:*** *A monkey selecting a coconut to twist off.*

The British arrived in Pahang in much the same way as they had entered the tin states of the west coast. Bendahara Tun Ali died in 1857 leaving a will which caused serious problems. He left his favourite son, Ahmad, with control of the Kuantan and Endau rivers, but his eldest son, Mutahir, wanted everything and chose to ignore the will. Bloodshed was only just avoided at the funeral when both sons arrived with bands of armed followers. Shortly afterwards Pahang was plunged into five years of civil war. The prosperity of Bendahara Tun Ali's day was swept away as his two sons, backed by their internal and foreign supporters, fought it out.

Ahmad was a far more resourceful character than Mutahir, added to which he was blessed with good fortune. On several occasions Ahmad found himself short of funds, resorting to his favourite sport of cock-fighting, where his birds won as much as RM1,000 in one contest alone. In 1862 Ahmad invaded Pahang from his base in Terengganu, and advanced down the Pahang River. He was unstoppable.

Mutahir's final stand came at Kampung Temai where he held out for five months, but his position was rendered hopeless when Ahmad captured Pekan. The civil war was over.

Ahmad celebrated his victory by setting out on an expedition into Ulu Pahang. After a few weeks he found himself in the legendary area of **Kota Gelanggi**. He had heard local tales of an *orang asli* princess who possessed the gift of immortality and was determined to investigate. Troops were sent into the jungle with instructions to capture all the local inhabitants they could find. The expedition proved a fiasco from the start. Four of the soldiers were savaged by tigers, while only eight *orang asli* were found. Of the princess there was no sign. Situated a few kilometres from Jerantut, Kota Gelanggi is well-known for its limestone caves. Locals believe that the caves once formed a thriving village, until a vengeful spirit turned all the inhabitants and houses into stone. Nature has indeed produced a series of dramatic rock formations within the caves. Perhaps they do form a village in ruins. Certainly there is a genuine sense of hustle and bustle. Stalactites and stalagmites appear almost alive, as they twist and writhe from the ceiling and the floor. Yet, as is so often the case, the experts have dispelled all such romantic notions. There is no trace of man having ever occupied the caves.

The British had stayed neutral during the civil war, but the Singapore business community remained convinced of the need to extend control over Pahang, believing the tales of a land of abundant gold and tin. Ahmad himself wished to encourage investment from Singapore, though not at the price of British control. In a move clearly designed to strengthen his own position, Ahmad assumed the title of Sultan of Pahang in 1881. Yet the pressure from Singapore was unrelenting and, four years later, Ahmad accepted a British agent

to help open the country to 'commerce and civilization'. The British had a foot in the door. Ahmad might say that he would rather see Pahang revert to jungle than be governed by the British, but the inevitable was not long in coming. The agent, Hugh Clifford, soon fell out with Ahmad and rumours swept Pekan of an impending British attack. Many of the Pahang chiefs wanted to fight, but Ahmad took the easy way out and 'invited' the British to send a Resident in 1888.

J.R. Rodger arrived in Pekan facing an extremely difficult task. Anti-British feeling was widespread. Rodger proceeded cautiously - he was no Birch - but his actions, limited as they were, made matters worse. Many of the contentious issues were the same as in Perak, for instance, the question of centralised tax collection and the payment of salaries to the chiefs. The establishment of a British district office at Kuala Lipis led to more trouble. The local chief, Haji Wan Daud, old in years but as proud and stubborn as they come, was going to have none of it. Determined to defend his land, he signalled his intentions by sitting on the promontory at the junction of the Jelai and Lipis rivers, and taking pot-shots at British boats passing up and down. The British thought him mad, and began negotiating with his sons who agreed to sell the land for RM200. However, when the British tried to take possession of Kuala Lipis, Wan Daud killed an official. A group of Malay chiefs was sent to persuade him to give up. Wan Daud responded by rushing at them with a spear. The accompanying soldiers promptly shot him dead.

Wan Daud was only the first of many Malay patriots to fight the British in what became the Pahang War (1891-1895). He was followed by Dato Bahaman, the Semantan chief who started the rebellion in 1891 and was its effective leader. A born jungle fighter, he excelled in the skirmishes

Opposite: *A backpacker boarding the boat for Mersing at one of Pulau Tioman's jetties.* ***Above:*** *The day draws to a close along the west coast of Pulau Tioman.*

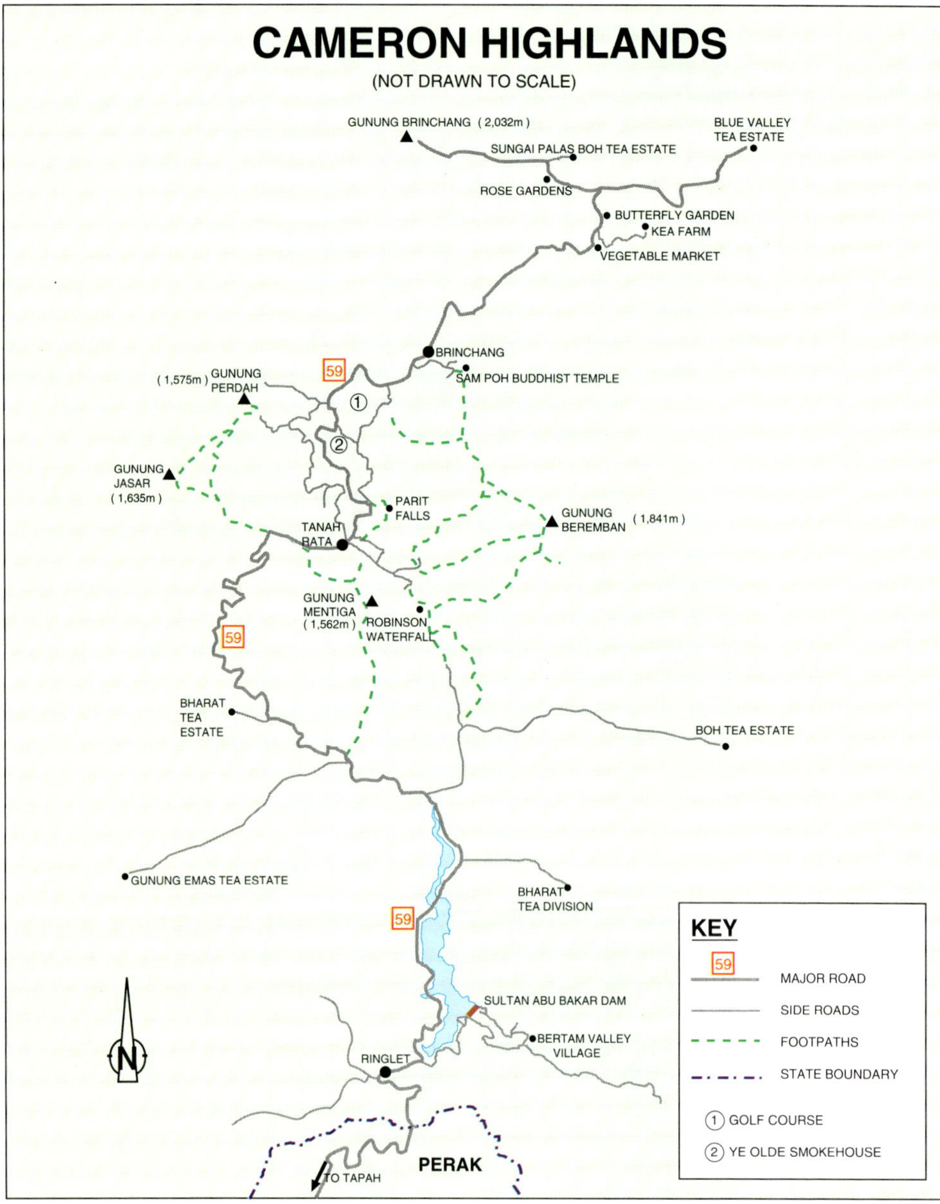

and ambushes that typified the war, but his importance pales beside that of Mat Kilau. The son of Tok Gajah, a leading Pahang chief, Mat Kilau took up arms against the British after their destruction of Budu on the River Lipis. He only just escaped with his life, but revenge proved sweet. Leading a hundred men, armed with spears, swords and muskets, Mat Kilau descended on Kuala Lipis in 1892, looting the shops and houses. As his fame grew, so Malays came to believe that he possessed magical powers. Recruits flocked to his cause and, for the British, the rebellion began to look as if it was getting out of hand.

Yet appearances were deceptive. The rebellion had reached its flood-tide and was beginning to ebb fast. The attitude of

Sultan Ahmad was crucial. At first he gave his tacit support to the rebels, but under pressure from the British, he turned against them. In desperation Mat Kilau and Dato Bahaman fled to Terengganu, where they met a renowned holy man, Engku Sayed of Paloh. He proclaimed a *jihad*, or holy war, against the infidel and assured them of victory and protection from all British weapons. The rebels returned to Pahang in 1894, storming the fort at Kuala Tembeling. Mat Kilau had made another dramatic entry into Pahang history. He and his men penetrated as far as Kampung Pulau Tawar, but support from the local Malay chiefs was not forthcoming. The British response was also gathering. They counter-attacked and overwhelmed the rebel stronghold at Jeram Ampai, near to Kuala Tembeling, forcing Mat Kilau and Dato Bahaman to flee again. The British commander, Hugh Clifford, was relentless, pursuing them into Terengganu and Kelantan. Yet he did not catch them, going to his grave in the belief that Mat Kilau had only escaped his clutches through being killed by the Siamese.

Pahang was a greatly changed place when Mat Kilau reappeared in 1969. The British had gone, but as in the west coast states, they had left their mark. Pahang was always poorer economically than Selangor and Perak, and in that respect the British found the state disappointing. Possibly the greatest contribution they made to Pahang was the discovery and development of two of the state's hill resorts. The most famous is the **Cameron Highlands**, dubbed the 'Garden of Malaysia', as it is the source of most of the temperate fruit, vegetables and flowers to be found in the country's markets and shops. The Highlands were first discovered by the British surveyor, William Cameron, during a mapping expedition in

Above: *The Cameron Highlands can only be reached from Tapah in Perak. The road winds its way up into the Highlands, giving magnificent views of the countryside below, including hillside villages belonging to the Semai, members of the Senoi group of orang asli.*

1885. He described his find as 'a fine plateau with gentle slopes, shut in by lofty mountains'. The tea planters soon came, as did the Chinese farmers, who found the soil ideal for growing vegetables. Finally, the British planters and officials arrived, seeking a weekend respite from the heat and humidity of the coastal plain.

The Cameron Highlands remain a popular retreat today, both with locals and tourists. The scenery is suggestive of Britain in the summer, with undulating hills, green valleys and mountains, and an abundance of brilliantly coloured flowers. Only the tea plantations spoil the illusion. This cannot be Britain and yet, in one sense, tea is synonymous with the long gone days of empire. Was the British Empire not sustained and invigorated by the whole notion of afternoon tea, that most British of institutions? Malaysians also have quite a taste for tea, drinking some eleven million cups a day.

Guided tours are given at the two **Boh Tea factories** which produce a variety of teas, including the refreshing Cameronian brew. Here visitors can see the whole production process. The leaves are first withered and rolled, before being fermented, dried and finally packaged. Firewood is used in the drying process to add to the flavour of the tea. Out on the tea estates the pickers no longer pluck the leaves from the bushes by hand. Automatic hedge trimmers are now common, while many of the pickers use a pair of shears, tossing the leaves over their heads into large baskets attached to their backs. Most of the hotels and restaurants in the Cameron Highlands are only too pleased to produce a 'cuppa' for visitors, suitably enriched by sandwiches, cakes and, if the cholesterol level can take it, scones, home-made strawberry jam and lashings of cream.

After that little lot, the numerous jungle treks and mountain tracks come as something of a relief. The highest mountain is **Gunung Brinchang** (2,032 metres) and, on a clear day, this and the other peaks give panoramic views across to Ipoh and the Straits of Malacca. It is important

to stick to the paths and not go wandering off. In 1967 the wealthy businessman, Jim Thomson, on holiday from his Thai silk empire in Bangkok, went off for a pre-dinner stroll. He never came back. The mystery of his disappearance remains unsolved. Did he fall? Was he attacked by a tiger? Perhaps he was kidnapped or even staged his own disappearance. Everyone has their own theory of what happened on that fateful evening.

The Cameron Highlands are spread over three districts, Ringlet, Tanah Rata and Brinchang, and connected by a winding mountain road. North of Brinchang are the terraced slopes of the vegetable farms, the scenic **Sungai Palas Boh Tea Estate** and the **Rose Gardens**, which include a green rose among their displays and sell rose jam. The famous golf course, with its undulating fairways and devilish stream - do not hook here - was originally laid out by the British in 1935. It was only five holes then and tigers evidently frequented the bunkers. Situated between Tanah Rata and Brinchang, the course is one of the most popular in the country.

Overlooking the fifteenth hole, a challenging par 5, is **Ye Olde Smokehouse**, the most English of all Malaysia's hotels. Resembling a typical English country inn with its mock Tudor exterior, latticed windows and beamed ceilings, Ye Olde Smokehouse serves up traditional fare, such as porridge and kippers for breakfast, and roast beef and yorkshire pudding followed by apple pie and custard for dinner. After that guests can order their favourite nightcap, sink into an armchair and warm their feet in front of a crackling log fire, before retiring to a four-poster bed for a good night's sleep. Completing the scene, an old red telephone box shipped over from northern England stands in the lane outside.

Fraser's Hill, like Rome, sits on seven hills. The resort is named after an English adventurer, Louis James Fraser, who lived alone in the hills at the end of

Opposite: *The Sungai Palas Boh Tea Estate.* ***Below:*** *The tea pickers at work.*

the 19th century prospecting for tin. After several years, he suddenly disappeared and was never seen again. As with Jim Thomson, no one knows what became of Fraser. In 1910 Bishop Ferguson-Davie of Singapore searched the hills for the prospector, but found no trace of him. What the Bishop did discover was the ideal place for a hill resort, and so Fraser's Hill was born. The area is famed for its bird life and plays host to the International Bird Race, a rather misleading title for what is in fact a bird-watching contest. The winner has to record the largest number of birds sighted and heard. This is all a far cry from the height of the 'Emergency' in 1951, when communist guerrillas assassinated the British High Commissioner, Sir Henry Gurney, along the narrow winding road at Fraser's Hill.

The third hill resort in Pahang is the most notorious. Las Vegas is located in the middle of the desert, but Malaysia's gambling capital is found 'on top of the clouds', the meaning of the Chinese word *genting*. Open twenty-four hours a day, the casino dominates the hill resort at the **Genting Highlands**, even though it is often shrouded by the clouds which swirl around the top. The tables seem to exert a fatal attraction and there is a steady stream of players from Kuala Lumpur. People tend only to disappear here when they lose everything and more. The summit can be reached by road or by cable car, a ride in which gives sweeping views of the surrounding hills. The cable car starts near the scenic Awana Golf and Country Resort, with arguably the best golf course in Malaysia.

Pahang used to be renowned for containing Malaysia's largest natural lake, **Tasik Bera**, located in the remote south-west of the state. Unfortunately, in the last thirty years a large part of the lake has been inundated by *rasau*, a wild plant from the *pandanus* family. Once a vast expanse of open water, much of the lake has been turned into a maze of narrow passages, navigable only by small boat, between the rampant *rasau*. Malaysia's largest lake is now in effect one of its smallest, though there is still an abundant

fish life, attracting growing numbers of fishermen.

Nestling in the jungle some 80 km from Kuantan, and nearly as far from the madding crowd as Tasik Bera, is **Tasik Chini**, in fact a chain of twelve lakes. An eerie atmosphere pervades the serene lake setting, particularly at dusk, as the waters turn black and a breeze rustles through the reeds. It is easy to understand why Chini is a lake of legends. The silent, still depths hold a number of secrets, which several expeditions to the area have failed to reveal.

Tasik Chini is at its most beautiful when the lotus blossoms are in bloom, becoming a floating garden of pink and white flowers. The lake is accessible by both boat and road, though the latter involves driving along seemingly endless dirt tracks through the oil palm plantations which have sprung up in recent years. The most popular way to reach the lake is by boat along the River Chini. The river is kept deliciously cool by the jungle canopy overhead, which creates a tunnel-like effect. Here and there light dapples the water where the foliage gives way to reveal the sun overhead. Glorious old gnarled trees, often draped in lianas and ferns, line the river, their roots gripping the banks like fingers, exposed to the knuckles by erosion. It is a wonder how they survive even the slightest breeze, but they do, or at least most do. In a few places a tree has lost the struggle and crashed down across the river. The principal destination for the boats is the Tasik Chini Resort, which offers fan-cooled rooms and a verandah restaurant overlooking the lake. Watch out for the pet monkey chained to a tree in front of the verandah. He has acquired a reputation for grabbing the possessions of unsuspecting visitors, with a particular penchant for

Ye Olde Smokehouse:
Opposite: *The tea room, complete with armchairs and a grandfather clock, is the perfect venue for a Devonshire cream tea.*
Below: *The hotel resembles a typical English country inn with its mock Tudor exterior.*

sunglasses, which he chews with great relish.

A number of *orang asli* settlements belonging to the Jakun people, one of the main Proto-Malay groups, are scattered around the lake. These people continue to lead a simple life and are very much in tune with nature. The forest and the lake are their local 'supermarket', supplying them with meat, fruit, fish and water. Blowpipes are used for hunting monkeys, squirrels and birds, but for larger animals, such as wild pigs, a spear is used. The hunters usually go out in small groups for the day, and share whatever they catch with their fellow villagers.

The Jakun have a rich oral heritage, and have grown up on legends about Tasik Chini and the surrounding jungle. One of their most famous tales concerns the creation of the lake. Many centuries ago the lake was the site of an old Jakun settlement. When the Jakun were still clearing the jungle, an old woman suddenly appeared and told them that the land belonged to her. The Jakun persuaded her to allow them to stay, but in return she planted her walking stick in the ground to support her claim. She warned them never to pull it out. All went well in the settlement until one day when a dog began to bark incessantly. A member of the tribe went to investigate, discovering a huge log. He plunged his spear into it and, to his amazement, blood began spurting out. The other tribesmen rushed up and began hurling their spears at the log. The skies darkened, thunder and lightning erupted across the heavens, and seconds later the rain lashed down. The Jakun scattered in the rush for shelter. Amidst the confusion, one of them accidentally knocked the walking stick from the ground. The rain was very heavy, but nothing compared to the water that now gushed from the hole left by the walking stick. As the land flooded, the earth caved in, forming Tasik Chini.

The Jakun believe that the log was an incarnation of the naga, a giant serpent-like creature, which they say lurks in the depths of Tasik Chini. At the water's edge on one of the smaller lakes, a rickety wooden jetty leads to a shady clearing and three wooden huts, known collectively as **Rumah Egai**. Three brothers live here, the eldest being Egai, together with their families. When Egai was a boy, his father told him tales of the naga. There have been a number of reported sightings of the strange beast, a possible relation of the Loch Ness Monster in Scotland. Egai remembers his father returning from a fishing expedition one day, excited and out of breath. He had seen the naga and told his children that its body was covered with silver-coloured scales. The younger generation of today are far more sceptical about the existence of such a beast, and want to see it for themselves before they will believe the stories of Egai and the other Jakun elders.

A short boat ride across the lake from the Tasik Chini Resort is **Kampung**

Gumum, a small Jakun village tucked away in the jungle. The clearing in the middle of the village is the main centre of activity. A small shop sells drinks, sweets and tins of food, while next to it is a shelter where the villagers congregate and the hunters make darts for their blowpipes, in preparation for the next day's hunting. They will gladly show visitors their blowpipe skills, while also encouraging them to have a go. Their advice to the novice is to blow from your chest and stomach, not your mouth. Keeping a watchful eye on everything from the roof of the shop is Molek, the village hornbill. Found as a chick in the jungle by some of the villagers, Molek has been brought up in Kampung Gumum. She has never learned to fend for herself and has to be fed daily by the villagers.

The *bomoh* at Kampung Gumum, Tok Sewa, is another gifted storyteller, capable of spending hours on his front porch talking to visitors about Tasik Chini and its many legends. At the end of a long evening, he might bring a touch of realism to his tales, by leaning forward and whispering that there is a place in the lake where fishermen have seen betel nuts and leaves suddenly appear on the surface. The Jakun believe that these have floated up from the original settlement sunk in the flood. There may be an element of truth in their tales, as archaeological and historical evidence suggests that a sunken Khmer city might lie at the bottom of the lake. A number of artefacts have been discovered around Tasik Chini, indicating the possibility of some earlier form of civilisation in the area, while there are cultural similarities between the Jakun and the Khmer people of Cambodia. We will probably never know for certain, as the still waters of the lake are very adept at keeping their many secrets, but the fact that there could be a sunken city only adds to the mystery of Tasik Chini.

Opposite: *Tasik Chini at sunset.*
Below: *A Jakun woman paddles her husband and their dog home across the still waters of Tasik Chini.*

COURTESY OF THE SARAWAK MUSEUM

SARAWAK

The Kingdom of the White Rajas

To the east of Johor, across the shimmering waters of the South China Sea, lies the mystical island of Borneo. For centuries this huge land mass was looked upon by outsiders as a land of adventure and danger. Shrouded in mystery, the island wore a cloak of impenetrable jungle. Tales abounded of the head-hunting practices of its aggressive interior tribes, while the coast was said to be infested by barbaric pirates. Borneo had the image of a wild and primitive land until the 19th century, when a remarkable Englishman came, saw and finally tamed large tracts of the northern part of the island. His name was James Brooke, the first White Raja of Sarawak.

Sarawak and its northern neighbour, Sabah, are today part of the Federation of Malaysia. They are separated from Peninsular Malaysia by over 650 km of sea, and together cover an area larger than all eleven states on the peninsula. Sarawak and Sabah share Borneo with the small sultanate of Brunei and Indonesian Kalimantan. It is not just the considerable expanse of sea which separates East Malaysia from the peninsula. There are in fact many striking differences between both parts of the country, resulting from their diverse cultural and historical backgrounds.

Sarawak is the largest state in Malaysia. Its swampy coastal plain extends for over 700 km, giving way to a broad belt of undulating lowlands intersected by numerous river systems, which have their source in Borneo's mountainous and remote interior. Sarawak's inception as a state, and its present borders, are a legacy of the work of James Brooke and his descendants, the famous Brooke dynasty. From 1841, the year when James became Raja, the dynasty ruled Sarawak for just over a hundred years. The kingdom had its own army, a national anthem called *God Bless the Raja Brooke*, its own postage stamps and an Order of Chivalry. The story of Brooke rule reads like an epic best-seller. It is all there - dashing heroes, fearsome rebels, passionate and enchanting women, personal tragedy and heated family squabbles - and all set in an exotic location.

As a young man, no one would have guessed that James Brooke, the son of a high court judge, was destined to become a king. Yet he proved ideally suited to the role of founder of a kingdom in a faraway and troubled land. A charismatic figure, he was fascinated by the East from an early age, and showed himself to be a man of adventure. In his handling of Sarawak's many problems, he also demonstrated the skills of a born diplomat. James was one of the great figures of the East, not just a colonial leader, but a man who showed a rare sensitivity and concern in his handling of the native population. Born in India in 1803, James began his career as a soldier in the British East India Company, but was badly wounded in the Anglo-Burmese War of 1825. Turning to trade, his first business

State crest: *The crest is formed by a stylised representation of a rhinoceros hornbill, its thirteen wing and tail segments symbolising the thirteen states of Malaysia. On each of the hornbill's legs is a hibiscus. The state motto is 'united, industrious, dedicated'.* ***Pages 248-249:*** *One of the striking tribal murals on display at the Sarawak Museum.* ***Opposite:*** *James Brooke, the first White Raja of Sarawak.*

venture was a disaster. James persevered and, benefiting to the tune of £30,000 from his father's will, a princely sum in those days, he purchased a schooner named the *Royalist*. He intended sailing to 'places where the keel of a European ship had never before ploughed the waters'. Hearing intriguing tales of Borneo from other travellers in Singapore, he set sail for Sarawak in 1839.

When James sailed up the Sarawak River several weeks later, he gazed for the first time on Kuching, the small town which would become his home and capital. Sarawak had historically been a dependency of Brunei, though for long periods it was largely self-governing. The discovery of antimony ore in the early 19th century led to a reassertion of authority from Brunei. In 1836 Sarawak erupted in revolt. The sultan was furious and despatched his uncle, Raja Muda Hasim, to crush the rebellion. Hasim found the task beyond him, and in desperation turned to James Brooke. He came up with an amazing offer: he would give James the area around the Sarawak River and the title of Raja in return for his help in ending the rebellion. James had already fallen in love with the country and readily agreed to the terms. In

a short time he had suppressed the rebellion.

Hasim took some time to honour his side of the bargain, but in 1841 James Brooke, at the age of 38, was installed as Raja of Sarawak. The Brooke dynasty had arrived and Sarawak, indeed Borneo for that matter, would never be the same again. His kingdom covered only a small part of modern Sarawak and was inhabited mainly by Malays and Land Dayaks, the latter now being known as Bidayuhs. James took his new responsibilities very seriously. It would have been only too easy for him to have exploited his position solely for self-interest, but what marked him out from nearly all his colonial contemporaries was that he did just the opposite. As he once said, 'Sarawak belongs to the Malays, the Sea Dayaks, the Land Dayaks, the Kayans and all the other tribes, and not to us', adding, 'It is for them we labour, not ourselves'.

James intended to preserve native customs and traditions, except where they undermined law and order. Two of the more dubious local customs were head-hunting and piracy, both of which James outlawed from the beginning. They terrorised the inhabitants and inhibited trade. His own subjects were generally willing to accept the new laws, but the areas to the north were infested with head-hunters and pirates, making it impossible to bring real peace to the new kingdom. Trouble tended to spill over the borders. These northern lands were inhabited by the Ibans, also known as the Sea Dayaks, Borneo's most notorious head-hunters. James led a series of expeditions against them. He was favoured by the fact that there were no strong cultural bonds between the various Iban groups. They identified themselves by river, rather than their ethnic origins, and were driven by territorial loyalty. James quickly became very adept at playing the groups off against each other, and order was gradually established in the Iban lands.

James built a series of wooden forts at strategic locations along the Batang Lupar, Saribas and Skrang rivers, in order to discourage any further trouble. Each fort had a storage room for any heads which were found in the possession of Iban raiding parties. They were all labelled with the date of capture, the tribe concerned and, if known, the name of the person to whom the head had originally belonged. James also created a new category of Iban leader, the *penghulu*. Recruited from amongst trusted Iban warriors, the *penghulu* was

given responsibility for all the longhouses along a particular stretch of river.

Although a gory practice, head-hunting was an ancient ritual. The principal purpose derived from the spiritual power believed to be contained in human heads, in itself a part of Iban animistic beliefs. Head-hunting expeditions were often timed for the end of the harvesting season and were characterised by detailed planning and preparation. When a longhouse was selected for attack, scouts were first sent out to assess the strength of the defences. Even then the Ibans would only proceed if the signs from the bird god, Sengalang Burong, were favourable. The Ibans usually attacked at first light, setting fire to the wooden stilts of the longhouse. The occupants fled into the open, where they stood little chance. The Ibans then slashed the heads off their victims and slightly roasted them, before wrapping them in palm leaves for the journey back to their own longhouse.

When the head-hunting party returned home, the heads were ceremoniously received into the longhouse, like important guests, by the womenfolk. The tribe thus took possession of each head's spirit. Their enemy's loss would be their gain. The Ibans 'prepared' a head by scooping out the brains through the nostrils

or the lower part of the skull. The cheek skin was torn off and eaten to ensure fearlessness, while the hair was ripped out and used by the warriors to adorn their spears and swords. The jaws were fastened up and the tongue was cut out, before the head was finally smoked over a fire. When it was ready, studs were placed in the eye sockets and wooden stoppers pushed up the nostrils. The head was usually hung over a fireplace or on the verandah of the longhouse. On ceremonial occasions, the head was 'fed' with rice, which was smeared on the jaws, ensuring future protection for the tribe.

Head-hunting was also a form of initiation into manhood. From the age of seventeen, Iban males were encouraged to prove their masculinity by participating in head-hunting raids, in much the same way as the Red Indians of the American Plains took scalps. Only when an Iban had claimed his first head could he take a wife, have his hands tattooed and be consulted on village matters.

The *Gawai Kenyalang,* or Hornbill Festival, was an integral part of Iban head-hunting activities. The rhinoceros hornbill was believed to be the messenger of the bird god, whose opinion had to be sought on all important tribal matters. The centre-piece of the ceremony was an elaborate stylised wood carving of the hornbill, its distinctive upturned casque transformed into a sweeping spiral. A similar representation of the hornbill has been adopted for the state crest. The Ibans paraded the hornbill up and down the longhouse verandah, while chanting various incantations, before

Opposite, above: *An elderly Iban woman and her granddaughter sitting in the cool communal passageway, or ruai, of their longhouse. The woman's forearms are adorned with tattoos, a form of body decoration practised by a number of Sarawak's ethnic groups.* ***Opposite, below:*** *Blackened skulls, trophies from the Iban head-hunting days, can still be seen hanging from the rafters in a few longhouses.* ***Above:*** *The hornbill has always been closely associated with Sarawak.*

COURTESY OF THE SARAWAK MUSEUM

presenting it with sacrificial tokens. The hornbill was then mounted on a pole and turned to face enemy territory. The Ibans believed that the soul of the bird would then fly off and attack the enemy.

Probably the most famous Iban warrior was Rentap. His name translates as 'one who makes the world shake', a name he certainly lived up to. From his fort on Bukit Sadok, near Betong, Rentap raided almost at will along the neighbouring rivers. The local people began to believe the 'Inland Raja', as Rentap called himself, was invincible. After two unsuccessful attacks on Bukit Sadok, James's men finally took the fort, forcing Rentap to flee into the jungle. He later surrendered and, after agreeing to abide by the law, was set free. The campaigns against Rentap and the other Ibans extended Brooke authority into areas which were nominally under the control of Brunei, and played a vital role in expanding the size of Sarawak. Never able to police these districts effectively, the sultan agreed to hand them over to James Brooke in return for an annual payment. Once started, this was a process that developed its own momentum.

James went home to England in 1847 to a hero's welcome, receiving a knighthood from Queen Victoria. However, his success had made him powerful enemies and, following his return to Sarawak, there was growing criticism of his activities against the Ibans. This reached a peak in 1849 when, after defeating a particularly brutal Iban band, he was accused of slaughtering innocent people. The fact that the Ibans had plundered and massacred at will was conveniently forgotten in the stampede to discredit him. A Commission of Inquiry was set up in London to investigate his conduct, which, after examining all the available evidence, cleared him, but his reputation had been damaged.

Unfortunately, more trouble lay ahead. In 1857 the Chinese goldminers from Bau, higher up the Sarawak River, rebelled. James had tried to regulate their trade in opium, while suppressing the secret societies. The miners reacted by marching on Kuching, with the intention of killing Brooke and all the British officials. Rumours reached the capital of an imminent attack, but for once James misjudged the situation. He refused to believe them and took no precautions.

The miners attacked at night. James was convalescing from malaria, but managed to escape from his residence by swimming across a small creek. One of his young officials, Harry Nicholets, who was staying with him at the time, was far less fortunate. Mistaking him for Brooke, the rebels cut off his head and paraded it around Kuching on a spear. They went on to kill all the British they could find. Meanwhile, James had left Kuching to organise a force to regain the capital. When the miners sighted the boats of this relief force, they panicked and fled the town. They were pursued as far as the neighbouring Dutch territory of Sambas, most of them being killed in the headlong flight.

It was a hollow victory for James. Kuching lay in ruins, while he was increasingly plagued by feelings of guilt and self-doubt. He had ignored warnings of an attack and, to make matters worse, some of his men clearly thought that his behaviour during the rebellion had verged on cowardice. His first task was to rebuild Kuching, but the treasury coffers were empty. Fortunately, the newly established Borneo Company stepped in and lent him £5,000. The Company was the only European merchant house permitted to operate in Sarawak during the 19th century, as James believed, no doubt correctly, that uncontrolled foreign investment would only bring ruthless exploitation of

Opposite: *Charles Brooke.*

FROM 'MY LIFE IN SARAWAK'

the country's natural resources. However, when the Borneo Company called in the loan, he was unable to pay. An even more unexpected source of help came to his rescue this time. James had become friendly with the wealthy British heiress, Angela Burdett-Coutts, who was enchanted by him and his tales of adventure in Sarawak. She now came up with the necessary funds. No wonder James referred to her as his 'guardian angel'.

James never married and was never known to have had a serious relationship with a woman. Speculation abounded that the wound he had received in Burma had deprived him of his manhood. This left James with the thorny problem of the succession. A young man did claim to be his illegitimate son, and James went as far as offering him a post in Sarawak, but he died before he arrived in Kuching. That left the two sons of his favourite sister, Emma, both of whom were already in his service. He decided to name the eldest as heir to the throne. Family quarrels were always to be a trait of the Brookes, particularly when it came to matters of the succession. James duly fell out with his eldest nephew, disinherited him and named his other nephew, Charles Brooke, as heir. The strains of leadership and illness had taken a heavy toll on James. He returned to England,

leaving Charles in charge of Sarawak. Even then he could not let go, despatching a steady stream of instructions to his nephew. He died in 1868, five years after he left Sarawak for the last time, and was buried in the churchyard at Sheepstor, in the county of Devon.

James had on occasions doubted whether Charles Brooke would be up to the task of ruling Sarawak, but he had chosen his successor well. A very different character from James, Charles possessed none of his uncle's charm and easygoing manner, being reserved and unbending. People found him difficult to like, but they always respected him. James had felt closest to the Malay community in Sarawak, but Charles was always at his happiest with the Ibans. He had spent many years living amongst them at remote stations, and he enjoyed their simple lifestyle, often wearing native dress. James had given him control of the difficult Batang Lupar region, where he worked to put down head-hunting. He wrote that some of the Ibans would plead to be allowed to go for heads like 'children crying after sugar plums'. Head-hunting was gradually stamped out during his rule, though there were reports of heads being taken in the upper reaches of the Rejang River as late as 1930. The practice did enjoy a brief, and legal, revival during the Second World War, when the Ibans were encouraged to take Japanese heads.

Above all, Charles was extremely good with money. Within a few years he had put Sarawak on a sound financial footing and, under his strong and caring rule, the country continued to grow and prosper. In the year after he became Raja, Charles married his distant cousin, Margaret de Windt, who had just turned twenty. He proposed while she was playing the piano, handing her a scruffy piece of paper with the message:

'With a humble demean

Opposite: *A portrait of Margaret Brooke wearing traditional Malay dress.*

Above: *An Iban boy smiles from one of the doors of his longhouse in Kapit.*

If the King were to pray
That You'd be his Queen,
Would *not* you say *Nay?*'

Margaret Brooke was an intelligent and charming woman, who fell in love with Sarawak, and was looked upon with great affection by the local people. While most other British women in Borneo and Malaya lived for the arrival of the mail boat or their next trip home, Margaret embraced her new world with unabashed enthusiasm. She quickly mastered the Malay language and discarded the frills, flounces and corsets of Victorian dress for more practical native attire. Margaret had a craving for adventure and, whenever possible, accompanied Charles on his trips into the interior. Meeting the different tribes pleased her most and she always said that she left a piece of her heart behind whenever she stayed at a settlement.

Margaret later wrote two books about her time in Sarawak, which contain many entertaining anecdotes drawn from her travels around the country. On one trip she discovered that each Iban warrior wore a lock of hair at the back of his neck, 'in a spirit of true courtesy, in case his head were taken by an enemy, when this lock would serve as a handle for them to carry his head by!' On another occasion she was lucky not to lose her own head at a Kayan village. The entertainment included a sword dance with a man brandishing a very long and very sharp *parang*. During the dance he came so close with his *parang*, she felt it cause a draft over her head. She was later told that he had once become so excited during a performance, he had accidentally lopped off a spectator's head!

After four years in Sarawak, Margaret's health began to cause considerable concern. Repeated attacks of malaria had left her desperately weak and she returned to England with Charles to convalesce. The voyage turned into a nightmare for both of them. All three of their children fell ill with cholera and died within hours of each other. Margaret was devastated, but she found the inner strength to overcome the tragedy and start a new family. She became pregnant while in England and

gave birth to a son, Vyner, who would one day succeed his father on the throne of Sarawak. He was later joined by two brothers, Bertram and Harry.

Margaret returned to Kuching in early 1875, and for the next twenty years divided her time between England and Sarawak. Charles was never an easy man to live with and, over the years, they grew ever more distant. He was a notorious womaniser and could be cruel. Margaret confided in her daughter-in-law, Sylvia, that Charles had on one occasion killed her pet doves and served them up in a pie for supper. The couple lived a frugal existence. Charles would never spend any money on what he considered unnecessary luxuries for himself and his wife, always exclaiming, 'I don't believe in fripperies!' By the end Margaret felt that Charles did not want her in Sarawak anymore, and in 1895 she went home to live permanently in England. It was always her belief that Charles had become bored with her and, perhaps most of all, he no longer wished to share the affection of his people.

Charles was always faithful to his uncle's style of rule. One of his earliest measures was to create the State Council, which gave a forum for community leaders to express their views on important national decisions. Charles also created a proper civil service. As was the case in British Malaya, he showed a marked preference for employing single men. Marriage was thought to reduce the efficiency of British officials. Charles liked to set a good example to his men by keeping to a strict timetable. Margaret once described him as 'the most punctual man alive'. His day would always begin at 5 am with the firing of a cannon from Fort Margherita as his alarm call.

Sarawak's borders continued to grow under Charles Brooke. His publicly stated goal was to incorporate all of Brunei into the kingdom and he almost succeeded. The sultans continued the policy of ceding

Opposite: *A boatman checks the cargo on the express boat to Kapit.* ***Below:*** *The Rejang and the port of Sibu at sunset.*

territory to the Brookes for money, until there was practically nothing left. Brunei became both surrounded by Sarawak and cut in two by it. Talks began for what was left, but the British felt the expansion of Sarawak had gone far enough, and called a halt. The Brooke kingdom was by then over twenty times its original size. The ultimate irony is that, while the Brookes almost squeezed Brunei out of existence, they did not get their hands on the richest part. Although oil was discovered in northern Sarawak at the turn of the century, the reserves never approached the scale of those just across the border in Brunei.

Charles was still holding the reins tight at the age of 85. He had become partially deaf and had lost an eye in a riding accident. A suitable replacement was found in a taxidermist's shop, Charles purchasing a glass eye originally meant for an animal! Like James before him, Charles was worried about the future of Sarawak after his death. He was not sure if his eldest son, Vyner, was capable of ruling the kingdom. In the end Charles decided that Vyner should be Raja, but that he must consult his brother, Bertram, on all major decisions. Charles returned to England in 1916, after a spell of illness, and died there in the following year. He had ruled Sarawak, almost single-handedly, for nearly fifty years, establishing a peaceful and flourishing kingdom. His last wish was to be buried in Sarawak, but the First World War intervened and he was laid to rest by the side of James at Sheepstor.

The romance and adventure which first lured James Brooke to the shores of Sarawak are still there today, although tempered by development and modernisation. The best way to experience Sarawak's many charms is to take a trip up one of its rivers. A look at any map will reveal that the state is very much a land of rivers, which still play a central role in everyday life. Road communications have come a long way since the days of the Brookes. A main road now runs the entire length of the state between Kuching and Miri, but the rivers remain the only means of communication for the inhabitants in the interior.

Several tour companies in Kuching offer longboat trips along the Skrang River, with an overnight stay at an Iban longhouse. As its name suggests, a longhouse is one long house, with a whole community living under one roof, sometimes as many as sixty or seventy families. Each family has its own apartment, which opens out on to a communal covered passageway, the *ruai*, at the front. This is the social centre of the community. In some longhouses the blackened skulls of long dead enemies still hang from the rafters. Most of Sarawak's indigenous groups share this communal lifestyle. The organised tours are very convenient for those who have limited time on their hands, but it is more rewarding to head into the interior under your own steam. This is far easier than it sounds.

River transport has speeded up a great deal since the time of the Brookes. Express boats operate along the main rivers at speeds of 30 knots. The boats are in fact recycled aircraft, with the wings removed and an engine fitted in the stern. Journey times have been cut from weeks to a matter of hours. The mightiest of all Sarawak's rivers is the Rejang, which rises in the heart of Borneo and cuts across the centre of the state, before flowing into the South China Sea. The starting point for trips up the Rejang is the lively, mainly Chinese, port of Sibu.

The Chinese first settled in **Sibu** during the time of Charles Brooke. He arranged for a thousand immigrants from Foochow to be brought to the area, providing them with farmland and loans. Priority was to be given to the planting of *padi*, but this did not prove a success. The settlers next turned to rubber and pepper cultivation, becoming Sarawak's first pepper planters. The state is today one of the world's largest producers of the spice. Nicknamed the 'New Foochow', Sibu is the second biggest town in Sarawak. A smart new esplanade has been built on reclaimed land at one end of the town, where locals and visitors alike can enjoy an evening stroll. On the hour Sibu's chiming clock tower comes to life, and plays an entertaining tune. At the other end of town, clearly visible from the esplanade, rises a colourful seven-storey pagoda.

Express boats depart regularly from Sibu to the upriver settlement of Kapit. Always full of locals, who sometimes spill out on to the rooftop, the boats carry supplies as well as people to the interior, as everything that does not go by air has to travel by river. The cargo usually consists of food and drinks, but there might also be furniture, even livestock. Sometimes the boatmen help themselves to a freight snack, particularly if a chicken lays an egg on the way. Raised on stilts, longhouses

Opposite: *A crew member on a logging boat checks all the logs on the raft are in place as it makes its way down the Rejang to the sawmills at Sibu.* ***Above:*** *An empty logging raft is towed back up the Rejang.*

dot the river banks. Their inhabitants can sometimes be seen covered in soap suds taking their daily river bath, or vigorously washing clothes with an equal amount of lather. They usually stop momentarily to wave the express boat on its way. The longhouses are reached by rickety, narrow log ladders, negotiated by the locals with a nimble ease which visitors find impossible to emulate.

The journey time to Kapit depends on the number of stops made on the way. Most boats call at the towns of Kanowit and Song, and will also stop at various longhouses and logging camps if requested. A trip up the Rejang quickly brings home to visitors the extent of logging activities in Sarawak. Timber is the mainstay of the economy, and the area around the Rejang is the centre of the state's logging industry. Huge log rafts, pulled by tugs, make their slow journey down the river, destined for Sibu and the sawmills. Members of the crew can sometimes be seen striding purposefully and confidently over the logs, checking that they are all still in place, and ensuring the raft's uninterrupted passage downstream.

Kanowit is a small, quiet town with a row of attractive shophouses. It is home to one of the eight forts which have survived from the Brooke era. **Fort Emma**, named after James Brooke's favourite sister, was built in 1851 and sits on a small rise overlooking the river. A simple rectangular wooden structure, it is the least imposing of the remaining forts. Yet its rather dreary appearance belies an eventful past. One morning in 1859 a local tribe of Dayaks, appropriately known as the Kanowits, overran the fort and killed two British officials. Charles Brooke, in overall command of the area at the time, was determined to bring the culprits to justice. He led a well-armed expedition against the Kanowits, besieging them in their jungle stockade. They put up a furious defence, showering Charles's men with poisoned darts. Charles was to be seen rushing around his Iban troops, administering brandy and forcing them to get up and walk about, a combination which

apparently acted as an antidote against the poison. The battle, his first major engagement, ended in victory. The murderers were captured, tried and sentenced to death.

Another Brooke stronghold, **Fort Sylvia**, sits high above the Rejang at **Kapit**. That is during the dry season. The water level marks painted on the walls of the fort show how high the river can rise in the wet season, on one occasion a staggering 20 metres. The biggest town up the Rejang, Kapit lies in the heart of Iban country. The Ibans are today Sarawak's largest indigenous group, making up nearly a third of the total population. Many are now employed in the logging industry, which moors a large number of its boats at Kapit. The waterfront is a meeting place for locals and travellers. Here you may strike up a conversation with an Iban, who brings the past alive with longhouse tales of his warrior ancestors, the bloody battles in which they fought, and the number of heads they took. Some of the longhouses around Kapit can be reached by a very bumpy road. The rest are accessible only by river. It is obviously more polite if you wait to be invited to a longhouse by one of the inhabitants, rather than simply turning up unannounced on the doorstep. The Ibans are a very hospitable people and will usually give visitors a warm welcome. It is customary to take along some small gifts, such as cigarettes, sweets or biscuits.

From Kapit the express boat travels further up the Rejang to Belaga. Permission must first be sought for the journey from the district office in Kapit, and then it is all speed ahead for Belaga. The river becomes narrower, and more difficult to navigate, and includes a series of rapids. The roar of the engines drowns out all conversation on board, as the boat battles against the strong current, leaving a

Opposite: *Two young boys at the landing stage at Belaga.* ***Left:*** *The Kenyah people are renowned for their elongated ear lobes and heavy earrings.* ***Above:*** *This orang ulu man has used hornbill feathers to decorate his distinctive hat.*

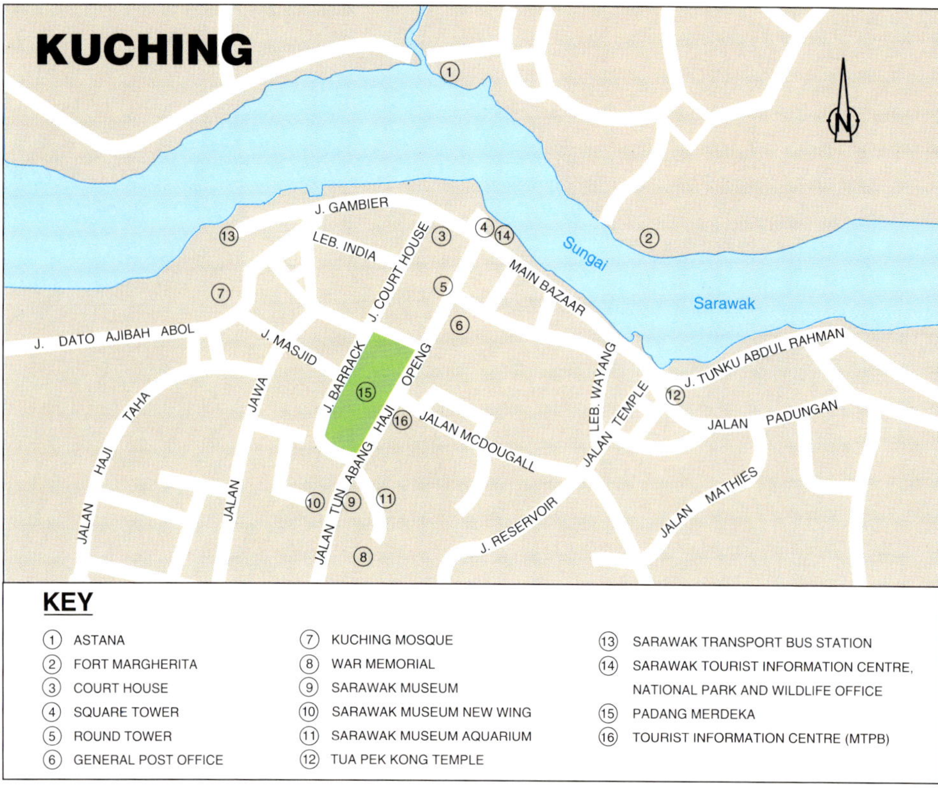

tremendous wake behind which washes right over the river banks. In the dry season the boats cannot always get through to Belaga, and at the series of rapids you can see why. Many of the passengers walk over the headland and rejoin the boat upstream, some from choice, others at the request of the crew to lighten the load. The rapids are an experience in themselves. Huge outcrops of rock protrude menacingly from the raging waters. On occasions they get rather too close for comfort and eyes turn nervously to the boatman, furiously grappling with the wheel. Fortunately, he is an old hand at this game, and he skilfully manoeuvres the boat between the rocks and through the various twists and turns of the rapids. Margaret Brooke went through these same rapids in a canoe, describing the exhilarating experience as 'the happiest time I have ever spent'. Beyond Belaga the journey upriver becomes even more adventurous as the rapids get bigger, too adventurous for the express boat service which terminates at the town.

Belaga comes as something of a surprise. This is the centre of Malaysian Borneo, with visitors probably expecting little more than a few longhouses and the odd shop. What they will find is a thriving little town. There is even a *padang* of sorts in front of the main street. Belaga is home to the Kenyahs and the Kayans, members of the *orang ulu*, or upriver people. *Orang ulu* is a collective term used for the various groups of upriver people found on both sides of the Malaysian-Indonesian border in central Borneo. The Kenyahs and Kayans are renowned for their tattoos and large heavy earrings, made of brass or lead. Their ears are pierced at an early age, and the lobes gradually stretched by adding heavier earrings until they reach shoulder

length. Elongated ear lobes are considered a form of beauty, though the practice is less common amongst the younger generation. Unlike many rural towns in Peninsular Malaysia, Belaga does not have a 'top-heavy' population. Young people, invariably dressed in T-shirts and jeans, are a common sight around the town. Kuching does not seem to hold the same attractions as Kuala Lumpur. Local employment prospects in the logging industry are also good and the tribal links remain strong.

In 1946, after twenty-nine years as Raja, Vyner Brooke travelled up the Rejang to convey an important message to the Iban communities around Kapit. He had come to announce the end of the Brooke dynasty. Vyner was always easy-going, with a good sense of humour, but he lacked self-confidence and was too sensitive. His style of leadership was far more relaxed than that of his father. Vyner spent several months of the year in England, during which time Bertram was left in charge. The two brothers acted quite well together, but contrary to his father's wishes, Vyner rarely consulted Bertram on important issues. The country continued to prosper, particularly as oil production, which had started at **Miri** in 1910, began to make a major contribution to state revenue.

Vyner had married Sylvia Brett, a renowned author and daughter of Lord Esher. She once sent a synopsis to Warner Brothers in Hollywood for a film based around the life of James Brooke, called 'The Great White Rajah'. Errol Flynn fancied the title role and wrote his own script, which Sylvia found trite and full of inaccuracies, portraying James as something of a casanova. The film was never made. Vyner and Sylvia had three daughters, but no sons. Vyner decided to make Bertram's son, Anthony, his successor. They did not always see eye to eye on matters, and Vyner revoked his appointment on more

Above: *The Astana in Kuching, now the residence of the Governor of Sarawak. Transport methods have changed somewhat since the time of Charles Brooke.*

than one occasion.

The comfortable existence of Sarawak was shattered by the Second World War. Kuching fell to the Japanese in December 1941, exactly one hundred years after James Brooke had become the first White Raja, and was not liberated until 1945. In April of the following year Vyner resumed control of Sarawak, but he did not stay for long. Sarawak had been badly damaged by the war and Vyner felt the task of rebuilding the kingdom was beyond the country's resources. On 1st July 1946 he ceded Sarawak to the British, and Brooke rule came to an abrupt end. Vyner was given a million pounds in exchange for his kingdom, leading to accusations that he had sold his birthright for the money.

Bertram and Anthony did all they could to reverse Vyner's decision and preserve Brooke rule. However, events had gone too far. Perhaps Vyner might have seen things differently with a son of his own, but there was no strong bond with his nephew. It was a sad end to the Brooke dynasty in Sarawak. Vyner and Sylvia retired to England, where they lived apart, though they remained friends. Vyner became a virtual recluse, a forgotten king in a shabby London house, dying at the age of 89 in 1963. He was buried alongside his two predecessors, far from their kingdom in the East.

Kuching is the Malay word for cat. Numerous theories have been advanced for this feline naming of the town, one of the most plausible being that it was named after a small river which once ran in front of the **Tua Pek Kong Temple**. Much of the centre of **Kuching** remains as it was during the time of the Brookes. On one side of the river stands the elegant **Astana**, built by Charles Brooke in 1870 for Margaret. Every day the Raja would take the short trip across the river in his royal boat to the **Court House**, the seat of government during Brooke rule. It is possible to take the same trip today in a *tambang*. These are Kuching's river taxis, which have been crossing and recrossing the Sarawak River for over a hundred years. In front of the Court House is a memorial

to Charles Brooke, erected by Vyner in 1924. Nearby is the **General Post Office**, a fine colonnaded building dating from 1931. At one time Vyner, who was a horse racing enthusiast, used it as a stable for his horses. Above the central columns are the Brooke coat of arms and the family motto, *Dum Spiro Spero,* which translates as 'That is our hope so long as we breathe'.

From the landing stage at the side of the Astana, it is a short uphill walk to **Fort Margherita**, built by Charles in the style of an English Tudor castle and named after Margaret. Occupying a highly strategic position overlooking the river, the fort saw little action until the arrival of the Japanese. By the late 19th century, Kuching was a peaceful and prosperous town. Nevertheless, the Brookes maintained a constant vigilance. A sentry was always stationed in the fort's lookout point. Every night, between 8 pm and 5 am, he would call out 'all's well' on the stroke of each hour. When he heard the call, the sentry at the Astana would pass it on to the sentry at the government offices across the river, who relayed it to the sentry at the Treasury. This hourly routine ensured that all the sentries stayed awake on duty. Today the fort houses the Police Museum. Among the exhibits is a reconstruction of an execution by *kris*. The executioner would stab the victim just below the right shoulder, and then draw the *kris* across the body, straight through the heart.

Situated on another rise, some distance away from the river, is the **Sarawak Museum**, which Charles Brooke built with the encouragement of Alfred Wallace (1823-1913), the naturalist who spent the best part of eight years exploring the jungles of Borneo. Several of his specimens are on display in the museum. At the same time as Charles Darwin, Wallace independently formulated the theory of evolution, but never received the credit he deserved.

Opposite: *Fort Margherita in Kuching.* ***Left:*** *A tambang, the traditional means of crossing the Sarawak River.* ***Above:*** *The magnificent kelirieng, or native burial pole, outside the Sarawak Museum.*

Charles Brooke had a passion for all things French and designed the facade of the museum in the style of a Normandy town hall.

The museum houses an excellent collection of local arts and crafts, including a striking mural painted by the Long Nawang Kenyahs. Among the natural history exhibits are a set of dentures and a large hairball, both retrieved from the stomach of a crocodile. It was common practice during the Brooke years to slit open the belly of a crocodile to search for any sign of human victims. The danger from crocodiles is much reduced today, though there are still reports of attacks. In 1990 a seventy-five year old Iban man narrowly escaped becoming crocodile fodder, while he was bathing in the Krian River. As he was dragged under water, he remembered old longhouse tales about fighting crocodiles, and stuck his fingers in the reptile's eyes. It let go long enough for him to swim to safety.

Several cultural artefacts are on display in the museum grounds, including an Iban war boat which was used in one of Charles Brooke's punitive expeditions in 1915. Pride of place must go to the magnificent *kelirieng*, or native burial pole. Several of the indigenous tribes used to inter the remains of their chiefs in these burial poles. Made from the trunk of a hardwood tree, the poles were elaborately carved, usually with niches up the side for the bodies of the chief's slaves. It was always the ancient custom in Sarawak that the chief should be accompanied into the next world by his slaves. The origins of head-hunting have in fact been associated with this custom. As slaves became more valuable, substitutes had to be found from hostile villages, leading to head-hunting expeditions. The heads were then brought to the dead chief's burial pole. His bones would be stored in a jar at the top. The burial pole on display at the museum was originally erected in the Belaga area by a local Kayan chief, as the final resting place for his young daughter. A few burial poles can still be seen out in the country. There is a good example, complete with the jar,

overlooking the river at **Pandan**, near Bintulu.

There are several beaches within easy reach of Kuching. Just over 30 km away is **Damai Beach**, site of the **Sarawak Cultural Village**. Nestling in the foothills of **Gunung Santubong**, the village is very much a living museum, where visitors can learn something about all the main ethnic groups of Sarawak. Replicas of the various native houses have been built around a lake, where a boatman waits to ferry people across in his *tambang*. In each house men and women demonstrate activities connected with their particular ethnic group, giving visitors a small gift to take home. Outside the Melanau tall house women make sago pearls from the pith of the sago tree. The Melanaus live mainly along the coast, between the Rejang and Baram rivers. They used to build these tall houses, mounted on very long stilts, as a precaution against attacks from pirates. At the Bidayuh longhouse there are demonstrations of sugar-cane crushing and the husking of *padi*, while the Iban women show off their skills at weaving and beadwork, and the Iban men entertain visitors with their storytelling.

At the Penan hut the men are dressed in loincloths and making blowpipes. Members of the *orang ulu* group, the Penans are traditionally a nomadic people, living in very simple, makeshift shelters in the remote upper reaches of the Rejang and Baram rivers. When food in the vicinity runs out, or there is a death in the family, they leave the shelter and move on. In recent years they have been encouraged to give up their nomadic ways and settle down permanently. The State Government has built longhouses and schools for them, in an effort to speed up the process.

The Baram River, which runs close to Sarawak's border with Brunei, is the starting point for trips to Gunung Mulu

The Sarawak Cultural Village:
Opposite: *The Iban men demonstrating their passion for cock-fighting.* ***Below:*** *An Iban woman in ceremonial dress.*

National Park, renowned for its magnificent caves. From Kuala Baram on the coast, it is a day's journey upriver to the park. Express boats operate as far as Long Terawan, stopping on the way at the small town of **Marudi**. This was the venue for the Baram Regatta, set up in the 1890s by the shrewd local Resident, Dr Charles Hose, as a substitute for tribal warfare. He decided that the tribes should settle their disputes by racing against each other in their war canoes. The regatta is still held on special occasions, although the venue has now moved to Kuching. Close to the jetty is **Fort Hose**, built by Charles Brooke in 1901. From Long Terawan, the river journey to park headquarters continues by longboat. Since the completion of Mulu's airstrip in 1992, visitors also have the option of flying to the park from the coastal town of Miri, cutting the journey time to half an hour. The flight gives some idea of the scale of the country, and how impenetrable much of it still is. Only the rivers provide relief. Glistening in the sun, they meander endlessly through the thick vegetation, branching off to the left and the right.

Much of **Gunung Mulu National Park** remains a mystery. Intrepid speleologists, or cave explorers, have discovered and surveyed around 200 km of cave passages in Mulu, but this is thought to represent less than half the caves contained within the park. Several of the caves are open to the public, but the remainder are considered too dangerous, including the **Sarawak Chamber**, the world's largest cave chamber, more than twice the size of its nearest rival. Rather than attempting to convey its size in metric units, more imaginative units of measurement have been employed. The Sarawak Chamber is capable of holding forty Boeing 747 aircraft, 7,500 buses or, if you are a sports fan, sixteen football pitches. Having taken in these statistics, the layman should next consider the proposition that the Sarawak Chamber should not be a cave at all. It is the bumble-bee of the cave world. Engineers argue that it is not structurally possible for such a large limestone cave to exist, but just as the disastrously aeronautically designed bee is able to fly, so the Sarawak Chamber does not 'cave' in.

Deer Cave, so-named because sambar deer used to visit the cave to lick the salt from its guano deposits, is another record breaker. The cave contains the world's largest cave passage, with enough room to accommodate St Paul's Cathedral in London five times over. American visitors will be particularly intrigued by the effects of nature on the entrance to Deer Cave, one side of which forms a perfect limestone profile of Abraham Lincoln, complete with prominent chin.

Perhaps Deer Cave should have been called 'Bat Cave', as it is the antics of these nocturnal creatures for which the cave is justifiably famous. Deer Cave is home to hundreds of thousands of bats, hence the guano. Every evening at dusk, they put on an amazing aerial display as they leave the cave in search of dinner. A bat observation station has been built for visitors to view the spectacle. There is a sudden rush of wings as the pathfinders emerge from the cave. They spiral through the air like ribbons of smoke. Every few minutes the stream stops for a short time, as the next squadron is lined up for action. As they fly overhead the beating of their wings sounds like the patter of rain. The exodus takes about an hour, with the last group of bats to leave the cave forming a perfect circle in the sky as they sign out for the night. Indeed they have been known to give spectators a real treat and form interlocking circles. On the walk back to park headquarters through the jungle, visitors are entertained by the chirps, burps, whistles, warbles and whoops of the forest's hidden inhabitants.

There are four caves, including Deer Cave, open to the public at Mulu. Created and sculpted by rainwater over millions of years, the caves are a natural art gallery. Stalactites cling to the roof like dripping icicles, while their counterparts rise majestically from the floor. Limestone curtains, fans and mushrooms add to the decoration. It is easy to imagine underground rivers, swollen by tropical storms, shaping the caves at Mulu, but the stalactites and stalagmites are formed by incessant drops of water falling from the ceiling. Each droplet contains a minute amount of dissolved calcite, which is either deposited on the ground or left clinging to the ceiling, gradually building into the dramatic limestone formations on display. Scientific experiments at Mulu indicate that the rate of growth varies between 1 to 10 mm per century.

The park also provides ideal opportunities for jungle trekking and river trips.

Opposite: *A Penan hunter. He is wearing leg coils, a traditional form of personal adornment.* ***Below, left:*** *A solitary bat hanging from the ceiling in Lang's Cave at Gunung Mulu National Park.* ***Below, right:*** *Hairy earwigs, a familiar sight in Deer Cave.*

On the banks of the Melanau River is the Penan settlement of **Batu Bungan**. Nearby, in the sheer cliff face, is a small cave, the setting for a sad Penan tale. A beautiful woman is said to have once lived in the cave. She was seen by a young Penan warrior, who came from a village on the other side of the river. Determined to take the woman as his wife, he paddled across the river and began to climb the cliff face. Despite numerous attempts, he could not reach the cave. He lost his temper and decided that, if he could not have the woman, no one would and killed her with his blowpipe.

Visitors pass Batu Bungan on their way to **Wind Cave**, famed for the King's Room, a section of the cave with very impressive limestone formations. Further along the Melanau River is **Clearwater Cave**, the longest cave in South East Asia at over 100 km. The cave is named after the river which flows through it. The waters of the river are not only renowned for their purity. According to the local people, they also possess the power of rejuvenation. Anyone who swims in the river is said to look and feel a year younger.

Where there are caves there must be mountains, and Gunung Mulu National Park offers two challenging climbs, the first to the Pinnacles on Gunung Api and the second to the summit of Gunung Mulu. The mountains of Mulu continue the record breaking tradition. **Gunung Api** (1,710 metres) is the highest limestone mountain between Thailand and New Guinea, though it is very gradually getting smaller, being constantly eroded or, more correctly, dissolved. In some ten million years time, give or take the odd million, Mount Api will have disappeared. It is estimated that a third of the original mountain has already gone. *Api* means fire in Malay and the mountain owes its name to the raging fires which have been observed on its slopes in the past. On one occasion these were mistaken for a volcanic eruption, and the story quickly spread that active volcanoes existed in the interior. The heavy rainfall has sculpted a stunning visual

spectacle on the slopes of Mount Api, a forest of razor-sharp limestone fangs called the **Pinnacles**. They rise above the tree tops in sinister, grey splendour, to a height of forty to fifty metres.

Gunung Mulu (2,376 metres) was first climbed by Edward Shackleton, later Lord Shackleton, in November 1932. He took as his guide Tama Nilong, a rhinoceros hunter who had discovered the route up the mountain. For years explorers had found their way blocked by 600 metre high rock cliffs. Tama Nilong was hot in the pursuit of a rhinoceros, when he found the way up through the cliffs which climbers use today. He emerged on the south-west ridge. From there it took him thirteen days, without food, to get back to his village. The journey to the summit of Gunung Mulu is far less arduous today, being suitable for anybody who is reasonably fit.

Sarawak is well endowed with caves, for along the coast, between Bintulu and Miri, are the famous limestone caves of **Niah National Park**. A 4 km plank walk through the jungle brings visitors to the mouth of the **Great Cave**, great not only in size, but also in terms of its archaeological importance. In the 19th century a so-called expert dismissed the site as being 'wholly without interest, except to local naturalists'. In 1954 a team from the Sarawak Museum, under the leadership of the curator Tom Harrison, decided to do some digging of its own. In the deep deposits of guano, Harrison unearthed a series of prehistoric treasures. The most exciting discovery, found over 2 metres below the surface, was a human skull, nearly forty thousand years old, making it the earliest evidence of the existence of *homo sapiens*

Opposite, left: *The entrance to Deer Cave and the profile of Abraham Lincoln.* ***Opposite, right:*** *Some of the magnificent limestone formations in Lang's Cave.* ***Below:*** *The Great Cave in Niah National Park. The poles hanging from the ceiling of the cave are used by the bird's nest collectors. At the entrance is the house where Tom Harrison and his wife lived during the excavations at Niah.*

in South East Asia. Close to the excavation site, just inside the cave's stalactite fringed entrance, is the small wooden house where Harrison and his wife lived during their time at Niah. The modern home of man thus stands dwarfed within the ancient home of early man.

The importance of the cave is not only archaeological, it is also home to a very large swiftlet and bat population. Swiftlet spit and bat droppings may sound distinctly unappealing, but they are an important source of income for the local population. The swiftlets possess specialised saliva glands which produce a 'nest cement'. This binds the material for their nests together, and is also strong enough to attach them to the cave wall. The saliva is a prized Chinese delicacy, forming the vital ingredient in the famous bird's nest soup. The excavations revealed that trade in the edible nests began around a thousand years ago. To reach the nests, the local villagers shin up poles hanging hundreds of feet from the cave roof. Just looking up at the poles is enough to make most people feel dizzy. The collectors take no safety precautions, risking a fatal fall every time they leave the ground. As you watch them make their precarious ascent, you find your own palms becoming moist and your mouth dry, and you can only wonder at the courage and fearlessness which enables them even to contemplate such a climb.

The nests are 'harvested' twice a year. In October they are collected before the swiftlets have had time to lay their eggs, forcing the birds to build a second nest. In May, when the young birds have flown, the replacement nests are collected. Before reaching the Great Cave, visitors pass through the **Traders' Cave**. This was once a thriving market place for the nests. The collectors, traders and their families lived there throughout the harvesting period. Improved access means that day trips are now possible and Traders' Cave is rarely used. It was also used as a base by Niah's guano collectors. The guano, deposited by the bats and birds on the cave floor for thousands of years, is much in demand as a fertiliser.

An eerie, timeless tranquillity pervades the mouth of the Great Cave. That is, until dusk, when it comes alive with the bats pouring out for the night shift, and the swiftlets returning to the cave after a day's work searching for food. Occasionally, a bird of prey may be seen soaring among them. Gliding majestically on the thermals at the cave mouth, it selects its target, and then, in a split second, swoops and catches a bat in mid-air. As they stream in overhead, the continual chirping of the swiftlets sounds almost like children giggling. Perhaps they are laughing at the folly of man, who is willing to take such risks and pay so much just for their spit! The Great Cave is linked to a series of smaller caves, which stretch to the other side of the limestone massif. Here, in an adjacent limestone outcrop, another exciting discovery was made.

In a small, shallow cave, Harrison found a series of haematite rock paintings, similar in style to the aboriginal cave paintings of Australia. Spread over sixty metres of cave wall, the murals depict an array of human figures, animals and boats. The cave was once used as a cemetery and the paintings are all associated with the death rituals practised at that time. Several 'death-ships' were found on the floor of the cave, and carbon dated to around twelve hundred years ago. Resembling small canoes, some of these coffin structures remain in the cave today. It is easy to understand why, in a land of rivers and at a time when boats were the only means of communication in this life, they should be used to carry the dead into the next world.

Opposite: *The stream of bats leaving Deer Cave in search of dinner.*

SABAH
P. BALAMBANGAN
P. BANGGI
0
50
100 km
KUDAT
SOUTH CHINA SEA
SULU SEA
Marudu Bay
S. Kinarut
KOTA MARUDI
KOTA BELUD
MT. KINABALU(4,101m)
TUARAN
PORING
P. GAYA
KUNDASANG
KOTA KINABALU
TANJUNG ARU
RANAU
SANDAKAN
PAPAR
S. Labuk
TAMBUNAN
K. PENYU
TELUPID
BEAUFORT
KENINGAU
S. Kinabatangan
LABUAN
S. Padas
PINANGAH
S. Segama
TENOM
LAHAD DATU
KEMABONG
RUNDUM
PENSIANGAN
SEMPORNA
LONG PASIA
SARAWAK
TAWAU
KALIMANTAN (INDONESIA)
CELEBES SEA
KEY
MAJOR ROADS
WEST COAST RAILWAY
AIRPORTS / AIRSTRIPS
STATE BOUNDARY
INTERNATIONAL BORDER
1 TUNKU ABDUL RAHMAN PARK
2 PENAMPANG
3 MAT SALLEH MEMORIAL
4 RAFFLESIA INFORMATION CENTRE
5 BAJAU FISHING VILLAGES
6 PULAU SIPADAN
7 KAMPUNG MOMPILIS
8 SEPILOK FOREST RESERVE
9 GOMANTONG CAVES
10 TURTLE ISLANDS PARK
11 PORING HOT SPRINGS

SABAH

The Land Below the Wind

While the British, in the guise of James Brooke and his family, made a positive contribution to the development of Sarawak, it was a very different story in Sabah, the country in the far north of Borneo. Here British rule was nowhere near as effective. All too often financial exploitation and personal gain were to ride roughshod over the customs and livelihoods of the local people. Not surprisingly, there was considerable opposition to colonial authority, bringing to the fore national heroes such as the legendary Mat Salleh. Visitors to Sabah today will see very few signs of British rule, as they left very little behind them when the Union Jack was lowered for the last time in 1963.

Two hundred years earlier the British had first set foot in Sabah, raising the flag on **Pulau Balambangan**, an island off the northern tip of the mainland. The subsequent tale of the settlement on Balambangan exhibited many of the worst aspects of colonial rule. The island had been ceded to the British East India Company (EIC) by the sultan of Sulu in 1762. At that time the British did not possess a port and trading centre in South East Asia, as Francis Light would not land on Penang for over twenty years. Balambangan appeared initially to fit the bill. The island had two good harbours, ample supplies of fresh water and timber, and was ideally located on the route taken by the Chinese junks in their annual passage south to trade in Brunei. However, the island also had its drawbacks, being largely low-lying and covered by mangrove swamps and poor sandy soils, and was never likely to attract trade away from the established ports in the region, such as Batavia.

After a long delay, John Herbert was appointed as the first governor. The EIC could scarcely have found a more unsuitable person if they had tried. Herbert took two years to take up the post, finally arriving in 1773, and then proceeded to swindle the EIC out of vast sums of money. He also cheated the native merchants and insulted the local lords, including a cousin of the sultan of Sulu. Disease had already reduced the EIC garrison to a quarter of its original strength, when in March 1775 a large force of Sulus and Ilanun pirates overran the British settlement. Herbert fled, though he was probably not too disappointed to see all the EIC records, and the evidence against him, going up in flames.

The British did not entirely give up on Balambangan. For over a quarter of a century the island was left alone, remote and apparently abandoned to the elements. Then in 1803, during the Napoleonic Wars, the British reoccupied it as a naval base, to counter the Spanish presence in the Philippines. Balambangan though had not changed its spots, and remained a deeply inhospitable place. The British troops were almost immediately short of food, the two ships carrying most of the supplies having sunk on the voyage to Borneo. Disease broke out and, as the number of dead grew, morale amongst the

State crest: *The two arms holding the state flag symbolise unity and cooperation between Sabah's ethnic communities. Below is the outline of Mount Kinabalu, the granite massif which dominates the state. The state motto is 'progressive and enlightened'.* ***Pages 278-279:*** *Mount Kinabalu's lofty peaks.*

garrison plummeted. In 1805 the British abandoned Balambangan for the last time.

There is an interesting postscript to the story of Balambangan. No merchandise was ever recovered from the island after the attack in 1775. Did the pirates get it all, or did Herbert and his men have time to hide it? Rumours soon spread that Herbert had buried some of the merchandise in a well. One or two expeditions even went to Balambangan to try and find it, but nothing was ever discovered. To the very end Balambangan had been a profound disappointment.

For today's visitors the coastal islands of Sabah are anything but a disappointment. The most popular are the group of islands lying in the South China Sea which form the **Tunku Abdul Rahman Park**. There are five islands in the park: Gaya, Mamutik, Mamutan, Sapi and Sulug. All of them can be reached by a short boat trip from the marina in Kota Kinabalu, the state capital, or from the jetty beside the luxurious resort hotel at Tanjung Aru. The islands are an ideal tonic for weary travellers, with their sandy beaches, inviting warm waters and coral reefs. Fish life abounds in the shallow, clear water, and you might well be treated to the sight and sound of parrot fish munching away on the coral.

On **Pulau Gaya**, the largest of the islands, a plank walk has been laid across an inlet of mangrove trees, allowing visitors to examine at close quarters this most distinctive of vegetations. Mangrove forest has always been a feature of the Sabah coastline and today it covers about 350 sq km of the state. It flourishes in a harsh environment, being subjected to inundation by the tides, strong winds and salt sprays. The soil is usually waterlogged and acidic, with a high level of salinity. The trees can reach a height of 25 metres, but what distinguishes a mangrove forest is the tangled and impenetrable mass of stilt roots, which support the trees in the unstable ground. Many of the trees produce seeds which germinate while still attached to the branches. Long roots grow out from the seeds which, after dropping from the tree,

anchor themselves in the soft mud. If they land in the water, they float until they find a suitable place to take root in the mud. Crabs, prawns and snails proliferate in mangrove forests, and at low tide mudskippers are a common sight. These are small fish which have learned how to walk, or more specifically waddle, on their fins.

The modern day peace and beauty of Tunku Abdul Rahman Park should not disguise the fact that the islands dotting the coastline were once the natural lair of pirate fleets. In any one of a thousand lonely bays and coves, deserted save for the birds, the pirates waited and watched, ever on the look out for a passing merchant ship. Having sighted their prey, the issue was seldom in doubt. The swift moving pirate vessels were quickly off in pursuit, easily overhauling their victim. Once they had pulled alongside, the pirates leapt on to the deck of the merchant vessel in their deadly quest for plunder. The most ferocious of all the pirates who infested the seas around Sabah were the Ilanun. Their principal base was on the island of Mindanau in the Philippines, but they also had settlements along the Sabah coast.

Ilanun ships, proud and mighty, can only have evoked fear in all who had the misfortune to set eyes upon them. Some were as long as thirty metres and weighed over sixty tons. They were powered by as many as a hundred slave oarsmen. The ships did not have masts, but were fitted with sheers which could be raised or lowered very rapidly. When raised, the sheers supported a huge mat sail. In the bow was the principal armament of the ship, a great brass cannon. Another less powerful piece was placed in the stern, while numerous swivel guns were also mounted on solid uprights along the sides. The Ilanun warriors were as fearsome a sight as their ships. They were dressed in tunics of vivid scarlet, surmounted by coats of mail, and wore feathered head-dresses. Their favoured

Opposite: *Pulau Sapi, one of the five islands in Tunku Abdul Rahman Park.*
Below: *A suspension bridge across one of Sabah's rivers.*

weapon was a great double-handed sword, or *kampilan*. The Ilanun custom was to insert a small brass stud in the blade to signify each kill. Some *kampilans* have been found with over twenty studs.

The Ilanun never had any reservations about attacking European merchant ships, with the crews often being put to the sword. They were still a menace in 1846 when the British returned to Sabah, acquiring the island of **Labuan** from the sultan of Brunei. Indeed one of the chief attractions of Labuan for the British was the island's potential as a naval base to combat the pirates. The name Labuan is derived from the Malay word *labuhan*, which means anchorage. The island never really flourished. The British had long had their eyes on the coal deposits at the northern end of the island. However, they discovered that the coal was of such a low quality as to be virtually worthless. The mines were also dogged by labour problems. Conditions were appalling, malaria was rampant and the workers, many of whom were convicts, resorted in desperation to a series of riots and strikes. Labuan is today a far happier place, a Federal Territory since 1984, and prospering as a free trade port and offshore financial centre.

This theme of opposition to British commercial exploitation was to be continued when Sabah came under the control of the privately owned British North Borneo Company later in the 19th century. The Company gave its name to the land of Sabah, calling it British North Borneo, but to the local population the country was always Sabah. The origins of the name are now unfortunately unknown. Sabah has also acquired other names, all of which testify to its attractions as a land. To seafarers of old it was the 'Land Below the Wind', due to its position to the south of the typhoon belt, while to early British pioneers Sabah was known as 'New Ceylon'. The country's climate and rich soil reminded them of the exotic island at the southern tip of India.

British North Borneo came into being in 1881. The sultan of Sulu ceded his rights in Sabah for an annual payment of

RM5,000, while the sultan of Brunei did rather better, getting RM15,000 a year. The situation seemed to be the same as in Sarawak, but the principal figure behind the British North Borneo Company, Alfred Dent, was no James Brooke. His intentions were clear from the outset: exploitation and administration. If the tales of great riches to be found in the interior of Borneo had turned out to be true, the Company might perhaps have done more to improve the lot of the local people. Unfortunately, Sabah never lived up to the expectations of Dent and his colleagues, and for much of its existence, the Company was beset by financial troubles.

Among the British North Borneo Company's few achievements was the construction of the **west coast railway**, completed in 1905. For over half a century the railway was the lifeline of the west coast communities, as the road was not built until the 1960s. The railway still runs today, covering the 154 km between Kota Kinabalu and Tenom, and is well worth a trip. There are two types of service operating on the line: the railcar, which runs between Beaufort and Tenom, and the local train. The railcar is faster, more comfortable and predominantly aimed at tourists, but taking the local train, which runs the whole length of the railway, is a more interesting experience. What the train lacks in sophistication, it more than makes up for in local colour. The journey is slow, bumpy and noisy, and on occasions the coaches can become very crowded as the train stops at the settlements along the route.

From Kota Kinabalu the line passes through attractive rural scenes, with *padi* fields and *kampungs*, to the sleepy town of **Papar**. From there the train rattles on to **Beaufort**, where most of Sabah's rubber estates were to be found during British times. Beaufort is situated on the banks of the Padas River, indeed on occasions in it,

Opposite: *St Michael's Church in Penampang, the oldest church in Sabah.* ***Below:*** *The local train running alongside the Padas River as it heads towards Tenom.*

as in the past the river has often flooded the town. After Beaufort the scenery becomes much more dramatic as the train enters the Padas Gorge. The line runs alongside the fast-flowing waters of the Padas River, a popular venue for the exhilarating sport of white-water rafting. You might even catch a glimpse of a raft shooting one of the many sets of rapids as you pass by. Suddenly, a seat in the train seems very safe and very dry. The line ends at Tenom in the heart of Murut country.

Sabah today has a population of some 1.4 million people, of almost bewildering racial and cultural diversity, with over 30 ethnic groupings, over 50 different languages and some 100 dialects. The demands of modern bureaucracy have led to many of the tribes being grouped together, while the ease of movement in recent years has also done much to break down earlier barriers and several groups have been absorbed by others. Sadly, some of the tribal names, as revealed in the first census of 1891, have now disappeared, such as the Booloodoopies, the Eraans and the intriguingly named Sabahans from Darvel Bay.

The Muruts are one of Sabah's four basic indigenous groups. Significantly, they do not use the term Murut, which means hill people, preferring to call themselves by their original tribal names. They mainly inhabit the interior divisions of Tenom, Keningau and Pensiangan. The Muruts are traditionally a semi-nomadic people, clearing an area by slash-and-burn, cultivating it for a few years and then moving on. Their staple diet is rice and tapioca, both of which they ferment into *tapai*, a highly potent brew. They have always been renowned hunters, being highly adept with both spear and blowpipe, and were the last people in Sabah to give up head-hunting.

The Muruts originally lived in longhouses, but as with their semi-nomadic practices, many have now abandoned the communal lifestyle. Murut longhouses are only found in the more remote areas to the south of Tenom. The old world and the new meet in the village of **Kemabong**. The inhabitants now live in individual family

homes, but they have maintained the spirit associated with the longhouse by building a community centre. Here they meet, entertain their friends and celebrate special occasions, all of which were the principal functions of the communal passageway in the original longhouses. They have even reproduced the unique feature of Murut longhouses, the *lansaran*, or sprung dance floor. The experience is something like bouncing around on a trampoline, while in a crowd. On festive occasions, money is often hung from the rafters and everyone tries to bounce high enough to grab it.

In the past certain rituals had to be followed when the Muruts built their longhouses, in order to prevent bad spirits, which might bring sickness, death or fire, from entering. These rituals were part of their animistic beliefs. Today most of the Muruts have converted to Islam or Christianity. The *amparawak* ceremony was carried out just before building operations commenced and was designed to drive away any spirits resting at the site. It was performed by a *mentuo*, one of the village elders, and involved the sacrifice of a white rooster. The blood was sprinkled on both the site and the feet of the builders. If certain animals, such as a mousedeer, a wild pig or a snake, were spotted at the site during construction, they were considered bad omens. Building ceased and another location was found.

In 1915 the Muruts from the **Rundum** district, to the south-east of Tenom, rebelled against the rule of the British North Borneo Company. They had a whole crop of grievances, including the level of taxation, in particular that imposed on their *tapai*, and the burden of compulsory, unpaid work. The British preferred to attribute the discontent to German spies. Hundreds of Muruts were killed by Company troops as the revolt was brutally suppressed. This disaster came in the wake of a drought in Rundum which had lasted

Opposite: *Kadazan children playing at the memorial in Tambunan to Mat Salleh, the greatest of Sabah's heroes.* ***Above:*** *An elderly Kadazan woman.*

for eight months, causing severe food shortages. Villages and longhouses were left deserted, as the inhabitants fled into the jungle. The name Rundum, which means cheerless in the Murut language, was well deserved.

From Tenom the main road heads to the north and the town of **Keningau**, the gateway to Kadazan country. The Kadazans are the largest indigenous group in Sabah, making up a third of the total population, though, as with the Muruts, the grouping includes several different tribes, who hold common cultural beliefs and speak similar languages. Some of the Kadazans prefer to be called Dusans, while others have kept their original tribal names, such as the Rungus from the Kudat area and the Lotuds who come from around Tuaran. Occupying the fertile plains along the west coast, the Kadazans have traditionally been *padi* farmers. Like the Muruts they have a healthy taste for *tapai*. This is never more so than every May, when the Kadazans celebrate the rice harvest in time-honoured fashion by consuming large quantities of the stuff. The Kadazan Harvest Festival has become a major event in Sabah with a two day public holiday.

The spiritual purpose of the festival is to give thanks to *Minamangun*, the creator of the world, and his wife *Suminundu*, for sacrificing their only daughter *Huminodun*, so that rice could grow from her body to feed the Kadazan people. The life force which sprang from her body is known as the *bambaazon*. It is the *bambaazon* which the Kadazans wish to bring into their homes during the Harvest Festival, thus ensuring prosperity in the year ahead. To achieve this each family calls upon the services of a *bobohizan*, or high priestess. Before the start of the harvest, she places seven stalks of ripe *padi*, representing the *bambaazon*, in the centre of each field. When the harvest is completed, the stalks are taken from the field to the owner's house and put in the family rice store, or *tangkob*. This is an enclosure made of tree bark and usually located in the attic. The family then gives thanks for a

COURTESY OF MUZIUM NEGARA

successful harvest and prays for more good harvests in the future, before starting the celebrations in the village.

To the north-east of Keningau is one of the historic sites of Sabah, the Tambunan valley. This is the heart of Kadazan country and where Mat Salleh, the greatest of Sabah's heroes, met his death at the hands of the British in January 1900. Mat Salleh was the son of a Sulu chief who controlled part of Sabah before the arrival of the British. Tales of Mat Salleh's feats still abound. As a youth he had been able to throw a buffalo by its horns. Flames were said to come out of his mouth. On one occasion he scattered rice which promptly turned into wasps. Mat Salleh was also reputed to possess the power of *kebal*. He had gained this by spending three days and nights in the jungle, fasting and praying to the spirits of his ancestors. On the third night his ancestors had given him special knowledge, making him invulnerable to all weapons. Given the many tales and legends circulating about Mat Salleh, it is hardly surprising that the local people, resentful of British rule, should support him in such numbers.

The British leaders who met Mat Salleh were struck by his appearance, one calling him the 'Rob Roy of British North Borneo'. He was a born jungle fighter and it took the British nearly five years to come to terms with the threat he posed in Sabah. On more than one occasion, they thought it wiser to negotiate with him rather than fight. His strategy was simple but very effective. He raided at will, before withdrawing to one of his forts. If the British threatened the fort, he fled into the jungle, reappearing later in another part of the country. Mat Salleh's most audacious raid was undoubtedly that on Pulau Gaya in 1897. He knew Gaya well, having spent part of his childhood there, and looted and burnt every house on the island. The end came at his fort in Tambunan three years later. The British

Opposite: *The Rafflesia, the world's largest flower.* ***Above:*** *Bajau women working in the padi fields.*

succeeded in surrounding the fort and launched a ferocious bombardment, during which Mat Salleh was killed.

A memorial to Mat Salleh has been erected in **Tambunan** at the site of his last stand. It is set in a small garden which is looked after by the local villagers, whose forefathers idolised Mat Salleh and fought alongside him. Some were probably among the three hundred who died with Mat Salleh during the British attack. From the Tambunan valley the road winds its way up into the **Crocker Range**, which runs like a spine through the state. There are stunning views of the rolling hills and countryside below. This is an area where the world's largest flower, the Rafflesia, is found. By the roadside is the **Rafflesia Information Centre**, which houses a permanent display on this extraordinary flower.

The Rafflesia is very rare, growing in only a handful of locations in South East Asia. Some varieties have not been sighted for nearly a hundred years and may already be extinct. The largest species, *Rafflesia arnoldii*, can grow to nearly a metre in diameter. The plant owes its name to Stamford Raffles, as it was first discovered during an expedition he led to western Sumatra in 1818. The discovery caused a sensation amongst the European scientific community, with some experts questioning whether it was a plant at all. The parasitic lifestyle of the Rafflesia is just as fascinating as its size. It lives on a host vine, the *Tetrastigma*, and has become so adept as a parasite that it consists solely of a single flower, without any roots, leaves or stem.

The Rafflesia takes nine months to blossom and, during this stage, it is much sought after by village *bomohs* and Chinese *sinsehs*, or traditional doctors, for its supposed medicinal qualities. In Peninsular Malaysia it is sometimes given to mothers to help them recover their strength following childbirth. The giant bud normally bursts open at night, but its magnificent, fleshy bloom lasts for only a few days. The rarity of the plant, combined with its short life span, makes the Rafflesia an uncommon sight. The

pollination process helps to explain its rarity. There are separate male and female flowers and pollination is carried out by insects. This requires the male and female flowers to blossom at roughly the same time in the same area. Some Rafflesia give off a strong smell of rotting meat to attract insects, an odour described by one explorer as 'more repulsive than any buffalo carcass in an advanced stage of decomposition'.

After the Kadazans, the next largest indigenous group in Sabah are the Bajaus. They are probably among the state's more recent arrivals, possibly coming from the Philippines only two centuries ago. The Bajaus were originally a seafaring people, also known as the 'sea gypsies', who lived along the coast. This changed when the British North Borneo Company came to Sabah. They associated the Bajaus with the Ilanun, forcibly resettled large numbers of them and made them earn a living as farmers. This inevitably brought about profound changes in Bajau society, which are most apparent on the west coast, in particular around the town of **Kota Belud**. Here the Bajaus are renowned for their skills as horsemen, which has earned them the nickname of the 'cowboys of Sabah'. On festive occasions they dress themselves and their horses in colourful costumes and parade through the town. Racing for many of the younger Bajaus is a passion, not just on their horses, but also on buffaloes.

On Sundays Kota Belud is the setting for one of Sabah's most popular *tamus*, or open-air markets. It is at its liveliest before 8 am. Business slows down as the sun rises in the sky, and by lunchtime everyone has packed up and gone home. People come from all the surrounding villages to meet their friends and exchange news and gossip. The local traders spread their wares on the ground for potential customers to view. Many of the Bajau women, old and young alike, enjoy chewing betel-nuts, so a friendly smile comes as something of a

Opposite: *The buffalo auction at Kota Belud.* ***Below:*** *A Bajau woman at the tamu in Kota Belud selling brightly coloured tudung saji, or food coverings.*

surprise for visitors. Their teeth and gums are stained deep red from the habit. There is a wide range of items on sale. You can even buy a buffalo at the cattle auction held in one corner of the market.

On the east coast of Sabah many of the Bajaus still follow the old traditions, living in water villages and earning a living from fishing. The best place to see Bajau fishing boats, with their billowing sails, is **Semporna**. The fishing villages, built on stilts, sprawl into the sea on either side of the main town. The people are always friendly and offer a cheery greeting as you negotiate your way along the rickety wooden pavements. Keep an eye out for the odd missing plank. Visitors should also keep a look out for the model wooden boats which some of the fishermen carve in their spare time.

The fishing grounds lie in the rich waters of the Celebes Sea. The waters off Semporna are studded with numerous islands, the most famous being **Pulau Sipadan**, which is formed by a limestone pinnacle, rising over 600 metres from the seabed and mushrooming out near the surface. A few metres from the shore, the sea suddenly turns from turquoise to deep blue, where there is a sheer drop down to the ocean floor. This is considered to be one of South East Asia's best diving locations, offering spectacular wall diving. The wall has colourful coral reefs, underwater cliffs and caverns, and abundant fish life. Among the many species found around Sipadan are sharks, barracuda, grouper, tuna and green turtles. Jacques Cousteau visited the island in 1988 and described it as 'an untouched piece of art'.

The vast majority of Sabah's rural population gained very few benefits from the years of the British North Borneo Company. To them it was always alien rule and mistrust was widespread. Many officials in the early years made no attempt to master the languages, or familiarise themselves with the customs of the various ethnic groups. Making a profit was always paramount. The rubber boom at the start of the 20th century led to the wholesale seizure of land for rubber estates, in many

cases with no compensation being paid to the local communities. The rule of the British North Borneo Company came to an end after the Second World War. The costs of reconstruction were far beyond the finances of the Company and in July 1946 Sabah, like Sarawak, became a British colony.

The British North Borneo Company chose the town of **Kudat** in the far north of the country as its first capital. The town had only just been founded and amounted to little more than a handful of atap houses built on stilts in the sea. The Company had high hopes for Kudat. It had a fine harbour on the western side of Marudu Bay, but still failed to attract any significant trade, and after two years the British moved on. Kudat remains a small, quiet town today. It can be reached by road from Kota Kinabalu, but the best and quickest way to get to Kudat is by the MAS Rural Air Service, which operates in Sabah and Sarawak linking the rural communities to the principal towns. In most cases there are no roads between the destinations. The flight to Kudat is in a rather cramped Twin Otter aircraft and takes around forty minutes. It is all great fun. There is a real sense of flying which you miss in the big carriers. You may well be asked your weight before you board and, if you are unsure, a set of scales is there to jog your memory. It is not that you are destined for the cargo hold, though that could hardly be more cramped than the cabin. There has to be a balanced and proportionate distribution of weight in the aircraft to ensure a safe take-off and landing.

The area around Kudat is where the Rungus, one of the Kadazan groups, are to be found. They are the only Kadazans who still live in longhouses. A particularly fine example is to be found at **Kampung Mompilis** in the Matunggong district,

Opposite: *Bajau boys at one of the fishing villages in Semporna.* ***Above:*** *A Rungus woman weaving a piece of cloth in the communal corridor of her longhouse at Kampung Mompilis. She is wearing brass coils on her forearms.*

some 46 km from Kudat. Rungus longhouses are built along an east-west axis to ensure a cool atmosphere. The longhouses are distinctive in that the walls lean outwards. Each family has its own unit called a *valai*. In the delightfully cool communal corridor, Rungus children can often be seen playing, while the women chat, prepare food, or make handicraft items. Rungus women are deservedly renowned for their weaving and fine beadwork. They used to wear brass coils around their necks, forearms and lower legs. Today the leg and neck coils are a rare sight, but the forearm coils are still worn, often with a knee-length black sarong.

In 1883 **Sandakan** on the eastern coast became the second capital of British North Borneo. Unlike Kudat, it grew in leaps and bounds, and the port was soon the busiest in the country. When there was no longer any land suitable for further building, a programme of reclamation was commenced. Most of the present town was in earlier times under water. The prosperity of Sandakan has always been associated with timber. On any flight into the town today, one of the first sights will probably be the logs floating in pens in the bay, though much of the timber industry has now moved elsewhere in Sabah and there is an air of past glories about the town. It was from Sandakan that the infamous death march to **Ranau** started in September 1944. Some 1,800 Australian and 600 British prisoners of war, all starving and many already sick, set out to march the 240 km to Ranau. It took nearly a year and only six Australians survived to recount the horrific story. Two of them managed to slip off down the Labuk River, reaching the sea where they were rescued. The other four fled from Ranau and were later found by the Kadazans in the Kundasang district.

Sandakan's greatest attraction for visitors is the **Sepilok Forest Reserve**, with its world famous Orang-Utan Rehabilitation Centre. The Centre looks after orang-utans rescued from captivity or displaced by forest clearance, and prepares them for life back in the wild. Orang-utans

became a protected species in Sabah in 1963, as concern mounted over their declining numbers. A law was introduced prohibiting the capture or killing of orang-utans, and the government set up the Rehabilitation Centre to take care of the confiscated apes. Since its inception over 130 orang-utans have been released back into the jungle. The Reserve covers some 4,000 hectares and provides the orang-utans with a protected environment, safe from man and his machines.

Sepilok offers a wonderful opportunity to see these shaggy russet-haired apes in their natural habitat. The orang-utan is unique to the islands of Borneo and Sumatra, and is the only representative of the world's great apes living outside central Africa. This intelligent, strong and slow moving primate, with its endearingly human facial characteristics and actions, is man's closest relative in the animal world. The name comes from the Malay words *orang hutan,* which mean 'man of the forest'. It is one of the few names of Malay origin which is used throughout the world, though it is ironically not the name used by the local inhabitants. In Sabah the orang-utan is known as the *kogiu*, while in Sarawak it is called a *mias*. Many of the local people believe that to look into the face of an orang-utan brings bad luck and, worse still, you will turn into stone if you laugh at one.

Fully grown male orang-utans are much larger than their female counterparts. They may reach almost 1.5 metres in height and weigh up to 100kg, though they can exceed twice this weight in captivity, where they tend to be overweight from too much food and a lack of exercise. Their long, powerful arms can span up to 2.4 metres. Orang-utans live in the trees, rarely descending to the ground. They make a treetop nest out of twigs and branches in which to sleep at night. As they are bulky and have no tail to help them balance, orang-utans never jump like monkeys. The

Opposite and above: *Some of the orang-utans in playful mood at the Sepilok Forest Reserve.*

risk of injury from a fall is too great. They move among the trees in a rather ponderous style by swinging from branch to branch. Orang-utans feed mainly on fruit and, like most Malaysians, have a marked taste for durian. They are solitary animals, but not territorial, living in overlapping ranges. When they do meet in the wild, they tend to ignore each other.

Orang-utans are slow growing, and only after five to seven years do they become independent of their mothers. Unfortunately, many of the orang-utans brought to Sepilok have been parted from their mothers at an early age. They have to be taught the skills they would have learnt from her in the wild, including climbing trees, nest building and searching for food. The process of rehabilitation to forest life is a slow one, usually taking several years. New arrivals are placed in quarantine for at least two months, to prevent any infectious diseases being passed on to the other apes. They are all given names, among them Bobby, Jessica and King, which make them seem more human than ever. Every day the young novices are fed on bananas and milk at a feeding platform just inside the forest, and it is here that visitors come to observe them.

Feeding time is a highly entertaining spectacle, as the orang-utans appear from the surrounding jungle. Each has its own character. One or two seem very impatient, and make their way past the assembled audience without so much as a hello. Some are real exhibitionists and like to show off their acrobatic skills in front of the camera, hanging and swinging amongst the trees like ungainly trapeze artists. They have a comic air about them with their childish antics and puckered-up impish faces. They are renowned for their inquisitive, naughty natures, and it is advisable to keep an eye on your personal belongings, such as hats and bags. They are particularly attracted to brightly coloured objects, and you might find yourself in a friendly tug of war over your knapsack. Indeed, on one occasion, a visitor was playfully stripped of his clothes! Park rangers keep a watchful eye

on proceedings and reprimand any misbehaving apes. Cheeky macaque monkeys join the orang-utans on the feeding platform for a free meal.

As their survival skills improve and they become more independent, the orang-utans are fed at another platform deeper in the forest. The meals provided are deliberately monotonous to encourage them to seek more and more food for themselves, and so become increasingly self-sufficient. The rehabilitation process is completed when they become fully independent. Although the Sepilok Forest Reserve has an important part to play in the protection of the species, prevention is obviously better than cure. The main threat to orang-utans today is destruction of the rain forests, and the most important way of ensuring the survival of the wild population is to conserve adequate areas of their natural habitat.

Other protected animals brought to Sepilok include elephants and the very rare two-horned Sumatran rhinoceros. This animal was once found throughout most of South East Asia, and during the early days of Sandakan they were even known to wander into the town. Today the picture is sadly very different. They have been relentlessly hunted for their horns, which are believed to possess certain medicinal qualities, as well as being thought an aphrodisiac. Scientific evidence offers no support for these claims. The natural habitat of the Sumatran rhinoceros has also rapidly disappeared in many places. The total number is now estimated at five hundred and still declining. One of their last breeding populations is located on Sabah's east coast. Sepilok has three males and a female, all captured by the Sabah Wildlife Department. The hope is to breed them in captivity as a precaution against their possible extinction in the wild.

Sandakan was badly damaged by

Opposite: *The modern town of Kota Kinabalu with the South China Sea in the background.* ***Below:*** *A young man displaying his deep sea wares at the wet market in Sandakan.*

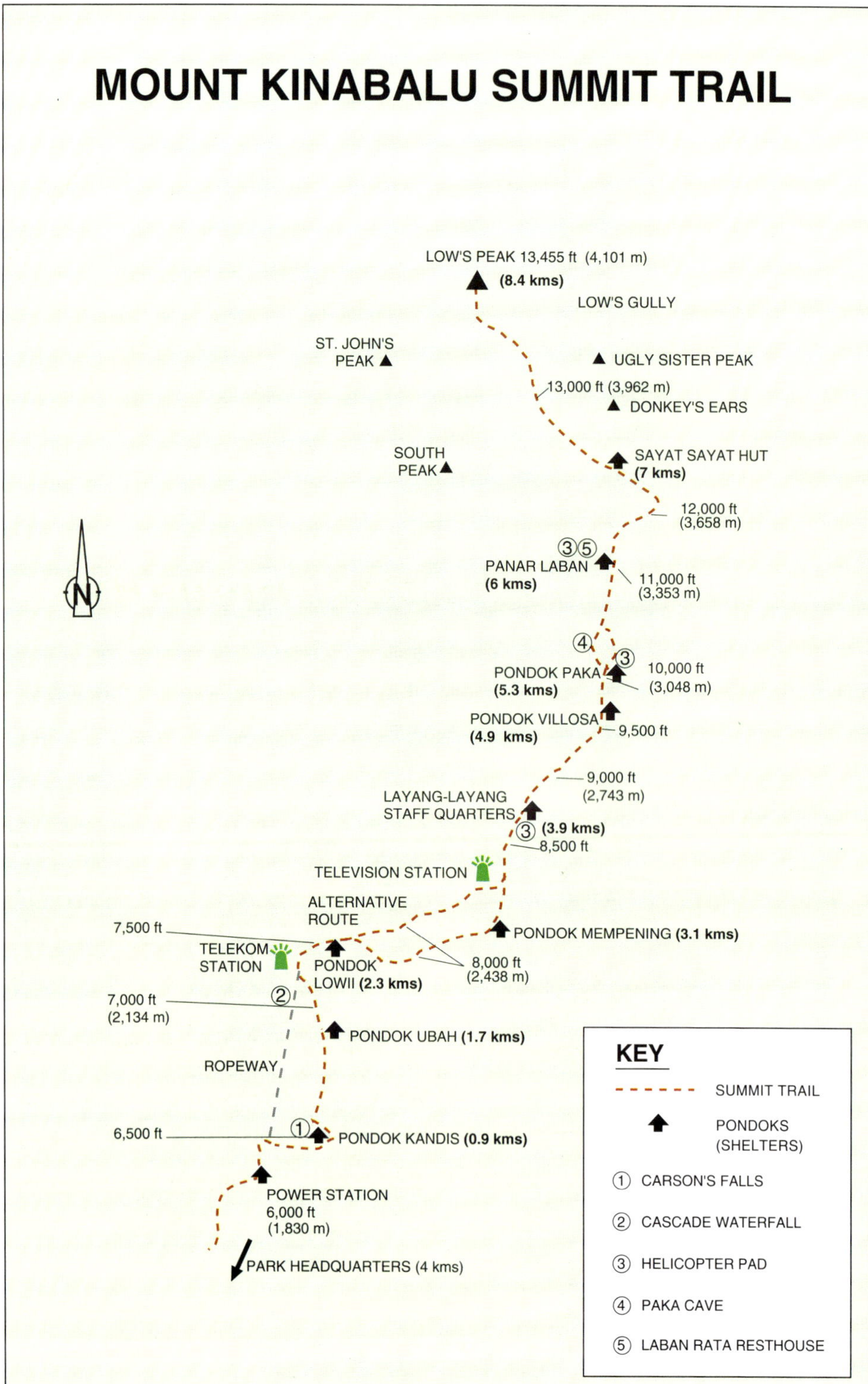
MOUNT KINABALU SUMMIT TRAIL
LOW'S PEAK 13,455 ft (4,101 m)
(8.4 kms)
LOW'S GULLY
ST. JOHN'S PEAK
UGLY SISTER PEAK
13,000 ft (3,962 m)
DONKEY'S EARS
SOUTH PEAK
SAYAT SAYAT HUT
(7 kms)
12,000 ft
(3,658 m)
③⑤
PANAR LABAN
(6 kms)
11,000 ft
(3,353 m)
N
④
③
PONDOK PAKA
(5.3 kms)
10,000 ft
(3,048 m)
PONDOK VILLOSA
(4.9 kms)
9,500 ft
9,000 ft
(2,743 m)
LAYANG-LAYANG STAFF QUARTERS
③ (3.9 kms)
8,500 ft
TELEVISION STATION
ALTERNATIVE ROUTE
7,500 ft
PONDOK MEMPENING (3.1 kms)
TELEKOM STATION
PONDOK LOWII (2.3 kms)
8,000 ft
(2,438 m)
②
7,000 ft
(2,134 m)
PONDOK UBAH (1.7 kms)
ROPEWAY
6,500 ft
①
PONDOK KANDIS (0.9 kms)
POWER STATION
6,000 ft
(1,830 m)
PARK HEADQUARTERS (4 kms)
KEY
SUMMIT TRAIL
PONDOKS (SHELTERS)
① CARSON'S FALLS
② CASCADE WATERFALL
③ HELICOPTER PAD
④ PAKA CAVE
⑤ LABAN RATA RESTHOUSE

bombing during the Second World War and the capital was moved to **Kota Kinabalu**, then named Jesselton, in 1946. The new capital had also been bombed during the war and much of it had to be rebuilt, creating the thriving modern town of today. The most striking symbol of the new town, indeed of the state itself, is the glass-encased **Sabah Foundation Building** overlooking Likas Bay. The town may not have the historic charm of Kuching, but it is located in a magnificent setting, with hills and mountains behind and the sweeping bay in front. The name Jesselton was never much used outside the British community. As far as the locals were concerned, the town was called Api Api. The town was renamed Kota Kinabalu in 1967, after the mountain of that name which dominates Sabah's landscape.

The granite massif of **Mount Kinabalu** rises abruptly from the Crocker Range. Towering 4,101 metres (13,455 feet) above the surrounding jungle, Kinabalu is the highest mountain between the Himalayas and the Snow Mountains of New Guinea. The terrain stretches upwards from lowland rain forest to montane oak forest, which gives way to mossy forest and then hardy alpine vegetation, before reaching the bare granite crown. The summit plateau is split in two by a dramatic chasm, known as **Low's Gully**. This was thought for many years to be the remains of a crater, and the mountain was assumed to be an old volcano. Recent evidence has revealed that Mount Kinabalu is in fact the world's youngest non-volcanic mountain. It originated as a granite pluton deep beneath the earth's crust, which was forced up through the overlying rocks of the Crocker Range about a million years ago. The mountain is still 'growing' at 5mm a year. During the Ice Age huge glaciers smoothed out the summit plateau, while leaving surface scratches and striations as they moved downwards. The jagged peaks, jutting out above the ice, were left untouched. The rock face has been further sculptured over the centuries by the wind

Above: *The summit trail.*

and rain. This has resulted in thin layers of granite flaking off, giving the summit plateau a tiled appearance.

The mountain plays a central role in the folklore and beliefs of the Kadazan people. The most widely accepted explanation of the name is that it derives from the Kadazan words *aki nabalu*, meaning the 'revered place of the dead'. The Kadazans believe that the summit is the sacred resting place of the spirits of their ancestors, and treat it with the utmost respect. The Rungus always sleep with their heads at right angles to the mountain, believing that this will ensure a long life. If they wake up facing the mountain, their life will be cut short. Another explanation of the name is that it comes from a Kadazan love tale and means Chinese widow, *kina* being a corrupted form of China and *balu* a native word for widow. The legend tells of a Chinese prince who climbed the mountain in search of a huge pink pearl, said to be on the summit and guarded by a ferocious dragon. The prince slayed the dragon, in true St George fashion, and took the pearl. He then married a local Kadazan girl but, feeling homesick, he left her and returned to China. His heartbroken 'widow' took to wandering the mountain and eventually turned to stone.

Such beliefs and stories, together with the cold, deterred the local Kadazans from climbing the mountain, and it was not until 1851 that the first recorded ascent of Kinabalu was made by Hugh Low, the future British Resident of Perak. He found no sign of the legendary lake. For many years it had been believed that a huge lake existed somewhere on the mountain. All the major rivers in Borneo were believed to flow from it. A British official, Alexander Dalrymple, wrote in 1760 of 'the lake of Kenny-ballo. It is said that this lake lies on the south side of the mountain, and is so large that the land is not visible across it.' Belief in its existence was so widespread that the lake was even marked on some maps. Needless to say, the lake has never been found, but it is easy to understand how the myth arose. No less than eight major rivers have their source on Mount

Kinabalu.

The mountain is part of **Kinabalu Park**, which covers an area of 754 sq km and is located 60 km to the east of Kota Kinabalu. For those who decide not to attempt the climb to the top, there are 11 km of graded trails around park headquarters to explore. These wind their way through montane oak and chestnut forest, and acorns and spiny chestnut cases lie scattered along the way. Here you may see a twig walk or a leaf jump. This is not your eyes playing tricks on you. The twig is a large bark-coloured stick insect, while the leaf is another master of camouflage, the horned frog. It has a leaf rib marking on its back and its horns resemble leaf tips to complete the disguise. The park is home to several species of frog, and the rather melancholy burping and belching of the frog chorus is a familiar forest sound.

The striking black and orange coated trilobite larva is another of the forest's inhabitants which can often be seen along the park trails, eating its way through decaying plant matter. The name comes from its resemblance to fossilised prehistoric marine creatures. For many years, the trilobite was something of an entomological enigma. It was obviously the larva of some insect, only nobody knew which one. Specimens were taken to England for study, but the larvae never developed and died. A Swedish naturalist, Dr Eric Mjoberg, finally solved the mystery of the trilobite in the 1920s. He discovered that the larvae were in fact fully developed females, which kept their larval shape for life. Mjoberg put some females on view to lure the male of the species, and discover its mystery identity. His simple ploy worked. He described the moment of truth as follows: 'Imagine, then, my delight and surprise, when next morning I saw a pitiable little creature sitting firmly on the pointed posterior of the female....I had at last succeeded in surprising the rare male *in flagrante*!' The female's partner, about a fifth of her size, was a steel blue beetle.

Mount Kinabalu is much easier to climb today than it was for Hugh Low and the other early explorers. There is a well-marked trail to the top and each year

Opposite: *A lookout point along the trail.* ***Above:*** *The lipstick plant, one of the many colourful flowers which grows in Kinabalu Park.* ***Below:*** *Nepenthes lowii, one of the most striking pitcher plants to be found on Mount Kinabalu. The plant was named after Hugh Low, who first climbed the mountain in 1851.*

thousands of visitors attempt the 8 km trek up to Low's Peak, the highest point on the mountain. Most people split the journey, making it a two day return trip. No special skills or equipment are needed. As long as you are fairly fit you can make it to the top, but it is no pushover. Local Kadazans continue to act as guides and porters, as they did for the early explorers. All climbers must be accompanied by a guide to ensure their safe arrival at the summit...and their return.

Most people spend the night at park headquarters before heading up the mountain. From here there are stunning views of Kinabalu's jagged granite peaks, rising above the trees into the heavens. They look stark and foreboding against the early morning cool blue sky, and you sense you are in the presence of a great force. By midday the mountain has performed a disappearing act, enveloped in a wall of clouds.

The best time to begin the climb is between 7 am and 8 am, as it often rains in the afternoon. The first day's target is the resthouse and huts at Panar Laban, where climbers spend the night before tackling the summit. This section of the trail takes four to eight hours. There is no need to rush, although there tends to be an element of competition between climbers as to how long they take. It is far better to reserve energy levels and take second place. There is also much to see along the way. The trail starts at the **Power Station** (1,830 metres). Surprisingly, it begins by dipping down into a valley. Enjoy it while it lasts. From here it is uphill all the way. The track is essentially a stairway to the heavens, composed of thousands of steps made from tree roots and branches. Progress can be monitored by the 'You Are Here' maps posted at various points on the route. Walking uphill, one kilometre seems like two or three, and as you weary, even more. Thankfully, there are open shelters, or *pondoks*, at intervals along the trail, providing a welcome respite from the seemingly endless uphill struggle. The first shelter, **Pondok Kandis**, offers a panoramic view to the south-west and the road back to Kota Kinabalu, winding its

way tentatively through the dramatic mountainous landscape.

Above this level the mossy, or cloud, forest begins. The slopes are often shrouded in saturating mist, and the trees are draped in mosses and ferns which thrive in the damp atmosphere. Brightly coloured orchids add further decoration. Squirrels are a fairly common sight along the summit trail, scurrying amongst the trees. As Mount Kinabalu novices puff and pant their way up, porters stride past with a sprightly step, despite being loaded down with rucksacks and other equipment. These hardy Kadazan men and women climb the mountain several times a week. Making their way back down are tired but exuberant climbers, who have already conquered the summit. They assure you that the climb is well worth the effort and remain helpfully vague about the gruelling trek ahead.

One of the most interesting and distinctive plants found on the mountain is the famous carnivorous pitcher plant. The leaf tips form colourful cups, which act simultaneously as a trap and a stomach. Insects are attracted to the nectar secreted by glands near the top of the pitcher. Once inside there is no escape. The insects slide down the slippery inner wall and drown in the liquid at the bottom. Their corpses are then digested and absorbed through the leaf wall for a nutritious meal. This ingenious method of obtaining nourishment enables the pitcher plant to survive in poor soils. The largest species is the spectacular *Nepenthes rajah*, found only on Mount Kinabalu. Stories tell of drowned rats being found in its clutches. The highest altitude pitcher plant found on the mountain is *Nepenthes villosa*. It grows between **Layang-Layang Staff Quarters**, which marks the halfway point for the first day, and Pondok Paka.

Along this stretch of the track the vegetation becomes noticeably shorter, and you find yourself walking in a dwarf

Opposite: *The Laban Rata Resthouse.*
Below: *The summit plateau of Mount Kinabalu looking towards South Peak.*

forest. The trees are gnarled, bent and stunted due to the poor soil conditions and exposure to the harsh winds. Although small, many of the trees are hundreds of years old. **Pondok Paka** at 3,048 metres is the last of the shelters. It takes its name from Paka Cave, situated to the left of the main trail. This is where the early explorers set up camp for the night before climbing to the summit. Beyond Pondok Paka the vegetation shrinks still further. A ghostly mist closes in and the landscape takes on an unreal appearance, resembling a mystical world from the pages of a children's book, inhabited by goblins and pixies.

Muscles ache. As the air gets thinner, you become more breathless. There seems to be no end in sight. Then suddenly, over a small rise, paradise - the **Laban Rata Resthouse** at Panar Laban. The only depressing sight is what lies ahead. The resthouse is on the edge of the tree line and, above it, rises a solid wall of granite. How, you wonder, is anyone supposed to climb that? Fortunately, there is a rather easier route to the top.

The sunsets at Panar Laban are legendary. The sun disappears into the valleys below, setting the clouds on fire in a blaze of oranges and reds. As the light fades, the fire goes out and the sky glows like dying embers. By 9 pm most people are in bed, as the following day's climb begins at what seems like a ludicrously early hour, when the rest of Sabah is still fast asleep. The guides have devised a simple system to ensure that everyone reaches the summit at about the same time. Basically, there are three divisions of climbers. The very fit leave at 3.30 am. The majority of climbers are in the solid and dependable middle division, which sets out at 3 am. Some poor souls are given their marching orders at 2.30 am. When you set off again, it is cold, pitch-black and everything aches. Soon you find yourself climbing on bare rock. From here thick ropes have been laid to mark the route and help climbers pull themselves up the steeper sections. All you can see ahead is a procession of torches, their beams searching out the darkness and signalling the route to the summit. It is on this part of the climb that you are most likely to experience a headache or nausea, signs of altitude sickness.

As the sky starts to lighten, the strange shapes of Mount Kinabalu's peaks begin to emerge. On the right the distinctive **Donkey's Ears** stand out, and to the left is **South Peak**, sweeping up in an elegant curve. Before you stretches the summit plateau, a barren expanse of grey, grooved granite slabs. The summit itself remains hidden from view until the upper part of the plateau is reached. After a short scramble up **Low's Peak**, you stand exhausted, but exhilarated, on the roof of South East Asia, watching the sun rise over the world below. Far away to the west is Kota Kinabalu. To the east you look straight down into Low's Gully. Across its gaping depths rise the peaks of the eastern

plateau, first conquered in the 1950s. In the distance, to the south, lie the hills of the Trusmadi Range. Clouds scud across them in an ever-changing landscape. The early explorers left signed and dated letters as proof of their ascent. Climbers today write their name in a book. Suddenly, clouds come racing up the mountain, enveloping the summit in an eerie mist within seconds. It is easy to understand why the Kadazans believe Mount Kinabalu to be a spirit world. You sense that man's intrusion is not welcome.

Thoughts turn to the long trek home, and all too quickly the guides announce that it is time to go. For the first time you see what you scrambled up in the early hours. Only a few hardy alpine plants can survive the harsh climatic conditions at this height, clinging to the cracks which criss-cross the granite slabs. After a short rest at Laban Rata, it is all the way back down to the starting point. For many this is the hardest part, as muscles finally rebel at the relentless strain they have been under. Once back at park headquarters, climbers can claim a certificate as proof of their conquest of Mount Kinabalu.

Nature has provided the perfect remedy for aching limbs at **Poring Hot Springs**, a few miles away. The hot sulphur water is piped from the springs to a series of spacious open-air tiled tubs, set in landscaped gardens. As you relax in a soothingly hot bath, immersed up to your chin and reflecting on the day's achievement, the water has an amazing effect on the aches and pains. Having hobbled to the springs, you emerge almost sprightly, though the effect is sadly only temporary. On the drive back to Kota Kinabalu, the stiffness returns, but the sight of Mount Kinabalu from the road, in all its glory, is ample compensation. Its lofty peaks tower dramatically over the surrounding countryside, conquered and yet unconquerable, still exerting a powerful influence on the people of Sabah and all those who come to climb the mountain.

Opposite: *The final section of the summit trail.* ***Above:*** *Sunset above the clouds at Panar Laban.*

GLOSSARY

adat	custom
air	water
air terjun	waterfall
anak	child
api	fire
arang	charcoal
atap	roofing thatch
aurat	parts of the body which should not be exposed according to Islamic law
baba	Straits-born Chinese (male)
bahasa	language
balai	audience hall
balik	return
balik kampung	to return to home town or village
batik	fabric design using molten wax
batu	stone
bendahara	chief minister
belacan	shrimp paste
belanga	pot
besar	big
bomoh	traditional Malay medicine man
buka	open
buka puasa	breaking fast
bukit	hill
bumiputera	sons of the soil or indigenous people
bumbun	animal observation hide
bunga	flower
cengal	a type of hardwood
cerita	story
cili	chilli
dewan	hall
feng-shui	Chinese geomancy
gasing	top spinning
gua	cave
gunung	mountain
halal	permissible according to Muslim laws
haram	forbidden
hikayat	form of Malay literature
hutan	jungle
ikan	fish
ipuh	a type of tree with poisonous sap
istana	palace
imam	presiding elder in mosque
jalan	road
jihad	holy war
kain songket	gold or silver woven cloth
kampung	village
kecil	small
kedai kopi	coffee shop
kelong	large fish trap
keramat	spirit
keropok	fish cracker
kopiah	Muslim cap
kota	fort
kris	Malay dagger
kuala	river mouth
kuah	gravy
kucing	cat
kuda	horse
kuih	cake
labu	gourd-shaped container made from clay
laksa	rice noodles
laksamana	admiral of the fleet
lama	old
laut	sea
lebuh	main street
lebuhraya	expressway

lorong	lane
makam	grave
mamak	Indian Muslim
mas	gold
masjid	mosque
mee	noodles
merantau	wanderings
merbuk	singing bird
merdeka	independence or freedom
moyang	ancestor, spirit
muazin	summoner to prayer
muzium	museum
naga	serpent, dragon
nasi	rice
negeri	state
negara	country
nipah	palm
nobat	royal orchestra
nyonya	Straits-born Chinese (female)
orang	man
padang	field
padi	rice
pakcik	uncle, term of respect when addressing older men
pandan	screw pines
pantai	beach
parang	machete
pasar	market
pasar malam	night market
pasir	sand
pecah	broken
penghulu	local chief, headman
perahu	boat
peranakan	Straits-born Chinese
pondok	shelter, hut
pulau	island
puteri	princess
raja	prince or ruler
rebana	a type of drum
rendang	spicy meat dish
rentak	beat or rhythm of music
ringgit (RM)	Malaysian unit of currency
rumah	house
rumah rehat	resthouse
seberang	opposite
sejarah	annals or history
sekolah	school
semangat	spirit of life
silat	Malay art of self-defence
songkok	Malay cap
sotong	squid
suku	clan
sungai	river
taman	park or garden
tamu	open-air market in Sabah
tanah	land
tanjung	cape
tarian	dance
tasik	lake
teh tarik	pulled tea
tekatan	gold thread embroidery
telaga	well
teluk	bay
tembaga	brassware
tuan	sir
ulu	upriver
unjang	fish house
wakaf	public shelter
wau	kite
wau bulan	moon kite
wayang kulit	shadow play

TRAVEL INFORMATION

The information given in this section on prices and schedules was gathered in early 1994. Prices and schedules change, and the data given is intended to give only a general indication of the cost and availability of certain items and services.

Opposite: *A sketch of the Melaka River by Abensha.*

LOCATION

Malaysia is situated in the central part of South East Asia between the latitudes formed by 1° and 7° north and longitudes 100° and 119° east. To the north are Thailand, Burma, Laos, Cambodia and Vietnam. To the south lie Singapore and Indonesia, while to the east are the islands of the Philippines. Between the East Malaysian states of Sabah and Sarawak lies the sultanate of Brunei.

TIME DIFFERENCE

Malaysia is 8 hours ahead of Greenwich Mean Time (7 hours ahead of British Summer Time). Peninsular Malaysia and East Malaysia are on the same time, but as Borneo is further east, the sun rises and sets about an hour earlier in Sabah and Sarawak (i.e. at approximately 6 am and 6 pm respectively).

At 9 am in the morning in Kuala Lumpur, the time in other major cities around the world is as follows:

London:	1 am (GMT)
Paris, Rome, Frankfurt, Amsterdam, Brussels:	2 am
Cairo, Athens, Johannesburg:	3 am
Moscow, Nairobi:	4 am
Bombay, Delhi:	6.30 am
Bangkok, Jakarta:	8 am
Singapore, Hong Kong, Manila, Beijing:	9 am
Sydney, Melbourne:	11 am
Tokyo:	10 am
Rio de Janeiro, Buenos Aires,	10 pm*
New York, Montreal:	8 pm*
Los Angeles:	5 pm*

* previous day

GETTING THERE

Air:

There are thirty-seven airlines serving Malaysia from all over the world. The national carrier, Malaysian Airline System (MAS), which operates the largest fleet of aircraft in South East Asia, has flights to

Malaysia from over fifty destinations around the world. Kuala Lumpur's international airport is at Subang, 22 km from the capital. A limousine taxi service operates from the airport using a coupon system. Customers pay for the journey at the counter outside the arrivals hall and are given a coupon which they pass on to the driver. The fare to the centre of Kuala Lumpur is RM20 to RM25. There is also a bus service (No. 47) from the airport to the centre of town, operated by Sri Jaya Kenderaan. The service is every half an hour and costs RM1.60. A new international airport is being built at Sepang, in the south of Selangor, to cope with the increasing number of visitors to the country. The airport is due to open in 1997. The popular holiday destinations of Penang and Pulau Langkawi also have international airports, as do the East Malaysian state capitals of Kuching and Kota Kinabalu.

Rail:

Peninsular Malaysia is served by two railway lines connecting the country to Singapore in the south and the Thai border in the north. Run by Keretapi Tanah Melayu Berhad (KTM), the trains which operate up and down the peninsula are inexpensive, comfortable and an ideal way to enjoy the Malaysian countryside. On-board services include video films, a restaurant car and telephone. There are three classes of travel. Only first and second class are air-conditioned.

There are five daily train services from Singapore to Kuala Lumpur, of which three are express trains, taking between 7 hours 15 mins and 8 hours 30 mins. Stops include Johor Bahru, Gemas and Seremban. The second class single fare is S$34. From Gemas another line runs up the centre of the peninsula, through Jerantut and Kuala Lipis, terminating on the east coast at Tumpat in Kelantan. There is a daily service from Bangkok to Kuala Lumpur, changing at the border town of Padang Besar in Perlis. Stops include Alor Setar, Butterworth and Ipoh. Journey time to Butterworth is around 21 hours 30 mins, and a further 8 hours to Kuala Lumpur. The second class single fare from Bangkok to Butterworth is 861 bahts. From Butterworth it costs a further RM34 to reach Kuala Lumpur. Visitors can also take the train from Bangkok to the east coast border town of Sungai Golok, as the railway branches off at Haadyai in southern Thailand.

For those who want to travel in real style, there is the Eastern and Oriental Express train service, which was launched in September 1993 and operates between Singapore and Bangkok. Like the Orient Express in Europe, the Eastern and Oriental Express offers luxury accommodation and fine cuisine on wheels. The train departs from Bangkok every Wednesday. The cost for a standard ticket to Kuala Lumpur is RM2,340. The Express leaves Singapore on a Sunday. The cost for a standard ticket to Kuala Lumpur is RM1,020.

Road:

There are regular air-conditioned express buses from Singapore to various destinations in Malaysia. Journey time to Kuala Lumpur is between 5 and 6 hours at a cost of about S$18. Long distance taxis also operate between Singapore and Malaysia. You will get a better rate if you cross the Causeway and hire a taxi from Johor Bahru. It is also possible to travel from Haadyai in Thailand to Malaysia's northern border by bus or taxi.

Sea:

There are boat services to several destinations in Peninsular Malaysia. These include: departures six days a week from Singapore to Pulau Tioman (journey takes approximately 5 hours and costs S$85); twice daily departures from Satun in southern Thailand to Pulau Langkawi (takes 1 hour 30 mins, fare 150 bahts); daily departures from Dumai in Sumatra to Melaka (takes 3 hours, fare 65,000 rupiah); and a service from Belawan in Medan, Sumatra to Penang four times a week (takes 4 hours 30 mins, fare 78,500 rupiah). There are also a number of cruises which include a Malaysian stop on their itinerary.

ENTRY FORMALITIES AND AIRPORT INFORMATION

All visitors to Malaysia must be in possession of a passport or other internationally recognised travel documents, valid for at least six months after the date of entry into the country. Travel documents are also essential for travel between

Peninsular and East Malaysia and between Sabah and Sarawak. Visitors are required to fill in a disembarkation card on arrival, which is handed over at the immigration checkpoint together with their passport.

Visa requirements:

No visa required: Commonwealth countries (except India, Pakistan, Bangladesh and Sri Lanka), British protected persons, Ireland, Liechtenstein, Netherlands, San Marino, Switzerland.

Three months visa free: Algeria, Austria, Bahrain, Belgium, Czech Republic, Denmark, Egypt, Finland, Germany, Hungary, Iceland, Italy, Japan, Jordan, Kuwait, Lebanon, Luxembourg, Morocco, Norway, Oman, Qatar, Saudi Arabia, Slovak Republic, South Korea, Sweden, Tunisia, Turkey, United Arab Emirates, United States of America, Yemen.

One month visa free: ASEAN countries, France, South Africa.

Two weeks visa free: Afghanistan, Albania, Iran, Iraq, Libya, Syria.

One week visa free: Bulgaria, Romania and Russia.

Visa required: Bangladesh, Bhutan, China, Cuba, India, Myanmar, Nepal, North Korea, Pakistan, Sri Lanka, Taiwan and all Certificate of Identity holders.

Visitors from countries not mentioned above (except Israel), can stay in Malaysia for up to a month without a visa. Visitors are issued with a visit pass upon arrival, lasting for either one, two or three months. Anyone who wishes to stay beyond the duration of their visit pass can apply for an extension at the nearest immigration office. Extensions are granted for up to three months.

Visitors are allowed to bring in 1 litre of wine or spirits, 200 cigarettes, toiletries to a value of RM200, gifts and souvenirs to a value of RM200, food items to a value of RM75 and personal possessions such as hairdryers, watches, cameras, and video cameras, duty-free. There are no limits on the amount of currency which can be brought into or taken out of the country. Trafficking in illegal drugs carries the death penalty in Malaysia.

The airport tax on departure from the country is RM20.

HEALTH

The standard of medical care in Malaysia is one of the highest in the region. There are government-run and private hospitals in the main towns, and clinics in all towns. A clinic will charge around RM15 to RM20 for a consultation, including the cost of medication. The main hotels have a doctor on call. In an emergency dial 999 for the ambulance service. It is a good idea to bring your own small first aid kit with you.

There is little or no risk of contracting malaria in the urban and coastal areas of Peninsular Malaysia and Sarawak. When visiting other parts of the country, in particular Sabah, precautions against malaria are recommended. Visitors should start taking anti-malarial tablets one week before entering the malarial area and continue taking them for four weeks after they leave it. Anti-malarial drugs do not give complete immunity, and it is therefore important to take precautions against getting bitten in the first place. Malaria is transmitted by the female anophelene mosquito. In typical vampire fashion, they are most active after the sun goes down. Cover up as much as possible after dusk or use mosquito repellent. Where there is no air-conditioning, sleep in a screened room or use a mosquito net if possible. Spray inside the net and tuck it in at the edges. Smoke coils and vaporising mats also deter mosquitoes. In its early stages malaria can feel very much like flu. If you feel unwell during your stay or up to three months after returning from a malarial area, it is advisable to have your blood tested for malaria.

The Malaysian authorities require

visitors from yellow fever epidemic zones, except children under one year of age, to be vaccinated against yellow fever. The London School of Hygiene and Tropical Medicine recommends that visitors to the region should be vaccinated against polio, tetanus, typhoid and hepatitis 'A'. During the wet season, those travelling to more rural areas in parts of East Malaysia may also be advised to have a vaccination against Japanese encephalitis, another disease transmitted by the mosquito.

The water is generally clean and safe to drink straight from the tap. However, many Malaysians prefer to boil their water before drinking it. When visiting more rural areas or eating out at hawker stalls, it is safest to stick to boiled, bottled or purified water. The larger hotels provide flasks of chilled drinking water in all their rooms.

MONEY MATTERS

The unit of currency is the Malaysian *ringgit* (RM), formally known also as the Malaysian dollar, which is divided into 100 *sen* or cents. Notes are issued in denominations of RM1 (being phased out), RM5, RM10, RM20, RM50, RM100, RM500, RM1,000. Coins are issued in denominations of 1 sen, 5 sen, 10 sen, 20 sen, 50 sen and RM1.

Listed below is a selection of the latest exchange rates available at the time of going to print. These are intended only as a general guide and are obviously subject to change.

(1 unit foreign currency)	Malaysian ringgit
Singapore dollar	RM1.68
Brunei dollar	RM1.68
US dollar	RM2.58
Sterling pound	RM3.90
Australian dollar	RM1.89
Canadian dollar	RM1.87
Deutschemark	RM1.57
Netherlands guilder	RM1.40
Swiss franc	RM1.84

(100 units foreign currency)	Malaysian ringgit
Austrian schilling	RM23.70
French franc	RM46.50
Italian lire	RM0.17
Swedish kroner	RM34.25
Chinese renminbi	RM29.85
Hong Kong dollar	RM33.80
Indian rupee	RM8.65
Indonesian rupiah	RM0.13
Japanese yen	RM2.49
Philippine peso	RM10.25
Thai baht	RM10.60

Most banks are open from 9.30 am to 3 pm on weekdays and from 9.30 am to 11.30 am on Saturdays. In Kedah, Kelantan and Terengganu, Thursday and Friday form the weekend, with banks being open from 9.30 am to 11.30 am on Thursdays and closed on Fridays. Money changers stay open longer and are situated in the main airports, shopping centres and high streets. Banks offer the best exchange rates for travellers cheques, while hotels give a generally poor exchange rate. Internationally recognised credit cards and travellers cheques are accepted at major stores, restaurants and hotels.

In most hotels and restaurants a service charge of 10% is added automatically to bills, in addition to the government tax of 5%. Tipping is therefore unnecessary

		JAN	FEB	MAR	APR	MAY	JUNE	JULY	AUG	SEP	OCT	NOV	DEC
Kuala Lumpur	Max.	32°C	33	33	33	33	32	32	32	32	32	31	31
	Min.	22°C	22	23	23	23	23	23	23	23	23	23	23
	Rain	159mm	154	223	276	182	119	120	133	173	258	263	223
	Sun	6hrs	7	7	7	7	6	6	6	5	5	5	5
Melaka	Max.	32°C	33	33	32	32	31	31	31	31	31	31	31
	Min.	22°C	23	23	23	23	23	23	23	23	23	23	23
	Rain	90mm	104	147	184	166	172	181	178	206	216	237	142
	Sun	7hrs	7	7	7	7	6	7	6	6	6	5	5
Penang	Max.	32°C	32	32	32	31	31	31	31	31	31	31	31
	Min.	23°C	23	24	24	24	24	23	23	23	23	23	23
	Rain	70mm	93	141	214	240	170	208	235	341	380	246	107
	Sun	8hrs	8	8	7	7	7	7	6	5	5	6	7
Kota Bharu	Max.	29°C	30	31	32	33	32	32	32	32	31	29	29
	Min.	22°C	23	23	24	24	24	23	23	23	23	23	23
	Rain	163mm	60	99	81	114	132	157	168	195	286	651	603
	Sun	7hrs	8	9	9	8	7	7	7	7	6	5	5
Kuala Terengganu	Max.	28°C	29	30	31	32	32	31	31	31	30	29	26
	Min.	22°C	23	23	23	24	23	23	23	23	23	23	23
	Rain	174mm	99	109	101	103	108	110	141	184	266	643	559
	Sun	7hrs	7	8	8	8	7	7	7	6	6	5	4
Kuantan	Max.	29°C	31	32	33	33	33	32	32	32	32	30	29
	Min.	21°C	22	22	23	23	23	23	23	23	23	23	22
	Rain	311mm	165	166	169	192	164	162	179	233	273	318	591
	Sun	5hrs	6	7	7	7	6	6	6	6	5	4	3
Johor Bahru	Max.	31°C	32	32	32	32	32	31	31	31	31	31	30
	Min.	21°C	22	23	23	23	23	22	22	22	22	22	22
	Rain	146mm	155	182	223	228	151	170	163	200	199	255	258
	Sun	6hrs	6	6	6	6	5	5	5	4	5	4	5
Cameron Highlands	Max.	21°C	22	23	23	23	23	22	22	22	22	22	21
	Min.	14°C	14	14	15	15	15	14	15	15	15	15	15
	Rain	120mm	111	198	277	273	137	165	172	241	334	305	202
	Sun	5hrs	5	5	5	5	5	5	4	4	4	3	3
Kota Kinabalu	Max.	30°C	30	31	32	32	31	31	31	31	31	31	31
	Min.	23°C	23	23	24	24	24	24	24	23	23	23	23
	Rain	133mm	63	71	124	218	311	277	256	314	334	296	241
	Sun	6hrs	7	8	8	7	7	7	6	6	6	6	6
Kuching	Max.	30°C	30	31	32	33	33	32	33	33	32	31	31
	Min.	23°C	23	23	23	23	23	23	23	23	23	23	23
	Rain	683mm	522	339	286	253	199	199	211	271	326	343	465
	Sun	4hrs	4	4	5	6	6	6	6	5	5	5	4
Mersing	Max.	28°C	29	30	31	32	31	31	31	31	31	29	28
	Min.	23°C	23	23	23	23	23	22	22	22	23	23	23
	Rain	319mm	153	141	120	149	145	170	173	177	207	359	635
	Sun	6hrs	7	8	7	7	7	6	6	6	6	5	4

1) Temperatures - mean maximum, mean minimum 2) Mean monthly rainfall 3) Mean daily sunshine hours

Courtesy of the Malaysia Tourism Promotion Board

unless the service is particularly good. Sometimes hotel rates are quoted inclusive of the 15%. Usually you will be quoted the basic room rate only. The additional tax and service charges are referred to as 'plus, plus'. In the larger hotels it is customary to tip porters and bellboys. Tipping at hawker stalls is not necessary. Tipping of taxi drivers is optional.

CLIMATE

The chart opposite is intended only as a general guide to the climate in various parts of Malaysia. The country's climate is discussed in the introduction to the book.

ACCOMMODATION

Malaysia offers accommodation to suit every pocket, from camping sites and hostels to luxury international class hotels. The Malaysia Tourism Promotion Board (formally the Tourist Development Corporation) produces a range of publications with information on accommodation around the country.

There is no hotel classification system in Malaysia, but the country's top hotels are among the best in the world. They include international chains, such as the Hilton and Holiday Inn, and local and regional chains like the Shangri-La. There is also plenty of choice in the medium and budget price range. Some rooms in the budget category, although basic, still come with attached bathroom and air-conditioning, while others have a ceiling fan and shared bathroom. Most of the budget hotels are Chinese-run, and are often located above coffee shops or restaurants. Many hotels offer discount rates and promotional packages during the off-peak season. In addition to the wide choice of hotel accommodation, a number of the islands and some of the mainland beaches have beachfront chalets and huts. The amenities are often quite basic, but the romantic setting more than makes up for any lack of creature comforts.

Many of the main towns have a government resthouse, or *rumah rehat*, a legacy of the colonial days. These are primarily for government officials, but providing it is not the school holidays, there are usually rooms available for visitors. These are clean and comfortable, and the room rates are very reasonable.

There are youth hostels in a number of the main towns and tourist destinations, including Kuala Lumpur, Melaka and Penang. Contact the Malaysian Youth Hostel Association for further information (tel: 03-230 6870). There is also dormitory-style accommodation for budget conscious travellers in several of the country's national parks. There are a number of campsites in Malaysia with locations ranging from beaches to a spot in the jungle.

BUDGET GUIDE

Below is a general guide to the cost of accommodation and meals. Actual prices will vary considerably depending on destination, facilities and the choice of food. The cost of living tends to be higher in East Malaysia than on the peninsula.

Accommodation	Double	Single
International class hotel	RM300	RM260
Medium range hotel	RM140	RM120
Budget hotel	RM30	RM25
Youth hostel/beach hut	RM15	RM15

Meals

Breakfast	
Hotel (buffet)	RM22.50
Kedai kopi	RM4
Hawker stall	RM2
Lunch	
Hotel (buffet)	RM30
Moderately priced restaurant	RM10
Hawker stall	RM3
Dinner	
Hotel (buffet)	RM30
Moderately priced restaurant	RM15
Hawker stall	RM4

(room rates and restaurant prices are given exclusive of government tax and service charge)

GETTING AROUND

Malaysia has a good transport infrastructure, with air, road, rail and sea networks linking the main towns and island resorts. Unless you plan to venture into the interior of Borneo, most places in Malaysia are easily accessible.

Air:

MAS has an extensive network of flights covering both Peninsular and East Malaysia (tel: 03-746 3000 for general flight information and ticket enquiries). Flights to a number of destinations, including Pulau Tioman, Taman Negara and Pulau Pangkor, are handled by a smaller Malaysian airline, Pelangi Air (tel: 03-262 4446/48). Below are standard class fares, together with frequency and duration of flights, from Kuala Lumpur to a number of destinations:

Destination	Price	No.*	Duration
Penang	RM104	17	45 mins
Langkawi	RM135	7	55 mins
Johor Bahru	RM93	8	45 mins
Kota Bharu	RM104	6	50 mins
Pulau Tioman	RM120	4	1 hr 5 mins
Kuching	RM262	5+	1 hr 40 mins
Kota Kinabalu	RM437	4+	2 hrs 35 mins

* daily flights
\+ direct flights

MAS offers various special fares on its domestic flights, for example, for group/family travel. Children under two years of age travel for 10% of the adult fare, while children over two travel for half the adult fare. In addition to Subang and the other international airports, there are thirteen major domestic airports and a number of smaller airports and landing strips. For the main domestic routes the baggage allowance is 20 kilos, but on the MAS rural air service and for destinations with airstrips, such as Pulau Tioman and Pulau Pangkor, the allowance is 15 kilos for Fokker aircraft and 10 kilos for Twin Otters, so check your ticket before flying, and pack accordingly. There are left luggage offices at the main airports, and hotels will usually store luggage for you. The domestic airport tax is RM5.

Rail:

Visitors to Malaysia can buy a ten or thirty day rail pass which can be used on all classes, and entitles the holder to unlimited rail travel in Peninsular Malaysia for the duration of the pass. They cost US$55 (RM151) and US$120 (RM329) respectively, but unless you plan to do a lot of rail travel, then it is often more economical to buy tickets when you need them, particularly if you are travelling second class. Contact the Kuala Lumpur Railway Station (tel: 03-274 7435/7442/7443) for information on schedules and availability.

Taxis:

In some areas, such as Kuala Lumpur and Georgetown, taxis operate on a meter system; in other parts of the country, for example, Pulau Langkawi, there are set fares to various destinations; while in certain places, including Melaka and Kuching, haggling is the order of the day. Always agree a price before you start the journey. There are taxi stands in the main towns. Taxis can also be hailed from the kerb by that universal sign: an outstretched arm.

The meter system operates on the basis of RM1.5 for the first 2 km, and 10 sen for every 200 metres after that. An additional charge of RM1 is made for taxis ordered by telephone and for every item of luggage placed in the boot. After midnight an extra charge of 50% is made on top of the meter reading. Make sure the meter is turned on before you set off.

Long distance, or 'outstation', taxis are good value, in most cases costing around double the express bus fare. There are outstation taxi stands in all the main towns. They usually operate on a fixed fare basis, but it is sometimes possible to haggle, for instance on the air-conditioning issue. They will reduce the fare if you (and they!) are willing to travel without air-conditioning. This is not as bad as it sounds if you are breezing along the highway with the windows rolled down, but it can get rather hot and sticky if you get stuck in a traffic jam. Most long distance taxis will quote you a per person rate, based on four people sharing the ride. Unless you are willing to charter the taxi and pay the full amount, you will have to wait for the driver to collect his quota. In Kuala Lumpur long distance taxis operate from the car park at Puduraya Bus Station. It is advisable to ignore the taxi drivers who wait for unsuspecting tourists on the road outside Puduraya, as they charge inflated prices.

Trishaws:

These bicycle-drawn carriages remain a popular form of transport in Melaka, Georgetown, Kota Bharu and Kuala Terengganu. They offer a relaxing way of enjoying the hustle and bustle of city life, and taking in the sites without wearing out your feet. Trishaws are designed to take two passengers, but they are often to be seen with a whole family squeezed in. Always negotiate the price up front.

Buses:

Air-conditioned express buses operate between all the main towns and provide an inexpensive way of getting around. On the longer journeys refreshment stops are made. In Kuala Lumpur the main bus station is Puduraya on Jalan Pudu near Chinatown (tel:03-230 0145). The largest company is Ekspres Nasional, but there are several smaller private companies operating on many of the same routes, so if you find that the bus you want is full, you may be able to get a seat on a slightly later bus with another company. East coast buses operate from Hentian Bas Putra (tel: 03-442 9530) opposite the Mall shopping centre. Below are adult one way express bus and per person taxi fares from Kuala Lumpur to selected destinations.

	Coach	Taxi
From K.L. to:		
Kota Bharu	RM25.00	RM45
Kuantan	RM12.10	RM25
Johor Bahru	RM16.50	RM40
Butterworth	RM17.10	RM42
Ipoh	RM 9.40	RM22
Cameron Highlands	RM10.00	RM32
Melaka	RM 6.65	RM17

The main cities and towns also have their own local bus services. For travel within Kuala Lumpur there is a *bas mini*, or minibus, network, although the buses become very crowded during the rush hour. The fare is 60 sen whether you are travelling one stop or the whole route.

Driving:

Peninsular Malaysia has a modern and extensive road network. There are a number of car rental agencies to choose from, including international chains such as Hertz and Avis, and local companies such as SMAS. Daily unlimited mileage rates start from around RM126. Drivers from countries outside ASEAN should have a valid International Driving Licence.

If you are driving at night in a rural area, keep an eye out for cyclists, cattle and stray animals on the road. At all times watch out

Alor Gajah	Alor Setar	Baling	Batu Pahat	Bukit Fraser	Bukit Ibam	Bukit Kayu Hitam	Butterworth	Brinchang	Dabong	Desaru	Dungun	Gemas	Grik	Gua Musang	Ipoh	Jeli	Johor Bahru	Kajang	Kangar	Klang	Kluang	Kota Bharu	Kota Tinggi	Kuala Kangsar	Kuala
582																									
541	114																								
119	704	660																							
219	443	402	338																						
194	700	659	219	324																					
630	48	162	752	491	748																				
489	93	91	608	350	607	141																			
334	378	337	443	195	315	426	285																		
676	349	235	795	488	595	397	350	452																	
316	898	857	194	535	291	946	805	650	795																
398	599	485	433	381	252	647	576	565	356	464															
70	630	589	153	267	112	678	537	382	656	283	328														
479	176	62	598	340	597	224	154	275	177	795	427	527													
392	504	395	521	222	436	557	491	401	266	675	374	390	337												
325	257	216	444	186	443	305	164	121	331	641	581	373	154	491											
612	296	182	734	434	542	344	273	399	53	767	303	603	124	213	278										
239	830	89	126	467	281	878	737	582	799	94	456	215	727	605	573	746									
99	484	443	221	121	217	532	391	236	578	415	412	144	381	312	227	525	347								
627	45	159	746	488	745	93	138	423	394	943	644	660	221	554	302	341	875	529							
153	495	454	272	132	271	541	400	247	567	469	423	201	392	323	236	514	401	55	507						
173	758	717	54	395	209	806	665	510	782	140	432	143	655	533	501	729	116	290	803	329					
583	409	295	705	406	485	457	386	512	166	697	246	574	237	184	391	113	689	496	454	507	658				
266	848	804	144	485	239	893	752	597	770	52	414	233	742	623	588	717	41	380	890	416	90	660			
375	207	166	494	236	493	255	114	171	281	691	531	423	104	441	50	228	623	277	252	288	551	341	638		
280	530	489	402	103	317	578	437	282	385	538	381	271	427	119	273	331	468	193	575	204	396	303	486	323	
120	462	421	239	99	238	510	369	214	556	436	390	168	359	290	205	503	368	22	507	33	296	474	383	255	171
187	446	405	306	166	305	494	352	214	520	503	457	235	343	357	189	467	435	89	491	47	363	541	440	239	238
475	521	407	500	453	317	569	498	633	278	529	78	405	349	296	503	225	521	477	566	488	505	168	492	453	446
268	684	616	304	253	121	726	591	436	487	333	131	197	558	369	427	434	325	281	729	292	294	371	283	477	250
408	278	273	527	269	526	336	170	204	414	724	639	454	216	553	83	340	656	310	320	319	584	453	671	120	356
212	608	567	326	181	143	656	515	360	559	397	207	177	505	293	351	506	388	205	653	216	316	440	345	401	174
24	606	565	98	243	206	654	513	358	689	292	422	94	503	423	349	636	224	123	651	177	152	607	242	399	304
279	815	774	158	436	151	863	722	567	678	142	328	247	712	548	558	625	134	329	860	386	104	568	92	608	429
69	651	610	53	288	259	694	558	403	734	247	467	139	548	468	394	681	179	168	696	222	107	652	197	444	349
664	82	196	783	525	782	130	175	460	431	980	681	712	258	586	339	379	912	566	37	540	840	491	927	289	612
557	393	279	628	390	445	441	370	496	150	656	206	533	221	168	375	97	649	565	438	491	632	40	620	325	287
161	503	462	280	140	279	551	410	255	597	477	431	209	400	331	246	544	409	83	548	8	337	515	424	296	212
195	777	733	73	411	292	825	681	526	849	142	506	226	671	594	517	796	61	294	819	345	127	739	92	567	475
88	552	511	192	189	206	600	459	304	646	404	420	133	449	380	295	593	318	75	603	115	279	564	369	345	261
250	383	342	369	198	368	431	290	153	457	566	520	298	280	420	126	404	498	152	428	110	426	520	513	176	283
99	659	618	124	292	95	707	566	411	685	254	309	29	556	419	402	632	186	176	704	230	114	584	204	452	300
56	526	485	172	163	174	574	433	478	620	372	388	101	423	354	269	566	304	43	571	97	247	538	337	319	235
145	486	446	264	124	263	534	394	239	581	461	415	193	384	315	230	528	393	47	532	9	321	499	408	280	196
396	263	261	515	257	514	314	170	192	402	712	652	442	204	541	71	328	644	298	308	307	572	441	659	108	344
524	58	56	643	385	642	106	35	320	291	839	540	572	118	451	199	238	772	426	103	437	700	351	787	149	470
411	183	181	530	272	529	231	90	207	309	727	559	454	132	469	86	256	659	313	228	322	587	369	674	36	359
14	574	533	136	211	168	622	481	326	641	332	384	53	471	385	317	598	262	91	619	145	190	569	280	367	256
286	347	306	405	162	404	395	254	117	421	602	530	334	244	456	90	368	533	188	392	146	462	481	549	140	247
162	558	517	280	131	193	606	465	310	549	412	255	127	455	297	301	510	342	155	603	167	270	481	360	351	178

DISTANCE CHART IN KILOMETRES

Courtesy of the Malaysia Tourism Promotion Board

for motor cyclists, who are quite likely to make a sudden move without any warning. While most Malaysian drivers are relatively safe, there are some seemingly suicidal motorists. Long distance taxi drivers are notorious for their hair-raising driving tactics. The speed limit on highways and expressways is 110 kmph, and 90 kmph on trunk roads. In towns and built-up areas the speed limit is usually 50 kmph. Seat belts are compulsory in Malaysia. Petrol costs around RM1.13 a litre. The chart below gives approximate distances in kilometres between selected destinations in Peninsular Malaysia. The distance between any two places is given by the intersection of the columns.

Ferry/boat services:

There are regular boat services to the most popular islands. Express boats operate up the principal rivers in Sarawak and are the main mode of transport away from the coast. There are hourly boat services up the Rejang during the morning from the jetty at Sibu to Kapit, at a cost of RM15. There is a daily boat service from Kapit to Belaga, which costs around RM20.

...ur · Kuala Selangor

	Kuala Terengganu	Kuantan	Lumut	Maran	Melaka	Mersing	Muar	Padang Besar	Pasir Puteh	Pelabuhan Klang	Pontian Kecil	Port Dickson	Sabak Bernam	Segamat	Seremban	Shah Alam	Sitiawan	Sungai Petani	Taiping	Tampin	Teluk Intan
Kuantan	209																				
Lumut	586	510																			
Maran	272	76	434																		
Melaka	508	292	432	236																	
Mersing	401	191	641	253	255																
Muar	544	336	477	281	45	210															
Padang Besar	603	760	360	690	688	897	733														
Pasir Puteh	128	337	437	400	581	528	626	475													
Pelabuhan Klang	496	300	329	224	185	394	230	585	483												
Pontian Kecil	571	375	600	399	171	184	126	859	699	337											
Port Dickson	503	291	384	231	94	321	139	634	554	123	265										
Sabak Bernam	585	389	209	313	274	550	318	465	501	118	514	226									
Segamat	376	180	485	202	120	218	168	741	504	238	197	165	327								
Seremban	471	259	352	199	80	289	125	608	522	105	251	32	194	133							
Shah Alam	480	284	313	208	169	378	214	568	483	17	337	121	118	222	90						
Sitiawan	574	498	12	422	420	629	465	348	425	317	588	372	197	473	340	301					
Sungai Petani	463	626	218	550	548	757	593	140	335	780	716	494	325	601	468	429	206				
Taiping	481	513	104	437	435	644	480	265	353	332	603	387	212	488	355	316	92	125			
Tampin	461	254	400	198	38	294	83	656	543	154	209	80	242	85	48	137	388	516	403		
Teluk Intan	593	402	173	326	310	514	355	320	465	154	478	262	36	363	230	155	161	278	176	278	
Temerloh	322	126	384	50	186	305	231	640	450	174	357	181	263	156	149	158	372	500	387	148	276

TOURIST INFORMATION OFFICES

The Malaysia Tourism Promotion Board (MTPB) has information offices in the main towns and tourist destinations around the country. In some instances these are backed up by state-run offices. The staff can help with queries on all aspects of your travel plans, and if they are unable to provide the answers themselves, they will point you in the right direction. If you are staying in Kuala Lumpur, the Malaysia Tourist Information Complex (MATIC) on Jalan Ampang is well worth a visit (tel: 03-242 3929). Based in an elegant mansion which once belonged to a wealthy tin miner, MATIC offers the most comprehensive facilities for tourists, including short videos on each state, a souvenir and handicraft shop, and a theatre where cultural shows are staged. The Complex also has ticketing counters for MAS and Ekspres Nasional.

The MTPB produces a range of informative publications, which are available free of charge at their offices. These include a road map of Malaysia, a calendar of events for the current year, fold-out leaflets on each of the states, and publications on the country's islands and beaches, hill resorts, golf courses, national parks and adventure activities.

TOUR AGENCIES

Ask at the nearest MTPB office or at your hotel reception for details of local tours and tour agencies. All reputable tour agencies are registered with the MTPB. Two of the most popular tours in Kuala Lumpur are the half day city and country tours, each costing RM22. They offer a good introduction to the city and its surrounding attractions. The city tour takes in Kuala Lumpur's main sites, while the country tour visits the Royal Selangor Pewter factory, a *batik* factory, the Batu Caves and a traditional Malay house.

WHAT TO WEAR

Cotton clothing and sandals are most comfortable in Malaysia's tropical climate. A jacket or jumper is advisable for the cool nights in the hill resorts (and for the occasional over air-conditioned hotel room!), and warm clothing, waterproofs and comfortable walking shoes are essential if you intend to climb Mount Kinabalu in Sabah.

One of the most important items to 'wear' while sightseeing and lazing on the beach is a sunscreen. The sun is very strong, and do not be fooled by a cooling sea breeze; it will still roast you if you fail to protect yourself. A hat and sunglasses are also recommended.

Shorts, T-shirts and swimwear are the standard attire for the beach resorts. A sarong is very versatile, particularly if you need to travel light. It can be used as a skirt, sheet, towel and a changing robe. As Malaysia is predominantly a Muslim country, it is advisable not to wear anything too revealing when away from the beach areas, particularly in the more conservative northern and east coast states. A more comprehensive attire also helps protect against sunburn. When entering mosques women must have their knees and arms covered.

For formal occasions men can wear either a lounge suit, or the local attire of a *batik* shirt worn loose over the trousers. Women can dress as they would for a similar function in their own country, although it is again advisable not to wear anything too revealing. The Chinese do not consider black appropriate for festive occasions, particularly Chinese New Year.

LAUNDRY AND DRY CLEANING

Laundry and dry cleaning services are available in the larger hotels and in the main towns.

SHOPPING

All the main towns have air-conditioned shopping complexes, which stock a wide variety of local and foreign goods at competitive prices. They are also a popular place for teenagers to 'hang out'. During major festivals, such as Chinese New Year and Hari Raya Puasa, the complexes really go to town on their decorations and often stage special shows such as lion dances. Exhibitions are often put on in the foyers.

For those who want to soak up more of the local atmosphere, there are plenty of old-fashioned shophouses selling everything from flip-flops to radios. The merchandise is often displayed in a rather higgledy-piggledy fashion, but that is all part of the shopping experience. There are also numerous markets, some daytime, others coming to life during the evening. There are wet markets, dry markets and bazaars, often all under the same roof. Wet markets sell meat, fish and vegetables. Even if you have no intention of buying anything, they are well worth taking a walk through, but do not wear your best shoes, as the floor is, as the name suggests, usually wet. Fish are gutted, and chickens killed and plucked on the spot. Dry markets sell spices, dried produce and commodities such as sugar and coffee. Bazaars sell an eclectic range of goods, including local handicraft items, watches, T-shirts and cassettes. The best known markets include Central Market in Kota Bharu, Kelantan, the night market in Kuala Lumpur's Chinatown, and the Sunday market in Kota Belud, Sabah.

By law prices have to be marked on goods, but it is still worth asking for a discount at most stores, except the large department stores, and always haggle at the market stalls. The night market in Chinatown is notorious for inflating prices. There are duty-free shops at the main international entry points. The islands of Labuan and Langkawi are also duty free.

A wide range of English language books and magazines is available in the main towns. In central Kuala Lumpur three of the best places to buy books are Bukit Bintang Plaza on Jalan Bukit Bintang, which has branches of MPH and Berita, Popular Book Shop on Jalan Hang Lekir in Chinatown and Times Books at Yaohan in the Mall.

Malaysia offers a wonderful variety of local handicraft items including pewterware, *batik*, silverware, wood carvings and pottery. In Kuala Lumpur the main handicraft outlets are Central Market and the Karyanika Handicraft Centre. Royal Selangor Pewter tankards sell at Central Market for between RM50 and RM110, while prices for *batik* silk scarves start at about RM18. You can also have your portrait painted at Central Market for around RM150. If you are visiting a *kampung* workshop or longhouse, you will be able to buy handicraft items from the villagers themselves.

If you forget to pack something you need during your stay, you should be able to buy it locally, particularly in the shopping complexes. This also means you have the option of travelling a little lighter, and stocking up on toiletries and other necessities once in Malaysia. You can usually find your favourite brand. Larger western clothes sizes for both men and women can be difficult to get, but Kuala Lumpur is a good place for men to purchase a made-to-measure suit. Prices start from around RM400.

BUSINESS HOURS

Offices in the private sector are generally open from 9 am to 5 pm Monday to Friday. Many also work a half day on Saturday. Government office hours are 8 am to 12.45 pm and 2 pm to 4.15 pm on Monday to Thursday. On Friday the lunch break is extended from 12.15 pm to 2.45 pm for Muslim Friday prayers. On Saturday government offices are open from 8 am to 12.45 pm. In Kedah, Kelantan and Terengganu government offices are open from 8 am to 12.45 pm on Thursday and are closed all day Friday. Shops are generally open from 9.30 am to 7 pm. Supermarkets, shopping centres and department stores are open daily from 10 am to 10 pm. In the main cities there are 7-Eleven and Hop-in stores, which are open twenty-four hours a day, and there are also twenty-four hour petrol stations.

COMMUNICATIONS

Media:

The main English language newspapers are the *New Straits Times*, *The Star* and the *Malay Mail*. Foreign newspapers are available at the main news stands and

hotels. There are three television channels, two of which are government-run. TV2 and the independent television channel TV3 are the most westernised in their programming output. Imported material is mainly American. The news in English is aired at 10.30 pm on TV3 and 11.30 pm on TV2. There are four government radio channels. The English language channel is Radio 4.

Telephone:

Malaysia has a good telecommunications system. There are both card and coin operated public telephones. Local calls cost 10 sen for the first three minutes. Coin telephones *(Koinfon)* take 10 sen, 20 sen, 50 sen and RM1 coins. Card phones (*Kadfon* or *Uniphone*) operate on prepaid cards which are available in units of RM3, RM5, RM10, RM20 and RM50. These can be bought from Telekom offices, airports, petrol stations, and most 7-Eleven and Hop-In outlets. Credit card phones are also available. International calls can be made by IDD (International Direct Dialing) from most hotels. They can also be made from credit card phones. Dial 007, then the country code, followed by the area code. For example, for a call to central London dial 007 44 71 plus the number required. The number for directory enquiries is 103 (108 for international enquiries). For general enquiries dial 102.

Telekom Malaysia standard rates per minute to selected countries are as follows:

USA, Canada	RM5.00
United Kingdom	RM4.00
France, Italy, Netherlands	RM6.00
Japan	RM5.40
Australia	RM3.90

Telekom Malaysia offers reduced international rates between midnight and noon, over the weekend and on festive public holidays. Hotels add their own telephone charges on top of these rates, which can be as high as 50%, but tend to be around 30%.

Postal services:

Malaysia has one of the most efficient postal systems in the region. Mail takes about five days to reach Europe and America, three days to reach Australia and two to three days to reach other Asian countries. There is a standard postal rate of 50 sen for postcards and aerogrammes to all countries. In the larger hotels, mail can be handed in at the reception counter for posting. There are also post offices (*pejabat pos*) in all the main towns. These are open from 8 am to 5 pm. Stamps can often be purchased at the small sweet and tobacco shops to be found on many street corners.

FOOD

One of the highlights of any visit to Malaysia is the country's delicious range of food, resulting from its multi-cultural make-up. Over the years, the Malays, Chinese and Indians have borrowed certain culinary ideas and ingredients from each other, creating some uniquely Malaysian dishes. A number of dishes, such as *mee goreng* (fried noodles) and *nasi goreng* (fried rice), are common to all races, although the style of cooking them differs.

The choice of eateries is as large as the range of dishes. You can eat for very little at a hawker stall or coffee shop, or dine out at a top restaurant. The hawker stalls offer the option of sitting down to eat your meal there or buying *bungkus*, take-away food wrapped in paper. The larger hotels offer a buffet breakfast, lunch and dinner, where you can eat as much as you like for a set price. These buffets are a good way to familiarise yourself with a range of local dishes. In addition to the numerous Malay, Chinese and Indian restaurants, there are a number of Japanese, Korean and Thai restaurants. Malaysia also has its

fair share of western fast food establishments, with the food adapted to suit local tastes and customs. For example, burger meat is *halal*, the Muslim equivalent of kosher. Below are some of the most popular local dishes.

Malay:

Malay food is generally quite spicy. A breakfast favourite is *nasi lemak*. It consists of rice cooked in coconut milk, *sambal* (shrimp paste cooked with chillies and onions), *ikan bilis* (anchovies), slices of cucumber and hard-boiled egg, and peanuts. Small packets of *nasi lemak* sell for 50 to 60 sen. *Nasi padang*, plain rice accompanied by a selection of meat, fish and vegetable dishes, makes a filling lunch or dinner. The food is served buffet style, with customers helping themselves to what they want from the dishes on offer. One of these is often beef *rendang*, tender chunks of spicy beef. Another tasty dish is *laksa*, rice noodles served in a spicy fish soup. *Satay*, Malaysia's answer to the shish kebab, is a popular snack.

Desserts include *sago melaka*, sago served with coconut milk and palm sugar syrup, and *ais kacang*, also known as *air batu campur* (usually shortened to ABC), which consists of a mound of shaved ice, sweetened with palm sugar, rose syrup and evaporated milk, and accompanied by red beans, sweet corn and cubes of jelly.

Chinese:

Cantonese, Szechuan, Hokkien, Teochew, Hainanese and Hakka dishes are all to be found in Malaysia. Hainanese chicken rice (rice cooked in chicken stock and served with roast or steamed chicken) makes a good lunch or dinner, as does clay pot, or *ngah poh fan*. The rice is cooked in a clay pot with spices, meat and vegetables. Another popular meal (particularly a brunch favourite) is *dim sum*, with a tempting array of steamed and fried bite-sized treats. The Chinese also use a lot of noodles in their cooking. Varieties include *kuey teow*, flat wide noodles, and *beehoon*, which are thin and fine. Steamboat, or Chinese-style fondue, is well worth a try. A large container of water is kept boiling in the centre of the table. Customers cook the food themselves, selecting from a range of meats, seafood, noodles and vegetables.

Indian:

Indian cuisine encompasses north Indian, south Indian and Indian Muslim fare. North Indian cuisine specialises in food cooked in a clay oven or *tandoor*. Tandoori chicken, marinated in yoghurt and spices, makes a delicious meal. *Naan* are another speciality of the region. The south Indian restaurants are known for their banana leaf curries. At the end of the meal the banana leaf is folded in half to indicate that you have finished eating. Some Indians say that, if the meal is very good or if it is a festive occasion, the leaf should be folded towards the body. The Indian Muslims are best known for their *nasi kandar*, rice served with a choice of curries and vegetable dishes. They are also renowned for their fish head curry, which, as the name suggests, is a fish head served in a curry sauce. The head is believed to be the best part of the fish. Another Indian Muslim dish is *rojak*, a salad consisting of flour-cake, beansprouts, cucumber, turnip, hard-boiled eggs, prawn fritters and squid, served with a sweet peanut sauce.

There are a number of Indian breads to choose from, which provide a cheap, tasty and filling meal at any time of the day. The most popular is *roti canai*, griddle-fried dough, which is usually served with *dhal* (a curry sauce made with lentils) or fish curry. Watching the *roti canai* maker at work is all part of the experience, as he tosses and twirls the dough to stretch it as far as possible before folding it into a square for frying. A *roti telur* has an egg added to the dough, while a *murtabak* is basically a *roti canai* filled with meat or vegetables.

DRINK

Fresh fruit juices are a popular and thirst quenching drink. Take-away drinks are sold at the hawker stalls in a plastic bag with a piece of string tied round the top and a straw. Fresh coconut juice served in the coconut makes a tasty and nutritious drink. Sugar cane juice is also refreshing. The juice is extracted by putting the cane through a mangle. Malaysians have a sweet tooth. When you order coffee or tea at a stall or coffee shop, it is often served with lots of sugar, so it is best to specify if you want it without sugar. Coffee without sugar is *kopi kosong*, while coffee without milk is *kopi-o*. Unsweetened black coffee is *kopi-o kosong*, and plain tea *teh-o kosong*. Evaporated or condensed milk is often used instead of fresh milk. Chinese tea is served hot or cold. *Teh tarik* is the Malaysian answer to cappuccino or a milk shake. The tea is poured between two cups from a great height for added flavour and froth....and sheer theatrics! Another popular local beverage is Milo. Wine and spirits are expensive in Malaysia because of the high taxes levied on them. The local beer is Anchor. Tiger, the Singapore brew, is also popular. The most widely available foreign beer is Carlsberg, though Guinness also has a loyal local following.

FRUIT

Malaysia offers a wide variety of delicious tropical fruits. A number of hawker stalls specialise in selling freshly cut fruit slices for a refreshing snack. Some fruits are seasonal, while others are available all year round. In addition to the infamous durian, local tropical fruits which need no introduction include the papaya *(betik)*, pineapple (*nenas*), mango (*mangga*), watermelon (*tembikai*), coconut (*kelapa*) and banana (*pisang*), the latter making tasty fritters. Other local fruits include:

Mangosteen:

While the durian has been dubbed the 'king of fruits', the purple-skinned mangosteen is often called the 'queen of fruits'. It has sweet, slightly acidic, white segments of juicy flesh. The best way to open a mangosteen is by squeezing it between both hands. Mangosteen stalls are often found next to durian stalls, as the mangosteen, known for its 'cooling' properties, is believed to balance the 'heatiness' of the durian. There are two main seasons, one from June to August, the other from November to January.

Rambutan:

This is a rather curious looking bright red or yellow hairy fruit, about the size of a ping-pong ball. It is aptly named, *rambut* meaning hair in Malay. The fruit, with its succulent and sweet translucent flesh, has a taste similar to that of the lychee. The main season is from June to September.

Jackfruit:

The jackfruit, or *nangka*, is a very large fruit, with a greenish-yellow skin. The pulpy flesh is yellow and sweet, and each segment has a shiny seed. The *cempedak* is a slightly smaller version of the fruit, which is normally deep-fried for a tasty fruit snack.

Pomelo:

The green-skinned pomelo, or *limau bali*, is the largest of the citrus fruits. It has a taste similar to that of a grapefruit, but not as tart.

Ciku:

This is a small brownish-skinned fruit, about the size and shape of a kiwi fruit, with soft sweet flesh. *Ciku* are popular for dessert.

ELECTRICITY

The electricity supply is 220 volts and 50 cycles.

TOILETS

There are public toilets (*tandas*) at the main tourist sites. The shopping complexes and most petrol stations also have toilets. A small charge, usually 10 sen, is often made. The provision of toilet paper is the exception rather than the rule, so it is advisable to carry your own supply with you. Small packets of tissues are widely available. In public places the toilets are often a mixture of the squat variety and western sit-down toilets.

WEIGHTS AND MEASURES

Malaysia has converted to the metric system. Fruit is sold in kilos, petrol by the litre and distances are given in kilometres.

PHOTOGRAPHY

It is polite to ask before you take a person's photograph. Usually people are happy for you to do so. Sometimes, particularly in the more remote areas where people have no access to a camera of their own, they may ask you to send them back a print of the photo. It is best to try and take pictures before 10.30 am, or later in the day, after 3 pm, as colours can easily become washed out when the sun is high in the sky. For jungle and cave photography use a faster film (ISO 400), which is more sensitive to light. ISO 100 is suitable for use on the beach or in towns. Photographic film is good value in Malaysia and a discount is usually negotiable. Always check the expiry date, particularly away from the main towns. Try to keep your camera and film in a cool place, if possible an air-conditioned room, and have films developed as soon as possible. If you are staying several months in Malaysia, you might consider buying an airtight box, together with silica gel bags, to protect equipment and film. If you are going snorkelling or diving, then you could try your hand at some underwater photography. Disposable waterproof cameras which sell for around RM35 can be used to a depth of 2.5 metres. One of the best photographic shops in Kuala Lumpur is Foto Shangri-La on Jalan Sultan Ismail (tel: 03-242 3088).

FESTIVALS, PUBLIC HOLI

Malaysia is often described as a land of festivals due to its cultural diversity. The major religious festivals are public holidays and, with the exception of Christmas, the dates change each year, as the Islamic, Chinese and Hindu calendars are based on the lunar year.

NATIONAL PUBLIC HOLIDAYS (DATES FOR 1995)

Chinese New Year (always falls in January, February or March)	31st January and 1st February
Hari Raya Puasa (marks the end of the fasting month)	*3rd and 4th March
Labour Day	1st May
Hari Raya Haji (holiday in honour of Muslims making a pilgrimage to Mecca)	*10th May
Wesak Day (Birthday of the Lord Buddha)	14th May
Awal Muharram (Muslim New Year)	31st May
Birthday of the Yang di-Pertuan Agong	3rd June
Birthday of the Prophet Muhammad	9th August
National Day	31st August
Deepavali (Hindu Festival of Lights, celebrating the victory of good over evil) (except Sarawak)	*23rd October
Christmas Day	25th December

* indicates dates which are subject to last minute change and depend on the sighting of the moon.

SELECTED STATE PUBLIC HOLIDAYS (DATES FOR 1995)

New Year's Day (except Johor, Kedah, Kelantan, Perlis and Terengganu)	1st January
Thaipusam (Johor, Negeri Sembilan, Perak, Penang and Selangor)	17th January
Federal Territory Day (Kuala Lumpur and Labuan)	1st February
Harvest Festival (Sabah and Labuan)	30th and 31st May
Gawai Dayak (Sarawak - Iban and Bidayuh harvest festival)	1st and 2nd June

The birthdays of the sultans and state governors are also celebrated with a public holiday in the state concerned, and are marked by various festivities and competitions. (Note: when a holiday falls on a Sunday, or Friday in Kedah, Kelantan and Terengganu, the following day becomes a public holiday).

AYS AND ANNUAL EVENTS

SELECTED ANNUAL EVENTS (DATES FOR 1995)

Perlis International Bird Singing Competition, 2nd - 4th January (Sungai Batu Pahat, Perlis).

Kuantan Challenge '95 International Boardsailing Regatta, 25th January - 6th February (Balok Beach, Kuantan, Pahang).

Langkawi Festival, March, dates to be confirmed (Pulau Langkawi, Kedah).

International Freshwater Fishing Competition, 21st - 24th April (Tasik Kenyir, Terengganu).

Malaysia World Motorcycle Grand Prix, April, dates to be confirmed (Shah Alam, Selangor).

Melaka Towards 600th Anniversary Celebrations, April, dates to be confirmed (Melaka town).

Pesta Air Papan, 1st May (Mersing, Johor).

Sabah Fest, 20th - 29th May (Kota Kinabalu, Sabah).

Malaysia International Kite Flying Festival, 25th - 29th May (Pantai Sri Tujuh, Tumpat, Kelantan).

MAS International Dragon Boat Festival 1995 Penang, 27th and 28th May (Gurney Drive, Georgetown, Penang).

MAS Sabah International Triathlon 1995, 28th May (Kota Kinabalu, Sabah).

Fraser's Hill International Bird Race, 3rd and 4th June (Fraser's Hill, Pahang).

Festa San Pedro, 27th - 29th June (Portuguese Settlement, Melaka).

Floral Festival, 2nd - 9th July (Kuala Lumpur).

Kelantan International Drum Festival, 27th - 31st July (Kota Bharu, Kelantan).

Kuching Festival 1995, 1st - 31st August (Kuching, Sarawak).

Port Dickson Festival, 13th - 31st August (Port Dickson, Negeri Sembilan).

Johor Carnival '95, 19th - 31st August (Johor Bahru, Johor).

Cameron Highlands Flower Fest, 20th - 24th August (Cameron Highlands, Pahang).

Terengganu Beach Festival, August, dates to be confirmed (Pantai Batu Buruk, Kuala Terengganu, Terengganu).

MAS Mount Kinabalu International Climbathon, 2nd and 3rd September (Kinabalu Park, Sabah).

Tioman International Regatta, 8th - 10th September (Pulau Tioman, Pahang).

Malaysia Fest, 9th - 23rd September (Kuala Lumpur).

MAS International Marathon Penang, October, date to be confirmed (Georgetown, Penang).

Penang Festival, 1st - 30th November (Sungai Nibong, Penang).

Another major event, currently held biannually, is the Langkawi International Maritime and Aerospace (LIMA) Exhibition, which is taking place on 5th to 10th December 1995. For a full list of annual events and holidays and more information on those listed above contact the MTPB.

SPORTS FACILITIES

Malaysia offers a wide range of sports facilities and adventure activities. Racket sports, swimming pools and gymnasiums are among the facilities at the main hotels and resorts. Watersports such as windsurfing, canoeing, parasailing and jet skiing are available at the main beach resorts.

Malaysia is well-known for its coral reefs, particularly off the east coast of the peninsula and Sabah. Snorkels and flippers can be hired at the main sites. Diving trips can also be arranged and beginners can undertake a diving course, one of the most popular locations being Pulau Tioman. There are several diving schools on the island, one of which is based at the Berjaya Imperial Beach Resort. The best time for diving off the east coast is April to October. For fishing enthusiasts, there are excellent opportunities for both deep sea and fresh water fishing. Those who like to get their adrenalin going can try their hand at white-water rafting, the main venue in the country being the Padas River in Sabah. Other adventure activities include cave exploration, mountain climbing and jungle trekking. Spectator sports include football, hockey, badminton, horse racing and local sports such as *gasing* and *sepak raga*.

The country is now a popular destination for golfers and boasts well over a hundred golf courses, some of which are attached to hotels. A number of the golf courses are floodlit at night, so keen golfers can enjoy a round after they have finished work, and avoid the enervating effects of the tropical sun. For more information contact the Malaysian Golf Association (tel: 03-457 7931).

NATIONAL PARKS

Malaysia has twelve national parks, ten of them in East Malaysia, covering a variety of terrain. Permits are required to visit the majority of the parks. If you are visiting a park on an organised tour package, the tour company will arrange the permits for you. Guides are compulsory for climbing Mount Kinabalu, Gunung Mulu, Gunung Api and Gunung Tahan. Some of the newer national parks which are still in the process of being fully established, have no visitor facilities, so visitors have to bring all their own provisions and equipment. However, the more established parks, such as Taman Negara and Gunung Mulu National Park, have excellent facilities. In addition to the national parks, Malaysia has a number of state parks and wildlife reserves, one of the most famous being the Sepilok Forest Reserve in Sabah with its Orang-Utan Rehabilitation Centre. Feeding times at the Centre are 10 am (9.30 am on Fridays) and 2.30 pm.

If you plan to go jungle trekking, always take along a bottle of water to replace fluid lost through sweating. Long-sleeved shirts and trousers are recommended and it is a good idea to bring along a spare pair of walking shoes. It is also advisable to take some form of leech protection, particularly after rainfall, and to use a mosquito repellent. If you are climbing Mount Kinabalu, in addition to warm clothes, gloves and waterproofs, you will need a torch, as the last section of the mountain is climbed before dawn. A torch is also essential for Gunung Mulu and Niah national parks. For further information on

Malaysia's national parks contact the Wildlife and National Parks Department, or the MTPB which also produces a brochure on the main national parks. The head office of the Wildlife and National Parks Department is in Kuala Lumpur (tel: 03-905 2872). MATIC also has a National Parks Department information counter. For Sabah's parks contact the Sabah Parks Office, tel: 088-212 719/518/ 508.

MUSEUMS AND CULTURAL COMPLEXES

Entrance to museums and cultural complexes is generally free of charge, but there are several notable exceptions. The Baba Nyonya Heritage Museum in Melaka charges RM7 for adults and RM4 for children. The Royal Abu Bakar Museum in Johor Bahru charges RM4 for Johorians, RM5 for other Malaysians and US$7 for foreigners (or ringgit equivalent). For Sarawakians the price of an adult ticket to the Sarawak Cultural Village near Kuching is RM20, while foreigners and other Malaysians pay RM45 (half price for children). The price includes small gifts from the various ethnic houses.

Opening hours vary, but most museums and cultural complexes are open during normal office hours. The times of cultural performances at selected venues are listed below.

MATIC in Kuala Lumpur:
Tuesday, Thursday, Saturday and Sunday at 3.30 pm (admission RM2 for adults, RM1 for children).

Gelanggang Seni in Kota Bharu:
Monday, Wednesday and Saturday at 3.30 pm; Wednesday and Saturday at 9 pm (admission free, closed during Ramadan and the monsoon season).

Pangkalan Budaya in Kuala Terengganu:
Saturday at 5 pm or 8 pm (admission free, closed during Ramadan and in bad weather during the monsoon season).

Sarawak Cultural Village:
Daily at 2 pm (price included in entrance admission).

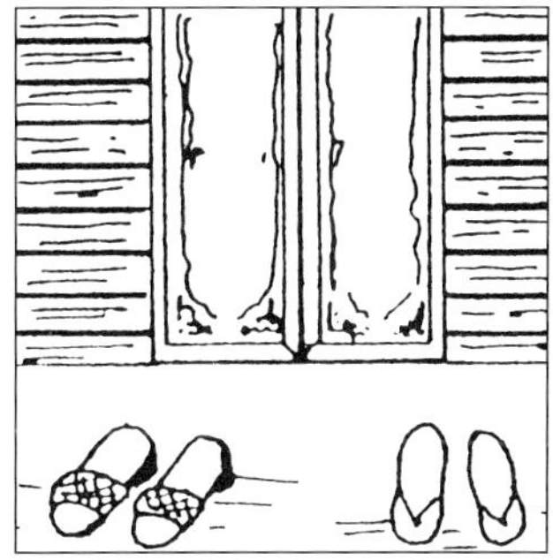

CUSTOMS AND TABOOS

As you would expect in a country which is home to all the world's major religions and races, there are many local customs and taboos. Some of the most important are highlighted below.

If you are invited into a Malaysian family's home, take your shoes off before entering. If your hosts say you can leave your shoes on, check to see whether they have left theirs on, then do as they have done. Shoes must also be removed before entering a mosque or Indian temple.

The Malay handshake, called the *salam*, is not a firm arm-wrenching vigorous shake. It is more of a hand touch. When a Malay gives you the *salam* handshake, he will touch your hand gently with both of his, and then bring his hands to his chest, which means he is greeting you from his heart. Some Malay men will not shake hands with women. The best advice for a woman introduced to a Malay gentleman is to wait for him to offer his hand. If he does not, then a nod of the head and a smile will do. The same is true when greeting an Indian gentleman. The traditional Indian greeting is to press the palms together, as in prayer, and bow the head.

It is considered bad manners to point with the forefinger. If you want to point at something or someone, then it is best to use the thumb of the right hand.

The issue of surnames is a confusing one for foreigners. There are no surnames as the west knows them. Malay names are followed by *bin* for men, an Arabic term meaning son of, or *binti* for women, meaning daughter of, and then the father's name. It is incorrect to address someone by their second name. For example, Ahmad bin Yusuf, is Encik Ahmad, or Mr Ahmad. Mr Yusuf is his father. Friends call him Ahmad. His sister, Azizah binti Yusuf, would be Cik Azizah, or Miss Azizah. Friends would call her Azizah. The same principle is applied when Malaysians address westerners. If your name is David Cook, you will not be referred to as Mr Cook, but as Mr David. Muslims who have been on a pilgrimage to Mecca have the title Haji for a man and Hajjah for a woman.

Chinese names have three parts: the family name, the generation name and the personal name. For example, Lim Ah Fatt would be addressed as Mr Lim, not Mr Fatt. Friends would call him Ah Fatt or Lim. In Malaysia many Chinese also have a Christian name (regardless of whether they are Christians), which is added to the front of their Chinese name, for example Robert Lim. Like the Malays, the Indians have a personal name followed by the father's name. For example, Ramesh Arumugam would be called Mr Ramesh or Ramesh. All Sikh men have their own individual name followed by Singh, for example Ranjit Singh, while Sikh women have Kaur after their first name.

While some Malays and Indians, particularly in the more urban areas, eat with cutlery, many still eat with their fingers. Only the right hand is used. The left hand is reserved for matters of the bathroom and is therefore considered unclean. Foreigners are usually offered cutlery, which for Malaysian meals is a fork and spoon. If you do decide to apply the 'when in Rome' principle, then wash your hands before and after you eat. In smaller Malay restaurants and many hawker stalls, a silver kettle, called a *kendi*, is provided on each table for washing your right hand, together with a perforated stand which the water is poured over. When eating with chopsticks, they should not be rested on or across your dinner plate or rice bowl. The top of the chopsticks should be placed on a rest stand or soy sauce dish, with the other end resting on the table.

It is *haram*, or forbidden according to Islamic law, for Muslims to eat pork, or animals not killed in accordance with religious rules. It is also *haram* for Muslims to drink alcohol. Hindus do not eat beef, as the cow is a sacred animal in Hinduism.

Among the Malays, Chinese and Indians it is customary for women to undergo a period of confinement after they have given birth. During this time the mother is put on a strict diet and is not allowed to leave the house. The traditional confinement period ranges from a month to forty-four days.

LANGUAGE

The national language is Bahasa Malaysia, or Malay, which is also spoken throughout Indonesia, and in southern Thailand and the southern Philippines. The other main languages are English, Chinese (Mandarin) and Tamil. Although English is widely spoken in the main towns and tourist destinations, it is well worth learning some basic Malay words and expressions. Malaysians are always pleased that you have made an effort to learn their language, and a basic command of Malay will be useful if you are travelling to more rural areas. It is also a helpful bargaining tool.

Although formal Malay is quite a complex language, basic Malay is fairly simple. The language is not tonal and uses the Roman alphabet. There are a few basic pronunciation rules to remember. The letter 'c' is pronounced 'ch', for example, ciku is pronounced chiku. The letters 'sy' are pronounced 'sh', for example, syariat becomes shariat; while 'g' is always hard as in good. Vowels are pronounced as follows: 'a' as in father; 'e' is usually soft and hardly pronounced at all, for example, besar becomes b-sar; 'i' as the 'ee' in sweet; 'o' as in so; 'u' as the 'oo' in soon.

There are no articles in Malay. For example, *anak* means 'the child' or 'a child'. Plurals are formed by repeating the noun. For example, *anak* becomes *anak-anak* for children. Adjectives always follow the noun, for example, *rumah* (house) and *kecil* (small) would be *rumah kecil*, meaning 'the small house'. Tenses are indicated using expressions of time, such as *semalam* (yesterday) and *besok* (tomorrow), or adverbs. For example, *sudah* (already) denotes the past tense, while *belum* means 'not yet', *akan* means 'will' and *tengah* means 'in the process of doing'.

A list of Malay words used in the book is provided in the glossary. Below are some other useful Malay words and expressions:

Pronouns:

I	*saya*
you	*anda, awak*
Mr	*Encik*
Miss	*Cik*
Mrs	*Puan*
we	*kami/kita*
he/she	*dia*
they	*mereka*

Greetings:

good morning	*selamat pagi*
good afternoon	*selamat tengahari*
good evening	*selamat petang*
good night	*selamat malam*
goodbye (to person staying)	*selamat tinggal*
goodbye (to person going)	*selamat jalan*
How do you do?	*apa khabar?*
Very well (usual reply)	*khabar baik*

Useful questions/answers and phrases:

thank you (very much)	*terima kasih (banyak)*
you're welcome	*sama-sama*
please can you help me?	*boleh anda tolong saya?*
how do I get there?	*bagaimana saya boleh ke sana?*
how much (price)?	*berapa harga?*
How far?	*berapa jauh?*
How long will it take?	*berapa lama?*
What is your name?	*siapa nama anda?*
My name is.....	*Nama saya.....*
Where do you come from?	*dari mana asal anda?*
I come from.....	*asal saya.....*
what?	*apa?*
what is this?	*apa ini?*
who?	*siapa?*
where?	*di mana?*
when?	*bila?*
why?	*mengapa?*
excuse me	*maafkan saya*
I am sorry	*saya minta maaf*

Useful words:

toilet	*tandas*
room	*bilik*

yes	*ya*
no	*tidak*
can	*boleh*
now	*sekarang*
hour	*jam*
day	*hari*
week	*minggu*
year	*tahun*
open	*buka*
closed	*tutup*
a little	*sedikit*
a lot	*banyak*
money	*duit/wang*
expensive	*mahal*
female	*perempuan*
male	*lelaki*
child	*anak*
chicken	*ayam*
prawn	*udang*
crab	*ketam*
egg	*telur*
fruit	*buah*
vegetables	*sayur*
meat	*daging*
drink	*minum*
eat	*makan*
coffee	*kopi*
tea	*teh*
milk	*susu*
sugar	*gula*
good	*baik*
wait	*tunggu*
sit	*duduk*
airport	*lapangan terbang*
post office	*pejabat pos*
rain	*hujan*
sunshine/hot	*panas*
cold	*sejuk*

Days of the week:

Monday	*hari Isnin*
Tuesday	*hari Selasa*
Wednesday	*hari Rabu*
Thursday	*hari Khamis*
Friday	*hari Jumaat*
Saturday	*hari Sabtu*
Sunday	*hari Ahad*

Numbers:

1	*satu*	10	*sepuluh*
2	*dua*	11	*sebelas*
3	*tiga*	12	*dua belas*
4	*empat*	20	*dua puluh*
5	*lima*	21	*dua puluh satu*
6	*enam*	30	*tiga puluh*
7	*tujuh*	40	*empat puluh*
8	*lapan*	100	*seratus*
9	*sembilan*	1,000	*seribu*

Directions/traffic signs:

north	*utara*
south	*selatan*
east	*timur*
west	*barat*
one way street	*jalan sehala*
turn	*belok*
right	*kanan*
left	*kiri*
keep left	*ikut kiri*
slow down	*kurangkan laju*
stop	*berhenti*
give way	*beri laluan*
speed limit	*had laju*
no overtaking	*dilarang memotong*
caution	*awas*
entrance	*masuk*
exit	*keluar*
detour	*lencongan*

The word *boleh*, meaning can, is often used instead of yes. *Tak boleh* means cannot, and is a common substitute for no. The word *lah* is often tagged on to the end of words, English as well as Malay, for added emphasis, for example, 'No *lah*!' There are a number of local usages of the English language. These include the expression 'last time', which is often used to express the past tense. For example, 'last time I lived in Australia' means 'I used to live in Australia'. Another notable example is 'going back' which means 'going home'

SELECT BIBLIOGRAPHY

Abbreviations:
MBRAS - Malaysian Branch of the Royal Asiatic Society.

Allen, C., (ed.) *Tales from the South China Seas* (London 1983).

Andaya, Barbara Watson, *Perak: the Abode of Grace, a Study of an 18th Century Malay State* (Oxford University Press, 1979).

Andaya, Barbara Watson & Leonard Y., *A History of Malaysia* (New York, St. Martin's Press, 1982).

Andaya, Leonard Y., *The Kingdom of Johor, 1641-1728* (Kuala Lumpur, Oxford University Press, 1975).

Apa Publications, *Insight Guides, Malaysia* (13th edition, 1990).

Berita (publisher) *Information Malaysia 1992 - 1993 Yearbook.*

Bird, Isabella L., *The Golden Chersonese. Travels in Malaya in 1879* (1883, reprint 1967).

Briggs, John, *Mountains of Malaysia* (Longman Malaysia, 1985).

Briggs, John, *Parks of Malaysia* (Longman Malaysia, 1991).

Brown, C.C., (ed.) *The Malay Annals* (Oxford University Press, 1970).

Brooke, Margaret, *My Life in Sarawak* (London, originally published by Methuen 1913, last reprint by Oxford University Press 1994).

Brooke, Lady Sylvia, *Queen of the Headhunters* (London, originally published by Sidgwick and Jackson 1970, last reprint by Oxford University Press 1993).

Cameron, I., *Magellan and the First Circumnavigation of the World* (London 1974).

Carey, Iskandar, *Orang Asli: the Aboriginal Tribes of Peninsular Malaysia* (Kuala Lumpur, Oxford University Press, 1976).

Cheah, Boon Kheng, *The Peasant Robbers of Kedah, 1900-1929* (Singapore, Oxford University Press, 1988).

Chin, Lucas, *Cultural Heritage of Sarawak* (Sarawak Museum 1980, revised edition 1987).

Clifford, Hugh, *Report of an Expedition to Trengganu and Kelantan in 1895* (MBRAS Reprint No. 13, Kuala Lumpur 1992).

Clodd, H.P., *Malaya's First British Pioneer: The Life of Francis Light* (London 1948, reprinted 1968).

Crowther, Geoff and Wheeler, Tony, *Malaysia, Singapore and Brunei, a travel survival kit* (Lonely Planet 3rd edition, 1988).

Falcon Press (publisher) *Petronas Heritage Mapbook of Peninsular Malaysia* (1990).

Fauconnier, Henri, *The Soul of Malaya* (London 1931, reprinted 1948).

Georgetown City Council, *Penang Past and Present* (Penang 1966).

Gullick, J.M., *The Story of Kuala Lumpur* (1857-1939) (Singapore, Eastern Universities Press, 1983).

Hill, A.H., (ed.) *The Hikayat Abdullah* (Oxford in Asia Historical Reprints, Kuala Lumpur, Oxford University Press, 1970).

Kamarudin Mat Salleh, *Rafflesia, Magnificent Flower of Sabah* (Kota Kinabalu, Borneo Publishing Co., 1991).

Knappert, Jan, *Malay Myths and Legends* (Kuala Lumpur, Heinemann Educational Books (Asia), 1980).

Kratoska, Paul H., *The Penang Guide* (Singapore, Graham Brash, 1986).

Leong, Cecilia, *Sabah: the First 100 Years.* (Kuala Lumpur, Percetakan Nan Yang Muda, 1982).

Lineham, W., *A History of Pahang* (MBRAS Reprint No. 2, Kuala Lumpur 1973).

Lo, Joan, *Glimpses from Sarawak's Past* (Kuching, Agas Sdn Bhd, 1986).

Maugham, Somerset, *Maugham's Malaysian Stories* (Kuala Lumpur, Heinemann Educational Books (Asia) 1969, reprinted 1975).

Middlebrook, S.M. and Gullick, J.M., *Yap Ah Loy* (MBRAS Reprint No. 9, Kuala Lumpur 1989).

Mjoberg, Eric, *Forest Life and Adventures in the Malay Archipelago* (1930, reprinted Oxford University Press, 1988).

Moore, Wendy, *Malacca* (Singapore, Times Editions, 1986).

Munan, Heidi, *Sarawak's Crafts: Methods, Materials and Motifs* (Singapore, Oxford University Press, 1991).

Nik Hassan Shuhaimi Nik Abd. Rahman and Othman Mohd. Yatim, *Antiquities of the Bujang Valley* (Kuala Lumpur 1990).

Payne, J. and Andau, M., *Orang-utan, Malaysia's Mascot* (Kuala Lumpur, Berita Publishing, 1989).

Payne, Robert, *The White Rajahs of Sarawak* (Singapore, Oxford University Press, 1986).

Purcell, V., *The Chinese in Malaya* (Oxford University Press, 1967).

Runciman, Steven, *The White Rajahs: a history of Sarawak from 1841 to 1946* (Cambridge University Press, 1960).

Salleh Mohd. Nor and Wan Portiah Hamzah (ed), *Marine Heritage of Malaysia* (Petronas, 1992).

Sheppard, M.C., *The Adventures of Hang Tuah* (Singapore, D. Moore, 1965).

Shepperd, M.C., *Tun Perak: Malacca's Greatest Bendahara* (Longman Malaysia, 1969).

Shepperd, M.C., *A Short History of Terengganu,* in Papers Relating to Terengganu (MBRAS Reprint No. 10, 1983).

Swettenham, Frank, *Footprints in Malaya* (London, Hutchinson & Co., 1941)

Swettenham, Frank, *Malay Sketches* (London, John Lane, 1903).

Talib, S., *After its own Image: the Trengganu Experience, 1881-1941* (Singapore, Oxford University Press, 1984).

Tan, Cecilia, *Penang* (Singapore, Times Editions, 1986).

Tan Ding Eing, *A Portrait of Malaysia and Singapore* (Oxford University Press, second edition 1983).

Tregonning, K.G, *A History of Modern Sabah: North Borneo, 1881-1963* (Kuala Lumpur, University of Malaya Press, 1965).

Turnbull, C. Mary, *A History of Malaysia, Singapore and Brunei* (Australia, Allen & Unwin, 1989).

Vlatseas, S., *A History of Malaysian Architecture* (Singapore, Longman, 1990).

Wallace, Alfred Russell, *The Malay Archipelago: the land of the orang-utan and the bird of paradise* (London, Macmillan, 1869, last reprint Singapore, Graham Brash, 1983).

Wheatley, P., *Impressions of the Malay Peninsula in Ancient Times* (Singapore, Eastern Universities Press, 1964).

Winstedt, R.O., *The Malays, A Cultural History* (reprinted Singapore, Graham Brash, 1981).

Winstedt, R.O., *A History of Johore* (MBRAS Reprints No. 6, Kuala Lumpur 1992).

Winstedt, R.O., *A History of Negri Sembilan* (Journal of the Malayan Branch, Royal Asiatic Society, 1934).

Winstedt, R.O. & Wilkinson, R.J., *A History of Perak* (MBRAS Reprint No. 3, Kuala Lumpur 1974).

Wolters W.O., *The Fall of Srivijaya in Malay History* (New York, Cornell University Press, 1970).

THE AUTHORS

Debbie Cook

Born in Liverpool in northern England, Debbie Cook studied economics at Newnham College, Cambridge, going on to teach A-level economics at Westminster School in London. Debbie left the teaching profession to work as a consultant, becoming a director of a London based political and public relations company. Since 1990 she has devoted all her time to writing. In addition to co-writing *Malaysia, Land of Eternal Summer*, she has worked as a journalist with Time-Life reporting on a wide range of stories and has contributed articles to a number of publications.

David Cook

David Cook was born and brought up in southern England. He read history at King's College, London and Lincoln College, Oxford. In 1979 David joined the teaching staff of Westminster School in London, later becoming Head of History. He is now a Housemaster at the School. David has written books on a number of historical subjects, including the War of the Roses and the Hundred Years War.

David and Debbie married in the summer of 1989, and spent their honeymoon in Malaysia. They fell in love with the country and have been coming back ever since.

ACKNOWLEDGEMENTS

We would like to thank the following for their help: Muzium Negara, Arkib Negara, the Sarawak Museum, the Malaysia Tourism Promotion Board (MTPB) and Royal Selangor Pewter for allowing us to use their photographs; Dewan Bahasa dan Pustaka for their advice regarding translations and spellings; the World Wildlife Fund Malaysia for their advice on plant and animal species; and the MTPB for permission to reproduce tables. We are also very grateful to Abdul Jalil Osman of the Melaka Historical Museum for his helpful comments on the text; Chan Eng Heng and Liew Hock Chark of Universiti Pertanian Malaysia for sharing their expertise on leatherback turtles; the staff at Sri Perdana, Perusahaan Otomobil Nasional Berhad, the Melaka Cultural Museum, the Royal Abu Bakar Museum, the Pan Pacific Hotel in Kuala Lumpur, the guardian of Sultan Abdul Samad's chest, Muzium Negara, the Kelantan Royal Museum and State Museum, Ye Olde Smokehouse, the Sarawak Museum and the Sarawak Cultural Village for permission to take photographs; Sekolah Sri Utama in Kuala Lumpur for allowing us to photograph some of their pupils; and Siti Fatimah Ujang and Anuar Ariffin for allowing us to photograph their wedding (congratulations on the new arrival!).

We would also like to say *terima kasih banyak* to all the people we have met during our travels in Malaysia for their help and hospitality. This book would not have been possible without them.

INDEX

Bold entries indicate a section on the subject. Underlined entries refer to a photograph or illustration.

MAPS